LEADERSHIP

LEADERSHIP

Research Findings, Practice, and Skills

Andrew J. DuBrin
Rochester Institute of Technology

HOUGHTON MIFFLIN COMPANY   Boston   Toronto
Geneva, Illinois   Palo Alto   Princeton, New Jersey

Associate Editor: Susan Kahn
Senior Project Editor: Margaret M. Kearney
Production/Design Coordinator: Carol Merrigan
Senior Manufacturing Coordinator: Marie Barnes
Marketing Manager: Bob Wolcott

Cover design: DesignHeads, Boston

To Melanie

Printed in the U.S.A.

Library of Congress Catalog Card Number: 94-76500

ISBN: 0-395-65634-6

123456789-DH-98 97 96 95 94

Contents

Preface   xvii

1   The Nature and Importance of Leadership   1

The Meaning of Leadership   2
  Leadership as a Partnership   2
  Leadership Versus Management   3

The Impact of Leadership on Organizational Performance   5
  Research and Opinion: Leadership Does Make a Difference   5
  Leader in Action: Phil Purcell of Dean Witter   6
  Research and Opinion: Formal Leadership Does Not Make a Difference   7

Leadership Roles   9
  Leadership Self-Assessment Exercise 1–1: Readiness for the Leadership Role   10
  Leader in Action: Bob Eaton of Chrysler   13

The Satisfactions and Frustrations of Being a Leader   14
  Satisfaction of Leaders   15
  Dissatisfactions and Frustrations of Leaders   16

A Framework for Understanding Leadership   17

Skill Development in Leadership   23

Summary   24
  Key Terms   25   Guidelines for Action and Skill Development   25
  Discussion Questions and Activities   26
  Leadership Case Problem: Does Bob Allen at AT&T Have the Right Stuff?   26
  Leadership Role Play: The Inspirational Leader   27

2   Traits, Motives, and Characteristics of Leaders   28

Personality Traits of Effective Leaders   29
  Leader in Action: High Tech Star Paul G. Stern   30
  General Personality Traits   30
  Leadership Self-Assessment Exercise 2–1: The Assertiveness Scale   33
  Leader in Action: Marcia Ann Gillespie, Ms. Editor   37
  Task-Related Personality Traits   38

Leadership Motives   41
The Power Motive   42
Drive and Achievement Motivation   43
Leadership Self-Assessment Exercise 2–2: How Strong Is
Your Achievement Motive?   43
Strong Work Ethic   44
Tenacity   45
Cognitive Factors and Leadership   45
Mental Ability and the Cognitive Resource Theory   46
Knowledge of the Business   47
Leader in Action: John Breen of Sherwin-Williams   48
Creativity   48
Insight into People and Situations   49
Farsightedness   49
Openness to Experience   50
Leadership Development Exercise 2–1: Group Feedback
on Leadership Traits   50
Physical and Background Factors   51
Energy and Physical Stamina   51
Height   51
Background Factors   51
The Influence of Heredity and Environment on Leadership   52
The Strengths and Limitations of the Trait Approach to Leadership   53
Summary   53
Key Terms   54   Guidelines for Action and Skill Development   55
Discussion Questions and Activities   55
Leadership Case Problem: What Traits Did Steve Ross Possess?
A Leadership Role Play: A Sense of Humor on the Job   57

3   *Charismatic and Transformational Leadership   58*
The Meanings of Charisma   59
Charisma: A Relationship Between the Leader and Group Members   60
The Effects of Charisma   60
Types of Charismatic Leaders   61
Characteristics of Charismatic and Transformational Leaders   62
Leader in Action: Richard Branson of the Virgin Group   63
The Communication Style of Charismatic Leaders   65
Management by Inspiration   65
Leadership Skill-Building Exercise 3–1: Becoming a Charismatic
and Transformational Leader   66
Management by Anecdote   67

How Transformations Take Place   68

   Leadership Skill-Building Exercise 3–2: Management by Anecdote   68

Empirical Studies on Charismatic and Transformational Leadership   70

   Leader in Action: Yvonne Scruggs-Leftwich, the People's Banker   71

Concerns About Charismatic and Transformational Leadership   72

   Challenges to the Validity of Charismatic Leadership   72

   The Dark Side of Charismatic Leadership   73

Summary   74

   Key Terms   75   Guidelines for Action and Skill Development   75

   Discussion Questions and Activities   75

   Leadership Case Problem: "I Have a Dream"   76

   Leadership Exercise: Visionary Speech   77

4   *Effective Leadership Behaviors and Attitudes*   *78*

Pioneering Research on Leadership Behaviors and Attitudes   79

   The Ohio State University Studies of Initiating Structure
   and Consideration   79

   The University of Michigan Studies of Effective Leadership Practices   81

Task-Related Attitudes and Behaviors   83

   Leader in Action: Chuck Daly, Basketball Coach   86

   Leadership Skill-Building Exercise 4–1: Feedback Skills   88

Relationship-Oriented Attitudes and Behaviors   89

   Leader in Action: Bill Gates, Software Mogul   91

Superleadership: Leading Others to Lead Themselves   92

Situational Influences on Effective Leadership Behavior   93

Summary   94

   Key Terms   95   Guidelines for Action and Skill Development   95

   Discussion Questions and Activities   96

   Leadership Case Problem: New Leadership at Compaq   97

   Leadership Exercise: Effective and Ineffective Leaders   98

5   *Leadership Styles*   *99*

The Leadership Continuum: Classical Leadership Styles   100

   The Boss-Centered Versus Employee-Centered Leadership Continuum   100

   The Autocratic-Participative-Free-Rein Continuum   102

   Leader in Action: Donald E. Petersen of Ford Motor Co.   103

   Leadership Self-Assessment Exercise 5–1: What Type of Leader
   Are You or Would You Be?   105

The Leadership Grid Styles 107
Key Grid Positions 107
Which Style is Best? 109
Team Leadership Versus Solo Leadership 109
The Entrepreneurial Leadership Style 110
Leader in Action: Walter Riley of G.O.D. 111
Gender Differences in Leadership Style 112
The Argument for Male-Female Differences in Leadership Style 112
The Argument Against Gender Differences in Leadership Style 113
Selecting the Best Leadership Style 113
Leader in Action: Donna Karan of Donna Inc. 114
Leadership Self-Assessment Exercise 5–2: How Flexible Are You? 116
Summary 116
Key Terms 117 Guidelines for Action and Skill Development 118
Discussion Questions and Activities 118
Leadership Case Problem: Is This Any Way to Treat Accountants? 119
Leadership Role Play: Contrasting Leadership Styles 120

6 *Contingency and Situational Leadership* 121

Fiedler's Contingency Theory of Leadership Effectiveness 122
Measuring Leadership Style: The Least Preferred Coworker (LPC) Scale 122
Leadership Self-Assessment Exercise 6–1: The Least Preferred
Coworker (LPC) Scale for Measuring Leadership Style 122
Measuring the Leadership Situation 124
The Leader-Match Concept and Overall Findings 124
Evaluation of Fiedler's Contingency Theory 125
The Path–Goal Theory of Leadership Effectiveness 126
Matching the Leadership Style to the Situation 126
Leader in Action: Robin Orr of Plantree 128
Leader in Action: Craig B. Barr, GM Plant Manager 129
How the Leader Influences Performance 129
The Hersey-Blanchard Situational Leadership Model 130
Basics of the Model 131
Evaluation of the Situational Model 133
Leader in Action: Vaughn D. Bryson of Eli Lilly 133
The Vroom–Yetton–Jago Decision-Making Model 134
Basic Premises of the Model 134
An Illustrative Use of the Model 135
Evidence and Opinion About the Model 137
Leadership Development Exercise 6–1: Using a Decision Tree
to Select an Appropriate Leadership Style 137

Summary   138

    Key Terms   139   Guidelines for Action and Skill Development   139
    Discussion Questions and Answers   140

    Leadership Case Problem: A Hard Decision at Nucor   140

    Leadership Exercise: The Hard-Hat Decision   141

7   *Power, Politics, and Leadership   142*

Sources and Types of Power   143

    Position Power   144
    Personal Power   144
    Power Stemming from Ownership   145
    Power from Providing Resources   145

    Leadership Self-Assessment Exercise 7–1: Rating a Manager's Power   146

    Power from Capitalizing on Opportunity   147
    Power Stemming from Managing Critical Problems   148
    Power Stemming from Being Close to Power   148

Developing a Plan for Increasing Power   149

Tactics for Becoming an Empowering Leader   149

    Empowering Practices   150

    Leader in Action: Dennis K. Pawley of Chrysler Corp.   151

    Practicing SuperLeadership   152

Factors That Contribute to Political Behavior   152

    Pyramid-Shaped Organization Structure   152

    Leadership Skill-Building Exercise 7–1: Becoming an
Empowering Manager   153

    Subjective Standards of Performance   154
    Environmental Uncertainty and Turbulence   154
    Emotional Insecurity   154
    Machiavellian Tendencies   155

    Leadership Self-Assessment Exercise 7–2: The Organizational
Politics Questionnaire   155

    Disagreement over Major Issues   158

Political Tactics and Strategies   158

    Ethical Political Tactics and Strategies   158

    Leader in Action: Felicia Anderson, Bank Manager and Input Seeker   161

    Unethical Political Tactics and Strategies   162

Exercising Control over Dysfunctional Politics   163

Summary   164

    Key Terms   164   Guidelines for Action and Skill Development   165
    Discussion Questions and Activities   165

    Leadership Case Problem: The Computerization Power Failure   166

    Leadership Exercise: Classroom Politics   166

8   Influence Tactics of Leaders   167

A Model of Power and Influence   168

Leadership Self-Assessment Exercise 8–1: Survey of Influence Tactics   170

Description and Explanation of Influence Tactics   171

Essentially Ethical and Honest Tactics   172
Essentially Dishonest and Unethical Tactics   176

Leader in Action: Jan Thompson, Marketing Vice President at Mazda   177

Leader in Action: Paul Kazarian, Former Sunbeam Chairman   179

A Study of the Effectiveness of Influence Tactics   182

Leadership Skill-Building Exercise 8–1: Identifying Influence Tactics   183

Summary   184

Key Terms   185   Guidelines for Action and Skill Development   185
Discussion Questions and Activities   186

Leadership Case Problem: The Tough-Minded Hank Greenberg   186

Leadership Exercise: Influence Tactics   187

9   Developing Teamwork   188

Advantages and Disadvantages of Group Work and Teamwork   189

Advantages of Group Work and Teamwork   190
Disadvantages of Group Activity   190

Leader Behavior and Attitudes That Foster Teamwork   191

Defining the Team's Mission   191
Developing a Norm of Teamwork   192
Emphasizing Pride in Being Outstanding   193
Serving as a Model of Teamwork   193

Leadership Skill-Building Exercise 9–1: Shelters for the Homeless   193

Using a Consensus Leadership Style   194
Overcoming the "We-They" Attitude   194

Leader in Action: Rod Canion, Consensus Leader   195

Establishing Urgency and Demanding Performance Standards   196
Emphasizing Group Recognition   196
Challenging the Group   197
Encouraging Group Competition   197
Encouraging the Use of Jargon   197
Initiating Ritual and Ceremony   198
Soliciting Feedback on Team Effectiveness   198

Team in Action: A Technical Group at Microsoft Corp.
Minimizing Micromanagement   199

Leadership Skill-Building Exercise 9–2: The Teamwork Checklist   200

Outdoor Training and Team Development   201

Features of Outdoor Training Programs   201
Evaluation of Outdoor Training for the Team Development   202

Leaders in Action: Electronics Company Staff at Outward Bound 202
The Leader-Member Exchange Model: A Partial Explanation of Teamwork 203
Summary 205
Key Terms 206 Guidelines for Action and Skill Development 206
Discussion Questions and Activities 207
Leadership Case Problem: The Unbalanced Team 208
Leadership Exercise: Learning Teamwork Through Ball Handling 209

10 Motivating and Coaching Skills 210

Behavior Modification and Motivational Skills 211
Behavior Modification Strategies 211
Rules for the Use of Behavior Modification 212
Expectancy Theory and Motivational Skills 213
An Overview of Expectancy Theory 213
Basic Components of Expectancy Theory 214
Leadership Skills and Behaviors Associated with Expectancy Theory 216
Leadership Skill-Building Exercise 10-1: Estimating Valances for Applying
Expectancy Theory 218
Coaching as a Leadership Philosophy 219
Leader in Action: Rick Pitino, Kentucky Wildcats Head Coach 222
Coaching Skills and Techniques 223
Leader in Action: Sam Rivera of Fel-Pro Inc. 225
Summary 226
Leadership Self-Assessment Exercise 10–1: Characteristics of an
Effective Coach 227
Key Terms 228 Guidelines for Action and Skill Development 228
Discussion Questions and Activities 229
Leadership Case Problem: The Financial Services Coach 230
Leadership Role Play: The Financial Services Coach Role Play 230

11 Creative Problem Solving and Leadership 232

Steps in the Creative Process 233
Characteristics of Creative Leaders 234
Knowledge 235
Leadership Self-Assessment Exercise 11–1: The Creative Personality Test 236
Intellectual Abilities 238
Personality 238
Social Habits and Upbringing 239
Overcoming Traditional Thinking as a Creativity Strategy 239
Leadership Skill-Building Exercise 11–1: Thinking Outside the Box 240
Leader in Action: Lyle Berman of Grand Casinos, Inc. 241

Leaders in Action: Cyndi Weiss and Diane Castellani of the Fit Company   241

Organizational Methods to Enhance Creative Problem Solving   242

Brainstorming   243

Leadership Skill-Building Exercise 11–2: Brainstorming   244

The Pet-Peeve Technique   245

The Forced-Association Technique   245

The Excursion Method   246

Evaluation of Creativity Training   246

Self-Help Techniques to Enhance Creative Problem Solving   247

Practicing Creativity-Enhancing Exercises   247

Staying Alert to Opportunities   248

Maintaining an Enthusiastic Attitude   248

Leadership Skill-Building Exercise 11–3: Word Hints to Creativity   249

Leader in Action: John Bryant, Urban Rebuilder   250

Speaking to Lead Users   250

Maintaining and Using an Idea Notebook   251

Playing the Role of Explorer, Artist, Judge, and Lawyer   251

Establishing a Climate for Creative Thinking   252

Summary   253

Key Terms   254   Guidelines for Action and Skill Development   254

Discussion Questions and Activities   254

Leadership Case Problem: The Ship-Jumping Engineer   255

Leadership Exercise: The Pet-Peeve Technique   255

12   Communication and Conflict Resolution Skills   257

Research Evidence About Communication and Leadership Effectiveness   258

Inspirational and Powerful Communication   258

Leadership Self-Assessment Exercise 12–1: A Test of Communication Effectiveness   259

Speaking and Writing   260

Leadership Skill-Building Exercise 12–1: Identifying Emotion-Provoking Words and Phrases   262

Nonverbal Communication   265

Supportive Communication   266

Leader in Action: Frederick C. Crawford, Former Chairman of TRW   269

Overcoming Cross-Cultural Communication Barriers   270

The Leader's Role in Resolving Conflict and Negotiating   273

Conflict Management Styles   273

Negotiating and Bargaining   274

Leader in Action: Elizabeth Elton, Product Manager   275

Summary   276

Key Terms   277   Guidelines for Action and Skill Development   277
Discussion Questions and Activities   278
Leadership Case Problem: Tough Day at Southern Tel   279
Leadership Exercise: Feedback on Verbal and Nonverbal Behavior   280

13   *International and Culturally Diverse Aspects of Leadership   281*

The Competitive Advantage of Managing for Diversity   283
Leader in Action: Sharon Allred Decker of Duke Power   285
Cultural Factors Influencing Leadership Practice   285
Key Dimensions of Differences in Cultural Values   286
Applying a Motivational Theory Across Cultural Groups   288
Leadership Skill-Building Exercise 13–1: Charting Your Cultural
Value Profile   289
Choosing the Most Appropriate Leadership Style for a National Group   291
Cultural Sensitivity   292
Leader in Action: Barry Romeril, Transnational Leader   294
Leadership Initiatives   294
Leader in Action: Bob Jacinto, Director of Fair Employment Practice   296
Developing the Multicultural Organization   297
Leadership Skill-Building Exercise 13–2: How Much Do I
Value Diversity?   298
Achieving Leadership Diversity   300
Summary   301
Key Terms   302   Guidelines for Action and Skill Development   302
Discussion Questions and Activities   303
Leadership Case Problem: "We're Working in Chicago, Not Stockholm"   304
Leadership Exercise: The Diversity Circle   304

14   *Leadership of Quality and Technology   306*

Leadership Practices That Foster Total Quality Management   307
Leadership Skill-Building Exercise 14–1: Principles of Total
Quality Management   307
Organizationwide Principles and Practices   309
Leader in Action: Horst Shulze of Ritz Carlton   310
Leadership Skill-Building Exercise 14–2: Do You Have the Right
Corporate Culture for TQM?   312
Team and Individual-Level Principles and Practices   313
Leader in Action: Richard Teerlink of Harley-Davidson   315

Leadership and the Baldrige Award   318

Leadership Self-Assessment Exercise 14–1: The Leadership Criterion of The Baldrige Award   319

Leader in Action: Arden C. Sims of Globe Metallurgical Inc.   321

Leadership Practices for Fostering Advanced Technology   321

Leadership Self-Assessment Exercise 14–2: Attitudes Toward Technology   322

Choosing an Appropriate Technological Strategy   323
Investing Heavily in Training   324
Using Automation to Assist Rather Than Replace People   324
Creating an Environment Suitable for Gold-Collar Workers   324

Leader in Action: Jill Shurtleff of Gillette Co.   325

Establishing a Reward System for Innovation   325

Summary   326

Key Terms   326   Guidelines for Action and Skill Development   326
Discussion Questions and Activities   327

Leadership Case Problem: Let the Chips Fall Where They May   328
Leadership Exercise: Developing a Mission Statement   329

15 *Leadership Development, Succession, and the Future   330*

Development Through Self-Awareness and Self-Discipline   331

Leadership Development Through Self-Awareness   331
Leadership Development Through Self-Discipline   333

Development Through Education, Experience, and Mentoring   333

Leadership Skill-Building Exercise 15–1: The Interpersonal Skills Checklist   334

Education   335
Experience   336

Leader in Action: Tanya Bridges, Human Resources Manager   337

Mentoring   338

Leadership Development Programs   339

Key Characteristics of a Leadership Development Program   339
Types of Leadership Development Programs   341

Leaders in Action: Life at the Advanced Management Program of Harvard University   343

Evaluation of Leadership Development Efforts   345

The Traditional Approach to Evaluation   345
Domains of Impact of a Leadership Development Program   346

Leadership Succession   347

Leading-Edge and Future Challenges   348

Leader in Action: Ernie Lofton of the UAW   350

Leadership Self-Assessment Exercise 15–1: Checklist for the Future   352

Summary 353

Key Terms 354   Guidelines for Action and Skill Development 354
Discussion Questions and Activities 355
Leadership Case Problem: "My Leadership Isn't Working" 355
Leadership Exercise: The Feedback Circle 356

Endnotes 357
Glossary 375
Name Index 381
Organization Index 383
Subject Index 384

Preface

*L*eadership has always been a key topic in management, organizational behavior, and industrial and organizational psychology. In recent years, however, leadership has become an important new course in schools and colleges of business, business administration, and public administration. Teaching and research about leadership have surged for two key reasons. One is that many business school faculty are convinced that effective leadership is required to meet most organizational challenges. Without effective leadership at all levels in private and public organizations, it is difficult to sustain profitability, productivity, quality, and good customer service. In dozens of different ways, researchers and teachers have demonstrated that leadership does make a difference. Many business school curricula therefore now emphasize the development of leadership skills.

An equally important reason behind the burgeoning study of leadership is that colleges of business and management are responding to environmental demands. Private and public organizations themselves, along with the business media, have placed renewed emphasis on the importance of leadership. Work organizations are unswerving in their belief that effective leaders are necessary to achieve such goals as improved profitability, productivity, quality, and customer service. Top management and other stakeholders believe that without effective leadership, the organization cannot remain competitive.

More so than previously, business organizations recognize that leadership transcends senior executives. As a result, they require people with appropriate leadership skills to inspire and influence others in small teams, task forces, and units at all organizational levels.

PURPOSE OF THE TEXT

The purpose of this text is implied by its title—*Leadership: Research Findings, Practice, and Skills.* It is designed for undergraduate and graduate courses in leadership that give attention to both stable research findings about leadership, the practice of leadership, and skill development. The text is also designed to fit courses in management development that emphasize the leadership function of management. It can also serve as a supplement to organizational behavior or management courses that emphasize leadership.

xvii

The student who masters this text will acquire an overview of the voluminous research literature about leadership. In addition, the student will acquire a feel for how leadership is practiced and also gain insights and information to enhance his or her leadership skills.

What the text is *not* also helps define its nature and scope. This book does not attempt to duplicate the scope and purpose of a leadership handbook by integrating theory and research from several thousand studies. At the other extreme, it is not an evangelical approach to leadership espousing one leadership technique. I have attempted to find a midpoint between a massive synthesis of the literature and a trade book promoting a current leadership fad. *Leadership: Research Findings, Practice, and Skills* is designed to be a mixture of scholarly integrity, examples of effective leadership in action, and skill development.

It is important to note that this book is not intended to duplicate or substitute for an organizational behavior text. Because almost all organizational behavior texts are survey texts, they will mention many of the topics covered here. My approach, however, is to emphasize skill development and prescription rather than duplicating basic descriptions of concepts and theories. I have tried to minimize overlap by emphasizing the leadership aspects of any concept presented here that might also be found in an organizational behavior or management text.

One area of intentional overlap with organizational behavior and management texts does exist: a review of all basic leadership theories. In such instances, however, I emphasize skill development and ideas for leadership practice stemming from these older theories.

FEATURES OF THE BOOK

To accomplish its purpose, this text incorporates nine features into each chapter in addition to summarizing and synthesizing relevant information about leadership:

1. Self-assessment exercises relating both to skills and to personal characteristics

2. Leader in Action inserts describing the leadership practices, behaviors, and personal attributes of real-life leaders

3. Boldfaced key terms, listed at the end of the chapter and defined in a glossary at the back of the text

4. Real-life and hypothetical examples throughout the text

5. Skill development and application exercises, including role plays, to emphasize the activities and skills of effective leaders

6. Discussion questions and activities suited for individual or group analysis

7. End-of-chapter Guidelines for Action, giving additional suggestions for improving leadership skill and practice

8. End-of-chapter summaries that integrate all key topics and concepts

9. Leadership Case Problems, which illustrate the major theme of the chapter, for individual or group analysis

10. Learning objectives to help focus the reader's attention on major outcomes

FRAMEWORK OF THE TEXT

The text is a blend of description, skill development, insight development, and prescription. Chapter 1 describes the meaning, importance, and nature of leadership including leadership roles. Chapter 2 identifies personal attributes associated with effective leaders, a subject that has received renewed importance in recent years. Charismatic and transformational leadership, an extension of understanding the personal attributes of leadership, is the subject of Chapter 3.

Chapter 4 surveys behaviors and practices associated with effective leadership in a variety of situations. Chapter 5 shifts to a description of various approaches to classifying leadership styles. Chapter 6 extends the style approach to leadership by describing the contingency and situational aspects of leadership. After Chapter 7 describes how leaders use power and politics, Chapter 8 extends the topic through an analysis of tactics leaders use to influence others. Chapter 9 describes how leaders foster teamwork and empower team members.

The next five chapters deal with specific leadership skills: motivating and coaching skills (Chapter 10), which constitute the basics of many leadership positions; creative problem solving (Chapter 11); communication (including nonverbal and cross-cultural communication) and conflict resolution skills (Chapter 12); leadership skills and attitudes required for providing effective leadership in international and culturally diverse settings (Chapter 13); and enhancing quality and capitalizing on technology (Chapter 14).

Chapter 15 concludes the book with an overview of approaches to leadership development and learning. In addition, it covers a group of leading-edge and future challenges facing the leader, such as providing leadership in a reengineered workplace and in a virtual corporation.

SUPPLEMENTS

An instructor's manual with text bank accompanies the text. Among its features are chapter outline and lecture notes, possible answers to discussion questions and case questions, comments on exercises in the text, and a comprehensive list of leadership videos. The instructor's manual also describes how to use Computer-Assisted Scenario Analysis (CASA). Especially designed for helping students develop a contingency point of view, CASA is a user-friendly technique that can be used with any word-processing software. It allows the student to insert a new scenario into the case and then re-answer the questions based on the new scenario. CASA helps to develop an awareness of contingency factor in making leadership decisions, as well as creative thinking. A briefer version of CASA was published in the October 1992 issue of *The Journal of Management Education.*

ACKNOWLEDGMENTS

Any project as complex as this one requires a team of dedicated and talented people to see that it achieves its goals. First, I thank the following professors who offered suggestions for improving the first draft of this project:

John Bigelow
Boise State University

Felipe Chia
Harrisburg Area Community College

Barry Gold
Pace University

George B. Graen
University of Cincinnati

Stephen G. Green
Purdue University

James R. Harris
North Carolina A & T State University

Nell Hartley
Robert Morris College

Winston Hill
California State University, Chico

Avis L. Johnson
University of Akron

Ralph Mullin
Central Missouri State University

Linda L. Neider
University of Miami

Randall G. Sleeth
Virginia Commonwealth University

Ahmad Tootoonchi
Frostberg State University

John Warner
University of New Mexico

David Van Fleet
Arizona State University, West

Writing without loved ones would be a lonely task. My thanks therefore also go to Carol Bowman, and my family members—Drew, Douglas, Melanie, Rosie, and Clare. Thanks also to members of Carol's family, Barbara, Tom, and Kristine.

LEADERSHIP

CHAPTER ONE

The Nature and Importance of Leadership

LEARNING OBJECTIVES

After studying this chapter, you should be able to

1. explain the meaning of leadership and how it differs from management.
2. describe how leadership influences organizational performance.
3. pinpoint several important leadership roles.
4. identify the major satisfactions and frustrations associated with the leadership role.
5. identify the major approaches to understanding leadership.
6. recognize how leadership skills are developed.

Carol Bartz advanced through a series of managerial positions to become number two at Sun Microsystems. She sought an even bigger challenge and became CEO at a troubled company, Autodesk, in Sausalito, California. The leadership assignment was particularly difficult. Bartz was the first woman outsider ever brought in to head a substantial high-tech company. Another issue was that many unruly programmers had been uncooperative with executives in the past. Bartz explained that she was not coming to Autodesk as a dictator, but neither did she believe in achieving consensus on all decisions.

Bartz spun off unprofitable operations and strengthened marketing. She also made certain that AutoCad, the firm's computer-aided design program, was released on time. After Bartz had been on the job one and one-half years, Autodesk sales surged 33 percent in one quarter.[1]

Our introductory chapter to the study of leadership begins with an explanation of what leadership is and is not. We then examine how leaders make a difference, the various roles they occupy, and the major satisfactions and frustrations they experience. The next section presents an overview of the book, which identifies the major approaches to understanding leadership. The chapter concludes with an explanation of how reading this book and doing the exercises will enhance your leadership skills.

THE MEANING OF LEADERSHIP

By helping her firm climb out of trouble, Carol Bartz exerted leadership. She made a difference in company performance through a combination of winning business strategies and personal influence. The fact that Bartz inspired, influenced, and motivated people to achieve constructive change means that she exercised leadership. To be a leader, one has to make a difference and facilitate positive changes.

You will read about many other effective organizational leaders throughout this text. The common characteristic of these leaders is their ability to inspire and stimulate others to achieve worthwhile goals. The people who can accomplish these important deeds practice leadership. Compatible with the theme of this text, **leadership** is the ability to inspire confidence and support among the people who are needed to achieve organizational goals.[2]

About 30,000 research articles, magazine articles, and books have been written about leadership so far this century. As a consequence, leadership has been defined in many ways. Several other representative definitions of leadership are as follows:

- Interpersonal influence directed through communication, toward goal attainment.
- The influential increment over and above mechanical compliance with directions and orders.
- An act that causes others to act or respond in a shared direction.
- The art of influencing a people by persuasion or example to follow a line of action.
- The principal dynamic force that motivates and coordinates the organization in the accomplishment of its objectives.[3]

Leadership as a Partnership

An important new thrust in understanding leadership is to regard it as a long-term relationship, or partnership, between leaders and group members. According to Peter Block, in a **partnership** the leader and the group members are connected in such a way that the power between them is approximately balanced. Block also describes partnership as the opposite of parenting (in which one person—the parent—takes the responsibility for the welfare of the other—the child). Partnership occurs when control shifts from the leader to the group member, in a move away from authoritarianism and toward shared decision making.[4] Four things are necessary for a valid partnership to exist:

1. *Exchange of purpose.* In a partnership every worker at every level is responsible for defining vision and values. Through dialogue with people at many levels, the leader helps articulate a widely accepted vision.

2. A *right to say no.* The belief that people who express a contrary opinion will be punished runs contrary to a partnership. Rather, a person can lose an argument but never a voice.

3. *Joint accountability.* In a partnership, each person is responsible for outcomes and the current situation. In practice this means that each person takes personal accountability for the success and failure of the organizational unit.

4. *Absolute honesty.* In a partnership, not telling the truth to each other is an act of betrayal. When power is distributed, people are more likely to tell the truth because they feel less vulnerable.[5]

Block's conception of leadership as a partnership is an ideal to strive toward. Empowerment and team building—two major topics in this book—support the idea of a partnership.

Leadership Versus Management

To understand leadership, it is important to grasp the difference between leadership and management. We get a clue from the standard conceptualization of the functions of management: planning, organization, directing (or leading), and controlling. Leading is a major part of a manager's job, yet a manager must also plan, organize, and control. Broadly speaking, leadership deals with the interpersonal aspects of a manager's job, whereas planning, organizing, and controlling deal with the administrative aspects. According to current thinking, leadership deals with change, inspiration, motivation, and influence. In contrast, management deals more with maintaining equilibrium and the status quo. Table 1–1 explains other differences between management and leadership.

According to John P. Kotter, a prominent leadership theorist, today's managers must know how to *lead* as well as manage. Without leading as well as managing, organizations face the threat of extinction. Kotter draws the following distinction between management and leadership:

■ Management is more formal and scientific than leadership. It relies on universal skills such as planning, budgeting, and controlling. Management is an explicit set of tools and techniques, based on reasoning and testing, that can be used in a variety of situations.

■ Leadership, in contrast to management, involves having a vision of what the organization can become.

TABLE 1–1   Leadership Versus Management

	Leadership	Management
Creating an Agenda	Establishes direction: develops a vision and the strategies needed for its achievement	Plans and budgets: establishes detailed steps and timetables for achieving needed results; allocate necessary resources
Developing a Network for Achieving the Agenda	Involves aligning people: Communicates direction by words and deeds to all those whose cooperation may be needed to help create teams and coalitions that understand the vision and strategies, and accepts their validity.	Organizes and staffs: Establishes structure for achieving the plans; staffs; delegates responsibility and authority for implementation; develops policies and procedures to guide people; creates monitoring systems
Execution	Motivates and inspires: Energizes people to overcome major political, bureaucratic, and resource barriers to change by satisfying basic human needs.	Controls and solves problems: Monitors results against plans, and then plans and organizes to close the gap.
Outcomes	Produces change, often to a dramatic degree: Has the potential of producing extremely useful change, such as new products desired by managers.	Produces a degree of predictability and order: Has the potential to consistently produce key results expected by various stockholders (such as meeting deadlines for customers and paying dividends to stockholders)

Source: John P. Kotter, *A Force for Change: How Leadership Differs from Management* (New York: The Free Press, 1990); Wayne K. Kirchner, book review of "A Force for Change," Personnel Psychology, Autumn 1990, p. 655.

Leadership requires eliciting cooperation and teamwork from a large network of people and keeping the key people in that network motivated, using every manner of persuasion.[6]

Building on Kotter's views, Edwin A. Locke and his associates draw another important distinction between leadership and management. The key function of the *leader* is to create a vision (mission or agenda) for the organization. The leader specifies the far-reaching goal as well as the strategy for goal attainment. In contrast to the leader, the key function of the *manager* is to implement the vision. The manager and his or her team thus choose the means to achieve the end that the leader formulates.[7]

If these views are taken to their extreme, the leader is an inspirational figure and the manager is a stodgy bureaucrat mired in the status quo. But we must be careful not to downplay the importance of management. Effective leaders have to be good managers themselves, or be supported by effective managers. A germane example is the inspirational entrepreneur who is so preoccupied with motivating employees and captivating customers that internal administration is neglected. As a result, costs skyrocket beyond income and such matters as funding the employee pension and paying bills and taxes on time are overlooked. Also, recall that part of Carol

Bartz's approach to turning around Autodesk was the strategy of jettisoning unprofitable operations. Such strategizing is part of the planning function of management.

THE IMPACT OF LEADERSHIP ON ORGANIZATIONAL PERFORMANCE

An assumption underlying the study of leadership is that leaders affect organizational performance. Leaders, through their actions and personal influence, bring about change. People who control organizations—the very top executives—make the same assumption. A frequent antidote to major organizational problems is to replace the leader, in the hope that the newly appointed leader will reverse performance problems. An example of this assumption in action is the frequent replacement of athletic coaches after one or two losing seasons. The owners, or school officials, assume that the leadership acumen of the new coach will vastly improve the ratio of wins to losses.

Here we will review some of the evidence and opinion, pro and con, about the ability of leaders to affect organizational performance. The accompanying Leader in Action vignette provides a positive example of the importance of effective leadership.

Research and Opinion: Leadership Does Make a Difference

The belief that leaders actually influence organizational performance and morale is so plausible that very little research and opinion even deal with this issue. Let us look at a sampling of what research and opinion there are.[8]

Psychoanalyst Michael Maccoby conducted in-depth interviews with business executives over fifteen years ago. He concluded that organizations required a higher level of leadership than ever before to survive and prosper. Among the challenges Maccoby saw confronting organizations were increasing competition, technological advances, changing governmental regulations, and changing worker attitudes. These observations are relevant because they persist today.

Two researchers examined the evolution of a retail firm over a sixty-year period. They found that a senior executive could successfully reorient the firm by changing strategies and organizational structures. For example, in the mid-1970s top management at J. C. Penney decided to upgrade the store's quality and fashion image. As a result of this visionary decision, Penney's has attracted a more upscale clientele, and the giant retailer has become highly profitable. A study of executive succession corroborated these results with retailing firms: a change in an executive accounts for up to 45 percent of the organization's performance. For example, within a year after a new CEO is appointed, profits might increase 45 percent. In another firm, profits might plunge by the same amount in the year following executive succession.

LEADER
IN
ACTION

Phil Purcell of Dean Witter

Philip J. Purcell now views the financial world from his smartly appointed office in the World Trade Center. He began his career as a consultant at McKinsey & Company. Purcell has always preferred that the facts speak for themselves rather than tooting his own horn. In 1978 he was hired by former Sears, Roebuck chairman Ed Telling to develop strategy. Purcell spearheaded the purchase of Dean Witter Reynolds (the financial services firm) and Coldwell Banker (real estate).

In 1982, Purcell was appointed chief operating officer of Dean Witter Financial Services to gain operating experience. He surprised outsiders by overhauling and revitalizing Dean Witter. Purcell spearheaded the launch of Discover Card in 1985. At the same time he focused Dean Witter on the individual investor and away from investment banking. Despite skeptics, the Discover Card has become a huge money maker, and the Dean Witter retail focus has been immensely successful.

Because of Purcell's sterling performance at Dean Witter Financial Services, outsiders think he should be appointed the CEO of the entire Sears, Roebuck. Between 1985 and 1992, virtually all of Sears' earnings came from financial services. Dean Witter and the Discover Card have been the only Sears divisions to experience earnings growth.

Purcell receives an annual compensation of close to $2 million as the COO of Dean Witter. According to friends and associates, however, his motivation for staying with the company transcends the financial. Purcell has always been intrigued by the challenge of revitalizing an American institution. Ed Telling says that there is no question that Purcell could run the entire Sears operation. The implication is that Purcell could help the troubled retailer return to its former glory.

Source: As reported in "A Star in the Gloom at Sears," *Business Week,* October 5, 1992, pp. 62–64; "Purcell, Philip James," Who's Who in America, 44th ed., Vol. I (Wilmette, Ill.: Marquis Who's Who, Macmillan Directory Division, 1990–91), p. 379..

Another study compared selected factors relating to senior managers in better performing minicomputer firms and those in poorer performing firms. The senior management in the more successful firms had previous experience in the electronics industry. In fact, the founder of the firm was likely to be the chief executive officer. The study implies that knowledge of the business *does* make a difference in leadership effectiveness. The same leadership attribute will be pursued in detail in Chapter 2.

In addition to tangible evidence that leadership makes a difference, the perception of these differences is also meaningful. An understanding of these perceptions derives from **attribution theory,** the process of attributing causality to events. Gary Yukl explains that organizations are complex social systems of patterned interactions among people. In their efforts to understand (and simplify) organizational events, people interpret them in simple human terms. One especially strong and prevalent explanation of organizational events is to attribute causality to leaders. They are viewed as heroes and heroines who determine the fates of their organizations.[9] The extraordinary success of Ford Motor Company during the early 1990s is thus attributed largely to its top executive, Harold A. Poling. If we accept the logic of attribution theory in a positive way, most organizational successes are attributed to heroic leaders.

Research and Opinion: Formal Leadership Does Not Make a Difference

Leadership has a smaller impact on organizational outcomes than do forces in the situation, according to the antileadership argument. To personalize this perspective, imagine yourself appointed as the manager of a group of highly skilled investment bankers. How well your group performs could be attributed as much to their talent and economic conditions as to your leadership. The two major arguments against the importance of leadership are substitutes for leadership, and leadership irrelevance.

Substitutes for Leadership.   At times competent leadership is not necessary, and incompetent leadership can be counterbalanced by certain factors in the work situation. Under these circumstances, leadership itself is of little consequence to the performance and satisfaction of team members. According to this viewpoint, many organizations have **substitutes for leadership.** Such substitutes are factors in the work environment that provide guidance and incentives to perform, making the leader's role almost superfluous.[10] Figure 1–1 shows four leadership substitutes: closely knit teams, intrinsic satisfaction, computer technology, and professional norms.

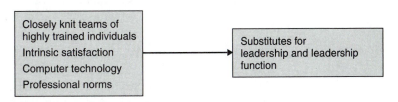

FIGURE 1–1

Substitutes for Leadership

Closely knit teams of highly trained members.   When members of a cohesive, highly trained group are focused on a goal, they may require almost no leadership to accomplish their task. Several researchers have studied air traffic controllers who direct traffic into San Francisco, and pilots who land jet fighters on a nuclear aircraft carrier. With such groups, directive (decisive and task-oriented) leadership is seemingly unimportant. When danger is the highest, these groups rely more on each other than on a leader.

Intrinsic satisfaction.   Employees engaged in work they find strongly self-motivating, or intrinsically satisfying, require a minimum of leadership. Part of the reason is that the task itself grabs the worker's attention and energy. The worker may require a minimum of leadership as long as the task is proceeding smoothly. Consultants observed a unique example of this principle at a manufacturer of camping equipment. The company manufactures sleeping bags of various qualities. At the top of the line are lightweight backpackers filled with down. At the other end are low-cost models filled with floor sweepings from a mattress factory.

Production workers must rotate among all the lines so no one group claims exclusive rights to working on one product. Management contends that supervisory direction is almost unnecessary for production employees assigned to the top of the line, yet product quality exceeds expectation. Workers say they are proud to work on this line and often team together to solve production problems. The production of bottom-of-the-line sleeping bags, on the other hand, is fraught with both quality problems and below-standard output. Close supervision is required to deal with these problems, thus raising indirect costs. Consultants to this company have concluded that when assigned to produce the low-quality backpackers, the workers lose intrinsic motivation. As a consequence, they require considerable supervision and leadership.

Computer technology.   Some companies today use computer-aided monitoring and computer networking to take over many of the supervisor's leadership functions. The computer provides productivity and quality data, and directions for certain tasks are entered into the information system. Even error detection and goal setting are incorporated into some interaction systems. Instead of asking a supervisor for assistance, some employees use the computer network to ask assistance from other workers. (We could argue here that the computer is being used to control rather than to lead workers.)

Professional norms.   Workers who incorporate strong professional norms often require a minimum of supervision and leadership.[11] A group of certified professional accountants may not need visionary leadership to inspire them to do an honest job of auditing the books of a client, or advising against tax fraud.

Although the leadership substitute concept has some merit, it reflects naiveté about the role of organizational leadership. Bass notes that self-management by groups and individuals requires delegation by a higher authority. In addition, higher-ranking managers provide guidance, encouragement, and support.[12]

Leader Irrelevance.   According to the theorizing of Jeffrey Pfeffer, leadership is irrelevant to most organizational outcomes. Rather, it is the situation that must be carefully analyzed. Pfeffer argues that factors outside the leader's control have a larger impact on business outcomes than do leadership actions.[13] An interesting example of this principle is the 1993 downturn in the Japanese automobile industry, which occurred even though the five top auto makers had not changed leadership. The primary contributors to this decreased demand were a business downturn in Japan and Europe. In addition, Japanese cars had become much more expensive than American-made cars in the United States. As a consequence, the Japanese share of the American automotive market eroded slightly.

Another aspect of the leader irrelevance argument is that high-level leaders have unilateral control only over a few resources. Furthermore, the leader's control of these resources is limited by obligations to stakeholders such as consumers and stockholders. Finally, firms tend to choose new organizational leaders whose values are compatible with those of the firm. The leaders therefore act in ways similar to previous leaders. When General Motors was experiencing financial difficulty, several critics suggested that GM exit the automotive business. Almost no chance existed, however, that the GM board would place people in executive positions who supported this point of view.

The leader irrelevance argument would achieve greater practical value if it were recast as a *leader constraint theory*, which would hold that leaders are constrained in what they can do, but that they still have plenty of room to influence others.

LEADERSHIP ROLES

Another way to gain an understanding of leadership is to examine the various roles carried out by leaders. A *role* in this context is an expected set of activities or behaviors stemming from one's job. Leadership roles are a subset of the managerial roles studied by Henry Mintzberg and others.[14] Before reading ahead to the summary of leadership roles, you are invited to do the accompanying leadership self-assessment exercise.

LEADERSHIP SELF-ASSESSMENT
EXERCISE 1–1   Readiness for the Leadership Role

Instructions: Indicate the extent to which you agree with each of the following statements, using the following scale: (1) disagree strongly; (2) disagree; (3) neutral; (4) agree; (5) agree strongly.

1. It is enjoyable having people count on me for ideas and suggestions.   1 2 3 4 5

2. It would be accurate to say that I have inspired other people.   1 2 3 4 5

3. It's a good practice to ask people provocative questions about their work.   1 2 3 4 5

4. It's easy for me to compliment others.   1 2 3 4 5

5. I like to cheer people up even when my own spirits are down.   1 2 3 4 5

6. What my team accomplishes is more important than my personal glory.   1 2 3 4 5

7. Many people imitate my ideas.   1 2 3 4 5

8. Building team spirit is important to me.   1 2 3 4 5

9. I would enjoy coaching other members of the team.   1 2 3 4 5

10. It is important to me to recognize others for their accomplishments.   1 2 3 4 5

11. I would enjoy entertaining visitors to my firm even if it interfered with my completing a report. 1 2 3 4 5

12. It would be fun for me to represent my team at gatherings outside our department.   1 2 3 4 5

13. The problems of my teammates are my problems too.   1 2 3 4 5

14. Resolving conflict is an activity I enjoy.   1 2 3 4 5

15. I would cooperate with another unit in the organization even if I disagreed with the position taken by its members.   1 2 3 4 5

16. I am an idea generator on the job.   1 2 3 4 5

17. It's fun for me to bargain whenever I have the opportunity.   1 2 3 4 5

18. Team members listen to me when I speak.   1 2 3 4 5

19. People have asked to me to assume the leader-
    ship of an activity several times in my life.   1   2   3   4   5
20. I've always been a convincing person.   1   2   3   4   5

Total score: _____

Scoring and interpretation: Calculate your total score by adding the numbers circled. A tentative interpretation of the scoring is as follows:

- 90–100   high readiness for the leadership role
- 60–89   moderate readiness for the leadership role
- 40–59   some uneasiness with the leadership role
- 39 or less low readiness for the leadership role

If you are already a successful leader and you scored low on this questionnaire, ignore your score. If you scored surprisingly low and you are not yet a leader, or are currently performing poorly as a leader, study the statements carefully. Consider changing your attitude or your behavior so that you can legitimately answer more of the statements with a 4 or a 5. Studying the rest of this text will give you additional insights that may be helpful in your development as a leader.

Leading is a complex activity, so it is not surprising that the researchers identified eight roles that can be classified as part of the leadership function of management.

1. *Figurehead.* Leaders, particularly high-ranking managers, spend some part of their time engaging in ceremonial activities, or acting as a figurehead. Four specific behaviors fit the figurehead role of a leader:
   a. entertaining clients or customers as an official representative of the organization
   b. making oneself available to outsiders as a representative of the organization
   c. serving as an official representative of the organization at gatherings outside the organization
   d. escorting official visitors

2. *Spokesperson.* When a manager acts as a spokesperson, the emphasis is on answering letters or inquiries and formally reporting to individuals and groups outside the manager's direct organizational unit. As a spokesperson, the managerial leader keeps five groups of people informed about the unit's activities, plans, capabilities, and possibilities (vision):
   a. upper-level management
   b. clients or customers
   c. other important outsiders such as labor unions
   d. professional colleagues
   e. the general public

Dealing with outside groups and the general public is usually the responsibility of top-level managers.

3. *Negotiator.* Part of almost any manager's job is trying to make deals with others for needed resources. Three specific negotiating activities are:
   a. bargaining with superiors for funds, facilities, equipment, or other forms of support
   b. bargaining with other units in the organization for the use of staff, facilities, equipment, or other forms of support
   c. bargaining with suppliers and vendors for services, schedules, and delivery times

4. *Coach.* An effective leader takes the time to coach team members. Specific behaviors in this role include
   a. informally recognizing team members' achievements
   b. providing team members with feedback concerning ineffective performance
   c. ensuring that team members are informed of steps that can improve their performance

5. *Team builder.* A key aspect of a leader's role is to build an effective team. Activities contributing to this role include
   a. ensuring that team members are recognized for their accomplishments, such as through letters of appreciation
   b. initiating activities that contribute to group morale, such as giving parties and sponsoring sports teams
   c. holding periodic staff meetings to encourage team members to talk about their accomplishments, problems, and concerns

6. *Team player.* Related to the team-builder role is that of the team player. Three such behaviors are
   a. displaying appropriate personal conduct
   b. cooperating with other units in the organization
   c. displaying loyalty to superiors by supporting their plans and decisions fully

7. *Technical problem solver.* It is particularly important for supervisors and middle managers to help team members solve technical problems. Two such specific activities are
   a. serving as a technical expert or advisor
   b. performing individual contributor tasks on a regular basis, such as making sales calls or repairing machinery

8. *Entrepreneur.* Although not self-employed, managers who work in large organizations have some responsibility for suggesting innovative ideas or furthering the business aspects of the firm. Three entrepreneurial leadership role activities are
   a. reading trade publications and professional journals to keep up with what is happening in the industry and profession

b. talking with customers or others in the organization to keep aware of changing needs and requirements

c. getting involved in situations outside the unit that could suggest ways of improving the unit's performance, such as visiting other firms, attending professional meetings or trade shows, and participating in educational programs

A common thread in the leadership roles of a manager is that the managerial leader in some way inspires or influences others. An important practical implication is that managers at every level can exert leadership. For example, a supervisory leader can make an important contribution to the firm's thrust for quality by explaining to team members how to minimize duplications in a mailing list. The accompanying Leaders in Action vignette provides additional insights into the various leadership roles. As you read it, seek to identify specific leadership roles of the two well-known executives described.

Up to this point we have described the meaning of leadership, how leadership affects organizational performance, and the many activities carried out by leaders. You have had an opportunity to explore your attitudes toward occupying the leadership role. Let's now further personalize information about leadership.

LEADER IN ACTION

Bob Eaton of Chrysler

In March 1992, the imperial reign of Lee A. Iacocca, the chairman of Chrysler Corp., was nearly over. He had announced his successor, a low-key former engineer named Robert J. Eaton, the president of General Motors Europe. Eaton was confident that he would be successful. "I have a strong background in product and manufacturing, and at least enough marketing and finance to run a successful business," he said (*Fortune*, p. 63). Within days of being appointed as the new chief executive, Eaton dispelled rumors that his low-key demeanor was a sign of indecisiveness or wimpiness.

At the outset, Eaton informed key staffers at Chrysler that he believed in participatory management, not consensus management. The message was that Eaton would be calling the shots. Nevertheless, Eaton's low-key approach differs radically from Iacocca's high-profile flash. Eaton says he will not appear on television commercials as did Iacocca.

A former colleague says about Eaton, "He laid out broad objectives, but he left it up to you how to achieve them" (Templeman, p. 96). Eaton's preference for the team-leader management style helped him attract and keep a high-caliber staff in Europe. He knows how to pump up profits in an automotive company already making a comeback. After taking over the top leadership position in Europe, Eaton racked up $5.5 billion in profits over three years.

High on the list of Eaton's goals for Chrysler is more efficient production. To achieve high productivity in Europe, Eaton squeezed more output from existing plants in Europe. A key part of his strategy was negotiating innovative labor deals. For example, at several plants he established union agreements that allowed twenty-four-hour-per-day production.

The Chrysler board hopes that Eaton will roll up his sleeves and engineer the same smooth-running operation for them as he did for GM Europe. After one year with Eaton in office, Chrysler's market share had increased. The new LH Series, Grand Cherokee, and minivans were doing well. Older models were also picking up market share.

Skill development: Jot down all the leadership roles you perceived in the vignette. Specify the activity and the role it reflects. Refer to the eight leadership roles described previously.

Eaton: _____

_____

_____

_____

_____

_____

Source: As reported in John Templeman, "Bob Eaton Is No Lee Iacocca—But He Doesn't Need to Be," *Business Week,* November 9, 1992, p. 96; "Detroit's Renaissance Man," *Newsweek,* June 28, 1993; "Iacocca's Last Stand at Chrysler," *Fortune,* April 20, 1992, p. 63.

THE SATISFACTIONS AND FRUSTRATIONS OF BEING A LEADER

The term *leader* has a positive connotation for most people. To be called a leader is generally better than to be called a follower or a subordinate. (Note that the term *follower* is rapidly falling into disuse in modern organizations. The term *subordinate* is also being used less frequently. The preferred term for a person who reports to a leader has become *team member* or *group member*.) Yet being a leader, such as a team leader, vice president, or CEO, does not always bring personal satisfaction. Some leadership jobs are more fun than others. The leader of a high-performing group has more fun than the leader of a low-performing one. The owner of a large, successful restaurant has more fun than the owner of a small restaurant facing bankruptcy.

Because most of you are contemplating becoming a leader or moving further into a leadership role, it is worthwhile to examine some of the potential satisfactions and frustrations many people find in being an organizational leader.

Satisfactions of Leaders

The type of satisfactions that you might obtain from being a formal leader depends on your particular leadership position. Factors such as the amount of money you are paid and the type of people in your group influence your satisfaction. Following are seven sources of satisfaction that leaders often experience.

A Feeling of Power and Prestige.   Being a leader automatically grants you some power. Prestige is forthcoming because many people think highly of people who are leaders. In many organizations, top-level leaders are addressed as Mr., Mrs. or Ms., whereas lower-ranking people are referred to by their surnames.

A Chance to Help Others.   A leader works directly with people, often teaching them job skills, serving as a mentor, and listening to personal problems. Part of a leader's job is to help other people become managers and leaders. A leader often feels as much of a "people helper" as does a human resources manager or a counselor.

High Income.   Leaders, in general, receive higher pay than team members, and executive leaders in major business corporations often earn several million dollars per year. If money is an important motivator or satisfier, being a leader has a built-in satisfaction. In some situations a team leader earns virtually the same amount of money as other team members. Occupying a leadership position, however, is a starting point on the path to high-paying leadership positions.

Respect and Status.   A leader frequently receives respect from group members. He or she also enjoys a higher status than people who are not occupying a leadership role. Status accompanies being appointed to a leadership position on or off the job. When an individual's personal qualifications match the position, his or her status is even higher.

Good Opportunities for Advancement.   Once you become a leader, your advancement opportunities increase. Obtaining a leadership position is a vital first step for career advancement in many organizations. Staff or individual contributor positions help broaden a person's professional experience, but most executives rise through a managerial path.

A Feeling of "Being in on" Things.   A side benefit of being a leader is that you receive more inside information. For instance, as a manager you are invited to attend management meetings. In those meetings you are given information not passed along to individual contributors. One such tidbit might be plans for expansion or downsizing.

An Opportunity to Control Money and Other Resources.   A leader is often in the position of helping to prepare a department budget and authorize expenses. Even though you cannot spend this money personally, it does provide some satisfaction in knowing that your judgment on financial matters is trusted. Many leaders in both private and public organizations control annual budgets of several million dollars.

Dissatisfactions and Frustrations of Leaders

About one out of ten people in the workforce is classified as a supervisor, administrator, or manager. Not every one of these people is a true leader. Yet the problems these people experience often stem from the leadership portions of their job. Many individual contributors refuse to accept a leadership role because of the frustrations they have seen leaders endure. The frustrations experienced by a wide range of people in leadership roles center around the problems described next.

Too Much Uncompensated Overtime.   People in leadership jobs are usually expected to work longer hours than other employees. Such unpaid hours are called *casual overtime.* People in organizational leadership positions typically spend about fifty-five hours per week working. During peak periods of peak demands, this figure can surge to eighty hours per week.

Too Many "Headaches."   It would take several pages to list all the potential problems leaders face. Being a leader is a good way to discover the validity of Murphy's law: "If anything can go wrong, it will." A leader is subject to a batch of problems involving people and things. Many people find that a leadership position is a source of stress, and many managers experience burnout.

Not Enough Authority to Carry Out Responsibility.   People in managerial positions complain repeatedly that they are held responsible for things over which they have little control. As a leader, you might be expected to work with an ill-performing team member, yet you lack the power to fire him or her. Or you might be expected to produce high-quality service with too small a staff and no authority to become fully staffed.

Loneliness. The higher you rise as a leader, the more lonely you will be in a certain sense. Leadership limits the number of people in whom you can confide. It is awkward to confide negative feelings about your employer to a team member. It is equally awkward to complain about one group member to another. Some people in leadership positions feel lonely because they miss being "one of the gang."

Too Many Problems Involving People. A major frustration facing a leader is the number of human resources problems requiring action. The lower your leadership position, the more such problems you face. For example, the office supervisor spends more time dealing with problem employees than does the chief financial officer.

Too Much Paperwork and Electronic Mail. As work organizations have become more formalized, an abundance of forms have been generated. A common complaint of leaders and managers at all levels is that paperwork and electronic mail take up too much of their time. Government regulations over matters such as employee health and safety and Equal Employment Opportunity Compliance are another source of substantial paperwork for managers. Even if a leader is seen primarily as a change agent and a visionary, he or she cannot escape all paperwork and electronic mail.

Too Much Organizational Politics. People at all levels of an organization, from the office assistant to the chairperson of the board, must be aware of political factors. Yet you can avoid politics more easily as an individual contributor than you can as a leader. As a leader you have to engage in political byplay from three directions: below, sideways, and upward. Political tactics such as forming alliances and coalitions are a necessary part of a leader's role.

A FRAMEWORK FOR UNDERSTANDING LEADERSHIP

Many different theories and explanations of leadership have been developed because of the interest in leadership as a practice and as a research topic. Several attempts have been made to integrate the large number of leadership theories into one comprehensive framework.[15] Unfortunately, such integrations become so complex that they are of limited practical value, and too multifaceted to validate. The framework presented here is basically

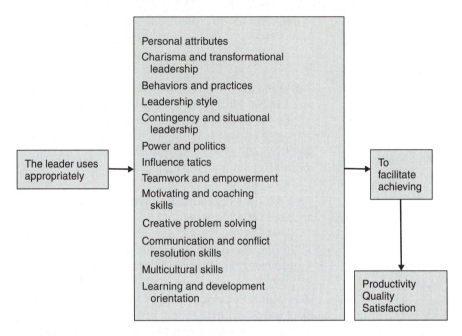

The leader uses appropriately →

Personal attributes

Charisma and transformational leadership

Behaviors and practices

Leadership style

Contingency and situational leadership

Power and politics

Influence tatics

Teamwork and empowerment

Motivating and coaching skills

Creative problem solving

Communication and conflict resolution skills

Multicultural skills

Learning and development orientation

→ To facilitate achieving

Productivity
Quality
Satisfaction

FIGURE 1–2

A Framework for Understanding Leadership

an overview of the major leadership topics selected for inclusion in this book, as shown in Figure 1–2. Its basic premise is that effective leaders use the right mix of appropriate personal characteristics, leadership behaviors, and techniques to facilitate productivity, quality, and satisfaction, and thus to attain goals.

To illustrate, a chief financial officer who wants to convince financial analysts that her company is a good investment might emphasize communicating a vision, personal magnetism, and creative thinking. A manufacturing supervisor striving to lead his group to attain a tough quality standard might emphasize motivational and coaching skills. The following paragraphs summarize the components of the framework, all of which are presented later as separate chapters.

Personal Attributes.   A starting point in understanding leadership is to recognize that leaders must rely on certain traits, motives, and characteristics to achieve their objectives. Certain personal attributes are frequently associated with leadership effectiveness. Among them are self-confidence, good problem-solving skills, ability, honesty and integrity, and assertiveness.

The earliest approaches to understanding leaders and leadership emphasized the **trait approach** (or **great person theory**), the observation that leadership effectiveness depends on certain personal attributes. For many years, researchers cast doubt on the trait approach. In recent years, though, research on and observation of leadership have gained a new appreciation of the importance of the personal qualities of leaders, as described in Chapter 2. For now, be mindful that a starting point in becoming an effective leader is to develop personal attributes associated with effective leadership.

Charisma and Transformational Leadership.   At times leaders can best achieve productivity, quality, and group member satisfaction by being magnetic, charming, and visionary. Leaders who are perceived in this way, and who bring about important changes, are said to exercise charismatic and transformational leadership. The study of charismatic and transformational leadership is both a subset and a modern version of the trait approach.

In recent years transformational leadership has become a major new emphasis in studying leadership, partly because so many organizations need to be transformed. Chapter 3 provides details about charismatic and transformational leadership, including examples of charismatic leaders. Martin Luther King, Jr. was an example of a charismatic leader in the public sector; his famous speech, "I Have a Dream," showed his charisma in action.

Effective Leadership Behaviors and Practices.   Personal attributes alone are insufficient for leaders to facilitate the accomplishment of objectives. The leader must also behave in certain ways and possess certain skills. Partly in response to the insufficiency of the trait approach, research in the post–World War II era began to focus on the relationships between leader behavior and employee performance. The intent of this research was to identify behaviors exhibited by effective leaders that were not displayed by their less effective counterparts.[16] The behaviors, skills, and practices of effective leaders are explored in Chapter 4. Among them are adaptability to the situation, setting high performance standards, providing emotional support to group members, and encouraging group members to participate in decision making.

A belief in the importance of leadership behaviors, skills, and practices has created the growth industry of leadership and management development. It is assumed that you can enhance your leadership effectiveness if you participate in appropriate leadership seminars and study the right information. Your personal attributes, however, will help you benefit from such leadership development experiences. For example, if you are intelligent and self-confident it will be easy for you to learn effective leadership practices. Following is the description of a course in a representative leadership development program, "The Effective Facilitator: Maximizing Involvement and Results," offered by the American Management Association:

> The facilitator is catalyst, coach, coordinator, and more. Like a conductor, the facilitator must bring out the best in individual players and orchestrate successful group efforts. It's a role that demands exceptional interpersonal skills, keen observation, insight, and tact. It can only be learned by doing. And at this course,

you'll gain maximum practice, group interaction, and feedback as you go along. Learning in a group meeting environment from the start, you'll see your own group's process and progress on videotape—and sharpen your own skills.[17]

Leadership Style.   A **leadership style** is a relatively consistent pattern of behavior that characterizes a leader. The concept of style is therefore a logical extension of understanding leadership through behaviors, skills, and practices. A leader must choose a leadership style that is appropriate for accomplishing results; it should also fit his or her personality.

The concept of leadership styles, described in Chapter 5, may already be familiar to you. Business leaders are typically described in terms of their style: an example is Bob Eaton of Chrysler, who sees himself as a "participatory not a consensus leader." The implication is that Eaton solicits input from team members before making a decision, and then takes action—but he does not wait until general agreement has been reached.

Contingency and Situational Leadership.   Taking the concept of leadership styles one step further, the framework indicates that leaders often practice **contingency and situational leadership**—that is, they choose the right style to match the situation. The situational theory of leadership begins with the assumption that there are no traits and behaviors that automatically constitute effective leadership. To be effective, the leader's style must fit the situation. For example, a low-key consultative style might work well with competent professionals but would be less effective with inexperienced team members with a weak work ethic.

The situational perspective on leadership, as described in Chapter 6, explains that leaders must correctly identify the behaviors required in a given situation. After diagnosing the situation, the leader must then be flexible enough to select a behavior to match the situation. Assume, for example, that an organizational unit is facing the crisis of a downsizing. The effective leader would diagnose the insecurity, ambiguity, and stress faced by team members. His or her response would be to support team members emotionally to help them through the crisis.

The example of the crisis manager illustrates an important point about the framework for understanding leadership: that the various perspectives on leadership are interrelated. A leader stands the best chance of correctly diagnosing a situation and then offering emotional support if he or she has high intelligence and personal warmth. The same example also reinforces the major proposition of the framework: that leaders emphasize various traits, and choose among various leadership approaches and skills in order to facilitate achieving productivity, quality, and satisfaction.

Power and Politics.   To facilitate the achievement of productivity, quality, and satisfaction, leaders must also make deft use of power and politics. Both power and politics are closely related to influence tactics. **Power** is the potential to influence decisions and control resources; **politics** refers to various methods people use to attain or maintain power, and to gain other advantages. Many influence tactics are political in nature, such as manipulating people by threatening to settle a dispute with a higher authority.

The leadership use of power and politics is explained in Chapter 7. Leaders must understand how to use power and politics effectively and ethically in order to achieve worthwhile ends. For example, a director of research and development whose budget and staff were threatened with drastic reduction made adept use of power and politics:

> Rumors were flying that the R&D [research and development] budget would be slashed next. I didn't mind helping the corporation by taking some reduction in our budget. And I wasn't concerned about job security. Being in such a visible spot in a high-technology leader, I regularly receive job offers. What worried me the most is the long-range health of our company. If we took the short-sighted view of squelching R&D we would be in big trouble in the near future.
>
> To head off big trouble, I made good use of my internal and external contacts. I had lunch separately with several board members including our CEO, our chairman, and two outsiders on the board. I presented data about how other high-tech companies that slashed research and development were seriously hurt in the long run.
>
> When the next downsizing was officially announced, we were asked to absorb only a five percent reduction in our operating budget. We were able to accomplish this goal readily with just a little selective pruning of people and projects.

Influence Tactics.   Leadership is universally considered to be an influence process. It therefore follows that to lead effectively the leader must choose among a combination of various influence tactics, as described in Chapter 8. Jerry M. Reinsdorf, the owner of the Chicago White Sox and the Chicago Bulls, exemplifies how a successful leader combines influence tactics to achieve important results. Above all, he uses rational persuasion. He can speak with authority on issues ranging from broadcasting to international marketing. The executive director of the Major League Baseball Players Association says of Reinsdorf, "Jerry is clearly the most powerful owner. He thinks, he plans, he pays attention to detail. He pleads, he cajoles, he urges, he threatens. He's able to do almost anything he wants."[18]

Teamwork and Empowerment.   To be an effective leader in most modern organizations, the manager must emphasize teamwork and empowerment. Teamwork, of course, concerns the group acting in concert with *esprit de corps* (team spirit). As described in Chapter 9, the leader can choose from among many strategies and tactics to achieve teamwork. To strengthen the team, and lead with an approach consistent with the major new thrust in organizations, the leader must be willing to empower the right team members. **Empowerment** refers to the process of sharing power with team members, thereby enhancing their feelings of personal effectiveness.

To empower employees, the leader must accept the team member as a partner in decision making. The empowering leader must therefore choose a leadership style consistent with power sharing. Simultaneously, the leader must emphasize personal traits consistent with power sharing, such as trust. A vice president of claims at an insurance company expresses her attitude toward empowerment in these terms:

> Without empowering our claims specialists, we would have an unmanageable backlog of unsettled claims. Our claims people have wide latitude in doing what is best for the customer. If our claims specialists had to clear each claim settlement through three levels of management, we would have the same bad reputation as many of our competitors.

Motivating and Coaching Skills.   Visionary leaders may be able to motivate people from a distance. Yet many other managers must perform their leadership function by working closely with team members to prompt them to work hard, and sustain good performance. To accomplish these ends, the leader must choose among various motivational and coaching techniques. Motivation and coaching are the nuts and bolts of a leader's job. Similar to a machine, an organization will soon fall apart if these nuts and bolts are given short shrift. Consider also that effective leaders see themselves as motivators. This is especially true because without sustained effort by employees, organizational goals will not be achieved. Chapter 10 describes specific motivating and coaching skills. (The theories of motivation already familiar to the reader are not repeated, however.)

Creative Problem Solving.   To facilitate achieving productivity, quality, and satisfaction, managers must frequently engage in creative problem solving. True leaders, however, also use creative problem solving to inspire and encourage people on the path toward increased productivity and quality. People do not have to be inspired to experience job satisfaction, but inspirational leadership may contribute to satisfaction. Chapter 11 provides information on improving creativity to meet the demands of managerial leadership positions.

One application of creative problem solving to inspiring people is to develop dramatic stunts to capture people's attention. T. J. Rodgers, the colorful chief executive of Cypress Semiconductors, uses imaginative thinking to dramatize a point. At one time a manager did not carefully follow the company procedures for employee selection. In retaliation, Rodgers cut a company rule book in half with a giant pair of scissors. He then sent the errant manager the "broken rule book," as a reminder of the manager's mistake. Rodgers also captures attention through a computer program he has developed to destroy the data and software of company managers who violate procedures. The program is called *killer software.*

Another example of inspiration is Jack Hollister, the former president of an industrial pump company in Massachusetts. Hollister promised to give each employee a $100 U.S. Savings Bond when the company reached $25 million in sales. To the surprise of many employees, every worker did receive the bond in the mail, ten days after the milestone was achieved.

Communication and Conflict Resolution Skills. Excellence in persuasive communication is required in almost every leadership act. Communication is the vehicle for inspiration, influence, motivation, and coaching. The spoken and written communication of charismatic leaders is marked by colorful analogies and powerful words, as will be described in Chapter 12. John Sculley, the former visionary head of Apple Computer, Inc., often uses phrases such as "We want this computer to be outrageously good," and "Our next generation of products will reshape the way the world communicates." Effective leadership also requires an ability to resolve conflict among group members and various constituencies.

Multicultural Skills. In the modern environment a leader is frequently required to work effectively with culturally diverse people. The diversity stems from working with people from other countries and with diverse groups within one's own country. As the workforce becomes increasingly heterogeneous, an appreciation of multiculturalism escalates in importance, as described in Chapter 13.

Learning and Development Orientation. A final element in the framework here is that to remain effective, leaders must continue to develop and learn. The knowledge base required to lead others effectively continues to increase. In addition, it behooves the leader to stay current with new developments in leadership theory, such as achieving partnerships with group members. Chapter 14 describes management development.

SKILL DEVELOPMENT IN LEADERSHIP

Developing leadership skills is more complex than developing a structured skill such as conducting an inventory audit or driving a golf ball. Nevertheless, you can develop leadership skills by reading this text, which follows a general learning model:

1. Conceptual knowledge and behavioral guidelines. Each chapter in this text presents useful information about leadership, including a section titled "Guidelines for Action."

2. Conceptual information demonstrated by examples and brief descriptions of leaders in action.

3. Experiential exercises. The text provides an opportunity for practice and personalization through cases, role plays, and self-assessment exercises.

Self-quizzes are emphasized here because they are an effective method of helping you personalize the information, that is, link conceptual information to yourself. For example, you will read about the importance of assertiveness in leadership and also complete an assertiveness scale. Readers who look for opportunities to practice some of the leadership skills outside the classroom will acquire new skills more quickly.

4. Feedback on skill utilization, or performance, from others. Feedback exercises appear at several places in the text. Implementing some of the skills outside of the classroom will provide additional opportunities for feedback.

Chapter 15, about leadership development, provides more information about how leadership skills are developed. As you work through the text, keep the four-part learning model in mind.

SUMMARY

Leadership is the ability to inspire confidence in and support among the people who are needed to achieve organizational goals. Leading is a major part of a manager's job, but a manager also plans, organizes, and controls. Leadership is said to deal with change, inspiration, motivation, and influence. In contrast, management deals more with maintaining equilibrium and the status quo. An important new development is to regard leadership as a long-term relationship, or partnership, between leaders and group members.

Some research evidence supports the widely accepted view that the leader affects organizational performance. It is also observed that many people attribute organizational performance to leadership actions. The concept of substitutes for leadership argues that factors in the work environment make the leader's role almost superfluous. Among them are closely knit teams of highly trained workers, intrinsic satisfaction with work, computer technology, and professional norms. Another antileadership argument is that the leader is irrelevant in most organizational outcomes because the situation is considered to be more important. Part of the leadership irrelevance argument is that the leader has unilateral control over only a few resources. Another part is that new leaders are chosen whose values are compatible with those of the firm.

Examining the roles carried out by leaders contributes to an understanding of the leadership function. Eight such leadership roles are the figurehead, spokesperson, negotiator, coach, team builder, team player, technical problem solver, and entrepreneur. An important implication of these roles is that managers at every level can exert leadership.

A leadership position is often a source of satisfaction to its holder, stemming from such factors as power, prestige, the opportunity to help others, high income, and the opportunity to control resources. At other times being a leader carries with it a number of frustrations, such as insufficient authority, dealing with human problems, and too much organizational politics.

The framework for understanding leadership presented here observes that the leader uses the appropriate personal characteristics, leadership behaviors, and techniques to facilitate productivity, quality, and satisfaction. The components of the framework then become the major topics in studying leadership. These include (1) the personal attributes of leaders, (2) charisma and transformational leadership, (3) leadership behaviors and practices, (4) leadership style, (5) contingency and situational leadership, (6) influence tactics, (7) power and politics, (8) teamwork and empowerment, (9) motivating and coaching skills, (10) creative problem solving, (11) communication and conflict resolution skills, (12) multicultural skills, and (13) a development and learning orientation. All of these aspects of leadership are directed toward productivity, quality, and satisfaction.

KEY TERMS

Leadership	Contingency and situational leadership
Partnership	
Attribution theory	Power
Substitutes for leadership	Politics
Trait approach (great person theory)	Empowerment
Leadership style	

GUIDELINES FOR ACTION AND SKILL DEVELOPMENT

Vast information has been gathered about leaders and leadership, and many different leadership theories have been developed. A definitive review of leadership research, *Bass & Stogdill's Handbook of Leadership: Theory, Research, & Managerial Applications* contains approximately 7,560 references.[19] Moreover, these references include very few magazine articles and trade books about leadership. Many leadership research findings and theories are confusing and contradictory. Nevertheless, through this thicket of information emerge many useful leadership concepts and techniques to guide you toward becoming a more effective leader.

As you work toward leadership effectiveness, first be familiar with the approaches to leadership described in this text. Then choose the formulation that seems best to fit the leadership situation you face. For example, if you are leading a team, review the information about team leadership. Typically an effective leader needs to combine several leadership approaches to meet the demands in a given situation. For instance, a leader might need to combine creative problem solving and emotional support to members to help the team rebound from a crisis.

DISCUSSION QUESTIONS AND ACTIVITIES

1. What would be a practical problem stemming from the idea that the leader creates a vision, whereas the manager implements it?

2. Why do you think the terms *subordinate* and *follower* are used less frequently than previously?

3. After reading this chapter, do you believe that a person who is not a "born leader" still has a chance of becoming an effective leader?

4. Identify a sports or business leader whom you think is charismatic. Present your observations to your class.

5. Why are persuasive skills so important for a leader?

6. Phil Purcell of Dean Witter achieved high grades at top business schools, yet many people argue that grades are a poor predictor of leadership success. What is your opinion?

7. Identify a force in society or an economic factor that has contributed to the growth of empowerment.

8. Why might the framework for understanding leadership presented in this text be considered *eclectic*?

9. Several surveys have indicated that leadership is the most important topic in organizational behavior and management. How do you explain this finding?

10. Why or why not are you suited for a leadership role?

LEADERSHIP CASE PROBLEM

Does Bob Allen at AT&T Have the Right Stuff?

A battle took place several years ago for the control of NCR Corp., the computer manufacturer. NCR Chairman Charles E. Exley, Jr., delighted reporters with biting quips about American Telephone & Telegraph's floundering computer strategy. Exley joked that AT&T's attempt to enter the computer field was analogous to an electric utility getting into the Mixmaster business. In comparison, AT&T Chairman Robert F. Allen appeared uncomfortable talking to reporters about his company's plans to enter the computer industry. Yet after an almost half-year struggle, Allen's perseverance, along with $7.4 billion in AT&T stock, won the contest.

Allen has a ramrod-straight style, matched by a seriousness of purpose. The combination has impressed many people, including Hale Irwin, his Pro-Am golfing partner, and the current NCR Chairman, Gilbert P. Williamson. Says Williamson, "He's a thoughtful person—unemotional, clinical. That's pretty good."

Allen's character was developed in Indiana. In his early days he worked on a farm and a railroad gang and played end on the Wabash College football team. His first professional job was as a traffic engineer for Indiana Bell. He gained experience with assignments at Bell of Pennsylvania, Illinois Bell, and the Chesapeake & Potomac Telephone companies. Allen was then assigned permanently to corporate headquarters in 1983.

A career in the heavily regulated Bell system was not the best experience for leading AT&T through deregulation and open competition. Allen admits that he floundered for a few months upon becoming chairman in 1988. Yet soon he acquired a management style that suited his temperament. He is seen as more collegial than inspirational. Instead of trying to tightly centralize AT&T, Allen has divided the company into twenty lines of business. To demonstrate the seriousness of the decentralization plan, he turned the organization chart upside down to show that AT&T top management actually supports the business unit presidents.

Last year, Allen took his decentralization plan one step further. He delegated day-to-day decisions to a five-person Operations Committee, of which he is not a member. He put the ambiguity in structure on purpose.

Allen demonstrated in the struggle with NCR that he can take decisive action. By going over Exley's head, he risked a group of mass resignations and creating confusion in both companies. Among top NCR people, only Exley has resigned. Furthermore, the merger between AT&T and NCR is progressing smoothly. In August of 1993, Allen spearheaded a major step toward making AT&T the dominant power in the new era of telecommunications. The company bought McCaw Cellular for $12.6 billion.

Some observers think that Allen's serious, straightforward style is just what is needed. The same people believe that flair and showpersonship will not keep the combination of AT&T and NCR on its long-term course.

1. How does this case relate to the framework for understanding leadership?

2. If Bob Allen is not considered a visionary, should he still be considered a leader?

3. In what way did Allen use organizational power and politics to achieve his goal?

4. Do you think Allen's personal style is well suited in the long run to being the CEO of AT&T?

Source: Based on facts in Peter Coy, "How Bob Allen Is Rewiring AT&T Management," *Business Week,* January 20, 1992, pp. 58–59; "AT&T's Bold Bet," *Business Week,* August 30, 1993, pp. 26–30.

LEADERSHIP ROLE PLAY

The Inspirational Leader

An important leadership characteristic is the ability to inspire others. To develop a preliminary feel for what it means to inspire a group, conduct the following role play. One person plays the role of a leader who is attempting to inspire a work group toward some important end, such as increasing sales or attaining new heights of quality. About five other people play the role of the inspirees (the people being inspired). After the leader makes his or her inspirational appeal, a group discussion is held of how well the appeal might have worked in reality.

Although it is early in the course to have learned how to inspire people, use this exercise as a baseline experience. Attempt to use whatever persuasive appeals you can.

CHAPTER TWO

Traits, Motives, and Characteristics of Leaders

LEARNING OBJECTIVES

After studying this chapter, you should be able to

1. identify general and task-related personality traits of leaders that contribute to leadership effectiveness.
2. identify key motives that contribute to leadership effectiveness.
3. describe cognitive factors associated with effective leadership, and summarize key points of the cognitive resource theory.
4. explain the relationship between leadership and physical and background factors.
5. discuss the heredity versus environment issue in relation to leadership effectiveness.
6. summarize strengths and weaknesses of the trait approach to understanding leadership.

While attending college, Len Calcone worked part-time and summers for Ryder, the truck rental firm. When graduation approached, Len never had to conduct a job search. Instead, he was offered an assistant manager's position at the same Ryder location. Len was told, "We've watched your work closely for two years. You've got what it takes to become a manager at Ryder. We like your take-charge attitude, and the way you deal with people. We see you as having leadership potential."

The incident just described illustrates a workplace reality. When people are chosen for leadership positions, or when leaders are evaluated, their personal traits and characteristics are scrutinized. Should somebody appear to be a good candidate for a position, or has performed well, the person is described by such adjectives as "compassionate," "honest," "take-charge," and "forward thinking." Many people believe intuitively that personal characteristics strongly determine leadership effectiveness.

The belief that certain personal characteristics and skills contribute to leadership effectiveness in many situations is the **universal theory of leadership.** According to this theory, certain leadership traits are universally important—that is, they apply in all situations. This and the following chapter concentrate on the personal characteristics aspect of the universal theory; Chapter 4 describes the behaviors and skills that are part of the universal theory. Recognize, however, that personal characteristics are closely associated with leadership skills and behaviors. For example, creative thinking ability (a characteristic) helps a leader formulate an exciting vision (leadership behavior). The Leader in Action essay on page 30 presents a case history supporting the belief that a leader can be effective in different leadership situations.

Characteristics associated with leadership can be classified into four broad categories: personality traits, motives, cognitive factors, and physical and background factors. These categories of behavior serve as helpful guides but are not definitive. A convincing argument can often be made that an aspect of leadership placed in one category could be placed in another. Nevertheless, no matter how personal characteristics are classified, they point toward the conclusion that effective leaders are made of the *right stuff*. Published research about the trait (*great person*) approach first appeared at the turn of the century; it continues today. A full listing of every personal characteristic ever found to be associated with leadership would take several hundred pages. Therefore, included here are the major and most consistently found characteristics related to leadership effectiveness.

PERSONALITY TRAITS OF EFFECTIVE LEADERS

Observations by managers and human resource specialists, as well as dozens of research studies, indicate that leaders have certain personality traits.[1] These characteristics contribute to leadership effectiveness in many situations as long as the leader's style fits the situation reasonably well. For example, Paul Stern, the former CEO of Northern Telecom, has performed admirably as a leader in companies involved in different aspects of telecommunications and with widely varying organizational cultures. Nevertheless, Stern might not fit well as a shop-floor leader; his intellectual style might make him a poor fit with production workers. Leaders' personality traits can be divided into two groups: general personality traits, such as self-

LEADER IN ACTION

High-Tech Star Paul G. Stern

Paul G. Stern was recently the chairman and CEO of Northern Telecom, a Canadian-based telecommunications giant. The company conducts 76 percent of its business internationally. Sales in the United States are double those in Canada.

Stern was born in Czechoslovakia and reared in Mexico City. After graduating from college in the United States, he earned a doctorate in solid-state physics at the University of Manchester in England. After graduation, he joined IBM in a research capacity, but he quickly moved into management. Stern was promoted five times during his seven years at IBM, leaving as a vice president. Stern left to join Braun, the German consumer appliance company, where he quickly became CEO. His flawless German earned him the nickname "the German American."

After four years at Braun, Stern moved on to become the president of Burroughs Corp. When Burroughs merged with Sperry to form Unisys, Stern became the first president of the new company. He had a personality clash with CEO W. Michael Blumenthal, and resigned to join the board of Northern Telecom. In March 1989, Stern was named CEO of Northern Telecom. After five profitable years, Northern Telecom reported its first loss in the second quarter of 1993. At that time Stern resigned abruptly to become an investment banker.

Paul Stern has developed the reputation of a professional executive who makes heavy demands on people yet inspires them toward high performance. Headhunters (executive recruiters) classify Stern as an executive in demand for many different industries.

Source: Based in part on information in "High-Tech Star: Northern Telecom Is Challenging Even AT&T," *Business Week,* July 27, 1992, pp. 54–58; "Ringing in a Change: Financial Shocks Hit Northern Telecom," *Maclean's,* July 12, 1993, pp. 32–37.

confidence and honesty, and task-related traits, such as an internal locus of control.

General Personality Traits

We define a general personality trait as a trait that is observable both within and outside the context of work. That is, the same general traits are related to success and satisfaction in both work and personal life. Figure 2–1 lists the general personality traits that contribute to successful leadership.

Self-confidence.   In virtually every leadership setting, it is important for the leader to be realistically self-confident. A leader who is self-assured without being bombastic or overbearing instills confidence in team members. Self-confidence was among the first leadership traits researchers identified. Recent research with leaders in many situations has continued to underscore the importance of this trait. In addition to being self-confident, the leader must project that self-confidence to the group.[2] Quite often he or she can do so by using unequivocal wording, maintaining good posture, and making appropriate gestures, such as pointing an index finger outward.

Self-confidence is not only a personality trait; it also refers to the behavior a person exhibits in a number of situations. It is akin to being cool under pressure. We can conclude that a person is a self-confident leader when he or she retains composure during a crisis such as managing a large product recall. Bernadine Healy, the director of the National Institutes of Health, exemplifies a self-confident leader. An associate dean at Johns Hopkins medical school, where Healy earlier served as a researcher and administrator, said, "You knew she was going to be the first woman dean of a major medical school or head of NIH."[3]

Honesty, Integrity, and Credibility.   Group members consistently believe that leaders must display honesty, integrity, and credibility. Leaders themselves believe that honesty makes a difference in their effectiveness. Researchers and outside observers also share these views. Warren G. Bennis, an established leadership authority, interviewed more than 100 corporate leaders and 50 private-sector leaders during a thirteen-year period. One of the common threads he found was the capacity of leaders to generate and

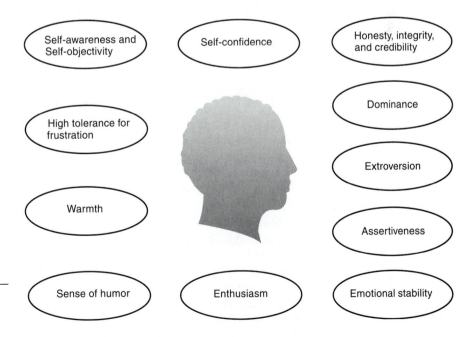

FIGURE 2–1

General Personality Traits of Effective Leaders

sustain trust. Under the umbrella term of *trust*, Bennis included competence, caring, reliability, predictability, and integrity. He observed a consistency among what leaders think, feel, and do. Bennis said it drives people crazy when bosses don't walk their talk.[4]

According to James M. Kouzes and Barry Z. Posner, leadership is in the eye of the follower (that is, the group member). This is why honesty, integrity, and credibility are so important. Kouzes and Posner asked more than 7,500 managers from private and public organizations to indicate what they looked for or admired in their leaders. Eighty-seven percent of the respondents selected honesty as a key leadership characteristic. In fact, in every survey conducted, honesty was the most frequently chosen leadership characteristic. Consistent with Bennis's observations, the managers in the Kouzes-Posner survey judged the honesty of their leaders by their behaviors:

> Leaders are considered honest by their constituents when the leaders do what they say they are going to do. Agreements not followed through, cover-ups, inconsistency between word and deed are all indicators of lack of honesty. Yet if a leader behaves in ways consistent with his or her stated values and beliefs, then we believe we can entrust to that person our careers, our security, even our lives.[5]

The importance of honesty also emerged in a study by the Center for Creative Leadership. Research showed that managers who become executive leaders are likely to espouse the following formula: "I will do exactly what I say I will do when I say I will do it. If I change my mind, I will tell you in advance so you will not be harmed by my actions."[6]

Dominance.   A dominant person imposes his or her will on others. As a consequence, a dominant leader is often seen as domineering or bossy. Whereas dominance was considered almost synonymous with leadership in the early days of leadership research, the more modern viewpoint recognizes that many other traits are involved.

Extroversion.   Extroversion has been recognized for its contribution to leadership effectiveness because it is helpful for leaders in most situations to be gregarious and outgoing. Also, extroverts are more likely to want to assume a leadership role and participate in group activities.[7] Even though it is logical to think that extroversion is related to leadership, many effective leaders are laid-back and even introverted. AT&T executive Bob Allen, for example, is quiet and reserved.

Assertiveness.   In recent years more attention has been paid to assertiveness than to dominance and extroversion as a leadership trait. **Assertiveness** refers to being forthright in expressing demands, opinions, feelings, and attitudes. Assertiveness helps leaders perform many tasks and achieve goals. Among them are confronting group members about their mistakes, demanding higher performance, setting high expectations, and making legitimate demands on higher management.

To be assertive differs significantly from being aggressive or passive. Aggressive people express their demands in an overly pushy, obnoxious, and abrasive manner; passive people suppress their own ideas, attitudes, feelings, and thoughts as if they were likely to be perceived as controversial. As a result of being passive, a person might not be recommended for large salary increases, good assignments, and promotions.

To determine how assertive you are, do the accompanying leadership self-assessment exercise.

LEADERSHIP SELF-ASSESSMENT EXERCISE 2–1 The Assertiveness Scale

Directions: Indicate whether each of the following statements is mostly true or mostly false as it applies to you. If in doubt about your reaction to a particular statement, think of how you would *generally* respond.

	Mostly True	Mostly False
1. It is extremely difficult for me to turn down a sales representative when he or she is a nice person.	____	____
2. I express criticism freely.	____	____
3. If another person is being very unfair, I bring it to that person's attention.	____	____
4. Work is no place to let your feelings show.	____	____
5. It's no use asking for favors; people get what they deserve.	____	____
6. Business is not the place for tact; say what you think.	____	____
7. If a person looks as if he or she is in a hurry, I let that person in front of me in a supermarket line.	____	____
8. A weakness of mine is that I'm too nice a person.	____	____
9. If my restaurant bill is even 50 cents more than it should be, I demand that the mistake be corrected.	____	____
10. If the mood strikes me, I will laugh out loud in public.	____	____
11. People would describe me as too outspoken.	____	____

12. I am quite willing to have the store take back a piece of furniture that was scratched upon delivery.   ____   ____

13. I dread having to express anger toward a co-worker.   ____   ____

14. People often say that I'm too reserved and emotionally controlled.   ____   ____

15. Nice people finish last in business.   ____   ____

16. I fight for my rights down to the last detail.   ____   ____

17. I have no misgivings about returning an overcoat to the store if it doesn't fit me right.   ____   ____

18. After I have an argument with a person, I try to avoid him or her.   ____   ____

19. I insist that my spouse (or roommate or partner) do his or her fair share of undesirable chores.   ____   ____

20. It is difficult for me to look directly at another person when the two of us are in disagreement.   ____   ____

21. I have cried among friends more than once.   ____   ____

22. If someone near me at a movie keeps up a conversation with another person, I ask him or her to stop.   ____   ____

23. I am able to turn down social engagements with people I do not particularly care for.   ____   ____

24. It is in poor taste to express what you really feel about another individual.   ____   ____

25. I sometimes show my anger by swearing at or belittling another person.   ____   ____

26. I am reluctant to speak up at a meeting.   ____   ____

27. I find it relatively easy to ask friends for small favors such as giving me a ride to work while my car is being repaired.   ____   ____

28. If another person is talking very loudly in a restaurant and it bothers me, I inform that person.   ____   ____

29. I often finish other people's sentences for them.   ____   ____

30. It is relatively easy for me to express love and affection toward another person.   ____   ____

Scoring Key

1. Mostly false	11. Mostly true	21. Mostly true
2. Mostly true	12. Mostly true	22. Mostly true
3. Mostly true	13. Mostly false	23. Mostly true
4. Mostly false	14. Mostly false	24. Mostly false
5. Mostly false	15. Mostly true	25. Mostly true
6. Mostly true	16. Mostly true	26. Mostly false
7. Mostly false	17. Mostly true	27. Mostly true
8. Mostly false	18. Mostly false	28. Mostly true
9. Mostly true	19. Mostly true	29. Mostly true
10. Mostly true	20. Mostly false	30. Mostly true

Interpretation: Score +1 for each of your answers that agrees with the scoring key.

0–15	Nonassertive
16–24	Assertive
25+	Assertive

Do this exercise again about thirty days from now to give yourself some indication of the stability of your answers. You might also discuss your answers with a close friend to determine if that person has a similar perception of your assertiveness.

Emotional Stability. Anyone who has ever worked for an unstable boss will attest to the importance of emotional stability as a leadership trait. **Emotional stability** refers to the ability to control emotions to the point that one's emotional responses are appropriate to the occasion. Emotions associated with low emotional stability include anxiety, depression, anger, embarrassment, and worry.

Emotional stability is an important leadership trait because group members expect and need consistency in the way they are treated. A sales manager had this to say about her boss, the vice president of marketing: "It was difficult to know whether to bring problems to Larry's attention. Some days he would compliment me for taking customer problems seriously. Other times he would rant and rave about the ineffectiveness of the sales department. We all worry about having our performance appraised on one of Larry's crazy days."

One study found that executive leaders who are emotionally unstable and lack composure are more likely to derail, that is, handle pressure poorly and give in to moodiness, outbursts of anger, and inconsistent behavior. Such inconsistency undermines their relationships with group members, peers, and superiors. In contrast, effective leaders are generally calm, confident, and predictable during a crisis.[8]

Enthusiasm.   In almost all leadership situations, it is desirable for the leader to be enthusiastic. Group members tend to respond positively to enthusiasm, partly because enthusiasm may be perceived as a reward for constructive behavior. Enthusiasm is also a desirable leadership trait because it helps build good relationships with team members. A leader can express enthusiasm both verbally ("Great job"; "I love it") and nonverbally (making a "high five" gesture). An executive newsletter made an enthusiastic comment about enthusiasm as a leadership trait:

> People look to you for [enthusiasm] to inspire them. It is the greatest tool for motivating others and for getting things done. As a leader, you have to get out in front of your people. Even the most enthusiastic employee is loath to show more of it than his or her boss. If you don't project a gung-ho attitude, everybody else will hold back.[9]

The accompanying Leader in Action insert presents a portrait of a leader known for her enthusiasm. Be alert also for other leadership traits this woman possesses.

Sense of Humor.   Some see a sense of humor as a trait, and some as a behavior. However you classify it, the effective use of humor is considered an important part of a leader's role. Humor serves such functions in the workplace as relieving tension and boredom and defusing hostility. Because humor helps the leader dissolve tension and defuse conflict, it helps her or him exert power over the group. Psychologist Barbara Mackoff contends, "Humor is the ultimate power tool on the job."[10]

Self-effacing humor is the choice of comedians and organizational leaders alike. By being self-effacing, the leader makes a point without insulting or slighting anybody.[11] A vice president of marketing at Sun Microsystems once said, "I want you people to design a work station so uncomplicated that even managers at my level could learn how to use it."

Warmth.   Being a warm person and projecting that warmth contribute to leadership effectiveness in several ways. First, warmth facilitates the establishment of rapport with group members. Second, the projection of warmth is a key component of charisma. Third, warmth is a trait that facilitates providing emotional support to group members. Giving such support is an important leadership behavior. Fourth, in the words of Kogan Page, "Warmth comes with the territory. Cold fish don't make good leaders because they turn people off."[12]

LEADER IN ACTION

Marcia Ann Gillespie, *Ms.* Editor

When Marcia Ann Gillespie was appointed editor in chief of *Ms.* magazine in 1993, she proclaimed, "I want stories that deal with extraordinary acts of everyday women. I want to see their faces and sing their praises." Influenced by her parents, Gillespie grew up with a sense of life's possibilities. At age 27 she became editor in chief of *Essence,* the first national magazine for black women. She joined *Ms.* as a contributing editor in 1980, and was appointed executive editor in 1988.

Gillespie sees herself as a person with a mission. The publisher and chief executive of *Essence* says that Gillespie provided the soul and sustenance of the magazine in its early years. In reflecting on her plans for *Ms.,* she says, "I'm determined to see before I die that feminist is not a dirty word." She sees the magazine as the home of feminism's big tent, pointing out that all feminists do not think alike.

A writer colleague says that "joyful" is the word used most frequently to describe Gillespie. Although not effusive and bubbly, she perceives her life as a feminist to be a joy, not a burden. Gillespie hopes that the color of her skin sends the message to black women that "there's room here for you, gal."

Source: Pat Guy, "*Ms.* Editor with a Mission," *USA Today,* August 11, 1993, p. 2B. Copyright 1993, *USA Today.* Reprinted with permission.

High Tolerance for Frustration.   Chris Piotrowski and Terry R. Armstrong took a creative approach to studying the personality characteristics of CEOs. They conducted a content analysis of data from televised interviews of leading chief executive officers on Cable Network News. Most of the personality traits revealed in the study parallel others mentioned in this chapter. The researchers also found that the most of the thirty executive leaders whose interviews were analyzed showed **high tolerance for frustration,** or the ability to cope with the blocking of goal attainment.[13] This trait is important because a leader encounters a great many frustrations.

Self-awareness and Self-objectivity.   Effective leaders are aware of their strengths and limitations. This awareness enables them to capitalize upon their strengths and develop their weaknesses. A leader might realize, for example, that he or she is naturally distrustful of others. Awareness of this problem cautions the leader not to distrust people without good evidence. Self-awareness and self-objectivity will be described further in Chapter 15.

Task-Related Personality Traits

Certain personality traits of effective leaders are closely associated with task accomplishment even though they still seem to fall more accurately in the trait category rather than the behavior category. The task-related traits described here are outlined in Figure 2–2.

Initiative.   Exercising **initiative,** or being a self-starter, refers to taking action without support and stimulation from others. A person aspiring to leadership assignments should recognize that initiative is a personality trait sought in potential leaders. Initiative is also related to problem-finding ability—you need to exercise initiative to search for worthwhile problems. An extraordinary example is John Sculley, the former CEO of Apple Computer. He took the initiative to spur his company to develop products beyond computers, such as personal digital assistants. Sculley's leadership along new product lines stemmed from his ability to recognize new potential opportunities in the external environment.

As conceptualized by Kirkpatrick and Locke, *initiative* refers to the proactive side of leadership. Rather than just reacting to events, effective leaders make choices and take action that leads to change.[14] The new president of a building supply company exemplifies such proactive leadership. He was appointed after a larger company bought the supply company,

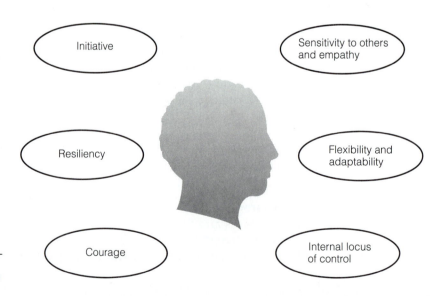

FIGURE 2–2

Task-Related Personality Traits of Leaders

allowing the former owner to retire. After four weeks on the job, the new president made some important changes:

> The company I was invited to run was doing quite well. But I wasn't there for more than ten days when I found out a lot of money was being thrown out the window. There were also a lot of good opportunities being neglected. Worst of all, the former owner had two relatives on the payroll who were being paid management salaries for doing practically nothing. One guy was called "customer relations coordinator," and did practically nothing but go to lunch and play golf with customers. A gal with the title "inventory manager" presided over a warehouse for basically unsalable merchandise. I offered both of these people honest jobs at much-reduced pay.
>
> I also found that nobody in the marketing department was cultivating new customers. The sales personnel stayed with their cozy relationships with established customers. New business development translated into waiting for the phone to ring. I immediately worked with the marketing people to set some tight quotas on pursuing new business leads.
>
> At first my changes brought me no love and admiration. Yet after awhile most people admitted that the changes I made were necessary. As bigger profits began to stream in, I became much more popular.

Sensitivity to Others and Empathy.   In an effort to influence others, it is instrumental for the leader to understand group members, their interests and attitudes, and how to reach them. According to Jeffrey Pfeffer, this type of **sensitivity to others** means understanding who the group members are, what their position on issues is, and how to best communicate with and influence them.[15] Achieving sensitivity to others requires **empathy,** the ability to place oneself in the other person's shoes.

To lack sensitivity to others is to risk becoming a failed leader. Researchers McCall and Lombardo compared derailed executives with those who had progressed to senior management positions. The leading category of fatal flaws was insensitivity to others, characterized by an abrasive, intimidating, bullying style.[16] Insensitivity to people is particularly self-defeating in a large, bureaucratic firm because such firms emphasize politeness. You can probably think of a tyrannical, yet powerful leader. It is important to realize, however, that such tyrants are the exception.

Sensitivity to others is an important leadership trait also because it enhances negotiating effectiveness. The sensitive leader can "read" the other side accurately, thus doing a better job in the negotiator role. Union leaders who bargain effectively are particularly well respected.

Flexibility and Adaptability.   A leader is someone who facilitates change. It therefore follows that a leader must be flexible and adaptable enough to cope with change. Corporate leaders must be able to adapt to changes such as when:

> Sophisticated technological advances have made it possible to speed up production.

New services are constantly being offered and developed to attract and retain customers.

Customers demand the latest products in the least amount of time.[17]

Flexibility, or the ability to adjust to different situations, has long been recognized as an important leadership characteristic. Leaders who are flexible are able to adjust to the demands of different situations, much like antilock brakes enable an automobile to adjust to changes in road conditions. Without the underlying trait of flexibility, a person could be an effective leader only in one or two situations. Paul Stern, the former Telecom CEO, showed the flexibility to provide powerful leadership in both deregulated and regulated companies.

Internal Locus of Control.   People with an **internal locus of control** believe that they are the prime mover behind events. Thus, an internal locus of control helps a leader in the role of a take-charge person because the leader believes fundamentally in his or her innate capacity to take charge. An internal locus of control is closely related to self-confidence. A strong internal locus facilitates self-confidence because the person perceives that he or she can control circumstances enough to perform well.

Supervisory leaders with an internal locus of control are favored by group members.[18] One reason is that an "internal" person is perceived as more powerful than an "external" person because he or she takes responsibility for events. The dean of a liberal arts college provides an example of how an internal locus of control contributes to effective leadership. Presented with declining enrollment figures, and the threat of a drastic cutback at her college, the dean said:

Indeed, our enrollment has been declining. Yet there are many liberal arts colleges that have stabilized enrollments. Even better, there are many other liberal arts colleges that are expanding in an era of declining enrollment. The reason these liberal arts colleges are succeeding is that they are offering something the world wants. Either their reputation is so glowing that a degree from them is worth the money, or they offer very useful, marketable degrees. We can't upgrade our prestige in the next year, but we can put together a program with a recession-proof demand.

The dean's pep talk, with its take-charge attitude, reflected the dean's internal locus of control and led to constructive change. The college developed a master's degree program in school psychology that met with high enough demand to stabilize enrollment and remove the environmental threat.

Courage.   Leaders need courage to face the challenges of taking prudent risks and taking initiative in general. They must also face up to responsibility, and be willing to put their reputations on the line. It takes courage for a leader to suggest a new undertaking because if the undertaking fails, the leader is often seen as having failed. The more faith people place in the power of leaders to cause events, the more strongly they blame leaders when outcomes are unfavorable. Beyond these reasons for the importance of courage, Peter Koestenbaum emphasizes, "It is on the personal side of leadership—in the sense of greatness and inspiration, focus on people, their meanings, their souls and hearts, their destinies—that the next break-through in business will occur."[19]

Resiliency.   An important observation about effective leaders, as well as managers in general, is that they are resilient—they bounce back quickly from setbacks such as budget cuts, demotions, and being fired. An intensive study of executive leaders revealed that they don't even think about failure; in fact, they don't even use the word. Instead, they rely on synonyms such as *mistake, glitch, bungle,* and *setback.*[20] In practice this means that the leader sets an example for team members by not crumbling when something goes wrong. Instead the leader tries to conduct business as usual.

LEADERSHIP MOTIVES

Effective leaders, as opposed to nonleaders as well as less effective leaders, have frequently been distinguished by their motives and needs. In general, leaders have an intense desire to occupy a position of responsibility for others and to control them. Figure 2–3 outlines four specific leadership motives or needs: power motive, drive and achievement motive, strong work ethic, and tenacity. All four motives can be considered task-related.

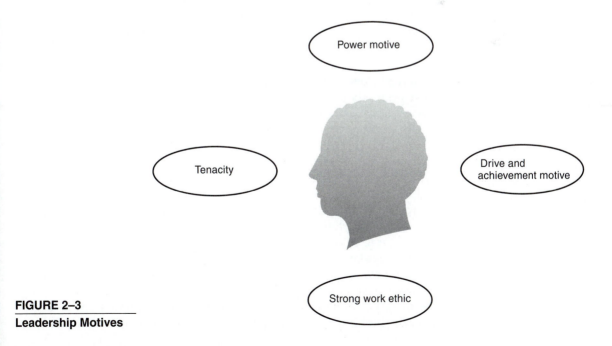

FIGURE 2–3
Leadership Motives

The Power Motive

Effective leaders have a strong need to control resources. Leaders with high power motives have three dominant characteristics: (1) They act with vigor and determination to exert their power; (2) they invest much time in thinking about ways to alter the behavior and thinking of others; and (3) they care about their personal standing with those around them.[21] The power motive is important because it means that the leader is interested in influencing others. Without power, it is much more difficult to influence others. Power is not necessarily good or evil; it can be used for the sake of the power holder (personalized power motive), or for helping others (socialized power motive).[22]

Personalized Power Motive.   Leaders with a personalized power motive seek power mostly to further their own interests. They crave the trappings of power such as status symbols, luxury, and money. In recent years, some leaders have taken up power boating, or racing powerful, high-speed boats. When asked how he liked his power boating experience, an entrepreneurial leader replied, "It's fun, but the start-up costs are about $350,000."

Donald Trump is seen as a leader with a strong personalized power motive because of his love of the trappings of power. He has a penchant for naming yachts, hotels, and office buildings after himself. Nevertheless, he gives his financial managers considerable latitude in managing his enterprises. Many of the financial troubles the Trump organization experienced at one time were partially attributed to the death of his chief financial officer in a helicopter crash. In contrast to Trump, some leaders with strong personalized power motives typically enjoy dominating others. Their need for dominance can lead to submissive subordinates who are frequently sycophants and yes-persons.

Socialized Power Motive.   Leaders with a socialized power motive use power primarily to achieve organizational goals or a vision. In this context, the term *socialized* means that the leader uses power primarily to help others. As a result, he or she is likely to provide more effective leadership. Leaders with socialized power motives, in contrast to leaders with personalized power motives, tend to be more emotionally mature. Also, they exercise power more for the benefit of the entire organization and are less likely to manipulate others through the use of power. Leaders with socialized power motives are less defensive, and are more willing to accept expert advice. Finally, they have longer-range perspectives.[23]

It is important not to draw a rigid dichotomy between leaders with personalized power motives and those with socialized power motives. The distinction between doing good for others versus doing good for oneself is often made on the basis of very subjective criteria. A case in point is H. Ross Perot, the highly successful business founder, social activist, and former candidate for U.S. president. Perot supporters attest to his genuine desire to create a good life for others and to serve them. His detractors, however, regard Perot as a leader obsessed with power and self-importance.

Drive and Achievement Motivation

Leaders are known for the strong effort they invest in achieving work goals. The importance of strong motivation for leadership is well accepted. **Drive** refers to a propensity to put forth high energy into achieving goals and to a persistence in applying that energy. Drive also includes **achievement motivation,** finding joy in accomplishment for its own sake. Entrepreneurs and high-level corporate managers usually have strong achievement motivations. A person with a strong achievement motivation has a consistent desire to:

1. achieve through one's own efforts and take responsibility for success or failure;
2. take moderate risks that can be handled through one's own efforts;
3. receive feedback on level of performance;
4. introduce novel, innovative, or creative solutions;
5. plan and set goals.[24]

To personalize the information just presented about the achievement motive, do Leadership Self-Assessment Exercise 2–2.

LEADERSHIP SELF-ASSESSMENT EXERCISE 2–2   How Strong Is Your Achievement Motive?

Directions: Answer the following questions Yes or No to compare your traits to those with a strong achievement motive (or need).

_____ 1. I am flexible enough to put work out of my mind when off the job.

_____ 2. I very much enjoy gambling, sports pools, lotteries, races, and so forth.

_____ 3. I dislike seeing things such as fuel and water wasted.

_____ 4. I give a good deal of respect to people in positions superior to mine.

_____ 5. I would prefer working with a congenial but somewhat incompetent partner to working with one who is difficult but highly competent.

_____ 6. I frequently have a compulsion to do things today rather than put them off until tomorrow.

_____ 7. I have a strong interest in the lives of successful people.

_____ 8. I feel secure enough to spend money without much planning for the future.

Explanation

Give yourself one point for each correct answer.

1. No. Whether you judge it as good or bad, strivers have a strong sense of involvement and continue to dwell on work problems long after quitting time.

2. No. Those with high aspirations rarely engage in the magical thinking that success comes through outside forces.

3. Yes. Achievers abhor waste in any form and try to avoid unnecessary motions.

4. Yes. Those with a strong need for achievement take on successful role models. If a person does not respect successful role models, he or she probably has a self-defeating attitude.

5. No. Most achievement-motivated people don't agree with this type of partner arrangement. They are willing to sacrifice congeniality for a partner who helps them make it to the top.

6. Yes. Achievers usually have a strong sense of time urgency. They keep ahead of their work by finishing assignments on time.

7. Yes (See No. 4 above.)

8. No. Most achievers are good planners. They use money in the same manner as they use their personal resources.

Interpretation

7–8 points   high achievement motive; you think and act like a striver
4–6 points   achievement motive equal to that of most people
0–3 points   low achievement motive

If your score was low, remember that achievement is a relative term. We have largely been discussing success in the workplace. You may find that your sense of success lies elsewhere.

_____

Source: Reprinted and adapted with permission from the files of psychologist Salvatore V. Didato, Ph.D., 1993.

Strong Work Ethic

Effective leaders typically have a strong **work ethic,** a firm belief in the dignity of work. People with a strong work ethic are well motivated because they value hard work; not to work hard clashes with their values. A strong work ethic helps the organizational leader believe that the group task is worthwhile. For example, the outside world might not think that a poultry-preparation factory is so important, but an effective leader of one of Frank Perdue's chicken factories said "Everybody works hard here and I set the example. We are making it possible for thousands of families to eat nutritious food."

The presence of a leadership work ethic is supported by Piotrowski and Armstrong's study of the characteristics of business executives based on television interviews. The CEOs seemed to harbor an unswerving, consistent value system with a propensity to be engaged and energized by their work. A downside was found, however, to this strong work ethic: hard work and persistence at their jobs leads to very long hours at the expense of quality time at home.[25]

Tenacity

A final observation about the motivational characteristics of organizational leaders is that they are *tenacious*. Leaders are better at overcoming obstacles (as mentioned in relation to resiliency) than are nonleaders. Tenacity multiplies in importance for organizational leaders because it can take so long to implement a new program. Many executives who have been responsible for upgrading quality have discovered that such change proceeds slowly. As one manager placed in charge of an Error-Free Work program said:

> I thought we could make quantum leaps in quality improvement immediately. Employees completed the training programs all charged up and ready to become TQM [total quality management] disciples. Shortly thereafter when progress was slow, I knew I had to fight for improved quality every day. Many workers lapsed back into their usual way of doing things. We are making progress, but it consumes a lot of my energy.

The Bennis study of 150 leaders reinforces the link between leadership effectiveness and tenacity. All interviewees embodied a strongly developed sense of purpose and a willful determination to achieve what they wanted. "Without that," said Bennis, "organizations and individuals are not powerful. The central ingredient of power is purpose."[26]

COGNITIVE FACTORS AND LEADERSHIP

Mental ability as well as personality is important for leadership success. To inspire people, bring about constructive changes, and solve problems creatively, leaders need to be mentally sharp. Problem-solving and intellectual skills are referred to collectively as **cognitive factors**. The term *cognition* refers to the mental process or faculty by which knowledge is gathered. We begin our discussion of cognitive factors and leadership with a description of mental ability and the cognitive resource theory. We then describe the specific cognitive factors shown in Figure 2–4: knowledge of the business, creativity, insight into people and situations, farsightedness and openness to experience.

Mental Ability and the Cognitive Resource Theory

A current theory of leadership supports what has been known for many years: Effective leaders have good problem-solving ability. **Cognitive resource theory** is based on two key assumptions: (1) Intelligent and competent leaders make more effective plans, decisions, and strategies than do leaders with less intelligence or competence. (2) Leaders of task groups communicate their plans, decisions, and action strategies primarily in the form of directive behavior. Cognitive resource theory is based on several hypotheses that focus on mental ability:

1. If a leader is experiencing stress, his or her intellectual abilities will be diverted from the task. As a result, measures of leader intelligence and competence will not correlate with group performance when the leader is stressed.

2. The intellectual abilities of directive leaders will correlate more highly with group performance than will the intellectual abilities of nondirective leaders.

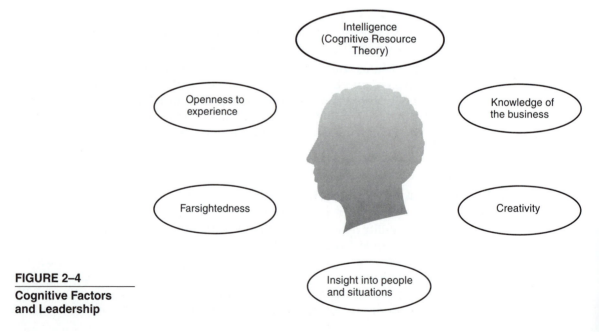

FIGURE 2–4

Cognitive Factors and Leadership

3. A leader's intellectual abilities will be related to group performance to the degree that the task requires the use of intellectual ability.[27]

The general thrust of the cognitive resource theory is plausible, and highlights the importance of intelligence in many leadership situations. Robert P. Vecchio critically examined the theory and found support for the second hypothesis. Intelligence makes a bigger contribution with a directive leader because such a leader makes more problem-solving suggestions than does a nondirective leader.[28] For example, a group member might ask a directive leader, "What new projects for next year should we be working on?" The directive leader might reply, "Here's what I want you to be working on. I'll prepare a list right now." The nondirective leader might reply, "What projects do you think you should be working on?"

Strong problem-solving ability is an asset to leaders because they must collect, integrate, and interpret enormous amounts of data. Computers add to the intellectual demands of a leader's job because more data are brought to his or her attention. Managerial leaders also need intelligence to run software. The accompanying Leader in Action essay illustrates the cognitive requirements of an executive leader's position.

Despite the importance of problem-solving ability for leadership, an advanced capacity for solving abstract problems and an overly intellectual style can create problems. A leader with too strong a penchant for gathering and analyzing information may suffer from *analysis paralysis*. The leader might keep analyzing problems at the expense of taking decisive action.

Knowledge of the Business

Intellectual ability is closely related to having knowledge of the business. An effective leader has to be technically or professionally competent in some discipline, particularly when leading a group of specialists. It is difficult for the leader to establish rapport with group members when he or she does not know what they are doing and when the group does not respect the leader's technical skills. At a minimum, the leader of specialists must be "snow proof," that is, not readily bluffed about technical matters.

The importance of knowledge of the business is increasingly being recognized as an attribute of executive leadership. John Breen of Sherwin-Williams is a good example. An important part of his leadership contribution to the organization consists of formulating winning strategy. Xerox Corp. uses a Management Resource Planning Evaluation form, on which each manager evaluates himself or herself. One key category is Knowledge of Field, which is defined as follows on the form:

> Has fundamental understanding of ideas, techniques, leading edge applied technologies, trends and discoveries (both inside and outside the Company) that pertain to assigned work responsibilities; seeks out and quickly understands new developments.

LEADER
IN
ACTION

John Breen of Sherwin-Williams

John G. Breen, the forceful CEO of Sherwin-Williams Corp., has developed a reputation as an excellent strategist during hard times. After many years of experience as a manufacturing executive, he joined Sherwin-Williams as the chief executive officer. Over a decade ago he spearheaded the strategy the paint company needed to make a comeback.

Back in the mid-1980s, Breen decided to go after market share because the paint industry showed little prospects of real growth. He reasoned, "the way we looked at it, there was no other way you could grow sales and profits" (*Business Week,* p. 111). To implement this strategy, Breen is credited with some clever marketing moves. Most important, Sherwin-Williams has targeted its individual brands at specific markets and priced them competitively. During a five-year period, Breen doubled the ad budget.

Other winning moves included buying the consumer paints assets of DeSoto Inc., a major supplier of private-label accounts, including Sears. Sherwin-Williams also increased the number of its own stores, where it sells its own famous brand, from 1,829 to 1,981. The company has also successfully differentiated its Dutch Boy from other brands of house paint. An ad campaign heralded Dutch Boy as "The look that gets the looks." The aesthetic appeal was different from the typical paint advertising, which focuses on washability and durability.

Breen's strategy has been a winner. The company's market share in architectural paint climbed from about 13 percent in 1986 to 18 percent or more at present. An industry analyst offers this explanation for Sherwin-Williams's success: "They hammered home on what was most important to them. It was paint—selling more paint."

Breen also lends his strategic thinking expertise to several firms as a member of the board, including the Mead Corporation. He lives in Shaker Heights, a suburb of Cleveland, and relies on ice skating for physical conditioning and relaxation.

Source: As reported in "Masters of the Game: CEOs Who Succeed in Business When Times Are Really Trying," *Business Week,* October 12, 1992, pp. 110–111; Breen, John Gerald," *Who's Who in America,* 44th ed., Vol 1 (Wilmette, Ill.: Marquis Who's Who, Macmillan Directory Division, 1990–91), p. 379.

Creativity

Many effective leaders are creative in the sense that they arrive at imaginative and original solutions to complex problems. Creative ability lies on a continuum; some leaders are more creative than others. At one end of the creative continuum are business leaders who think of innovative products and services. Two examples are Steven Jobs of NeXT, Inc., and Michael Eisner, a senior executive whose chief duty it is to lead the Disney empire creatively. At the middle of the creativity continuum are leaders who explore imaginative—but not breakthrough—solutions to business problems. At the low end of the creativity continuum are leaders who inspire group members to push forward with standard solutions to organizational problems.

An example of a creative business leader is August A. Busch IV, the brand manager for Budweiser at Anheuser-Busch Companies, Inc. One of Busch's key roles is to make suggestions for advertising campaigns and to approve of campaigns developed by advertising agencies. Busch, himself in his late twenties, was instrumental in developing a series of Budweiser ads to attract young beer drinkers. His successful creative input was to downplay sexually oriented advertising.[29]

Creativity is such an important aspect of the leader's role in the modern organization that the development of creative problem-solving skills receives chapter-length attention in this book (see Chapter 11).

Insight into People and Situations

Another important cognitive trait of effective leaders is **insight,** a depth of understanding that requires considerable intuition and common sense. Insight is therefore related to creativity because of its intuitive component. Insight into people and situations involving people is an essential characteristic of managerial leaders. A manager with keen insight is able to make wise choices in selecting people for key assignments. Furthermore, insight enables a manager to make better work assignments and do a better job of training and developing team members. The reason is that such a manager makes a careful assessment of the strengths and weaknesses of team members. Another major advantage of being insightful is that the leader can size up the situation and adapt his or her leadership approach accordingly. For instance, in a crisis situation group members welcome directive and decisive leadership.

Insight also helps a leader solve business problems and make observations that others might not see. For example, beer wholesalers at first objected to August Busch IV's proposal to develop clever ads that do not display scantily-clad women. Yet Busch's insights told him that young people would welcome non-sexually oriented appeals.

You can gauge your insight by charting the accuracy of your hunches and predictions about people and business situations. For example, size up a new coworker or manager the best you can. Record your observations and test them against how that person performs or behaves many months later. The feedback from this type of exercise helps sharpen your insights.

Farsightedness

To develop visions and corporate strategy, a leader needs **farsightedness,** the ability to understand the long-range implications of actions and policies. Ray

J. Friant, Jr., among many other critics, is concerned that too many business leaders are shortsighted. For example, the "get-rich-quick" philosophy of many business executives and investment bankers has left many companies with burdensome debt loads.

Friant recommends that to develop as future business leaders, junior executives should be given long-term assignments in long-range planning and implementation. At the same time they should go through their usual developmental rotations such as intermediate-term assignments in marketing and manufacturing. In addition, they should spend at least five years doing projects that change the character of the business. Such assignments would help business leaders of the future understand both the need for and the difficulty of balancing long-term and short-term results.[30]

Openness to Experience

Yet another important cognitive characteristic of leaders is their openness to experience, or their positive orientation toward learning. People who have a great deal of openness to experience have well-developed intellects. Traits commonly associated with this dimension of the intellect include being imaginative, cultured, curious, original, broad-minded, intelligent, and artistically sensitive.

To help personalize the information about key leadership traits presented so far, do Leadership Development Exercise 2–1.

LEADERSHIP DEVELOPMENT EXERCISE 2–1   Group Feedback on Leadership Traits

Your instructor will organize the class into groups of about seven people. A volunteer sits in the middle of each group. Each group member looks directly at the person in the "hot seat" and tells him or her what leadership trait, characteristic, or motives he or she seems to possess. It will help if the feedback providers offer a few words of explanation for their observations. For example, a participant who is told that he or she has self-confidence might also be told, "I notice how confidently you have told the class about your success on the job." The group next moves on to the second person, and so forth. (We assume that you have had some opportunity to observe your classmates prior to this exercise.)

Each member thus receives positive feedback about leadership traits and characteristics from all the other members in the group. After all members have had their turn at receiving feedback, discuss as a group the value of the exercise.

PHYSICAL AND BACKGROUND FACTORS

Another perspective on understanding the personal qualities of effective leaders is to examine their physical characteristics and biographical or background factors. A major limitation to this approach, however, is that it is based on physical and cultural stereotypes that are changing as more diverse people gain power. The physical and background factors reviewed here are energy and physical stamina, height, and biographical factors.

Energy and Physical Stamina

Being an effective organizational leader requires considerable energy and physical stamina. Among the demanding physical challenges facing leaders are long working hours, frequent travel, and making presentations to various constituents. Many executives in business and government work sixty to sixty-five hours per week. Also, executives frequently arrive at work up to two hours early in order to take care of paperwork before the day's round of meetings begins.

Physical energy is helpful both in inspiring group members and in sustaining high levels of productivity. As Jeffrey Pfeffer observes about leaders, "Without endurance and the ability to persevere, other skills and attributes are not worth much."[31]

Height

Common wisdom is that leaders are taller than nonleaders, and that being tall is an asset for commanding the attention and respect of others. Although the mean height of leaders may be higher than that of nonleaders, there are exceptions. Many top executive leaders are below average in height. Among them are H. Ross Perot of Electronic Data Systems, Al Neuharth, formerly of the Gannett Co., and T. J. Rodgers of Cypress Semiconductor. Robert Reich, the Secretary of Labor in the Clinton administration, is under five feet tall. As more women and Asians are promoted to key positions in American and Canadian corporations, the mean height advantage of leaders will continue to shrink.

Background Factors

Business Week tabulated biographical background factors of the 1,000 most highly placed executives in American-based corporations. Among the findings:

1. *Education.* Nine hundred and sixteen took an undergraduate degree of some kind, and the rest (55) attended some college. More than half received a bachelor of science degree, the majority of them in business or related fields. Over one-half the CEOs attended graduate schools, earning doctorates in physical science, law degrees, and MBAs.

2. *School attended.* Yale headed the list as the undergraduate school most frequently attended by a top executive (37 executives). Next were Princeton (31) and Harvard (29). The Ivy League schools collectively were attended by 159 CEOs; 63 attended Big Ten schools. Overall, the CEOs attended 312 colleges. Harvard was the most frequently attended graduate school with 98 top executives having attended its Business School or Law School.

3. *Seniority.* Staying with one firm for a long time is an asset to becoming a top executive. The average service at the company for a CEO is 22.5 years. Among recently appointed CEOs, the average tenure is less than 17 years.[32]

Background factors make their largest contribution to understanding leadership to the extent that they reflect underlying traits, motives, characteristics, and skills. For example, people who received advanced degrees may have a hunger for knowledge and good problem-solving skills. People who attend well-known schools may make extensive use of networking.

THE INFLUENCE OF HEREDITY AND ENVIRONMENT ON LEADERSHIP

Does heredity or environment contribute more to leadership effectiveness? Are leaders born or made? Do you have to have the right stuff to be a leader? Many people ponder these issues now that the study of leadership is more in vogue than ever. The most sensible answer is that the traits, motives, and characteristics required for leadership effectiveness are a combination of heredity and environment. Personality traits and mental ability traits are based on certain inherited predispositions and aptitudes that require the right opportunity to develop. Mental ability is a good example. We inherit a basic capacity that sets an outer limit as to how much mental horsepower we will have. Yet people need the right opportunity to develop their mental ability so they can behave brightly enough to be chosen for a leadership position.

The physical factor of energy also sheds light on the nature-versus-nurture issue. Some people are born with a biological propensity for being more energetic than others. Yet unless that energy is properly channeled it will not help a person become an effective leader.

The nature-versus-nurture issue also surfaces in relation to the leadership characteristic of creativity and innovation. Important genetic contributors to imaginative thinking include brain power and emotional expressiveness. Yet these traits require the right environment to flourish. Such an environment would include encouragement from others and ample opportunity to experiment with ideas.

THE STRENGTHS AND LIMITATIONS OF THE TRAIT APPROACH TO LEADERSHIP

A compelling argument for the trait approach is that the evidence is convincing that leaders possess personal characteristics that differ from those of nonleaders. Based on their review of the type of research reported in this chapter, Kirkpatrick and Locke concluded: "Leaders do not have to be great men or women by being intellectual geniuses or omniscient prophets to succeed. But they do need to have the 'right stuff' and this stuff is not equally present in all people."[33]

Understanding the traits of effective leaders serves as an important guide to leadership selection. If we are confident that honesty and integrity, and creativity and imagination are essential leadership traits, then we can concentrate on selecting leaders with those characteristics. Another important strength of the trait approach to leadership is that it can help people prepare for leadership responsibility. A person might seek experiences that enable him or her to develop characteristics such as self-confidence, good problem-solving ability, and assertiveness.

A limitation to the trait approach is that it does not tell us which traits are absolutely needed in which leadership situations. We also do not know how much of a trait, characteristic, or motive is the right amount. For example, some leaders get into ethical and legal trouble because they allow their ambition to cross the borderline into greed and gluttony. Too much focus on the trait approach can breed an elitist conception of leadership. People who are not outstanding on key leadership traits and characteristics might be discouraged from seeking leadership positions.

A balanced perspective on the trait approach is that certain traits, motives, and characteristics increase the probability that a leader will be effective. Yet they do not guarantee effectiveness, and the leadership situation often influences which traits will be the most important.[34]

SUMMARY

A universal theory of leadership contends that certain personal characteristics and skills contribute to leadership effectiveness in many situations. The trait approach to leadership studies the traits, motives, and other characteristics of leaders. General personality traits associated with effective leadership include the following: (1) self-confidence, (2) honesty, integrity, and credibility, (3) dominance and extroversion, (4) assertiveness, (5) emotional stability, (6) enthusiasm, (7) sense of humor, (8) warmth, and (9) a high tolerance for frustration.

Some personality traits of effective leaders are closely associated with task accomplishment. Among them are (1) initiative, (2) sensitivity to others,

(3) flexibility and adaptability, (4) an internal locus of control, (5) courage, and (6) resiliency.

Certain motives and needs associated with leadership effectiveness are closely related to task accomplishment. Among them are (1) the power motive, either personalized or socialized, (2) drive and achievement motivation, (3) a strong work ethic, and (4) tenacity.

Cognitive factors are also important for leadership success. Cognitive resource theory underscores the contribution of intelligence to planning and decision making. The theory also emphasizes that plans, decisions, and action strategies are communicated through directive behavior. Good problem-solving ability is an asset to leaders because they must collect, integrate, and interpret enormous amounts of data.

Intellectual ability is closely related to the leadership requirement of possessing knowledge of the business or being technically competent. Creativity is another important cognitive skill for leaders, but effective leaders vary widely in their creative contributions. Insight into people and situations, including the ability to make effective judgments about business opportunities, also contributes to leadership effectiveness. The cognitive skill of farsightedness helps leaders understand the long-range implications of actions and policies.

Physical characteristics and background factors are also related to occupying leadership positions. Energy and physical stamina make an important contribution to meeting the physical demands of a leader's job. Height is loosely related to occupying a leadership position, but many people of below-average height occupy key positions. Background factors such as education and the school attended are associated with holding executive positions. Yet background factors make their largest contribution to understanding leadership to the extent that they reflect underlying personal attributes.

The issue of whether leaders are born or bred frequently surfaces. A sensible answer is that the traits, motives, and characteristics required for leadership effectiveness are a combination of heredity and environment.

The trait approach to leadership is supported by many studies showing that leaders are different from nonleaders, and effective leaders different from less effective leaders. Nevertheless, the trait approach does not tell us which traits are the most important in which situations, and the amount of the trait required.

KEY TERMS

Universal theory of leadership	Initiative
Assertiveness	Sensitivity to others
Emotional stability	Empathy
High tolerance for frustration	Flexibility

Internal locus of control   Cognitive factors
Drive   Cognitive resource theory
Achievement motivation   Insight
Work ethic   Farsightedness

GUIDELINES FOR ACTION AND SKILL DEVELOPMENT

An important application of the trait theory of leadership is to choose a leadership trait as a personal development goal. Assertiveness is one such trait amenable to development. To become a more assertive person, follow these steps:

1. **Observe your own behavior.** Are you asserting yourself adequately? Or are you being pushy or abrasive? Do you believe you get what you want, when you want it, without stepping on the rights of others?

2. **Concentrate on a specific situation.** Imagine how you would handle a specific incident such as asking to be considered for a task force assignment.

3. **Observe an effective model.** Observe another person who appears to be assertive. Observe the person's style as well as what he or she says.

4. **Try it out.** You are now prepared to try out an assertive behavior in a specific problem situation or two. Possibilities include asking for an interesting assignment, getting an error corrected by a bank, or turning down a luncheon request.

5. **Evaluate your performance.** Review how well you performed in behaving assertively, and therefore improving your trait of assertiveness.

6. **Practice and obtain social reinforcement.** Continue your assertive behavior in a variety of situations. Observe the beneficial consequences in order to receive reinforcement in a real situation (social reinforcement).[35]

DISCUSSION QUESTIONS AND ACTIVITIES

1. How much faith does the public place in the trait theory of leadership when they elect public officials?

2. When managers are polled, they claim honesty is an essential leadership trait. To what extent do you think these managers are just making a response they think the researchers want to hear?

3. Why is a high tolerance for frustration an important leadership trait?

4. Why is personal warmth an important leadership trait?

5. How does an internal locus of control help a leader become a good crisis manager?

6. A company president made the following comment about leadership and intelligence: "Sometimes a less than top IQ is an advantage because that person doesn't see all the problems. He or she sees the big problem and gets on and gets it solved. But the extremely bright person can see so many problems that he or she never gets around to solving any of them." What is your reaction to his comment?

7. Find an article or book about a successful executive leader, and look for evidence that knowledge of the business is an important success factor for that person.

8. Visualize the least effective leader you know. Identify the traits, motives, and personal characteristics in which that person might be deficient.

9. We purposely did not mention weight as a physical factor associated with leadership. Have you noticed any relationship between leadership success and weight?

10. A disproportionate number of top business executives are graduates of Harvard Business School or Harvard Law School. Would you then conclude that attending these two schools helps a person develop the right stuff?

LEADERSHIP CASE PROBLEM

What Traits Did Steve Ross Possess?

"I'm not a manager," Steven Jay Ross once said. "I'm more of a dreamer" (*Time*, p. 51). When Ross died from cancer at age 65, he was the chairman and chief co-executive of Time Warner Inc., the entertainment and information conglomerate. His admirers saw Ross as a visionary company builder with an uncanny instinct for the art of the deal. A managing editor who had worked with Ross said, "he had extravagant charm, an intense generosity, and a whole-hearted view of leadership" (*Fortune*, p. 4). The former Warner Brothers chairman said of Ross, "Steve was not perfect, but in the sense of being a chief executive, running a major corporation, the human part of Steve was as important as the deal-making" (Bruck, p. 91).

To his detractors, Ross was a symbol of corporate excess: a ridiculously overpaid executive with a flamboyant lifestyle. People who

knew Ross agreed that he projected an aura larger than life. Steve Ross was tall and physically robust, with a perpetual tan, neatly styled hair, and impeccably dressed. In most situations Ross had a relaxed, charismatic charm. He had a superquick mathematical mind and developed deals of extraordinary complexity.

As an executive he was intuitive rather than cerebral and happily let others run the details of his enterprises. Ross would put the most talented people he could find in charge of ventures. He would encourage them to take risks, and rewarded them generously if they succeeded. When his key people made a mistake, Ross protected them. People who worked for Ross were unswervingly loyal. Ross often signed his business memos, "Love, Steve."

Ross's early jobs included stockboy and salesman in New York City's garment district. Later, while working at a family funeral home,

Ross began to build his empire, a conglomerate named Kinney Services. Its businesses included parking garages, cleaning services, and limousine rentals. While working at the funeral home, Ross encountered many people at an emotional low. This gave him the opportunity to develop his talent for persuading others that they were important to him.

In 1969 Ross purchased Warner Bros.–Seven Arts, the once-great Hollywood studio. He immediately took to the Hollywood glitz, and he became a confidant of several leading Hollywood stars. Ross's empire grew rapidly, but in 1973 he experienced a setback. Two of his close aides were convicted in a racketeering scheme involving a theater in which Warner had invested. Ross was identified as an unindicted co-conspirator. Ten years later Ross had another setback when Warner nearly went bankrupt when its Atari video games division failed.

Ross encountered more controversy when his company acquired Time Inc. in 1990. The deal paid off extraordinarily well for Ross and other Warner executives. His compensation package exceeded $78 million in 1990—the cost to Time Inc. of buying out Ross's stake in Warner. Under Ross's leadership, Warner grew from a has-been to an entertainment superpower. Friends and critics alike believed that Ross was a world-class salesperson.

1. Identify the traits, motives, and personal characteristics of Steve Ross from the above description.
2. How might Steve Ross have developed fewer enemies?
3. How would you rate Steve Ross on the leadership dimension of sensitivity to people?

Source: As reported in "The Merchant of Dreams: Steven Jay Ross 1927–1992," *Time,* January 4, 1993; "Steven J. Ross, 1927–1992," *Fortune,* January 25, 1993; Connie Bruck, "A Mogul's Farewell," *The New Yorker,* October 18, 1993, pp. 70–93.

A LEADERSHIP ROLE PLAY

A Sense of Humor on the Job

One person plays the role of the company president who has scheduled a staff meeting. The president's task is to inform employees that the seventh top manager in the last year has just resigned. You want to make effective use of humor to relieve some of the tension and worry. Make a couple of humorous introductory comments. Five other people should play the roles of the remaining staff members. Make effective use of humor yourself in response to the president's comments.

Charismatic and Transformational Leadership

LEARNING OBJECTIVES

After studying this chapter you should be able to

1. achieve a comprehensive understanding of the meaning of charismatic and transformational leadership.
2. differentiate among several types of charismatic leaders.
3. describe many of the traits and behaviors of charismatic leaders.
4. explain how leaders create transformations.
5. explain the communication style of charismatic leaders.
6. describe the concerns about charismatic leadership from the scientific and moral viewpoint.

*S*hortly after taking office, U.S. Attorney General Janet Reno acquired many followers inside and outside the Justice Department. Reno was planning a revolution in law enforcement. She wanted government agencies to understand the root causes of crime, and she wanted the country to have both less crime and less punishment. Senators claimed she was the most impressive member of the Clinton cabinet. When fans surround the table when she's eating dinner with a movie star, it's Reno's autograph they request.[1]

Janet Reno exemplifies leaders who are so exciting, so appealing, so magnetic, so dynamic, and so visionary that their constituents eagerly accept their leadership. As you already know, such leaders are said to be charismatic. The same leaders are described as transformational because they facilitate major changes in organizations. The study of charismatic and transformational leadership is another manifestation of the trait theory.

In this chapter we examine the subtypes of charismatic leadership, the personal attributes of charismatic leaders, how charismatic leaders communicate, and research on the effects of charismatic leadership. We also look at suggestions for developing charismatic qualities.

THE MEANINGS OF CHARISMA

Charisma, like leadership itself, has been defined in various ways. Nevertheless, there is enough consistency among these definitions to make charisma a useful concept in understanding and practicing leadership. To begin, *charisma* is a Greek word meaning divinely inspired gift. In the study of leadership, **charisma** is a special quality of leaders whose purposes, powers, and extraordinary determination differentiate them from others.[2]

The various definitions of charisma have a unifying theme. Charisma is a positive and compelling quality of a person that makes many others want to be led by him or her. The term *many others* is chosen carefully. Few leaders are perceived to be charismatic by *all* their constituents. A case in point is Lee Iacocca, the former chairman of Chrysler Corp. whose name surfaces frequently in discussions of charisma. Despite his wide appeal, many people considered Iacocca to be brash, outspoken, sexist, and vulgar—hardly the characteristics of an inspiring leader.

Table 3–1 presents a sampling of additional definitions of charisma. These definitions point to different subtleties of charisma.

TABLE 3–1 Definitions of Charisma and Charismatic Leadership

1. A devotion to the specific and exceptional sanctity, heroism, or exemplary character of an individual person, and of the normative patterns revealed or ordained by that person.

2. Endowment with the gift of divine grace.

3. The process of influencing major changes in the attitudes and assumptions of organization members, and building commitment for the organization's objectives.

4. Leadership that has a magnetic effect on people.

5. In combination with individualized consideration, intellectual stimulation, and inspirational leadership, a component of transformational leadership.

Sources: (1) Max Weber, cited in S. N. Eisenstadt, *Max Weber: On Charisma and Institution Building* (Chicago: University of Chicago Press, 1968); (2) Bernard M. Bass, "Evolving Perspectives on Charismatic Leadership," in *Charismatic Leaders,* eds. Jay A. Conger, Rabindra N. Kanungo, et al (San Francisco: Jossey-Bass, 1988), p. 40; (3) Gary A. Yukl, *Leadership in Organizations,* 2nd ed. (Englewood Cliffs, N.J.: Prentice Hall, 1989), p. 204; (4) James M. Kouzes and Barry Z. Posner, *The Leadership Challenge: How to Get Extraordinary Things Done in Organizations* (San Francisco: Jossey-Bass, 1987), p. 123; Bernard M. Bass, cited in Kenneth E. Clark and Miriam B. Clark (eds.), *Measures of Leadership,* A Center for Creative Leadership Book (West Orange, N.J.: Leadership Library of America, 1990).

Charisma: A Relationship Between the Leader and Group Members

A key dimension of charismatic leadership is that it involves a relationship or interaction between the leader and the people being led. (The same, of course, holds true for all types of leadership.) Furthermore, the people accepting the leadership must attribute charismatic qualities to the leader. John Gardner believes that charisma applies to leader-constituent relationships in which the leader has an exceptional gift for inspiration, and nonrational communication. At the same time the constituent's response is characterized by awe, reverence, devotion, or emotional dependence.[3] The late Sam Walton, founder of Wal-Mart Stores, had this type of relationship with many of his employees. Walton's most avid supporters believed he was an inspired executive to whom they could trust their careers.

Charismatic leadership is possible under certain conditions. The beliefs of the constituents must be similar to those of the leader, and unquestioning acceptance of and affection for the leader must exist. The group members must willingly obey the leader, and they must be emotionally involved both in the mission of the charismatic leader and in their own goals. Finally, the constituents must have a strong desire to identify with the leader.[4]

The Effects of Charisma

Robert J. House developed a theory of charismatic leadership that defined charisma in terms of its effects. A charismatic leader, according to House, is any person who brings about certain outcomes to an unusually high degree. The nine charismatic effects are as follows:

1. Group member trust in the correctness of the leader's beliefs
2. Similarity of group members' beliefs to those of the leader
3. Unquestioning acceptance of the leader
4. Affection for the leader
5. Willing obedience to the leader
6. Identification with and emulation of the leader
7. Emotional involvement of the group member or constituent in the mission
8. Heightened goals of the group member
9. Feeling on the part of group members that they will be able to accomplish, or contribute to, the accomplishment of the mission[5]

Jane A. Halpert factor-analyzed (statistically clustered) these nine hypothesized outcomes into three groups or dimensions, as outlined in Figure 3–1. The first six effects refer to the power exerted by the leader. Three of them (similarity of beliefs, affection for the leader, identification with and emulation of the leader) are related to referent power. **Referent**

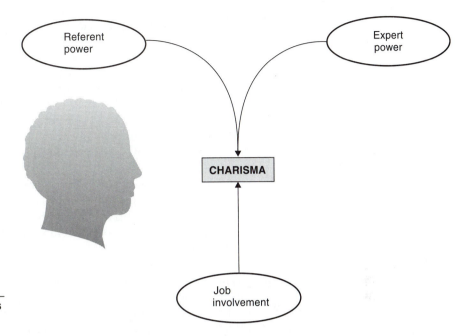

FIGURE 3–1

Halpert's Dimensions of Charisma

power is the ability to influence others that stems from the leader's desirable traits and characteristics. Three other effects (group member trust, unquestioning acceptance, and willing obedience) are related to expert power. **Expert power** is the ability to influence others because of one's specialized knowledge, skills, or abilities.

The last three effects are perceptions related to the task or mission. Halpert noted also that the job-related effects (emotional involvement, heightened goals, and perceived ability to contribute) are concerned with *job involvement.* As a result, charismatic leaders will encourage group members to be job involved.

In summary, the nine charismatic effects in House's theory can be reduced to three dimensions: referent power, expert power, and job involvement.[6] Such information is useful for the aspiring charismatic leader. To be charismatic, one must exercise referent power and expert power and must get people involved in their jobs.

TYPES OF CHARISMATIC LEADERS

The everyday use of the term *charisma* suggests that it is a straightforward and readily understood trait. As already explained, however, charisma has different meanings and dimensions. As a result, charismatic leaders can be categorized into five types: socialized charismatics, personalized charismatics, office-holder charismatics, personal charismatics, and divine charismatics.[7]

Following the distinction made for the power motive, some charismatic leaders use their power for the good of others. A **socialized charismatic** is a leader who restrains the use of power in order to benefit others. This type of leader also attempts to develop a value congruence between himself or herself and constituents. The socialized charismatic formulates and pursues goals that fulfill the needs of group members and provides intellectual stimulation to them. Followers of socialized charismatics are autonomous, empowered, and responsible.

A second type of charismatic leader is the **personalized charismatic.** Such individuals exercise few restraints on their use of power so they may best serve their own interests. Personalized charismatics impose self-serving goals on constituents, and they offer consideration and support to group members only when it facilitates their own goals. Followers of personalized charismatics are typically obedient, submissive, and dependent.

Another type of charismatic leader is the office-holder charismatic. For this type of leader, charismatic leadership is more the property of the office occupied than his or her personal characteristics. The chief executive officer of General Electric, for example, might have considerable luster but would lose much of it immediately after leaving office. By occupying a valuable role, office-holder charismatics attain high status. Office-holder charisma is thus a byproduct of being placed in a key position.

In contrast to office-holder charismatics, personal charismatics gain very high esteem through the extent to which others have faith in them as people. A personal charismatic exerts influence whether occupying a low- or high-status position because he or she has the right traits, characteristics, and behaviors.

A historically important type of charismatic leader is the divine charismatic. Originally, charismatic leadership was a theological concept: a divine charismatic is endowed with a gift of divine grace. In 1924 Max Weber defined a charismatic leader as a mystical, narcissistic, and personally magnetic savior who would arise to lead people through a crisis. When H. Ross Perot ran for U.S. president in 1992, many of his constituents reacted to him as if he were a divine charismatic.

The accompanying Leader in Action portrayal describes a charismatic executive. After reading the excerpt, categorize this leader into one of the five types just described.

CHARACTERISTICS OF CHARISMATIC AND TRANSFORMATIONAL LEADERS

Earlier it was stated that charismatic leaders are often **transformational leaders**—that is, leaders who bring about positive, major changes in organizations. They differ significantly from **transactional leaders**—managers

LEADER IN ACTION

Richard Branson of the Virgin Group

[First appeared in *Success* November 1992. Written by Echo Montgomery Garrett. Reprinted with permission of *Success* Magazine. Copyright © 1992 by Hal Holdings Corporation.]

Richard Branson has built a $1.5 billion empire by knowing when to take the plunge. Ever since his early days, he has valued the media. A photo or an article was free advertising, made much more effective if he was speedboating across the Atlantic or hot-air ballooning from Japan to the Canadian Arctic. Risking his life was part of running a business.

In the business world Branson has been larger than life. His reputation as an "adventure capitalist" has placed him in the spotlight as a glamour boy who mingles with the jet set and rules over a $1.5 billion kingdom. Branson's ability to recognize opportunity, as well as to know when to get out of a business when still on top, has befuddled the British financial community. Many of these people have accused Branson of being all show and no substance.

In 1991 Branson sold Virgin Music Group to Thorn EMI for $980 million, the biggest sale of an independent label in record business history. Although this deal catapulted Branson into the ranks of the business elite, he doesn't look the part. Often clad in jeans, and grinning frequently, Branson appears as a thrill seeker who acts on a whim and who has an unprecedented share of luck.

Branson labels himself "the ultimate consumer." He believes his tastes reflect those of the general public. When his intuition told him the music scene was headed toward the unconventional, he signed up raw talent, such as Culture Club and the Sex Pistols.

Branson has worked hard at self-improvement. "I once did a radio interview and the interviewer sent over two tapes. On one he'd been kind enough to clean up my 'ums' and 'ahs.' He left the other one exactly the way I spoke. It made me work hard."

When Branson launched Virgin Atlantic Airways in 1984, he had to compete with British Airways. Branson thought that the way to compete was to give the media access to his personal life. His solution was to do things he knew would be written about all over the world. In all of these stories, his company was mentioned. He is a three-time Guinness world record holder, having won for such feats as his hot-air ballooning. Branson's strategy has worked. According to a recent poll of students, Branson is the third most-admired person in England, just behind the pope and the Prince of Wales.

Every one of the 6,000 Virgin employees has Branson's home phone number and calls him by his first name. When on a Virgin Atlantic flight,

Branson bounds up and down the aisles pouring orange juice, chatting with passengers and crew. An executive who works for Branson said, "Keeping up with Richard is almost impossible. The ideas constantly pop out of his brain."

The nerve center for the Virgin empire of more than 100 companies is a four-story mansion in London. While working in the living room, Branson stays focused on one company at a time. Branson is able to deal with his collection of companies as a whole by never letting any one part of his empire become large and unwieldy. Virgin consists of self-sufficient small companies, each run by a director loyal to Richard Branson.

who mostly carry on transactions with people, such as taking care of administrative work and offering rewards for good performance.

Charisma and transformational leadership are closely intertwined. Remember, though, that not all charismatic leaders are transformational. Unless you significantly change an organization, you are not a transformational leader. As we look specifically at the characteristics of charismatic and transformational leaders, you will note that many of these characteristics apply to leaders in general.

1. *Vision.* A charismatic leader offers an exciting image of where the organization is headed and how to get there. A vision is more than a forecast because it describes an ideal version of the future of an entire organization or an organizational unit.

2. *Masterful communication skills.* To inspire people, the charismatic leader uses colorful language and exciting metaphors and analogies. (More about the communication skills of charismatic leaders is presented in the next section.)

3. *Ability to inspire trust.* Group members and constituents believe so strongly in the integrity of charismatic leaders that they will risk their careers to pursue the chief's vision.

4. *Ability to make group members feel capable.* One technique for helping group members feel more capable is to enable them to achieve success on relatively easy projects. The leader then praises the group members and gives them more demanding assignments.

5. *Energy and action orientation.* Like entrepreneurs, most charismatic leaders are energetic and serve as a model for getting things done on time.

6. *Emotional expressiveness and warmth.* A key characteristic of charismatic leaders is the ability to express feelings openly. A bank vice president claims that much of the charisma people attribute to her can be explained simply: "I'm up front about expressing positive feelings. I praise people, I hug them, and I cheer if necessary. I also express my negative feelings, but to a lesser degree." Nonverbal emotional expressiveness, such as warm gestures and frequent (nonsexual) touching of group members, is also characteristic of charismatic leaders.

7. *Willingness to take personal risks.* Charismatic leaders are typically risk takers, and risk taking adds to their charisma. Richard Branson of the Virgin Group is an exemplary risk taker in his buying and selling of companies.

8. *Use of unconventional strategies.* Part of being creative is to use unconventional strategies to achieve success. The charismatic leader inspires others by formulating unusual strategies to achieve important goals. Anita Roddick, the founder of the worldwide chain of cosmetic stores called the Body Shop, accomplishes her goals unconventionally. She travels around the world into native villages searching out natural beauty products that in the manufacturing process do not harm the environment or animals.

9. *Self-promoting personality.* Charismatic leaders are hardly diffident; they toot their own horns and allow others to know how important they are. Richard Branson, for example, has relied on self-promotion to help build his empire.

10. *Propensity to emerge during crises.* Early formulations of charismatic leadership emphasized that the charismatic leader arises in response to a crisis. Such emergence is more evident with political and union leaders because they may arise to power when economic conditions are at their worst. James R. Hoffa, the long-time head of the Teamsters Union, rose to power when truck drivers were lowly paid and overworked.

11. *Minimum internal conflict.* Charismatic leaders are confident and determined that they are right, even through setbacks. They appear to have less internal conflict between their emotions, impulses, and feelings and their consciences than do most people. Because they are convinced they are right, they experience less guilt and discomfort in reprimanding group members.[8]

Most people can work toward developing charisma, or becoming more charismatic. To that end, try doing Leadership Skill-Building Exercise 3–1.

THE COMMUNICATION STYLE OF CHARISMATIC LEADERS

Charismatic and transformational leaders communicate their visions, goals, and directives in a colorful, imaginative, and expressive manner. In addition, they communicate openly with group members and create a comfortable communication climate. To set agendas that represent the interests of their constituents, charismatic leaders regularly solicit their viewpoints on critical issues. They encourage two-way communication with team members while still promoting a sense of confidence.[9] Here we describe two related aspects of the communication style of charismatic leaders: management by inspiration and management by anecdote.

Management by Inspiration

According to Jay A. Conger, the era of managing by dictate is being replaced by an era of management by inspiration. An important way to inspire others

LEADERSHIP
SKILL-BUILDING
EXERCISE 3–1   Becoming a Charismatic and Transformational Leader

Directions: Indicate the extent to which you possess each charismatic characteristic, using a 1–5 scale: (1) way below average (2) below average, (3) average, (4) above average, (5) way above average.

   If you are dissatisfied with your answer, sketch an action plan you think might help you develop in the desired direction. For example, if you think that your emotional expressiveness is insufficient, you might carefully observe people who are emotionally expressive and then model their behavior. For several of the characteristics, such as minimum internal conflict, developing an action plan will be difficult.

Charismatic Characteristic	Degree to Which You Possess the Trait
1. Vision *Action plan:*	1 2 3 4 5
2. Masterful communication skills *Action plan:*	1 2 3 4 5
3. Ability to inspire trust *Action plan:*	1 2 3 4 5
4. Ability to make group members feel capable *Action plan:*	1 2 3 4 5
5. Energy and action orientation *Action plan:*	1 2 3 4 5
6. Emotional expressiveness and warmth *Action plan:*	1 2 3 4 5
7. Willingness to take personal risks *Action plan:*	1 2 3 4 5
8. Use of unconventional strategies *Action plan:*	1 2 3 4 5
9. Self-promoting personality *Action plan:*	1 2 3 4 5
10. Propensity to emerge during crises *Action plan:*	1 2 3 4 5
11. Minimum internal conflict *Action plan:*	1 2 3 4 5

is to articulate a highly emotional message. Conger has observed two major rhetorical techniques of inspirational leaders: the use of metaphors and analogies, and the ability to gear language to different audiences.[10]

Metaphors and Analogies.   A well-chosen analogy or metaphor appeals to the intellect, to imagination, and to values. The charismatic Mary Kay Ash, the founder of Mary Kay Cosmetics, has made frequent use of metaphors. To inspire her associates toward higher performance, she often said: "You see, a bee shouldn't be able to fly; its body is too heavy for its wings. But the bumblebee doesn't know that and it flies very well." Mary Kay explains the message of the bumblebee metaphor in these terms: "Women come to us not knowing they can fly. Finally, with help and encouragement, they find their wings—and then they fly very well indeed."[11]

Gearing Language to Different Audiences.   Metaphors and analogies are inspiring, but effective leaders must also choose the level of language to suit the audience. The challenge of choosing the right level of language is significant because constituents vary widely in verbal sophistication. One day, for example, a CEO might be attempting to inspire a group of Wall Street financial analysts, and the next day she or he might be attempting to inspire first-level employees to keep working hard despite limited salary increases.

Conger has observed that an executive's ability to speak on a colloquial level contributes heavily to creating appeal. A person with the high status of an executive is expected to use an elevated language style. When the person unexpectedly uses the everyday language of an operative employee, it may create a special positive response. Part of Lee Iacocca's appeal appears to be his tough-guy talk.

Management by Anecdote

Another significant aspect of the communication style of charismatic and transformational leaders is that they make extensive use of memorable anecdotes to get messages across. **Management by anecdote** is the technique of inspiring and instructing team members by telling fascinating stories. The technique is a major contributor to building a strong company culture. David Armstrong, an executive at Armstrong International, uses the following anecdote to reinforce the importance of listening to customers:

> Bill, our sales manager, wanted to add an obsolete feature to our company's new fish finder. We thought he was crazy. Bill knew that we preferred only to offer high-end, advanced products in order to hold on to our market share. The "flasher mode" he wanted to add to our fish finders was outdated, since it only told the fishers that fish were nearby—while our new computerized models would also indicate the fish's location and size.
>
> Who on earth would want the old-fashioned fish finder? Our customers, as it turned out. Many of them were old-time fishermen and didn't feel comfortable

with the newfangled model, which confused them. They wanted the kind of machine they were used to.

Nobody agreed with Bill at first, but eventually he got his way. We put the "flasher" back on the fish finder. Customers are still calling us to tell us how much they like this feature. We've sold a lot more units, because we listened to the market.

After Armstrong tells this story, he explains the lessons illustrated by the story. One is, "Listen, listen, listen to your salespeople and your customers. Get direct feedback and don't second-guess them." Another is, "Ask yourself if this feature is necessary. Technology is not an end in itself." The third lesson is that classic products can outsell new products. Experts told the Coca Cola Bottling Company to change its formula, but Coca-Cola drinkers didn't agree."[12]

To get started developing the skill of management by anecdote, do Leadership Skill-Building Exercise 3–2.

HOW TRANSFORMATIONS TAKE PLACE

Leaders often encounter the need to transform organizations from low performance to acceptable performance, or from acceptable performance to high performance. At other times, a leader is expected to move a firm from a crisis mode to high ground. To accomplish these lofty purposes, the transformational leader attempts to overhaul the organizational culture or

---

LEADERSHIP
SKILL-BUILDING
EXERCISE 3–2   **Management by Anecdote**

Directions: Gather in a small problem-solving group to develop an inspiring anecdote about something that actually happened, or might have happened, at a present or former employer. Here are some guidelines:

1. Make up a list of core values the firm holds dear, such as quality, service, or innovation.

2. Think of an incident in which an employee strikingly lived up to (or violated) one of these values. Write it up as a story with a moral.

3. Share your stories with other members of the class, and discuss whether this exercise could make a contribution to leadership development.

Source: The guidelines are from "Management by Anecdote," *Success*, December 1992, p. 35.

subculture. His or her task can thus be as immense as the process of organizational change. To focus our discussion specifically on the leader's role, let's look at several ways in which transformations take place.[13] (See Figure 3–2.)

1. *Raising people's awareness.* The transformational leader makes group members aware of the importance and values of certain rewards and how to achieve them. He or she might point to the pride workers would experience should the firm become number one in its field. At the same time, the leader should point to the financial rewards accompanying such success.

2. *Helping people look beyond self-interest.* The transformational leader helps group members look to "the big picture" for the sake of the team and the organization. The executive vice president of a bank told her staff members, "I know most of you dislike word processing your own memos and letters. Yet if we hire enough staff to makes life more convenient for you, we'll be losing money. Then the government might force us to be taken over by a larger bank. Who knows how many management jobs would then have to be cut."

3. *Helping people search for self-fulfillment.* The transformational leader helps people go beyond a focus on minor satisfactions to a quest for self-fulfillment. The leader might explain, "I know that making sure you take every vacation day owed you is important. Yet if we get this proposal out on time, we might land a contract that will make us the envy of the industry." (Being the envy of the industry satisfies the need for self-fulfillment.)

4. *Helping people understand the need for change.* The transformational leader must help group members understand the need for change both emotionally and intellectually. The problem is that change involves dislocation and discomfort. An effective transformational leader recognizes this emotional component to resisting change and deals with it openly. Organizational change is much like a life transition. Endings must be successfully worked through before new beginnings are possible. People must become unhooked from their pasts.

Dealing with the emotional conflicts of large numbers of staffers is obviously an immense task. One approach taken by successful leaders is to conduct discussion groups, in which managers and workers are free to discuss their feelings about the changes. This approach has been used quite effectively when firms are downsized. Many of the "survivors" feel guilty that

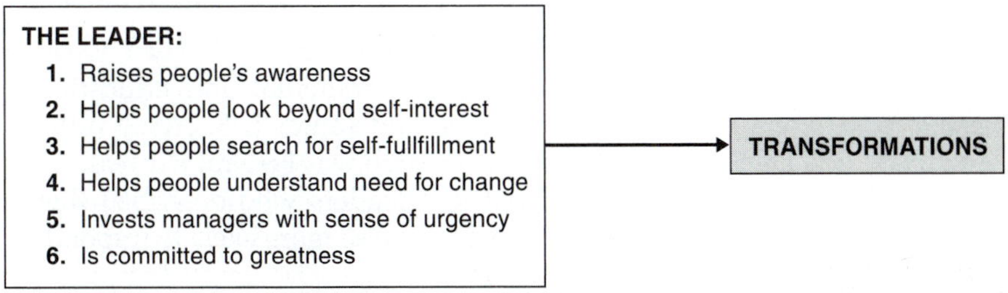

FIGURE 3–2
How Transformations Take Place

THE LEADER:
1. Raises people's awareness
2. Helps people look beyond self-interest
3. Helps people search for self-fullfillment ⟶ TRANSFORMATIONS
4. Helps people understand need for change
5. Invests managers with sense of urgency
6. Is committed to greatness

they are still employed while many competent coworkers have lost their jobs. Clearly, conducting these sessions requires considerable listening skill on the manager's part.

5. *Investing managers with a sense of urgency.* To create the transformation, the leader assembles a critical mass of managers and imbues in them the urgency of change. The managers must also share the top leader's vision of what is both necessary and achievable. To sell this vision of an improved organization, the transformational leader must capitalize on available opportunities. When Paul Stern joined Northern Telecom, he already had a vision of the company as a world-class player in telecommunications. He kept repeating his vision to lower-ranking managers. The managers bought his vision, and Stern's persistence achieved its intended results

6. *Committing to greatness.* Peter Koestenbaum argues that business can be an opportunity for individual and organizational greatness. By adopting this greatness attitude, leaders can ennoble human nature and strengthen societies. Greatness encompasses striving for business effectiveness such as profits and high stock value, as well as impeccable ethics. An emphasis on ethical leadership instills a desire for customer service and quality and fosters feelings of proprietorship and involvement.[14] (A commitment to greatness is, of course, important for all leaders, not just those who are charismatic.)

The accompanying Leader-in-Action box describes a leader who directly and indirectly uses some of the transformational techniques just described.

EMPIRICAL STUDIES ON CHARISMATIC AND TRANSFORMATIONAL LEADERSHIP

A concern some scholars have about transformational leadership is that it sounds too mystical and "soft." Fortunately, some empirical research has been conducted about the effects of charismatic and transformational leadership in work settings. Of particular significance is Bass's charismatic leadership scale. which measures both the leader's behavior and the group members' reactions. The following are three sample items:

> I have complete faith in [the leader].
>
> [The leader is] a model for me to follow.
>
> [The leader has] a sense of mission that is transmitted to me.[15]

Using this scale, Bass surveyed over 1,500 general managers, leaders of technical teams, governmental and educational administrators, upper-middle managers, and senior U.S. Army officers. One of the companies involved in the research was Federal Express.

Subordinates of leaders who described their managers as being more transformational were also more likely to respond that the organizational units

LEADER IN ACTION

Yvonne Scruggs-Leftwich, the People's Banker

[First appeared in *Success* January 1991. Written by Don Wallace and Michael Maren. Reprinted with permission of *Success* Magazine. Copyright © 1991 by Hal Holdings Corporation.]

Yvonne Scruggs-Leftwich left public service in 1987 to join an investment banking firm. Her career had included positions as a faculty member at the Wharton School of Economics, deputy assistant secretary of the Department of Housing and Urban Development, and deputy mayor of Philadelphia. As a member of the investment banking community, Scruggs-Leftwich kept thinking that she should be helping poor and struggling people with their financial problems. She committed herself to find a way to earn money, yet still help people whom the investment banking community had written off.

Grappling with a problem that had baffled governments and private enterprise alike, Scruggs-Leftwich developed the idea of the country's first nondepository bank. Customers would be able to purchase money orders and stamps and pay their bills in cash. The new bank would then transfer the funds to utility companies.

She established the bank in her hometown of Buffalo, New York. She staffed the bank exclusively with people from the community, which her colleagues believed to be a poor decision. Yet owing to the community's participation, the financial center also functioned as a community center. Local artists displayed their works on the center's walls, and neighborhood organizations held meetings at the center. Business flourished as more and more community members enjoyed doing business with Scruggs-Leftwich. As profits grew, she opened two more centers in the state. Soon these centers were serving about 45,000 people monthly.

Scruggs-Leftwich describes her innovative business strategy as looking for disinvestment by traditional institutions. She is the most bullish on "urban cottage industries," such as ones that buy and rehabilitate housing using local labor.

they led were more highly effective. The leaders who were described as transformational were judged to be more effective than those described as transactional. First, they were judged to have better relationships with higher-ups. Second, their team members exerted more effort for them. If leaders were judged to be only transactional, the organizations were seen as less effective.

Leaders who were described as charismatic by their team members also tended to be appraised highly by their superiors. Being perceived as

TABLE 3–1   Correlations Between Ratings of Charisma by Team Members and Appraisals by Superiors

Superior's Appraisal	Subordinates' Evaluation of Charisma
Judgment and decision making	.33*
Financial management	.36†
Communication	.32*
Persuasion	.33*
Risk taking	.45†

*p < .05.
†p < .01.

Source: Derived from data presented in John J. Hater and Bernard M. Bass, "Supervisors' Evaluations and Subordinates' Perceptions of Transformational and Transactional Leadership," *Journal of Applied Psychology*, November 1988, p. 701.

charismatic was significantly correlated with five dimensions of managerial performance, as shown in Table 3–1.

Another study demonstrated that the performance appraisals of group members were higher if their leaders had been described as transformational.[16] A possible bias here is that people who receive higher performance ratings may develop more positive perceptions of that leader. Have you noticed the same effect in student evaluation of faculty members?

CONCERNS ABOUT CHARISMATIC AND TRANSFORMATIONAL LEADERSHIP

Up to this point, an optimistic picture has been painted of both the concept of charisma and charismatic leaders. For the sake of fairness and scientific integrity, contrary points of view must also be presented. The topic of charisma and transformational leadership has been challenged from two major standpoints: the validity of the concept, and the misdeeds of charismatic leaders.

Challenges to the Validity of Charismatic Leadership

One reason so few studies of charismatic leadership have been conducted is that most leadership researchers doubt that charisma can be accurately defined and measured. Conducting research about charisma is akin to conducting research about total quality: you know it when you see it, but it is difficult to define in operational terms. Furthermore, even when one leader is deemed to be charismatic, he or she has many detractors. According to the concept of **leadership polarity,** leaders are often revered or vastly unpopular. People rarely feel neutral about them.[17]

Another problem with the concept of charisma is that it may not be necessary for leadership effectiveness. Warren Bennis and Burt Nanus have observed that very few leaders can accurately be described as charismatic. The organizational leaders the two researchers studied were "short and tall, articulate and inarticulate, dressed for success and dressed for failure, and there was virtually nothing in terms of physical appearance, personality, or style that set them apart from followers."

Based on these observations, Bennis and Nanus hypothesized that instead of charisma resulting in effective leadership, the reverse may be true. People who are outstanding leaders are granted charisma (perceived as charismatic) by their constituents as a result of their success.[18]

The Dark Side of Charismatic Leadership

Some people believe that charismatic leadership can be exercised for evil purposes. This argument was introduced previously in relation to personalized charismatic leaders. Years ago, Robert Tucker warned about the dark side of charisma, particularly with respect to political leaders:

> The magical message which mesmerizes the unthinking (and which can often be supplied by skilled phrase makers) promises that things will become not just better but perfect. Charismatic leaders are experts at promising Utopia. Since perfection is the end, often the most heinous actions can be tolerated as seemingly necessary means to that end.[19]

More recently it has been observed that some charismatic leaders are unethical and lead their organizations toward illegal and immoral ends. People are willing to follow the charismatic leader down a quasi-legal path because of his or her referent power.[20] For example, the legendary dealmaker Michael Milken was convicted of illegal securities transactions and sentenced to jail. Nevertheless, he inspired hundreds of people. Many of his admirers claimed that by promoting high-risk, high-yield bonds (junk bonds) Milken facilitated the growth of small business.

Another way of framing the issue of the dark side of charisma is that some charismatic and transformational leaders neglect their social responsibility. **Social responsibility** is an obligation to groups in society other than owners or stockholders and beyond that prescribed by law or union contract. When charismatic leaders behave in socially responsible ways, concerns are lessened about abusing the gift of charisma.

A charismatic leader's ability to influence constituents multiplies the importance of his or her having a strong sense of social responsibility. For example, a company president who invests substantial personal time in helping community groups will inspire workers throughout the firm to do the same. Leaders who are not particularly charismatic also have an obligation to behave in socially responsible ways, thus serving as a positive model.

SUMMARY

Charisma is a special quality of leaders whose purposes, powers, and extraordinary determination differentiate them from others. Charisma is also a positive and compelling quality of a person, which creates a desire in many others to be led by him or her. The relationship between group members and the leader is significant because they must attribute charismatic qualities to the leader.

Charismatic leadership can be understood in terms of its effects, such as group members' trust in the correctness of the leader's beliefs. One study showed that the effects of charismatic leadership can be organized into three dimensions: referent power, expert power, and job involvement.

Charismatic leaders can be subdivided into five types: socialized, personalized (self-interested), office-holder, personal (outstanding characteristics), and divine. Charismatic and transformational leaders have characteristics that set them apart from noncharismatic and transactional leaders. Those studied here are (1) vision, (2) masterful communication skills, (3) ability to inspire trust, (4) ability to make group members feel capable, (5) energy and action orientation, (6) emotional expressiveness and warmth, (7) willingness to take personal risks, (8) use of unconventional strategies, (9) self-promoting personality, (10) propensity to emerge during crises, and (11) minimum internal conflict.

Charismatic and transformational leaders communicate their visions, goals, and directives in a colorful, imaginative, and expressive manner. Communication effectiveness allows for management by inspiration. One communications technique to inspire others is through metaphors, analogies, and organizational stories. Another is gearing language to different audiences. Charismatic and transformational leaders also extensively use memorable anecdotes to get messages across.

To bring about change, the transformational leader attempts to overhaul the organizational culture or subculture. The specific change techniques include raising people's awareness of the importance of certain rewards. Another is to get people to look beyond their self-interests for the sake of the team and the organization. The transformational leader also assembles a critical mass of managers who share his or her sense of urgency and makes a commitment to greatness.

Empirical research indicates that leaders who are perceived to be charismatic are more likely to run highly effective units. Charismatic leaders are also more likely to be rated high on several important work dimensions, such as judgment and decision making.

One concern about charismatic and transformational leadership is that the concept is murky. Many noncharismatic leaders are effective. Another concern is that some charismatic leaders are unethical and devious, suggesting that being charismatic does not necessarily help the organization. By behaving in a socially responsible manner, charismatic leaders can avoid abusing their influence over others.

KEY TERMS

Charisma
Referent power
Expert power
Socialized charismatic
Personalized charismatic

Transformational leaders
Transactional leaders
Management by anecdote
Leadership polarity
Social responsibility

GUIDELINES FOR ACTION AND SKILL DEVELOPMENT

Robert Dawson offers several suggestions to help a person act in a charismatic manner, thus creating charismatic appeal. All of them relate to well-accepted human relations techniques.

1. *Make everybody you meet feel that he or she is quite important.* For example, when at a company meeting shake the hand of every person you meet.

2. *Multiply the effectiveness of your handshake.* Shake firmly without creating pain, and make enough eye contact to notice the color of the other person's eyes. When you take that much trouble, you project care and concern. Think a positive thought about the person whose hand you shake.

3. *Thank people frequently, especially your own group members.* Thanking others is still infrequently practiced; thus it gives you a charismatic edge.

4. *Smile frequently even if you are not in a happy mood.* A warm smile seems to indicate a confident, caring person, which contributes to a perception of charisma.[21]

DISCUSSION QUESTIONS AND ACTIVITIES

1. Identify a business, government, education, or sports leader whom you perceive to be charismatic. Explain the basis for your judgment.

2. Can a first-level supervisor be charismatic?

3. Identify a well-known leader who is definitely *not* charismatic.

4. Explain how job involvement can be part of charisma.

5. Why do you think British students rated Richard Branson to be one of the three most admired people in England?

6. What similarity do you see between the goals of organization development practitioners and transformational leaders?

7. What should a leader do who is not effective at developing inspirational metaphors and anecdotes?

8. Furnish an example of how some workers need to transcend their self-interests for the good of the organization.

9. A concern has been expressed that leaders who are charismatic are often incompetent. They simply get placed into key positions because they create such a good impression. What do you think of this argument?

10. Design a research study or survey to determine if you are charismatic.

LEADERSHIP CASE PROBLEM

"I Have a Dream"

Martin Luther King, Jr., delivered the following address on the steps of the Lincoln Memorial in Washington, D.C. on August 28, 1963.

I say to you, my friends, that in spite of the difficulties and frustrations of the moment I still have a dream. It is a dream deeply rooted in the American Dream.

I have a dream that one day this nation will rise up and live out the true meaning of its creed: "We hold these truths to be self-evident; that all men are created equal."

I have a dream that one day on the red hills of Georgia the sons of former slaves and the sons of former slave owners will be able to sit down together at the table of brotherhood.

I have a dream that one day even the state of Mississippi, a desert state sweating in the heat of injustice and oppression, will be transformed into an oasis of freedom and justice.

I have a dream that my four little children will one day live in a nation where they will not be judged by the color of their skin but the content of their character.

I have a dream today.

I have a dream that one day the state of Alabama, whose governor's lips are presently dripping with the words of interposition and nullification, will be transformed into a situation where little black boys and girls will be able to join hands with little white boys and white girls and walk together as sisters and brothers.

I have a dream today.

I have a dream that one day every valley shall be exalted, every hill and mountain shall be made low, the rough places will be made plains, and the crooked places will be made straight, and the glory of the Lord shall be revealed, and all flesh shall see it together.

This is our hope. This is the faith with which I return to the South. With this faith we will be able to transform the jangling discords of our nation into a beautiful symphony of brotherhood. With this faith we will be able to work together, to pray together, to struggle together, to go to jail together, to stand up for freedom together, knowing that we will be free one day.

This will be the day when all of God's children will be able to sing with new meaning, "My country 'tis of thee, sweet land of liberty, of thee I sing. Land where my fathers died, land of the pilgrim's pride, from every mountainside, let freedom ring."

And if America is to be a great nation this must become true. So let freedom ring from the prodigious hilltops of New Hampshire. Let freedom ring from the mighty mountains of New York. Let freedom ring from the heightening Alleghenies of Pennsylvania!

Let freedom ring from the snowcapped Rockies of Colorado!

Let freedom ring from the curvaceous peaks of California!

But not only that; let freedom ring from the Stone Mountains of Georgia.

Let freedom ring from every hill and mole-hill of Mississippi. From every mountainside, let freedom ring.

When we let freedom ring, when we let it ring from every village and every hamlet, from every state and every city, we will be able to speed up that day when all of God's children, black men and white men, Jews and Gentiles, Protestants and Catholics, will be able to join hands and sing in the words of that old Negro spiritual, "Free at last! Free at last! Thank God almighty, we are free at last!"

1. How would you rate the charismatic appeal of King's speech? (If feasible, listen to the speech on tape to better comprehend the nonverbal aspects of the speech.)

2. What specific charismatic elements can you identify in this famous speech?

3. Would a speech of this emotional intensity be appropriate in a work setting? Explain your reasoning.

LEADERSHIP EXERCISE

Visionary Speech

Write a brief speech about a dream that you or someone else could use in a work setting. Make the dream so inspiring that workers will eagerly help the organization attain the vision you have articulated. Remember to make several emotional appeals to strengthen your speech.

Effective Leadership Behaviors and Attitudes

LEARNING OBJECTIVES

After studying this chapter, you should be able to

1. summarize the pioneering research on leadership behaviors and attitudes conducted at the Ohio State University and the University of Michigan.
2. describe at least seven task-oriented leadership behaviors and attitudes.
3. describe at least seven relationship-oriented leadership attitudes and behaviors.
4. explain the meaning and significance of SuperLeadership.
5. describe how the situation influences the choice of effective leadership behavior.

---

*L*inda Gosnell, a travel agency owner, has held together a stable and productive work force of twenty-five to thirty workers for more than twenty years. Asked about her successful practices, Gosnell explained that her most important leadership skill is to give her agents the right amount of emotional support. She said, "The technical aspects of an agent's job center around proper use of our on-line computer systems. It takes time to learn the systems, but they are menu driven, which means they can be self-taught. What I emphasize is dealing with the emotions of my staff.

"I'll give you an example. Booking reservations for the Holiday season is emotionally draining. My agents could sell three times as many trips if there were hotel and air space available. My agents have to deal with the frustration and impatience of our clients. To help my agents preserve their sanity, I have to calm them down and reassure them they are doing a good job."

The traits and personal characteristics described in the two previous chapters contribute substantially to effective leadership. Success as a leader, however, also depends on the right behaviors (including skills) and attitudes. For example, to be effective, Linda Gosnell—whether or not she is charismatic—must emotionally support her agents during hectic times. This chapter describes a number of key behaviors and attitudes that contribute to a manager's ability to function as a leader. It also describes how the right leadership behaviors and attitudes can get team members to lead themselves, and how the situation influences the leader's actions.

Frequent reference is made in this chapter, and at other places in the text, to leadership effectiveness. A working definition of an **effective leader** is one whose actions facilitate group members' attainment of productivity, quality, and satisfaction.

PIONEERING RESEARCH ON LEADERSHIP BEHAVIORS AND ATTITUDES

Beginning in the 1950s, extensive research was conducted at Ohio State University and the University of Michigan on effective leadership practices. This pioneering research laid the foundation for understanding the difference between successful and unsuccessful leaders. The same research led to modern conceptions of leadership styles. Despite the contributions of this early leadership research, it has limitations for a modern understanding of high-level leadership. Most of the surveys and interviews were conducted with bomber airplane commanders and production and office supervisors.

The Ohio State University Studies of Initiating Structure and Consideration

After World War II, a major leadership research program was conducted at the Bureau of Business Research at the Ohio State University. The study identified 1,800 specific examples of leadership behavior, which were reduced to 150 questionnaire items of leadership functions.[1] The functions are also referred to as *dimensions of leadership behavior.* A major thrust of the research was to ask team members to describe their supervisors by responding to questionnaires. Leaders were also asked to rate themselves on leadership dimensions.

Two Key Leadership Dimensions.   A series of studies identified two leadership dimensions that accounted for 85 percent of the variance in descriptions of leadership behavior: initiating structure and consideration. **Initiating structure** is the degree to which the leader organizes and defines relationships in the group by activities such as assigning specific tasks, specifying procedures to be followed, scheduling work, and clarifying expectations of team members.

Leaders who score high on the initiating structure dimension define the relationship between themselves and the staff members, as well as the role that they expect each staff member to assume. Such leaders also endeavor to establish well-defined channels of communication and ways of getting the job done. Five self-assessment items measuring initiating structure are as follows:

1. Try out your own new ideas in the work group.
2. Encourage the slow-working people in the group to work harder.
3. Emphasize meeting deadlines.
4. Meet with the group at regularly scheduled times.
5. See to it that people in the work group are working up to capacity.

Consideration is the degree to which the leader creates an environment of emotional support, warmth, friendliness, and trust. The leader creates this environment by being friendly and approachable, looking out for the personal welfare of the group, keeping the group abreast of new developments, and doing small favors for the group.

Leaders who score high on the consideration factor are typically friendly, trustful, earn respect, and have a warm relationship with team members. Leaders with low scores on the consideration factor are typically authoritarian and impersonal in their relationships with group members. Five questionnaire items measuring the consideration factor are as follows:

1. Do personal favors for people in the work group.
2. Treat all people in the work group as your equal.
3. Be willing to make changes.
4. Back up what people under you do.
5. Do little things to make it pleasant to be a member of the staff.

An important output of research on initiating structure and consideration was to categorize leaders with respect to how much emphasis they place on the two dimensions. As implied by Figure 4–1, the two dimensions are not mutually exclusive. A leader can achieve high or low status on both dimensions. For example, an effective leader might contribute to high productivity yet still place considerable emphasis on warm human relationships. The four-cell grid of Figure 4–1 is a key component of several approaches to describing leadership style. We return to this topic in Chapter 5.

Some Research Findings and Implications.   Many practical implications have been derived from research conducted on the relationship between these two leadership dimensions and effectiveness criteria. A general finding is that the most effective leaders emphasize both initiating structure and consideration. In summarizing some of the earliest research, Andrew W. Halpin wrote, "In short, our findings suggest that to select a leader who is

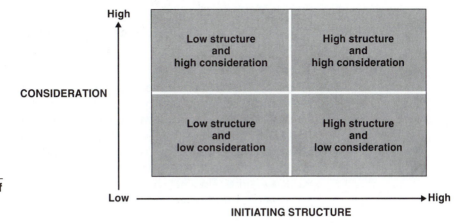

FIGURE 4–1

Four Combinations of Initiating Structure and Consideration

likely to satisfy both his men [only male aircraft pilots were studied], we do best by choosing an aircraft commander who is above average on both leader behavior dimensions."[2]

Another consistent finding from the Ohio State studies was that group members desire more in the way of consideration. In contrast, the managers to whom the supervisory leaders reported preferred a greater emphasis on initiating structure. The higher the level of management, the greater the emphasis on initiating structure. Additional data supported the idea that group members value consideration. It was discovered that employee turnover was lowest and job satisfaction highest under leaders who were rated high in consideration. Conversely, leaders who were rated low in consideration and high in initiating structure had high grievance and turnover rates among their employees. Research also indicated that leaders high on structure were generally rated highly by superiors. They also had higher producing work groups than did leaders who scored lower in initiating structure.

Another important implication for organizational leaders is that the situation influences whether the leader should emphasize initiating structure or consideration. In some situations, group members rated leaders with a strong emphasis on initiating structure as being more effective. For example, Air Force commanders who rated high on consideration were rated as *less* effective than were commanders rated high on structure. A plausible reason for this finding is that the organizational culture of the Air Force supports a demanding leader.

The University of Michigan Studies of Effective Leadership Practices.

During the time of the Ohio State studies, researchers at the Survey Research Center of the University of Michigan were also studying leadership effectiveness. Interviews and questionnaires were used extensively to contrast the behavior of leaders from high-producing units with that of leaders from low-producing units.[3]

Two Key Approaches to Leadership.　Supervisory leaders were categorized into two groups, depending on whether they emphasized production or employees. **Production-centered leaders** set tight work standards, organized tasks carefully, and prescribed the work methods to be followed. They also closely supervised the work of group members. **Employee-centered leaders** encouraged subordinate participation in goal setting and in other work decisions. They also helped to ensure high performance by engendering trust and mutual respect. The production-centered versus employee-centered difference parallels the distinction between initiating structure and consideration, with one exception. A leader is classified as either production-centered or employee-centered, which is a one-dimensional classification. The classification of structure and consideration is two-dimensional with four possible categories, as previously explained.

Some Research Findings and Implications.　A dominant finding of the University of Michigan studies was that most productive work groups tend to have leaders who are employee-centered rather than production-centered. Also, the most effective leaders are those who have supportive relationships with group members. They emphasize group rather than individual decision making, and encourage team members to set and achieve high performance goals. Despite the general consistency of the contribution of employee-centered leadership, the studies produced some mixed findings.

Later research by the Michigan group shed new light on the complexity of the relationship between the type of leadership and productivity. One group of employees in a life insurance company was managed by employee-centered leaders. A comparable group was managed by production-centered leaders. Contrary to expectations, both groups showed a significant increase in productivity. The employee-centered leadership approach, however, fostered an increase in favorable attitudes toward the supervisors and the company. In contrast, the production-centered group showed a marked decrease in favorable attitudes toward supervision and management. Another study was conducted with 20,000 employees in a firm that manufactures earth-moving equipment. It was concluded that supervisors with the best production records were both production- and employee-centered.

An important implication from both the Ohio State and Michigan studies is that effective leaders emphasize both high productivity and good interpersonal relationships. The same theme surfaces in many of the approaches to leadership studied throughout this book. In almost any leadership situation you face, you will need to juggle the two dimensions of task orientation and people orientation.

TASK-RELATED ATTITUDES AND BEHAVIORS

The task-related versus relationship-related classification remains useful as a framework for understanding leadership attitudes, behaviors, and practices. This section identifies and describes task-related attitudes and behaviors characteristic of effective leaders, as outlined in Table 4–1. *Task-related* in this context means that the behavior, attitude, or skill focuses more on the task to be performed than on the interpersonal aspect of leadership. Most task-related activities would be included under initiating structure. Before reading further, do Leadership Self-Assessment Exercise 4–1.

TABLE 4–1   Task-Related Leadership Attitudes and Behaviors

1. Adaptability to the situation	5. Ability to interpret conditions
2. Direction setting	6. Frequent feedback
3. High performance standards	7. Stability of performance
4. Risk taking and bias for action	8. Strong customer orientation

LEADERSHIP SELF-ASSESSMENT EXERCISE 4–1   How Effective Are You as a Leader?

Directions: Circle the number on the 1–5 scale that best indicates how you really feel. If you are not now a manager, project how you would react if you were a manager.

1. I'll wait until things settle down.	1 2 3 4 5	I really like change.
2. Most of my staff meetings are about internal procedures and budgeting.	1 2 3 4 5	I spend much of my time talking to and about customers.
3. If there's a way, I'll find it.	1 2 3 4 5	Top management should make the first move.
4. I'll wait for orders from above.	1 2 3 4 5	Let's get it done right now.

5. I seek responsibility beyond my job description. 1 2 3 4 5 I fulfill my job description.

6. How can I enhance revenue? Add value? 1 2 3 4 5 I'll stay within my budget plan.

7. My people should "challenge the system." 1 2 3 4 5 I carefully review subordinates' work.

8. If I haven't been told *yes*, I can't do it. 1 2 3 4 5 If I haven't been told *no*, I can do it.

9. I'll take responsibility for my failures. 1 2 3 4 5 I usually make excuses for my failures.

10. I won't take risks because I may fail. 1 2 3 4 5 I'll take my risks although I may fail.

11. We've got to do things faster. 1 2 3 4 5 We can't turn things around that fast.

12. I want to know what other departments are doing and what their needs are. 1 2 3 4 5 I protect my own department.

13. I talk mainly to those people who are formally linked to me. 1 2 3 4 5 I'll go beyond the organization chart to share information and resources.

14. Leave my people and me alone and let us get our job done. 1 2 3 4 5 I'll cross department lines to get the job done.

15. I trust only a few people within the firm. 1 2 3 4 5 I volunteer to share ideas and resources with people in other departments.

Scoring and interpretation: Measure your effectiveness as a managerial leader as follows: For questions numbered 1, 2, 4, 8, 10, 13, 14, and 15, simply add up the scores. For questions 3, 5, 6, 7, 9, 11 and 12, flip the scale so that a response score of 1 becomes 5, 2 becomes 4, 4 becomes 2, and 5 becomes 1. A total score of 60 means you have the mindset of an effective manager. If you scored below 45, you have some work to do.

Source: Adapted from Oren Harari and Linda Mukai, "A New Decade Demands a New Breed of Manager," *Management Review*, August 1990, p. 23. Used by permission of the author.

Adaptability to the Situation. Effective leaders adapt to the situation. Adaptability reflects the contingency viewpoint: a tactic is chosen based on the unique circumstances at hand. (Chapter 6 describes the major contingency theories of leadership.) Assume that a leader was responsible for psychologically immature group members. The leader would find it necessary to supervise them closely. If the group members were mature and self-reliant, they would require less supervision. The adaptive leader also selects an organization structure best suited to the demands of the situation, such as choosing between a brainstorming group and a committee.

The ability to size up people and situations, and adapt tactics accordingly, is a vital leadership behavior. It stems from insight and intuition, both of which reflect a talent for direct perception of a situation, unrelated to any specific reasoning process. Adaptability is a leadership behavior that includes attention to both task and interpersonal factors. The accompanying Leader in Action profile describes a heralded adaptive leader.

Direction Setting. John Kotter reasons that since the function of leadership is to produce change, the leader must set the direction of that change. Setting the direction goes beyond planning, which is a management process designed to produce orderly results rather than change. Kotter explains that setting a direction is more inductive. Leaders gather voluminous data and search for patterns, relationships, and linkages that help explain events.

Direction setting creates vision and strategies rather than a plan. In turn, the vision describes a business, technology, or corporate culture in terms of what it should become. The strategy describes a feasible way of achieving the vision. (Many would argue that a strategy *is* a plan.) An example of successful direction setting took place at Scandinavian Airline Systems (SAS) several years ago. CEO Jan Carlzon articulated the vision to make SAS the best airline in the world for the frequent business traveler. Focusing on the business customer gave the airline a competitive advantage.[4]

High Performance Standards. Effective leaders consistently hold group members to high standards of performance. Setting such standards increases productivity, as people tend to live up to the expectations set for them by superiors. This is called the Pygmalion effect, and it works in a subtle, almost unconscious way. When a managerial leader believes that a group member will succeed, the manager communicates this belief without realizing that he or she is doing so. Conversely, when a leader expects a group member to fail, that person will not disappoint the manager. The manager's expectation of success or failure becomes a self-fulfilling prophecy. The manager's perceptions contribute to the success or failure.

A plausible explanation for the Pygmalion effect is that the leader sends nonverbal signals that indicate how much confidence he or she has in the group member. The signals, in turn, elevate or lower the group member's confidence level.

LEADER IN ACTION

Chuck Daly, Basketball Coach

Chuck Daly is the head coach for the New Jersey Nets and was the coach for the U.S. Olympic Basketball Team of 1992. He says, "I've coached at every level. I know that you take what you have and you work with it." In college that may mean screaming and hollering and teaching. With the Detroit Pistons it meant pedal to the metal one night, foot covering the brake the next. With the "Dream Team" (the 1992 Olympic men's basketball team) it meant realizing that the best players ever just need a little nurturing.

"He's made the whole thing enjoyable," said Michael Jordan, a Dream Team player. "We needed someone to meld all these personalities together. He can put into words, and get a player to accept a certain responsibility. He makes it so easy to accept a role without animosity. There's been no ego problem, and no ball-hogging either. . . . Even we were a little concerned about potential problems, but it's been smooth sailing from Day 1."

Daly said that when coaching a group of superstars, "You have to give them some structure, but that's about it. You don't diagram plays, you give them some ideas and they go from there. I learned when I coached the NBA all-star game that professional players have a great deal of pride."

Sportswriter Michael Wilbon adds that there never was a more logical choice than to pick the man who has the perfect touch for most every situation.

Source: Michael Wilbon, "Dream Team Really Has Dream Coach," *Washington Post* syndicated story, August 8, 1992. © 1992 *The Washington Post*. Reprinted with permission.

Gary C. Wendt, chief executive of GE Capital Services Inc., exemplifies an executive leader who sets high performance standards. Wendt is known to set a high bar for his managers to reach. Following his pattern, Wendt's staff managers set high standards for the people who report to them. The high standards set are considered the key reason that GE Capital has become the major finance company in the United States. Among these high standards are outwitting competitors by moving faster, buying cheaper, and servicing customers more rapidly. Another standard is to deal with problems the minute they arise.[5]

Risk Taking and Bias for Action.   A bias for action rather than contemplation has been identified as a characteristic of a successful organization.[6] Combined with risk taking, a bias for action is also an important leadership behavior. To bring about constructive change, the leader must take risks and be willing to implement these risky decisions. Xerox Corp.'s performance appraisal includes risk taking and a bias for action as an evaluation characteristic. On the evaluation form, the characteristic is defined as follows:

> Willing to take personal risks to advance new ideas and programs for the success of the Company; has the courage to commit sizable resources based on a blend of analysis and intuition; is comfortable with making the percentages, rather than achieving success with each initiative; trusts own judgment and instincts without requiring definitive proof; prefers quick and approximate actions to slow and precise approaches.

Ability to Interpret Conditions.   According to the consulting firm Forum, leaders must interpret internal and external conditions that affect the leader and the organizational unit. A leader who interprets conditions is carrying out the management role of environmental sensing. When significant trends are observed, the leader helps the group develop an action plan to capitalize on or defend against the trends. The five interpreting practices are as follows:

1. Seeking information from as many sources as possible
2. Knowing how one's own work supports the organization's strategy
3. Analyzing how well the members of the group work together
4. Knowing the capabilities and motivations of the individuals in the work group
5. Knowing one's own capabilities and motivations[7]

John Sculley, formerly of Apple Computer, exemplifies a leader who interprets conditions. He sensed that the consumer need for information handling is beginning to transcend single-use devices such as fax machines, electronic mail, and cellular telephones. Sculley therefore spearheaded a strategic alliance of six companies—AT&T, Sony, Apple, Matsushita, Motorola, and Philips—called General Magic. General Magic is developing a telephone for the year 2000, which combines the three personal communication devices just mentioned.[8]

Frequent Feedback.   Giving group members frequent feedback on their performance is another vital leadership behavior. The leader can rarely influence the actions of group members without appropriate performance feedback. Feedback of this nature has two aspects. First, group members are informed how well they are doing so they can take corrective action if needed. Second, positive feedback serves as a reinforcer that prompts group members to continue favorable activities. Leadership Skill-Building Exercise 4–1 provides practice in developing feedback skills.

LEADERSHIP SKILL-BUILDING EXERCISE 4–1 Feedback Skills

After small groups have completed an assignment such as answering the case questions or discussion questions, hold a performance feedback session. Also use observations you have made in previous problem-solving activities as the basis for your feedback. Each group member provides some feedback to each other member about how well he or she thinks the other person performed. To increase the probability of benefiting from this experience, feedback recipients must listen actively. Refer to the section in Chapter 10 about giving feedback and active listening.

A convenient method to do this exercise is for everyone to sit in a circle. Choose one feedback recipient to begin. Going clockwise around the circle, each group member gives that person feedback. After all people have spoken, the feedback recipient gives his or her reactions. The person to the left of the first recipient is the next one to give feedback.

After everyone has had a turn receiving performance feedback, hold a general discussion. Be sure to discuss three key issues:

1. How helpful was the feedback?
2. What was the relative effectiveness of positive versus negative feedback?
3. Were some group members better than others in giving feedback?

Stability of Performance.   Effective leaders are steady performers, even under heavy workloads and uncertain conditions. Remaining steady under conditions of uncertainty contributes to effectiveness because it helps team members cope with the situation. When the leader remains calm, group members are reassured that things will work out satisfactorily. Stability is helpful for another reason: it helps the managerial leader appear professional and cool under pressure.

In early 1993, a bomb exploded inside the underground garage of the World Trade Center. Key executives at Coopers & Lybrand, an accounting and consulting firm, provided steady performance to help workers cope with the situation. Almost overnight, operations from the Coopers & Lybrand offices in the World Trade Center were transferred temporarily to nearby offices of the firm. Without the calm leadership of the executives, company clients would have experienced severe disruption in services. Furthermore, the company would have lost substantial revenue.

Strong Customer Orientation.   Effective leaders are strongly interested in satisfying the needs of customers, clients, or constituents; this approach helps inspire employees to satisfy customers. A customer orientation is natural in a consumer products business but can be equally important for an industrial company. John W. Snow became the president of CSX, a financially troubled conglomerate, in 1988. Snow sold off all non-transportation-related businesses. In addition, he eliminated many jobs and helped the company develop a customer focus. Snow met with major shippers, listened to their complaints about poor service, and then made internal changes. CSX quickly returned to profitability, much of which has been attributed to Snow's customer focus.[9]

RELATIONSHIP-ORIENTED ATTITUDES AND BEHAVIORS

Leadership involves influencing people, so it follows that many effective leadership attitudes, behaviors, and practices deal with interpersonal relationships. Table 4–2 lists seven relationship-oriented attitudes and behaviors, which we will discuss next. (Most other parts of this book describe the interpersonal aspects of leadership.)

Alignment of People.   According to John Kotter, aligning people is more of a communications challenge than a problem of organization design. To get people pulling together, it is necessary to talk to more people than are required in organizing. The target population can involve many different stakeholders. Among them are immediate subordinates, higher-ups, peers, and workers in other parts of the organization, as well as suppliers, government officials, and even customers. Anyone who can help implement the vision and strategies or who can block implementation must be aligned.[10]

Another perspective on alignment is that it represents organizational members pulling together toward a higher purpose. This stands in contrast to being organized into units in which people stay within the confines of tight job descriptions. Alignment enables people to have a clear sense of

TABLE 4–2   Relationship-Oriented Attitudes and Behaviors

1. Alignment of people	5. Satisfaction of human needs
2. Mobilization	6. Formulation of vision and strategy
3. Concert building	7. Emotional support
4. Inspiration	

direction because they are pursuing a vision. As long as their behavior supports the vision, they are less likely to be reprimanded by superiors.

Mobilization.   Whereas alignment of people takes place at almost a spiritual level, mobilization is more involved with getting the group working together smoothly. Mobilizing people is getting individuals with different ideas, skills, and values to carry out the work of the group. Mobilizing practices include:

1. Communicating expectations clearly
2. Appealing to people's hearts and minds to lead them in a new direction
3. Demonstrating care for team members
4. Demonstrating confidence in the abilities of others
5. Letting people know how they are progressing toward the group's goal.[11]

Concert Building.   A new concept of the leader's role, **concert building,** involves both aligning and mobilizing. The concert builder functions as an orchestra leader. His or her goal is to produce a system that is self-evaluating, self-correcting, self-renewing, and ongoing. David S. Brown describes concert-building leadership in these terms:

> The system can be thought of as a large modern orchestra with a number of professionals playing quite different instruments and performing separate—and often very difficult—tasks. Each instrumentalist, like so many in large organizations, is indeed a specialist in a particular field whose work must be integrated with the work of others to make up the whole.[12]

Becoming an organizational concert builder requires many of the skills and insights described throughout this book. Building teamwork, as described in Chapter 9, is particularly relevant.

Inspiration.   As described in the discussion of charismatic and transformational leadership, inspiring others is an essential leadership practice. Based on surveys and focus groups, the Forum Group has identified five inspiring practices:

1. Promoting the development of people's talents
2. Recognizing the contribution of others
3. Enabling others to feel like leaders
4. Stimulating others' thinking
5. Building enthusiasm about projects and assignments[13]

What it takes to inspire people depends considerably on the characteristics of the group members being inspired. The accompanying Leader in Action vignette describes a tactic the wealthiest man in America used to inspire a well-educated, highly intelligent work force.

LEADER IN ACTION

Bill Gates, Software Mogul

Microsoft Corp. founder Bill Gates inspires employees by holding out the promise of a great future such as a global marketing strategy. He also inspires employees with dramatic stunts. For example, one day 5,000 Microsoft employees are assembled in the Kingdome in Seattle, Washington. While the houselights dim, a spotlight follows a red Corvette with the word "Windows" written across its door. The executive vice president steps out from the car. He pumps his fist into the air, and leads the crowd in a boisterous chant: "Windows, Windows, Windows, Windows." The spotlight then shifts to an Edsel making its way into the arena. "OS/2," the name of IBM's competing software, emblazons the failed automobile.

Next, as the song "Leader of the Pack" blares from the loudspeakers, ten motorcyclists clad in leather roar into the Kingdome on Harleys. The crowd greets lead biker Bill Gates with the same roar typically reserved for rock stars. After his flamboyant entrance, the 36-year-old chairman presents his overview of the computer market and Microsoft for the current year and beyond.

Source: As reported in "Microsoft: Bill Gates's Baby Is on Top of the World. Can It Stay There?" *Business Week*, February 24, 1992; Michael Warshaw, "Power in Practice," *Success*, June 1994, p. 39; "Microsoft: Mark II," *The Economist*, March 19, 1994, p. 81.

Satisfaction of Human Needs.   To inspire people, effective leaders motivate people by satisfying higher level needs. John Kotter explains that motivation and inspiration energize people by satisfying needs for achievement, a sense of belonging, recognition, self-esteem, and a feeling of control over one's life. A strictly managerial—rather than leadership—approach would be to push people in the right direction through control mechanisms.[14] An example would be suspending people who did not achieve sales or quality quotas. Specific motivational skills used by leaders are described in Chapter 10.

Formulation of Vision and Strategy.   An effective leader shapes or formulates the vision and strategy to provide meaning for the work of the group. Shaping is important to involve team members in goal accomplishment. One of the purposes of Bill Gates's address after his motorcycle entrance was to provide specifics about what his vision of Microsoft would mean to employees. Part of this shaping includes maintaining the most stringent hiring standards for new employees. The following are ways to shape vision and strategy:

1. Involve the right people in developing the work group's strategy.
2. Stand up for what is important.
3. Adjust plans and actions as necessary in turbulent situations.
4. Communicate the strategy of the organization as a whole.
5. Create a positive picture of the future for the work group.[15]

Emotional Support to Group Members.   Supportive behavior toward team members usually increases leadership effectiveness. A supportive leader gives frequent encouragement and praise. The emotional support generally improves morale and sometimes improves productivity. Being emotionally supportive comes naturally to the leader who has empathy for people and who is a warm person.

SUPERLEADERSHIP: LEADING OTHERS TO LEAD THEMSELVES

Charles C. Manz and Henry P. Sims, Jr. have formulated what they refer to as the SuperLeadership Theory. A **SuperLeader** is one who leads others to lead themselves, by acting as a teacher and a coach, not a director.[16] Unlike a charismatic leader, who maintains a high profile indefinitely, a SuperLeader inspires others to motivate themselves. And when people are self-directing, they require a minimum of external control.

SuperLeadership requires the leader to take a risk on people: to believe that if given a chance to be self-directing, workers will rise to the occasion. Over a decade ago, Lincoln Electric Co., a renowned welding equipment manufacturer, faced a severe sales slump. To maintain its no-layoff policy, company leadership asked production workers for some help. Fifty production workers volunteered to help out in sales. After a brief sales training program, the workers called on body shops throughout the United States to sell a small welder. The new temporary sales representatives brought in $10 million in new sales and established the small arc welder as an industry leader. The SuperLeadership in this example centers on taking a risk with workers and showing faith in their resourcefulness.

The key aspect of SuperLeadership deals with teaching the right thought patterns. Manz and Sims contend that the leader must teach team members how to develop productive thinking. The purpose of productive, or constructive, thinking is to enable workers to gain control over their own behavior. The SuperLeader serves as a model of constructive thought patterns. For example, the leader should minimize expressing pessimistic, self-critical thoughts to team members. Instead, he or she should reward employees when they think constructively.[17]

Manz recommends several specific ways of establishing and altering thought patterns in desirable ways, as outlined in Figure 4–2 and described

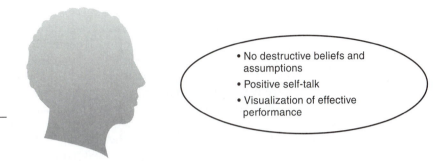

FIGURE 4–2

Productive Thinking as Part of SuperLeadership

- No destructive beliefs and assumptions
- Positive self-talk
- Visualization of effective performance

next. Leaders and individual contributors alike should be able to practice self-leadership by incorporating the following attitudes and behaviors:

1. *Identification and Replacement of Destructive Beliefs and Assumptions.* Negative thoughts are identified and then replaced with more accurate and constructive ones. For example, an employee might regard the manager's criticism as an indicator of personal dislike. A more productive way to view the criticism is to think that the manager is just trying to help him or her perform at a higher level.

2. *Positive and Constructive Self-Talk.* Negative thoughts are converted into positive ones. For example, instead of saying, "My communication skills are too poor to make a presentation to higher management," one would say, "In order to make an impressive presentation to management, I will have to improve my oral communication skills. I'll get started tonight."

3. *Visualization of Methods for Effective Performance.* One imagines oneself moving effortlessly through a challenging assignment using methods that have worked in the past. Visualize making a hard-hitting presentation to management, similar to a presentation of lesser stake that you have made in the past. The idea is that the visualization is practice for the real event and will help one believe in one's capacity to be effective.

In summary, the SuperLeader helps create conditions whereby team members require very little leadership. Achieving such a goal is important because organizations have reduced the number of managers. Also, organizational structures such as work teams and horizontal structures require a high degree of self-management.

SITUATIONAL INFLUENCES ON EFFECTIVE LEADERSHIP BEHAVIOR

As mentioned briefly in connection with the Ohio State studies, the situation can influence which leadership behavior an effective leader emphasizes. Both the internal and external environments have a significant impact on leader effectiveness. For example, the quality of the work force and the competitiveness of the environment could influence which behaviors the leader emphasizes. A manager who supervises competent employees might be able to practice SuperLeadership readily. And a manager who faces a competitive environment might find it easier to align people to pursue a new vision. Chapter 6 describes several contingency leadership theories, specifying which approaches to leadership work best in which situations.

Recent research comparing entrepreneurial leaders with those from large corporations illustrates situational influences on leadership. One of the research questions asked was whether chief executive officers from different corporate environments differ in the attributes, skills, and abilities they possess. A sample of thirty-five *Fortune* 500 (large-company) CEOs and thirty-five *Inc.* (small-company) CEOs was assessed on a psychological assessment battery of nine different inventories. The battery evaluates higher level personnel ranging from supervisors and nonmanagerial professionals to presidents and chief executive officers.

The profiles of the large company and small company CEOs were then compared. Many significant differences between the two groups were found. The skills of small company CEOs appeared to be centered primarily on production-oriented areas. For example, *Inc.* CEOs significantly exceeded *Fortune* 500 CEOs on a measure of developing and implementing technical ideas. Small company CEOs were significantly stronger in measures of coping with difficulties and emergencies, and in handling outside contacts. The researchers explained that the environment of the entrepreneurs requires them to perform tasks that their *Fortune* 500 counterparts delegate to others.

The large company CEOs had a significantly better developed subset of interpersonal skills. They scored higher than their small company counterparts on measures of communications, developing group cooperation and teamwork, developing employee potential, and supervisory practices. The large company CEOs also scored better on a measure of leadership and group participation.[19]

One interpretation of these findings is that the heavy pressures and understaffing faced by small company CEOs compel them to emphasize task-related attitudes and behaviors. In large, successful firms, the CEOs have more opportunity to develop the interpersonal aspects of leadership.

SUMMARY

Effective leadership requires the right behaviors, skills, and attitudes, as emphasized in two pioneering sets of studies. The Ohio State University studies identified two major dimensions of leadership behavior, initiating structure and consideration.

Initiating structure is the degree to which the leader organizes and defines relationships in the group by such activities as assigning tasks and specifying procedures. Consideration is the degree to which the leader creates an environment of emotional support, warmth, friendliness, and trust. The most effective leaders emphasize both initiating structure and consideration. The situation, however, often influences which leadership dimension should be emphasized.

The University of Michigan studies classified leaders as production-centered versus employee-centered. Among the key findings were that employee-centered leaders were the most effective. Yet it was also found that emphasizing both types of leadership can lead to high productivity.

Many task-related attitudes and behaviors of effective leaders have been identified. Among them are (1) adaptability to the situation, (2) direction-setting, (3) high performance standards, (4) risk taking and a bias for action, (5) ability to interpret environmental conditions, (6) frequent feedback, (7) stability of performance, and (8) strong customer orientation.

Many relationship-related attitudes and behaviors of leaders have also been identified. Among them are (1) alignment of people, (2) mobilization, (3) concert building, (4) inspiration, (5) satisfaction of human needs, (6) formulation of vision and strategy, and (7) emotional support.

A SuperLeader is one who leads others to lead themselves. Teaching team members to develop productive thought patterns helps develop self-leadership. For example, the leader encourages people to talk to themselves positively and constructively.

The situation can influence which behaviors an effective leader emphasizes. Recent research suggests that entrepreneurial leaders are faced with an environment that prompts them to emphasize production-oriented behaviors. In contrast, large company CEOs work in an environment more conducive to emphasizing interpersonal behaviors and skills.

KEY TERMS

Effective leader	Employee-centered leaders
Initiating structure	Concert building
Consideration	SuperLeader
Production-centered leaders	

GUIDELINES FOR ACTION AND SKILL DEVELOPMENT

One practical way to increase your leadership effectiveness is to select appropriate leadership behaviors to implement when you carry out a leadership assignment. Here is a checklist of the leadership behaviors described in this chapter. Choose several that would appear to be relevant to the leadership situation you face. Remember, however, that all leadership situations call for some combination of initiating structure and consideration. Adapting to the situation is the essence of situational leadership and is required almost universally.

Develop an action plan for developing each leadership behavior or attitude you choose. Typically the action plan will call for first understanding the meaning of the attitude or behavior, then using appropriate self-discipline or monitoring to engage in such behavior. Assume, for example, that you perceive "strong customer orientation" as an area for growth. To achieve a stronger customer orientation, you might engage in such behaviors as the following:

- Reviewing your daily work activities and asking, "How would this help our customers?
- Holding brief discussions with group members to review the importance of satisfying customer needs.
- Accompanied by a group member, call on customers to discuss the quality of your firm's service.

Leadership Behaviors and Attitudes

1. Initiating structure
2. Showing consideration
3. Adaptability to the situation
4. Setting a direction
5. Setting high performance standards
6. Giving frequent feedback
7. Exhibiting performance stability
8. Showing a strong customer orientation
9. Aligning people
10. Mobilizing people
11. Engaging in concert building
12. Inspiring people
13. Satisfying human needs
14. Shaping vision and strategy
15. Giving emotional support
16. Being a SuperLeader

DISCUSSION QUESTIONS AND ACTIVITIES

1. How does initiating structure relate to the traditional functions of management?
2. Why is consideration so closely associated with the human relations movement?
3. Explain how a leader could realistically be both production-centered and employee-centered.
4. What implications does the information in this chapter have for leadership development?

5. Which leadership traits and characteristics would be particularly important in helping a leader be adaptable to the situation?

6. An important leadership behavior is to have a customer orientation. Describe the opposite behavior.

7. What is the difference between aligning people and the traditional organizing function of assigning jobs?

8. Ask an experienced leader how he or she gives emotional support to team members. Be prepared to discuss your findings in class.

9. Identify two leadership behaviors and attitudes that Bill Gates appears to emphasize.

10. One critic said about SuperLeadership, "It sounds like so much psycho-babble to me." What is your reaction to her criticism?

LEADERSHIP CASE PROBLEM

New Leadership at Compaq

In his first two years in office, Eckhard Pfeiffer, the CEO of Compaq Computer, engineered a stunning turnaround for his company. In 1993, Compaq made more money than its two major rivals, Apple and IBM, combined. Company insiders contend it was Pfeiffer's ability to communicate his vision and a sense of urgency that made the quick turnaround possible. Pfeiffer was promoted to president in late 1992.

The presidency had been vacated after the board forced out the president and cofounder, Rod Canion. The board contended that Canion had misdiagnosed Compaq's downturn in sales by blaming it on the recession. Compaq had experienced its first-ever quarterly loss prior to Canion's departure.

Pfeiffer believed that something more sinister than a recession was responsible for Compaq's problems. He concluded that the company was facing the type of corrosive downward pricing spiral experienced with calculators in the 1970s. First as head of Compaq's European subsidiary, and then as the company's chief operating officer, Pfeiffer cham-pioned cost cutting. He reasoned that by focusing heavily on improving PC performance, the company was turning away from large segments of the market. He said, "The business we left behind was wide open to the competition, and they went after it with a vengeance," (*Business Week*, p. 147).

Pfeiffer's message met with a mixed reception. The engineering-oriented key people at Compaq had difficulty acknowledging that their PCs had become overengineered and overpriced. When Pfeiffer took over as president, he laid down strict policies. Bloated costs had to be slashed. Gold-plated technology had to be forgotten unless it really made a difference. Engineers were ordered to produce high-quality computers at low prices. At one point Pfeiffer declared that Compaq would match any manufacturer in the world on price.

By the end of 1992, Compaq could not keep up with the demand for its new low-priced line of personal computers, especially the ProLinea model. Distribution channels were increased from 3,300 to 8,300 outlets worldwide. Shipments were leaping at an annual 40 percent clip, and revenues and profits were increasing.

Pfeiffer's long-range strategy is to stick with what Compaq does best. He will continue pursuing the corporate PC market with Compaq's traditional line. At the same time Compaq will use ProLineas to build a new high-volume business among small business owners and consumers.

1. What leadership behaviors has Pfeiffer demonstrated?

2. What leadership attitudes has Pfeiffer demonstrated?

3. To what extent is Compaq backing off on the importance of quality?

Source: As reported in "Compaq: How It Made Its Impressive Move out of the Doldrums," *Business Week*, November 2, 1992, pp. 146–151; Stephanie Losee, "How Compaq Keeps the Magic Going," *Fortune*, February 21, 1994, pp. 90–92; "Score One for Compaq," *Forbes*, September 13, 1993, p. 232.

LEADERSHIP EXERCISE

Effective and Ineffective Leaders

Prepare a written description of either the best boss or the worst boss you have ever had. Relate your description to the behaviors and attitudes described in this chapter. After all class members have completed their descriptions, assemble into groups of "bad bosses" or "good bosses." Working in groups, search for patterns of behaviors, skills, and attitudes characteristic of very good or very bad leaders. To help prepare your descriptions, use the checklist presented in the "Guidelines for Action and Skill Development."

Leadership Styles

After studying this chapter, you should be able to

1. describe the leadership styles included in the leadership continuum and the Leadership Grid®.
2. differentiate between the team and solo styles of leadership.
3. present the case for the entrepreneurial style of leadership.
4. present the case for gender differences in leadership style.
5. determine how to choose the most appropriate leadership style.

Paul Enright is the founding partner of the small, successful accounting firm Enright, Goldstein, and Pasquale. Asked by a business student why his firm is so successful, Enright replied with a smile, "Our patron saint is the Internal Revenue Service. Because they keep changing tax laws so regularly, business firms need our help to stay in compliance. Beyond the IRS and plain luck, I think our leadership philosophy helps. The two other partners and I believe that every employee in this firm is an intelligent, good-spirited adult. We believe strongly in participative leadership. We involve several people in every significant decision we make. Let me give you an example. The satellite office we put in the inner city was the brainchild of our two newest CPAs."

The comments by Paul Enright illustrate the widespread acceptance of thinking about leadershp in terms of style. Phrases such as "he's a real autocrat" and "she's a consensus manager" have become commonplace. Most

99

experienced workers are thus familiar with the concept of **leadership style,** the relatively consistent pattern of behavior that characterizes a leader. The study of leadership style is an extension of an understanding of leadership behaviors and attitudes. As described in Chapter 4, most classifications of leadership style are based on the dimensions of initiating structure and consideration.

This chapter describes two well-known classifications of leadership style, the leadership continuum and the Leadership Grid. It then examines other style-related issues such as team leadership, the entrepreneurial leadership style, sex differences in leadership style, and choosing the best style. Chapter 6 continues the exploration of leadership style by presenting several leadership theories that sharply focus on contingency factors. Two chapters about leadership style are presented to enhance leadership effectiveness through the understanding of one's style and adapting it to circumstances.

THE LEADERSHIP CONTINUUM: CLASSICAL LEADERSHIP STYLES

The original concept of leadership style traces back to research conducted with Boy Scout leaders. In 1938, Lewin and Lippitt suggested that leadership behavior could be classified in terms of how much involvement leaders have with people-related versus work-related issues.[1] Research into initiating structure and consideration, and work-centered versus employee-centered leadership extended these ideas. Here we examine two related explanations of the leadership continuum: the boss-centered versus employee-centered continuum, and the autocratic–participative–free-rein continuum.

The Boss-Centered Versus Employee-Centered Leadership Continuum

Robert Tannenbaum and Warren H. Schmidt advised managers how to choose a leadership pattern from among a range of leadership behaviors.[2] Choosing from among these behaviors characterizes different leadership styles. As shown in Figure 5–1, the selection is made along a continuum of boss-centered versus employee-centered leadership. To select the most appropriate style, the leader takes into account certain forces in the manager, subordinates, and the situation, as well as time constraints.

Forces in the Manager.   Managers who believe strongly that team members should have a say in decision making will move toward the right side of the continuum. Managers who have confidence in the capabilities of team members will grant them more freedom. A leader's natural inclinations are also important. Some people are directive by nature, whereas others feel comfortable sharing decision making. Emotionally secure leaders are more comfortable releasing decision making to team members.

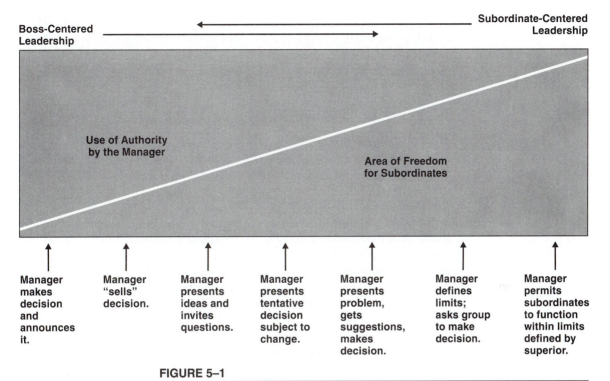

**Boss-Centered
Leadership**

**Subordinate-Centered
Leadership**

Use of Authority
by the Manager

Area of Freedom
for Subordinates

Manager
makes
decision
and
announces
it.

Manager
"sells"
decision.

Manager
presents
ideas and
invites
questions.

Manager
presents
tentative
decision
subject to
change.

Manager
presents
problem,
gets
suggestions,
makes
decision.

Manager
defines
limits;
asks group
to make
decision.

Manager
permits
subordinates
to function
within limits
defined by
superior.

FIGURE 5–1

Continuum of Leadership Behavior

Source: Reprinted by permission of *Harvard Business Review.* An exhibit from "How to Choose a Leadership Pattern" by Robert Tannenbaum and Warren H. Schmidt, May/June 1973. Copyright © 1973 by the President and Fellows of Harvard College; all rights reserved.

Forces in the Subordinate.   Each team member, similar to the leader, is influenced by many personality variables. Generally speaking, team members can be granted more decision-making latitude if they are independent, can tolerate ambiguity, are competent, and identify with organizational goals. Team members who expect to share in decision making can be more readily granted authority.

Forces in the Situation.   The values and traditions of the organization in regard to shared decision making influences how much authority can be granted to team members. Effective work groups can handle more freedom. At times the team has the requisite knowledge to handle the problem; at other times only the manager has enough competence to solve the problem. For example, the manager might have a network contact that enables him or her to get a budget issue resolved.

The Pressure of Time.   The more the manager feels the need for an immediate decision, the more difficult it is to involve others in decision making. Employee-centered leadership is time consuming despite its merits.

Tannenbaum and Schmidt's leadership continuum summarizes a wealth of knowledge about participative decision making. Other leadership theories, such as the Vroom–Yetton–Jago model described in Chapter 6, incorporate many of its basic ideas.

The Autocratic–Participative–Free-Rein Continuum

The Schmitt and Tannenbaum model gradually evolved into a leadership continuum with more specific anchor points on the continuum. Three key points on the continuum represent autocratic, participative, and free-rein styles of leadership, as shown in Figure 5–2.

Autocratic Leadership Style.   **Autocratic leaders** retain most of the authority for themselves. They make decisions confidently and assume that group members will comply; they usually are not concerned with group members' attitudes toward the decision. Autocratic leaders are considered task-oriented because they place heavy emphasis on getting tasks accomplished. Typical autocratic behaviors include telling people what to do, asserting themselves, and serving as a model for team members.

Robert Crandall, the CEO of American Airlines, represents a positive example of an autocratic leader. Nicknamed "Fang" or "Darth Vader" by some, Crandall is considered the industry's fiercest competitor. He is also known as a tough and demanding boss. Every Monday morning he grills his staff on details such as on-time records and baggage deliveries. His oft-repeated question is "Are we doing better than competitors?" Staff members fear meeting with Crandall if they have not done their homework for these meetings.[3]

Participative Leadership Style.   **Participative leaders** share decision making with group members. Participative leadership encompasses so many behaviors that it can be divided into three subtypes: consultative, consensus, and democratic. **Consultative leaders** confer with group members before making a decision. However, they retain the final authority to make

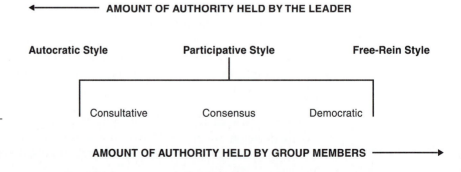

FIGURE 5–2

**The Authoritarian–
Participative–
Free-Rein Continuum**

decisions. **Consensus leaders** are called that because they strive for consensus: they encourage group discussion about an issue and then make a decision that reflects general agreement and will be supported by group members. All workers who will be involved in the consequences of a decision have an opportunity to provide input. A decision is not considered final until all parties involved agree with the decision. **Democratic leaders** confer final authority on the group. They function as collectors of group opinion and take a vote before making a decision.

The participative style encompasses the teamwork approach. Predominant behaviors of the participative leader include coaching team members, negotiating their demands, and collaborating with others. The accompanying Leader in Action vignette provides insight into a successful executive's perception of the importance of participative management.

LEADER
IN
ACTION

Donald E. Petersen of Ford Motor Co.

Highly regarded Donald E. Petersen was president of Ford Motor Co. from 1980 to 1985, and chairman of the board and CEO from 1985 to 1990. His pathfinding participatory leadership style contributed to the biggest comeback recorded in the U.S. auto industry.

Petersen found the greatest resistance to participative management among lower ranking managers who were not fully qualified to become high-level managers. According to Petersen, these people often have self-doubt and low confidence because they see themselves not continuing to grow. He also noticed that people who do not contribute their share in a participative environment are soon rejected by the team.

To get a company started on participative management, Petersen recommends a small pilot group. At a Ford parts depot in Richmond, California, the hourly employees suggested that the managers stay home for a week so they could run the unit. The depot set many records that week for accuracy and timeliness in filling orders. It's also important for the CEO to make on-site visits.

Petersen believes that the teamwork required of participatory leadership still allows room for individual freedom. For example, a person with outstanding leadership characteristics can still rely heavily on input from the group.

The participative leadership style is well suited to managing competent people who are eager to assume responsibility. Such people want to get involved in making decisions and giving feedback to management. The majority of graduates from business and professional programs expect to be involved in decision making. Participative leadership works well with the new breed of managers and professionals. Formal participation programs, such as one at Procter & Gamble, have increased productivity as much as 40 percent.[4] Finally, participative leadership is an important component of empowerment and work teams. As a consequence, participative leadership fits the modern thrust in managing people.

Participative leadership does have some problems. It often results in extensive and time-consuming committee work. Sometimes participative management is carried to extremes. Team members are consulted about trivial things that management could easily handle independently. Another problem is that many managers still believe that sharing decision making with team members reduces their power.[5]

Maryellen Kelly and Bennett Harrison conducted a study of how well the employee involvement form of participative management worked in more than 1,000 factories. They discovered that involvement programs often failed in large, bureaucratic firms, because these programs were unable to intervene in rule making and decision making at many levels.[6] Such evidence, however, does not negate the importance of participative management in most work settings.

Free-Rein Leadership Style.   **Free-rein leaders** turn over virtually all authority and control to the group. (A synonym for free rein is *laissez-faire*, a French term meaning "leave to do.") Leadership is provided to the group indirectly rather than directly. Group members are presented a task to perform and are given free rein to figure out how to perform it best. The leader does not get involved unless requested. Team members are allowed all the freedom they want as long as they do not violate policy. In short, the free-rein leader delegates completely.

The free-rein leadership style sometimes works effectively with well-motivated and experienced employees. These people are self-sufficient and may not need help or emotional support from the manager. A problem with free-rein leadership, however, is that group members perceive the free-rein leader as uninvolved and indifferent. Yet free-rein leaders believe they are helping subordinates develop self-sufficiency.

Part of your skill development as a leader is to attain insight into your own leadership style or potential style. To this end, do Leadership Self-Assessment Exercise 5–1.

The leadership continuum and the other approaches to describing leadership styles presented in this and the next chapter provide useful suggestions for being an effective leader. Most approaches to classifying leadership styles, however, overlook a major aspect of leadership: inspiring people, being innovative, and initiating positive change.

LEADERSHIP _____
SELF-ASSESSMENT
EXERCISE 5–1   What Type of Leader Are You or Would You Be?

Directions: Answer the following questions, keeping in mind what you have done, or think you would do, in the situations described.

	Mostly Yes	Mostly No
1. Do you enjoy the authority leadership brings?	____	____
2. Do you think it is worth the time and effort for a manager to explain the reasons for a decision or policy before putting the policy into effect?	____	____
3. Do you tend to prefer the planning functions of leadership, as opposed to working directly with team members?	____	____
4. A stranger comes into your work area, and you know the person is a new employee. Would you first ask, "What is your name?" rather than introduce yourself?	____	____
5. Do you keep team members up to date on developments affecting the work group?	____	____
6. Do you find that in giving out assignments, you tend to state the goals, and leave the methods up to your team members?	____	____
7. Do you think leaders should keep aloof from team members, because in the long run familiarity breeds lessened respect?	____	____
8. It comes time to decide about a company event. You have heard that the majority prefer to have it on Wednesday, but you are pretty sure Thursday would be better for all concerned. Would you put the question to a vote rather than make the decision yourself?	____	____
9. If you had your way, would you make communications an employee-initiated affair, with personal consultation held only on request?	____	____
10. Do you find it fairly easy to give negative performance evaluations to group members?	____	____

11. Do you feel that you should be friendly with the members of your work group? _____ _____

12. After considerable time, you determine the answer to a tough problem. You pass along the solution to your team members, who find many errors. Would you be annoyed that the problem is still unsolved, rather than become upset with the employees? _____ _____

13. Do you agree that one of the best ways to avoid discipline problems is to provide adequate punishment for rule violations? _____ _____

14. Your employees are criticizing the way you handled a situation. Would you sell your viewpoint, rather than make it clear that as the manager, your decisions are final? _____ _____

15. Do you generally leave it up to the team members to contact you as far as informal, day-to-day communications are concerned? _____ _____

16. Do you feel that everyone in your work group should have a certain amount of personal loyalty to you? _____ _____

17. Do you favor the practice of using task force teams and committees rather than making decisions alone? _____ _____

18. Do you agree that differences of opinion within work groups are healthy? _____ _____

Scoring and skill development: On the scoring matrix below, place a check mark next to each question you answered Mostly Yes.

1. ___	2. ___	3. ___
4. ___	5. ___	6. ___
7. ___	8. ___	9. ___
10. ___	11. ___	12. ___
13. ___	14. ___	15. ___
16. ___	17. ___	18. ___
Authoritarian total ___	Participative total ___	Free-rein total ___

You favor one of the three styles if your total for that style is three or more points higher than your total for either of other styles. The quiz you just completed is also an opportunity for skill development. Review the eighteen questions and look for implied suggestions for engaging in leadership and management practices. For example, question 17 might prompt you to make better use of task forces and committees.

Source: Adapted and updated from George Manning and Kent Curtis, *Leadership: Nine Keys to Success* (Cincinnati: South-Western, 1988), pp. 51–53; Naomi Miller, Northern Kentucky University, 1981; Auren Uris, *Techniques of Leadership* (New York: McGraw-Hill, 1953), pp. 49–52; 78–89.

THE LEADERSHIP GRID® STYLES

A popular method of classifying leadership styles suggests that the best way to achieve effective leadership is to integrate the task- and relationship-orientations. The **Leadership Grid**® (formerly known as the Managerial Grid) is a framework for simultaneously specifying the concern for production and people dimensions of leadership. The grid is also a comprehensive system of leadership training and organization development. Grid leadership styles are based on the extent of a person's concern for production and people (see Figure 5–3).[7]

Concern for production, rated on the horizontal axis, includes such matters as results (including high quality), the bottom line, performance, profits, and mission. Concern for people, rated on the vertical axis, is reflected in such matters as showing support for team members, getting results based on trust and respect, and worrying about employees' job security. Each concern is rated on a 1–9 scale.

Key Grid Positions

The benchmark styles on the Leadership Grid are described here and also defined in Figure 5–3.

> *Authority-Compliance (9,1).* The authority-compliance style, in the lower right corner, is characterized by a maximum concern for production combined with a minimum concern for people. A leader with this orientation concentrates on maximizing production by exercising power and authority, and dictating to people.
>
> *Country Club Management (1,9).* The "country club" style, in the top left corner, shows a minimum concern for production and a maximum concern for people. Primary attention is placed on good feelings among team members and coworkers, even at the expense of achieving results.
>
> *Impoverished Management (1,1).* The lower left position is impoverished management: a minimum concern for both production and people.

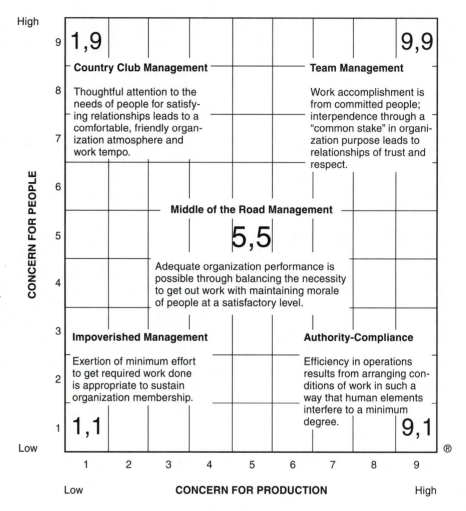

FIGURE 5–3

**The Leadership Grid®
Leadership Styles**

Source: The Leadership
Grid® Figure for *Leader-
ship Dilemmas—Grid
Solutions,* by Robert R.
Blake and Anne Adams
McCanse. (Formerly the
Managerial Grid figure by
Robert R. Blake and Jane
S. Mouton) Houston: Gulf
Publishing Co., p. 29.
Copyright © 1991, by
Scientific Methods, Inc.
Reproduced by permis-
sion of the owners.

Such a leader does only the minimum required to remain a member of
the firm. (According to the current definition of leadership, this type of
manager does not qualify as a leader.)

Middle-of-the-Road Management (5,5). In the center is the 5,5 orientation.
Leaders with this middle-of-the-road style do their job but avoid making waves and conform to the status quo.

Team Management (9,9). In the upper right corner is the 9,9 orientation,
team management, which integrates concern for production and people.
It is a goal-directed team approach that seeks to gain optimum results
through participation, involvement, and commitment.

Managers generally have one dominant leadership style as well as a
back-up style. Leaders tend to use the backup style when the dominant style
does not achieve the desired results. For instance, you might use the 9,9

approach only to find that most team members are unenthusiastic about implementing a total quality program. It might then be necessary to shift to a 9,1 approach.

Which Style Is Best?

The creators of the Grid argue strongly for the value of team management (9,9). They present evidence that the team management orientation usually results in improved performance, low absenteeism and turnover, and high employee satisfaction. In one study, two matched subsidiaries of the same parent company were compared on performance. Measures were taken of profitability before and after a ten-year period. One subsidiary engaged in an extensive Grid program emphasizing team management. The experimental subsidiary increased its profitability four times more than did the comparison subsidiary.[8]

A synthesis of a number of studies indicates that effective leaders score highly on both concern for people and production. The researchers who analyzed the studies caution, however, that each leadership situation should be investigated before prescribing the best leadership style.[9] Similarly, the Leadership Grid does not dictate that the manager mechanically use one style in trying to lead very different groups. Instead, he or she should use principles of human behavior to size up the situation. Many researchers criticize the Leadership Grid for dictating one best style, yet the team style includes adapting to the situation.

TEAM LEADERSHIP VERSUS SOLO LEADERSHIP

Many other writers have touted the team style of leadership. Meredith Belbin, for one, contrasts the team and solo leader (see Figure 5–4).[10] Team leaders share power and deemphasize individual glory. They are flexible and adaptable, thus welcoming change. Team leaders function as facilitators who bring out the best in others while still being inspirational. The team-style leader, in general, conforms closely to the consensus and 9,9 styles. The team style of leadership is required under a system of Total Quality Management because TQM requires input from team members about improvements.

The solo style of leader is the traditional leader in a bureaucracy. Basically an autocrat, the solo leader receives much of the credit for the success of his or her firm. Some of this credit is frequently undeserved. The solo leader may not recognize how dependent he or she is on the team. An example is Donald Trump, who readily fits the solo style of leader. At one point Trump had to sell many valuable properties when his empire was faltering. Some of his troubles stemmed from the loss of key people who had died in a helicopter crash. Trump admitted that without input from one of them, his chief financial officer, he made some poor financial decisions.

SOLO LEADER	TEAM LEADER
1. Plays unlimited role (interferes)	1. Chooses to limit role (delegates)
2. Strives for conformity	2. Builds on diversity
3. Collects acolytes	3. Seeks talent
4. Directs subordinates	4. Develops colleagues
5. Projects objectives	5. Creates mission

FIGURE 5–4

The Solo Leader and the Team Leader

Source: From Meredith Belbin, "Solo Leader/Team Leader: Antithesis in Style and Structure," in Michel Syrett and Clare Hogg, *Frontiers of Leadership*, p. 271. Copyright © 1992. Used by permission of Blackwell Publishers, Oxford, England.

THE ENTREPRENEURIAL LEADERSHIP STYLE

Many entrepreneurs and intrapreneurs use a similar leadership style that stems from their key personality characteristics and circumstances. (An *intrapreneur* is a corporate employee who takes on an entrepreneurial project for the firm, such as a business startup.) A general picture emerges of a task-oriented and charismatic leader. Entrepreneurs drive themselves and others relentlessly, yet their personalities inspire others.

Entrepreneurs and intrapreneurs often use a leadership style that incorporates certain behaviors described in the following paragraphs.[11] Recognize, however, that authorities disagree about whether an entrepreneurial personality exists. For example, Howard H. Stevenson of Harvard Business School says, "You can't build a single psychological profile of the entrepreneur because there are too many examples that break the rules." Instead, Stevenson regards entrepreneurship as a behavior focusing on the pursuit of opportunity without regard to the resources currently under control.[12]

1. *Strong achievement motive.* Entrepreneurs have stronger achievement motives than do most managers (see Chapter 2). Building a business is an excellent vehicle for accomplishment.

2. *High degree of enthusiasm and creativity.* Related to the achievement need are enthusiasm and creativity. Entrepreneurs' enthusiasm, in turn, makes them persuasive. As a result, they are often perceived as charismatic. Some entrepreneurs are often so emotional that they are regarded as eccentric.

3. *Tendency to act quickly when opportunity arises.* Entrepreneurs are noted for seizing upon opportunity. When a deal is on the horizon, they push themselves and those around them extra hard. As the founder of an information systems firm told his staff after receiving an important inquiry, "Cancel all your weekend plans. We work until this proposal is completed to my satisfaction and that of our prospect."

4. *Constant hurry.* Entrepreneurs and intrapreneurs are always in a hurry. When engaged in one meeting, their minds typically begin to focus on the next meeting. Their flurry of activity rubs off on group members and those

around them. Entrepreneurs often adopt a simple dress style in order to save time, and they typically allow very little slack time between appointments.

5. *Visionary perspective.* Entrepreneurs and intrapreneurs, at their best, are visionaries. They see opportunities others fail to observe. Specifically, they have the ability to identify a problem and arrive at a solution. The Leader in Action vignette on Walter Riley illustrates this characteristic.

6. *Dislike of hierarchy and bureaucracy.* Entrepreneurs are not ideally suited by temperament to working within the mainstream of a bureaucracy. Many successful entrepreneurs are people who were frustrated by the constraints of a bureaucratic system. Intrapreneurs, by definition, fit reasonably well

LEADER IN ACTION

Walter Riley of G.O.D.

[First appeared in *Success* January 1992. Written by Michael Maren and Don Wallace. Reprinted with permission of *Success* magazine. Copyright © 1992 by Hal Holdings Corporation.]

On April 6, 1983, a law went into effect legalizing the use of double trailers on interstate highways. Walter Riley, the young entrepreneur behind G.O.D. (Guaranteed Overnight Delivery) seized the moment. He had calculated his efficiencies to the last cent. Tandem trailers enable him to run the company with half the drivers, half the cabs, and half the miles. The system Riley chose for his business was the highly efficient Federal Express hub-and-spoke network. He went to FedEx headquarters in Memphis, watched its operation, took notes, and applied the system wholesale to trucks instead of airplanes. "It was such a brilliant system. I'd have been crazy not to use it," Riley says. The result was the first overnight freight service in the United States.

Riley attributes much of G.O.D.'s success to the high-quality process he developed. The company has only one loading dock, one modest office, and no need for warehouse space. Instead, Riley rents some secure spaces to park his trucks at critical points across the northeast United States. During the day his drivers take freight to these central points. The trailers are then linked together and driven to the Kearney, N.J., headquarters by the evening shift of the long-haul drivers.

Instead of using full-size offices, G.O.D. rents a couple of square feet of space of a gas station or a convenience store and sets up a fax machine. The bills of lading are faxed back to headquarters, and the information is entered into the computer. Trucks are then routed via computer.

Riley believes he had the vision to overcome the conventional wisdom that nobody can guarantee overnight delivery for commercial freight and expect to make a profit.

into a bureaucracy, yet they do not like to be restrained by tight regulations. The implication for leadership style is that entrepreneurs and intrapreneurs deemphasize rules and regulations when managing people.

7. *Preference for dealing with external customers.* One of the reasons why entrepreneurs and intrapreneurs have difficulty with bureaucracy is that they focus their energies on products, services, and customers, rather than on employees. Some entrepreneurs are gracious to customers and money lenders but brusque with company insiders.

GENDER DIFFERENCES IN LEADERSHIP STYLE

Controversy continues as to whether men and women have different leadership styles. Several researchers and observers argue that women have certain acquired traits and behaviors that suit them for relations-oriented leadership. Consequently, women leaders frequently exhibit a cooperative, empowering style that includes nurturing team members. According to this same perspective, men are inclined toward a command-and-control, militaristic leadership style. Women find participative management more natural than do men because they feel more comfortable interacting with people. Furthermore, it is argued that women's natural sensitivity to people gives them an edge over men in encouraging group members to participate in decision making.

Let us look briefly at some of the evidence and reasoning that gender differences do and do not exist between the leadership styles of today's organizational leaders. We emphasize the present because many more women hold formal leadership positions today than in previous decades. Also, sex roles are less rigid today.

A significant side issue here is that the terms *sex* and *gender* arouse controversy for both scientific and political reasons. As the term is used by many researchers, *gender* refers to perceptions about the differences among males and females.[13] An example would be believing that women managers tend to be better listeners than their male peers. Sex differences, however, refer to actual (objective and quantitative) differences such as the fact that the mean height of men exceeds that of women. Despite these observations, the terms *gender* and *sex* are still used interchangeably in general usage and to some extent in scholarly writings. In this era of celebrating diversity, we hope no reader will be offended by either term.

The Argument for Male-Female Differences in Leadership Style

In an article that stimulated considerable debate, Judy Rosener concluded that men and women do tend toward opposite styles. Based on self-reports, she found that men tended toward a command-and-control style. In contrast, women tended toward a transformational style, relying heavily on interpersonal skills.[14] Reporting from Britain, Cary Cooper contends that men tend to manage by punishment and women by rewards. He observes that women are socialized to manage people and relationships in the home, and have taken their skills from the home and transformed them to the workplace. Relying more on data, Cooper reports:

> Our studies have shown that women tend to be more participatory in their management style and they are seen by both male and female subordinates to be much more caring than male counterparts. In practical terms, this means that men's style of management contributes to stress, by putting much pressure on people and stopping them from producing their best.[15]

Based on some of his more recent research, Bass has found some specific male-female differences in leadership style. Data collected from subordinates suggest that women are less likely to practice management-by-exception (intervening only when something goes wrong). Yet women and men appear to use contingent recognition with equal frequency. Even when the women leaders studied do practice management-by-exception, they typically temper criticism with positive feedback. Bass also found that women leaders are slightly more likely to be described as charismatic. In a survey of sixty-nine world-class leaders (nine women included), women scored higher on the transformation factor than did men.[16] The Leader in Action vignette on page 114 describes a leader who is charismatic and task-oriented.

The Argument Against Gender Differences in Leadership Style

Based on a literature review, Jan Grant concluded that there are apparently few, if any, personality or behavioral differences between men and women managers. Yet as women move up the corporate ladder, their identification with the male model of managerial success becomes important; they consequently reject even the few managerial feminine traits they may have earlier endorsed.[17] Studies reviewed by Bass (other than his own research) indicate no consistent pattern of male-female differences in leadership style.[18]

Whether male and female differences in leadership style do exist, they must be placed in proper perspective. Both men and women leaders differ among themselves in leadership style. Plenty of male leaders are relations-oriented, and plenty of women practice command and control (the extreme task orientation).

SELECTING THE BEST LEADERSHIP STYLE

An underlying theme of this and the following chapter is that there is no one best or most effective style of leadership. As explained in the Tannenbaum and Schmidt leadership continuum, the leader examines certain forces to determine which style best fits the situation. Although the Leadership Grid has been accused of touting one style, the one style espoused includes

LEADER IN ACTION

Donna Karan of Donna Inc.

Donna Karan, CEO of an apparel conglomerate, stalks the model's runway where she is presenting her spring collection to fashion buyers. As the models prepare to move down the runway, Karan stays on top of every detail. She is in constant motion behind the curtain, tucking, smoothing, and adjusting angles unnoticeable to others. She has been described by a fashion reporter as "a combination of Auntie Mame, Everywoman and personal shopper extraordinaire—a woman who *knows* her merchandise" (Agins, p. 66).

Karan's devotion to detail and her insatiable drive has made her a powerful executive in the fashion business. She is the only well-known woman in the male-dominated group of U.S. clothing designers. Karan has shaped a sexy yet comfortable, distinctive style. She has also built a full-line apparel conglomerate. Her sales forecast for 1995 is $500 million. Her business units include top-of-the-line fashion for both men and women, sportswear, and children's clothing.

Karan attracts talented people who become fiercely loyal to her and who are willing to put up with her incessant demands. Karan has unusually devoted employees. Two of her key executives have been with her since her days at Anne Klein. Her executive assistant says, "Donna draws you in. She's this irresistible force" (*Time*, p. 57). Most of the staff has become somewhat of a Donna Karan cult. A vice president for design says, "There's no question that everyone loves what she does and wants to dress like her and be like her" (*Time*, p. 57).

Source: Based on facts in "Donna Inc.," *Time,* December 21, 1992, pp. 54–57; Teri Agins, "Woman on the Verge," *Working Woman,* May 1993, p. 66; Bill Saporito, "Unsuit Yourself: Management Goes Informal," *Fortune,* September 20, 1993, pp. 118–119.

adaptability to the situation. Paul Hersey and Kenneth H. Blanchard explain that there is no one best way to lead because leadership is situational.[19] Over twenty years ago Ralph Stogdill made a statement about selecting a leadership style that holds today:

> The most effective leaders appear to exhibit a degree of versatility and flexibility that enables them to adapt their behavior to the changing and contradictory demands made on them.[20]

More recently, Thomas R. Horton has observed that CEOs practice many different styles to achieve their objectives. Among these styles are public person or private, loose cannons or reflective thinkers, and autocrats or participative leaders.[21]

Table 5–1 presents useful information for choosing between an autocratic and participative leadership style, depending on needs of the group members and other forces in the situation.

Leadership Self-Assessment Exercise 5–2 provides an opportunity to think about your own willingness to adapt to circumstances as a leader. By developing such flexibility, you increase the chances of becoming an effective leader—one who achieves high productivity, quality, and satisfaction.

TABLE 5–1   Choosing a Leadership Style to Fit the Situation

Consider Being Autocratic Under These Conditions:

Leader/manager	Has high power and limited restraints on its use
	Has a way of saving matters in an emergency
	Has some unique knowledge
	Is firmly entrenched in her or his position
Group members	Are leader-dependent
	Are rarely asked for an opinion
	Are readily replaced by other workers
	Recognize emergencies
	Are autocrats themselves
	Have low need for independence
Work situation	Features tight discipline
	Is characterized by strong controls
	Is marked by low profit margins or tight cost controls
	Includes physical dangers
	Requires low skills from workers
	Requires that changes be made frequently and quickly

Consider Being Participative Under These Conditions:

Leader/manager	Has limited power and authority, and restraints on its use
	Risks rejection of his or her authority
	Has few existing time pressures
	Has limited sanctions that he or she can exert
Group members	Expect to have some control over methods used
	Have predominantly middle-class values
	Possess relatively scarce skills
	Like system, but not authority
Work situation	Is characterized by overall organizational objectives
	Involves shared responsibility for controls
	Has some time pressures
	Consists of gradual changes or regularly spaced changes
	Involves actual or potential hazards occasionally
	Values teamwork skills

Source: Reprinted, by permission of publisher, from *Personnel,* July/Aug. 1981 © 1981, American Management Association, New York. All rights reserved.

LEADERSHIP SELF-ASSESSMENT EXERCISE 5–2   How Flexible Are You?

To succeed as a managerial leader, a person needs a flexible style: an ability to be open to others and a willingness to listen. Where do you stand on being flexible? Test yourself by answering often, sometimes, or rarely to the following questions.

____ 1. Do you tend to seek out only those people who agree with your analysis of issues?

____ 2. Do you ignore most of the advice from coworkers about process improvements?

____ 3. Do your team members go along with what you say just to avoid an argument?

____ 4. Have people referred to you as "rigid" or "close-minded" on several occasions?

____ 5. When presented with a new method, do you immediately look for a flaw?

____ 6. Do you make up your mind early on with respect to an issue, and then hold firmly to your opinion?

____ 7. When people disagree with you, do you tend to belittle them or become argumentative?

____ 8. Do you often feel you are the only person in the group who really understands the problem?

Check Your Score: If you answered "rarely" to seven to eight questions, you are unusually adaptable. If you answered "sometimes" to at least five questions, you are on the right track, but more flexibility would benefit your leadership. If you answered "often" to more than four questions, you have a long way to go to improve your flexibility and adaptability. You are also brutally honest about your faults, which could be an asset.

SUMMARY

Leadership style is the relatively consistent pattern of behavior that characterizes a leader. The concept of leadership style is an extension of understanding leadership behaviors. One of the earliest classifications of leadership style places the style on a boss-centered through employee-centered continuum. The leader selects a style by taking into account forces in the manager, subordinates, and situation, and also time pressures. For example, a more employee-centered style is appropriate if team members are independent, can tolerate ambiguity, and are competent.

A related leadership continuum has three key anchor points: autocratic, participative, and free rein. Autocratic leaders retain most of the authority for themselves. Participative leaders share decision making with group members. The participative style can be subdivided into consultative, consensus, and democratic leadership. The participative style is well suited to managing competent people, eager to assume responsibility. Yet the process can be time consuming, and some managers perceive it to be a threat to their power. The free-rein leader turns over virtually all authority and control to the group.

The Leadership Grid styles classify leaders according to how much concern they have for both production (task accomplishment) and people. Team management, with its high concern for production and people, is considered the best. Another conception of the team leader contrasts him or her to the solo leader. Team leaders share power and deemphasize individual glory. The solo style of leader is the traditional, autocratic leader in a bureaucracy.

Another important style of leader is the entrepreneur or intrapreneur. The entrepreneurial style stems from the leader's personal characteristics and the circumstances of self-employment. The entrepreneurial/intrapreneurial style includes these elements: strong achievement motive, high degree of enthusiasm and creativity, rapid response to opportunity, hurriedness, visionary perspective, dislike of hierarchy and bureaucracy, and preference for dealing with external customers.

Male-female differences in leadership style have been observed. Women have a tendency toward relationship-oriented leadership, whereas men tend toward command-and-control. Some people argue, however, that male-female differences in leadership are inconsistent and not significant.

Rather than searching for the one best style of leadership, managers are advised to diagnose the situation and then choose an appropriate leadership style to match. To be effective, a leader must be able to adapt his or her style to the circumstances.

KEY TERMS

Leadership style	Consensus leaders
Autocratic leaders	Democratic leaders
Participative leaders	Free-rein leaders
Consultative leaders	Leadership Grid®

GUIDELINES FOR ACTION AND SKILL DEVELOPMENT

Most leadership style classifications are based on the directive (task-oriented) dimension versus the nondirective (relationship-oriented) dimension. In deciding which of these two styles is best, consider the following questions:

1. *What is the structure of your organization and the nature of your work?* You might decide, for example, that stricter control is necessary for some types of work, such as dealing with proprietary information.

2. *Which style suits you best?* Your personality, values, and beliefs influence how readily you can turn over responsibility to others.

3. *Which style suits your boss and organization?* For example, a boss who is highly directive may perceive you as weak if you are too nondirective.

4. *How readily will you be able to change your style if good results are not forthcoming?* Morale can suffer if you grant too much latitude today and have to tighten control in the future.

5. *Is there high potential for conflict in the work unit?* A directive leadership style can trigger conflict with independent, strong-willed people. A more nondirective style allows for more freedom of discussion, which defuses conflict.[22]

DISCUSSION QUESTIONS AND ACTIVITIES

1. How would you characterize the leadership style of your favorite athletic coach or professor? Document your answer.

2. The idea of a leadership continuum originated almost sixty years ago. Why has this basic idea lasted so long?

3. The Japanese human resources management style heavily emphasizes work group harmony. How would you characterize the leadership style of a typical Japanese organizational leader? Use the task and people dimensions in your answer.

4. Have you ever worked with people who would respond poorly to participative leadership? Describe the situation.

5. Describe an example of a the 9,9 style of leader from personal experience or from your reading.

6. What would be some of the dysfunctional consequences to the organization if the vast majority of the managers were 5,5 leaders?

7. Find an article on Microsoft's Bill Gates or another business founder. Report to your class how well that person fits the entrepreneurial leadership style.

8. Cynthia Fuchs Epstein made the following comment in response to the controversy over male-female differences in leadership style: "It is time to reconsider the excessive and inappropriate sex typing that takes place, whether offered in the service of improving women's situations or restricting them."[23] Where do you stand on this issue?

9. What is your reaction to Cary Cooper's contention that the male leadership style is responsible for so much work stress?

10. How might being a free-rein leader damage your career?

LEADERSHIP CASE PROBLEM

Is This Any Way to Treat Accountants?

Jon Madonna is CEO of Peat Marwick, one of the "Big Six" accounting firms. In recent years accounting firms have experienced a shrinking client base. Madonna believes that accounting firms should take a fresh look at how they operate because they have become too undisciplined and overstaffed.

Madonna was formerly in charge of the San Francisco office of Peat Marwick. After four month as CEO, he reduced the firm's partner roster by 15 percent, cutting both senior and junior personnel. Madonna uses the term "or else" in influencing others. Auditors who are generalists are required to develop expertise in certain industries or else be fired. The CEO is integrating staff professionals in industry-specific teams. An industry such as steel would therefore be served by auditors, tax specialists, and business consultants, all with steel business expertise.

Under Madonna a layer of managers responsible for supervising regional offices was forced into the field. The head of the firm's consulting practice was demoted. Some partners are concerned that Madonna is too impetuous. Many experienced staff members fear doing something wrong. When partners want to study a Madonna proposal carefully, he accuses them of suffering from a study-it-to-death syndrome.

Madonna sees himself in the role of a coach who makes a difference in whether a team wins. The CEO of a rival accounting firm says that Madonna's partner cuts were a major public relations blunder. Yet profits are beginning to climb despite flat yearly revenues of about $1.8 billion. And the editor of an accounting magazine said, "Under Madonna, Marwick is operating more like a business and not some professional club."

Tax accountant John Zobkiw offers this analysis of Madonna's way of running Peat Marwick: "Madonna is trying to make the firm cope with a changed world. It's very competitive today. The big firms are going after the business of little firms."

1. How would you characterize Madonna's leadership style?

2. How effective do you think his managerial and leadership approach will be in the long run?

3. Is Madonna a transformational leader?

4. What advice can you offer Madonna to enhance his leadership effectiveness?

Source: As reported in Ron Stodghill II, "Who Says Accountants Can't Jump?" *Business Week,* October 26, 1992, pp. 98–100; personal communication with John Zobkiw, tax accountant, Rochester, New York, May 1994.

LEADERSHIP ROLE PLAY

Contrasting Leadership Styles

One student plays the role of a new associate working for a financial services firms that sells life insurance and other investments. The associate has completed a six-week training program and is now working full-time. Four weeks have passed and the associate still has not made a sale. The associate's boss is going to meet with him or her today to discuss progress. Another student plays the role of a task-oriented leader. The two people participate in the review session.

Before playing (or assuming) the role of the associate or the boss, think for a few minutes how you would behave if placed in that role in real life. Empathize with the frustrated associate or the task-oriented leader. A good role-player is both a script writer and an actor.

Another two students repeat the same scenario except that this time the manager is a strongly relationship-oriented leader. Two more pairs of students then have their turn at acting out the task-oriented and relationship-oriented performance reviews. Another variation of this role play is for one person to play the roles of both the task-oriented and relationship-oriented boss. Other class members observe and provide feedback on the effectiveness of the two styles of leadership.

Contingency and Situational Leadership

LEARNING OBJECTIVES

After studying this chapter, you should be able to

1. present an overview of the contingency theory of leadership effectiveness.
2. explain the path-goal theory of leadership effectiveness.
3. explain the situational leadership theory.
4. use the Vroom–Yetton–Jago model to determine the most appropriate decision-making style in a given situation.

*D*onald R. Rumsfeld, CEO of the giant pharmaceutical firm G. D. Searle & Company, was asked his advice about leadership effectiveness. He replied, "There's a certain balance to maintain. The length of the leash varies with different people, depending on your knowledge of them, your own comfort in dealing with the subject matter they are dealing in, or your assessment of them. The leashes may vary with the same person with respect to different subjects."[1]

Rumsfeld's comments point to the core of contingency and situational leadership—specifying the factors that determine which style of leadership will achieve the best results in a given situation. Contingency and situational leadership builds further upon the study of leadership styles. It does so by adding more specific guidelines about which style to use under which circumstances. This chapter describes the four best known contingency theories of leadership: Fiedler's contingency theory, path-goal theory, the Hersey-Blanchard situational leadership theory, and the Vroom–Yetton–Jago decision-making model. Although the presentation of four theories about the same topic may appear baffling, you will notice that they share many elements.

FIEDLER'S CONTINGENCY THEORY OF LEADERSHIP EFFECTIVENESS

A **contingency theory of leadership** specifies the conditions under which a particular style of leadership will be effective. Fred E. Fiedler developed the most widely researched and quoted contingency model, which holds that the best style of leadership is determined by the situation in which the leader is working.[2] Here we examine how the style and situation are evaluated, and the overall findings of Fiedler's contingency theory.

Measuring Leadership Style: The Least Preferred Coworker (LPC) Scale

Fiedler's theory classifies a manager's leadership style as relationship-motivated or task-motivated. The intermediate style—which receives little mention—is labeled socioindependent. According to Fiedler, leadership style is a relatively permanent aspect of behavior and thus difficult to modify. He reasons that once leaders understand their particular leadership style, they should work in situations that match their style. Similarly, the organization should help managers match leadership styles and situations.

The least preferred coworker (LPC) scale measures the degree to which a leader describes favorably or unfavorably his or her least preferred coworker— that is, an employee with whom he or she could work the least well. A leader who describes the least preferred coworker in relatively favorable terms tends to be relationship-motivated. In contrast, a person who describes a coworker in an unfavorable manner tends to be task-motivated, or less concerned with human relations. In short, if you can tolerate your antagonists, you are relationship-motivated. You can use this scale to measure your leadership style by doing Leadership Self-Assessment Exercise 6–1.

LEADERSHIP SELF-ASSESSMENT EXERCISE 6–1   The Least Preferred Coworker (LPC) Scale for Measuring Leadership Style

Throughout your life you will have worked in many groups with a wide variety of different people—on your job, in social groups, in church organizations, in volunteer groups, on athletic teams, and in many other situations. Some of your coworkers may have been very easy to work with in attaining the group's goals, while others were less so.

Think of all the people with whom you have ever worked, and then think of the person with whom you could work *least well.* He or she may be someone with whom you work now or with whom you have worked in the past. This does not have to be the person you liked least well, but should be the person with whom you had the most difficulty getting a job done, the *one* individual with whom you could work *least well.*

Describe this person on the scale that follows by placing an "X" in the appropriate space. Look at the words at both ends of the line before you mark your "X." *There are no right or wrong answers.* Work rapidly: your first answer is likely to be the best. Do not omit any items, and mark each item only once.

Now describe the person with whom you can work least well.

Scoring

	8	7	6	5	4	3	2	1		
Pleasant									Unpleasant	____
Friendly	8	7	6	5	4	3	2	1	Unfriendly	____
Rejecting	1	2	3	4	5	6	7	8	Accepting	____
Tense	1	2	3	4	5	6	7	8	Relaxed	____
Distant	1	2	3	4	5	6	7	8	Close	____
Cold	1	2	3	4	5	6	7	8	Warm	____
Supportive	8	7	6	5	4	3	2	1	Hostile	____
Boring	1	2	3	4	5	6	7	8	Interesting	____
Quarrelsome	1	2	3	4	5	6	7	8	Harmonious	____
Gloomy	1	2	3	4	5	6	7	8	Cheerful	____
Open	8	7	6	5	4	3	2	1	Guarded	____
Backbiting	1	2	3	4	5	6	7	8	Loyal	____
Untrustworthy	1	2	3	4	5	6	7	8	Trustworthy	____
Considerate	8	7	6	5	4	3	2	1	Inconsiderate	____
Nasty	1	2	3	4	5	6	7	8	Nice	____
Agreeable	8	7	6	5	4	3	2	1	Disagreeable	____
Insincere	1	2	3	4	5	6	7	8	Sincere	____
Kind	8	7	6	5	4	3	2	1	Unkind	____
									Total	____

Scoring and Interpretation: To calculate your score, add the numbers in the right column; write the total at the bottom of the page. If you scored 64 or higher, you are a high LPC leader, meaning that you are relations-motivated. If you scored 57 or lower, you are a low LPC leader, meaning that you are task-motivated. A score of 58 to 63 places you in the inter-mediate range, making you a socioindependent leader. Compare your score to your score in Leadership Self-Assessment Exercise 5–1.

Source: Adapted from Fred E. Fiedler, Martin M. Chemers, and Linda Mahar, *Improving Leadership Effectiveness,* p. 7. Copyright © 1976. Reprinted by permission of John Wiley & Sons, Inc.

Measuring the Leadership Situation

The contingency theory classifies situations into three categories: high control, moderate control, and low control. (An earlier version of the model used the term *favorability* instead of *control*, because an easily controlled situation is favorable to the leader.) The control classifications are determined by rating the situation on its three dimensions, as follows:

1. *Leader-member relations* measure how well the group and the leader get along. (Sample question: "There seems to be a friendly atmosphere among the people I supervise.")

2. *Task structure* measures how clearly the procedures, goals, and evaluation of the job are defined. (Sample question: "Is there a book, manual, or job description that indicates the best solution or the best outcome for the task?")

3. *Position power* measures the leader's authority to hire, fire, discipline, and grant salary increases to group members. (Sample question: "Can the leader directly or by recommendation affect the promotion, demotion, hiring, or firing of subordinates?")

Leader-member relations contribute as much to situation favorability as do task structure and position power combined. The leader therefore has the most control in a situation in which his or her relationships with members are the best.

The Leader-Match Concept and Overall Findings

The major proposition in contingency theory is the **leader-match concept:** leadership effectiveness depends on matching leaders to situations in which they can exercise more control. It states that task-motivated leaders perform the best in situations both of high control and low control. Relationship-motivated leaders perform the best in situations of moderate control. A less-publicized finding is that socioindependent leaders tend to perform the best in situations of high control.

Task-motivated leaders perform better in situations that are highly favorable for exercising control, because they do not have to be concerned with the task. Instead, they can work on relationships. In moderately favorable situations, the relationship-motivated leader works well because he or she can work on relationships and not get involved in overmanaging. Also, in very low-control situations, the task-motivated leader is able to structure and make sense out of confusion. The relationship-motivated leader wants to give emotional support to group members or call a committee meeting.[3]

Figure 6–1 presents a summary of the findings on which the leader-match concept is based. To interpret the model, look first at the situational characteristics at the top of the figure. Leader-member relations can be good or poor; task structure can be high or low; and position power may be strong or weak. The eight possible situations (labeled I through VIII) range

SITUATIONAL CHARACTERISTICS

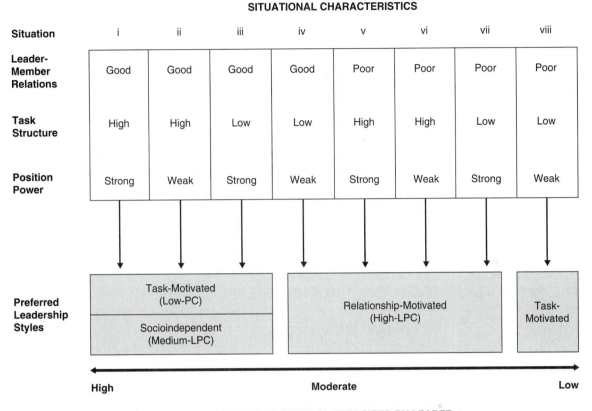

Situation	i	ii	iii	iv	v	vi	vii	viii
Leader-Member Relations	Good	Good	Good	Good	Poor	Poor	Poor	Poor
Task Structure	High	High	Low	Low	High	High	Low	Low
Position Power	Strong	Weak	Strong	Weak	Strong	Weak	Strong	Weak

Preferred Leadership Styles:

Task-Motivated (Low-PC) / Socioindependent (Medium-LPC)

Relationship-Motivated (High-LPC)

Task-Motivated

High ——————— Moderate ——————— Low

AMOUNT OF CONTROL EXERCISED BY LEADER

FIGURE 6–1

Fiedler's Findings on Leadership Performance and Favorability of the Situation

from very favorable for exercising control (cells I through III*) to very unfavorable for exercising control (cell VIII).

The bottom portion of the figure shows the leadership style most strongly associated with effective group performance in each situation. For example, task-motivated (low-LPC) leaders perform the best in situations of high control and low control (cells I, II, III, and VIII), and relationship-motivated leaders are the most effective when the situation is moderately favorable.

Evaluation of Fiedler's Contingency Theory

A major contribution of Fiedler's work is that it has prompted others to conduct studies about the contingency nature of leadership. It has also alerted

---

*Cell III is classified as favorable even though the leader has to deal with an unstructured task. This is true because leader-member relations and position power are so favorable.

leaders to the importance of sizing up the situation to gain control. For instance, an unfavorable situation could be made more favorable by granting the leader more position power or by increasing task structure.

Despite its potential advantages, the contingency theory is too complicated to have much of an impact on most leaders. A major problem centers on matching the situation to the leader. In most situations, the amount of control the leader exercises varies from time to time. For example, if a relationship-motivated leader were to find the situation becoming too favorable for exercising control, it is doubtful that he or she would be transferred to a less favorable situation or attempt to make the situation less favorable.

Nevertheless, the contingency theory can provide a few useful suggestions for becoming a more effective leader. Furthermore, as with the leadership theories presented in Chapters 4 and 5, remember that a leader has two primary dimensions to work with: task orientation and people orientation. The leader should emphasize either one or both, as the situation dictates.

THE PATH-GOAL THEORY OF LEADERSHIP EFFECTIVENESS

The **path-goal theory** of leadership effectiveness, as developed by Robert House, specifies what the leader must do to achieve high productivity and morale in a given situation. In general, a leader attempts to clarify the path to a goal for a group member so that he or she receives personal payoffs. At the same time, job satisfaction and performance increase.[4] Similar to the expectancy theory of motivation on which it is based, path-goal theory is complex and has several versions. Its key features are summarized in Figure 6–2.

The major proposition of path-goal theory is that the manager should choose a leadership style that takes into account the characteristics of the group members and the demands of the task. Two key aspects of this theory will be discussed: matching the leadership style to the situation, and steps the leader can take to influence performance and satisfaction.

Matching the Leadership Style to the Situation

Path-goal theory emphasizes that the leader should choose among four different leadership styles to achieve optimum results in a given situation. Two important sets of contingency factors are the type of subordinates and the type of work they perform. The type of subordinates is determined by how much control they think they have over the environment (locus of control) and by how well they think they can do the assigned task.

Environmental contingency factors consist of factors that are not within the control of group members but that influence satisfaction and task accomplishment. Three broad classifications of contingency factors in the environment are (1) the group members' tasks, (2) the authority system within the organization, and (3) the work group.

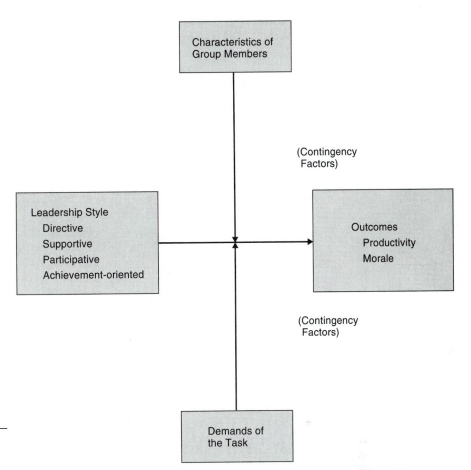

FIGURE 6–2

**The Path-Goal
Contingency Theory
of Leadership**

To use path-goal theory, the leader must first assess the relevant variables in the environment. Second, she or he selects one of four styles to fit those contingency factors best: directive, supportive, participative, or achievement-oriented. For example, if the manager is leading capable people performing a creative task, the participative style would be most appropriate.

Directive Style.   The directive leader emphasizes formal activities such as planning, organizing, and controlling. (The directive style is similar to the task-motivated or autocratic style.) The leader gives the group specific guidelines, rules, and regulations and carefully tells the group what is expected of them. The directive style improves morale when the task is unclear.

Supportive Style.   The supportive leader (similar to the relationship-motivated leader) displays concern for group members' well-being and creates an emotionally supportive climate. The leader also emphasizes developing mutually satisfying relationships among group members. He or she enhances morale when group members work on dissatisfying, stressful, or frustrating tasks. Group members who are unsure of themselves prefer the supportive leadership style.

Participative Style.   The participative leader consults with group members to gather their suggestions, and then takes these suggestions seriously when making a decision. The participative leader is best suited for improving the morale of well-motivated employees who perform nonrepetitive tasks. The Leader in Action essay below describes a leader who has found a new application for participative leadership.

Achievement-Oriented Style.   The achievement-oriented leader sets challenging goals, pushes for work improvement, and sets high expectations for team members. Group members are also expected to assume responsibility. The achievement-oriented leadership style works well with achievement-oriented team members, and also with those working on ambiguous and nonrepetitive tasks.

The Leader in Action profile on page 129 describes a manager who honed his leadership style to adapt to unusual circumstances, thus illustrating the importance of the contingency approach.

LEADER IN ACTION

Robin Orr of Plantree

Robin Orr is national director of hospital projects at Plantree, a consumer health care organization in San Francisco. The firm works with hospitals to create patient-centered services. Orr has designed a system that gives patients greater control in their treatments. They are allowed to read and write on their own medical charts. Nursing stations—which represent a physical barrier between patients and caregivers—have been abolished. Family members are encouraged to administer drugs to hospitalized patients. They are also encouraged to change bandage dressings and stay overnight in hospital rooms.

Orr explains that at Plantree, sick people are empowered to work and get well. She believes that many men mistakenly believe that leadership means control. From her viewpoint, leadership is really about inspiration and influence.

Source: Based on facts in Mary Billard, "Do Women Make Better Managers?" *Working Woman,* March 1992, pp. 68–69.

LEADER IN ACTION

Craig B. Barr, GM Plant Manager

Craig B. Barr is at his best closing down automotive plants for General Motors Corp. A recent assignment was to close the Pontiac-West assembly plant. Several years earlier his job was to close down the nearby Pontiac-Central plant. With General Motors so busy closing plants these days, Barr is consulted frequently. He says with a shrug, "I've become the encyclopedia that people refer to."

Barr struggles to maintain productivity and morale as the plant phases down. Yet he realizes the going is difficult. "The world and the company treat you as lepers," he says.

Barr gets out on the floor to interact with workers. On one occasion, an assembly worker told him about her postal carrier's problem with a panel light on a GM truck that the dealer couldn't repair. Barr had the truck fixed at his factory. He keeps the plant spotless and freshly painted. Since the announcement that the plant would shut in a couple of years, quality has actually improved. Barr has helped inspire workers to go out in style.

Production workers like Barr's style. One of them said, "In the 26 years I've been here, he's the most people-oriented manager." Barr believes strongly in being visible during a plant phasedown. He recommends that the manager in charge of the closing be visible. Barr recommends that the manager "take personal responsibility for guiding people through the change. Don't just have an 'open door' policy; wander around outside your office."

Source: As reported in James B. Treece, "Doing It Right, till the Last Whistle," *Business Week,* April 6, 1992, pp. 58–59.

How the Leader Influences Performance

In addition to recommending the leadership style to fit the situation, the path-goal theory offers other suggestions to leaders. Most of them relate to motivation and satisfaction, including the following:

1. Recognize or activate group members' needs over which the leader has control.

2. Increase the personal payoffs to team members for attaining work goals. The leader might give high-performing employees additional recognition.

3. Make the paths to payoffs (rewards) easier by coaching and providing direction. For instance, a manager might help a team member be selected for a high-level project.

4. Help group members clarify their expectations of how effort will lead to good performance, and how performance will lead to a reward. The leader might say, "Anyone who has gone through this training in the past came away knowing how to implement a total quality program. And most people who learn how to implement TQM wind up getting a good raise."

5. Reduce frustrating barriers to reaching goals. For example, the leader might hire a temporary worker to help a group member catch up on paperwork and electronic mail.

6. Increase opportunities for personal satisfaction if the group member performs effectively. The "if" is important because it reflects contingent behavior on the leader's part.

7. Be careful not to irritate people by giving them instructions on things they already can do well.

8. To obtain high performance and satisfaction, the leader must provide structure if it is missing, and must also supply rewards contingent upon adequate performance. To accomplish this, leaders must clarify the desirability of goals for the group members.[5]

As a leader, you can derive specific benefit from path-goal theory by applying these eight methods of influencing performance. A contribution of path-goal theory is that it highlights the importance of achievement-oriented leadership, which is becoming more important in high-technology organizations.[6] Despite the theory's potential contributions, however, the criticisms of Fiedler's contingency theory apply. Path-goal theory contains so many nuances and complexities that it has attracted little interest from managers.

THE HERSEY–BLANCHARD SITUATIONAL LEADERSHIP® MODEL

The two contingency approaches to leadership presented so far take into account collectively the task, the authority of the leader, and the nature of the subordinates. Another explanation of contingency leadership places its primary emphasis on the characteristics of group members. The **situational leadership model** of Paul Hersey and Kenneth H. Blanchard explains how to match the leadership style to the readiness of the group members. The term *model* rather than *theory* is deliberately chosen because situational leadership does not attempt to explain why things happen (as would a theory). Instead, the situational leadership model offers some procedures that can be repeated.[7]

Basics of the Model

Leadership style in the situational model is classified according to the relative amount of task and relationship behavior the leader engages in. The differentiation is akin to initiating structure versus consideration. **Task behavior** is the extent to which the leader spells out the duties and responsibilities of an individual or group. It includes giving directions and setting goals. **Relationship behavior** is the extent to which the leader engages in two-way or multiway communication. It includes such activities as listening, providing encouragement, and coaching. As Figure 6–3 shows, the situational model places combinations of task and relationship behaviors into four quadrants. Each quadrant calls for a different leadership style.

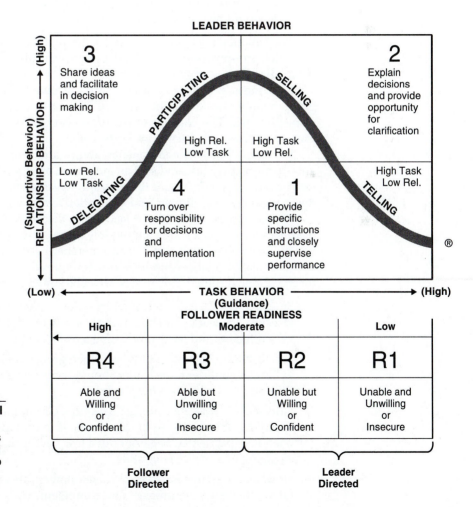

FIGURE 6–3

Expanded Situational Model

Style 1—High task and low relationship. The "telling" style is very directive because the leader produces a lot of input but a minimum amount of relationship behavior. An autocratic leader would fit here.

Style 2—High task and high relationship. The "selling" style is also very directive but in a more persuasive, guiding manner. The leader provides considerable input about task accomplishment but also emphasizes human relations.

Style 3—High relationship and low task. In the "participating" leadership style, there is less direction and more collaboration between leader and group members. The consultative and consensus subtypes of participative leader generally fit into this quadrant.

Style 4—Low relationship and low task. In the "delegating" leadership style, the leader delegates responsibility for a task to a group member and is simply kept informed of progress. If carried to an extreme, this style would be classified as free-rein.

The situational leadership model states that there is not one best way to influence group members. The most effective leadership style depends on the readiness level of group members.

Readiness in situational leadership is defined as the extent to which a group member has the ability and willingness or confidence to accomplish a specific task. The concept of readiness is therefore not a characteristic, trait, or motive—it relates to a specific task.

Readiness has two components, ability and willingness. *Ability* is the knowledge, experience, and skill an individual or group brings to a particular task or activity. *Willingness* is the extent to which an individual or group has the confidence, commitment, and motivation to accomplish a specific task.

The key point of situational leadership theory is that as group member readiness increases, a leader should rely more on relationship behavior and less on task behavior. When a group member becomes very ready, a minimum of task or relationship behavior is required of the leader. Guidelines for the leader, outlined in Figure 6–3, can be summarized as follows:

Situation R1—Low Readiness. When followers are unable, unwilling, or insecure, the leader should emphasize task-oriented behavior and be very directive and autocratic, using a *telling* style.

Situation R2—Moderate Readiness. When groups members are unable but willing or confident, the leader should focus on being more relationship-oriented, using a *selling* style.

Situation R3—Moderate-to-High Readiness. Group members are able but unwilling or insecure, so the leader needs to provide a high degree of relationship-oriented behavior but a low degree of task behavior, thus engaging in a *participating* style.

Situation R4 —High Readiness. When followers are able, willing, or confident, they are self-sufficient and competent. Thus the leader can grant them considerable autonomy, using a *delegating* style.

Evaluation of the Situational Model

The situational model represents a consensus of thinking about leadership behavior in relation to group members: competent people require less specific direction than do less competent people. The model is also useful because it builds on other explanations of leadership that emphasize the role of task and relationship behaviors. As a result, it has proved to be useful as the basis for leadership training. The situational model also supports common sense and is therefore intuitively appealing. You can benefit from this model by attempting to diagnose the readiness of group members before choosing the right leadership style.

Nevertheless, the model presents categories and guidelines so precisely that it gives the impression of infallibility. In reality, leadership situations are less clear-cut than the four quadrants suggest. Also, the prescriptions for leadership will work only some of the time. For example, many supervisors use a telling style with unable and unwilling or insecure team members (R1) and still achieve poor results.

Research evidence for the situational model has been mixed. A major concern is that there are few leadership situations in which a high-task, high-relationship orientation does not produce the best results.[8] Robert P. Vecchio conducted a comprehensive test of the Hersey-Blanchard model involving 303 teachers and their principals. The results were mixed, suggesting that the model may hold for only certain types of employees. For one thing, Vecchio found that more recently hired employees may need and appreciate greater task behavior from superiors.[9]

The accompanying Leader in Action box illustrates how organizations sometimes hope to improve results by selecting a leader with a style different from his or her predecessor's. In this sense, the company was practicing a form of contingency management and leadership.

LEADER IN ACTION

Vaughn D. Bryson of Eli Lilly

After years of excellent profits, Eli Lilly and Company's tradition-bound, slow-moving management style is beginning to have adverse affects. After surviving legal battles over whether its top-selling Prozac induced violent behavior, the antidepressant drug is facing tough competition. To make matters worse, Lilly's medical device and diagnostics business is encountering difficulty with government regulators. In one instance, the federal Food and Drug Administration turned up violations such as poor monitoring and recordkeeping.

Over the years, Lilly's routine success bred a rigid, bureaucratic leadership style, which slowed the company's response to emergencies. For example, it took Lilly one year to respond to allegations about the negative side-effects of Prozac. The company's relatively new CEO, Vaughn D. Bryson, hopes to loosen up the stiff organizational culture. Unlike the command-and-control style of his predecessor (who retired), he encourages decision making at the middle levels. Bryson makes a point of eating in the company cafeteria and otherwise mingling with lower-ranking workers.

Source: As reported in "Lilly Looks for a Shot of Adrenalin," *Business Week,* November 23, 1992, pp. 70–75.

THE VROOM–YETTON–JAGO DECISION-MAKING MODEL

Another contingency viewpoint is that leaders must choose a style that elicits the correct degree of group participation when making decisions. This perspective makes sense because much of a leader's relationships with team members involves decision making. The **Vroom–Yetton–Jago model*** views leadership as a decision-making process.[10] A leader examines certain factors in the situation to determine which decision-making style will be the most effective.

Basic Premises of the Model

The Vroom–Yetton–Jago model identifies five decision-making styles, each reflecting a different degree of participation by group members. As shown in Table 6–1, the decision-making styles follow the leadership continuum closely. The first two styles, AI and AII, are autocratic because the leader makes the decision with a minimum of group input. The second two styles, CI and CII, are consultative. The fifth style, GII, is group-directed because the leader turns over considerable authority to the group, and group consensus is achieved before a decision is reached.

The manager diagnoses the situation in terms of several variables. Based on those variables, the manager follows the paths through a decision tree to a recommended course of action. The model includes four decision trees: two for group-level decisions and two for individual-level decisions. (An individual-level decision involves only one subordinate.) One of each tree is for use when time is critical. Also, one of each is for use when time is less important and when the leader wants to develop a team member's decision-making capabilities.

Figure 6–4 depicts the decision tree for time-driven group problems, that is, when time is a critical factor. The situational variables, or problem attributes, are listed above the decision tree. To use the model, the decision maker begins at the left side of the diagram and asks the first question regarding

---

*The model was originally developed by Victor H. Vroom and Philip W. Yetton, and later refined by Vroom and Arthur G. Jago.

TABLE 6–1   Decision-Making Styles in the Vroom–Yetton–Jago Model

Decision-Making Style	Description
Autocratic I (AI)	Leader solves problem alone using information that is readily available.
Autocratic II (AII)	Leader obtains additional information from group members, then makes decision alone. Group members may or may not be informed.
Consultative I (CI)	Leader shares problem with group members individually, and asks for information and evaluation. Group members do not meet collectively, and leader makes decision alone.
Consultative II (CII)	Leader shares problem with group members collectively, but makes decision alone.
Group II (GII)	Leader meets with group to discuss situation. Leader focuses and directs discussion, but does not impose will. Group makes final decision.

Key: A—autocratic, C—consultative, G—group

quality requirement (QR). To begin, he or she asks, "How important is the technical quality of this decision?" If the answer is "high" the manager proceeds to CR, the commitment requirement and answers another question: "How important is subordinate commitment to the decision?" The answer to each question takes the user to another node. The process continues until the group leader reaches a terminal node. At that point, the leader is told which decision-making (or leadership) style is best. Assume that following the right paths took the group leader to CII. He or she would make the second type of consultative decision described in Table 6–1.

The complete Vroom–Yetton–Jago model is more complex than the version just described. Several of the questions allow for more than yes or no answers. Because of its complexity, the authors of the model have also developed a software version to help managers diagnose a situation. As with the decision trees, the manager then makes an appropriate decision about the correct amount of group participation.

An Illustrative Use of the Model

Assume that you are vice president of the claims division of a medical insurance company. You think it would benefit the company and the employees involved to begin a telecommuting (work-at-home) program for claims specialists. You wonder how much to involve the group in this decision. You decide to use the Vroom–Yetton–Jago model for time-driven group problems. Referring to Figure 6–4, proceed as follows:

1. You begin at the QR node: "How important is the quality of the decision?" You decide that quality importance is high. The wrong decision could result in poor-quality claims service. Answering "high" takes you to the CR node.

2. At the CR node, you ask: "How important is subordinate commitment to the decision?" Again, you answer "high," because the magnitude of

QR	*Quality Requirement:*	How important is the technical quality of this decision?
CR	*Commitment Requirement:*	How important is subordinate commitment to the decision?
LI	*Leader's Information:*	Do you have sufficient information to make a high-quality decision?
ST	*Problem Structure:*	Is the problem well structured?
CP	*Commitment Probability:*	If you were to make the decision by yourself, is it reasonably certain that your subordinate(s) would be committed to the decision?
GC	*Goal Congruence:*	Do subordinates share the organizational goals to be attained in solving this problem?
CO	*Subordinate Conflict:*	Is conflict among subordinates over preferred solutions likely?
SI	*Subordinate Information:*	Do subordinates have sufficient information to make a high-quality decision?

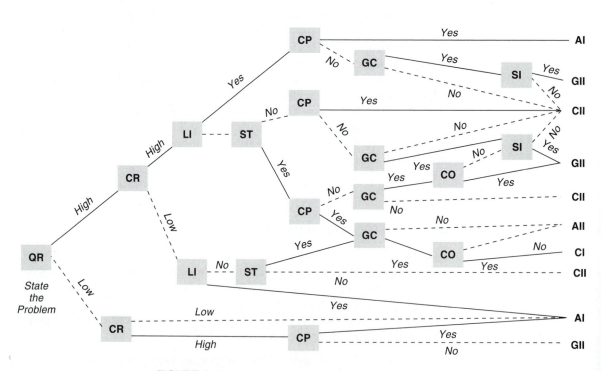

FIGURE 6–4

The Vroom–Yetton–Jago Model for Time-Driven Group Problems

Source: Reprinted from *The New Leadership: Managing Participation in Organizations* by Victor H. Vroom and Arthur G. Jago, 1988, Englewood Cliffs, N.J.: Prentice Hall. Used with permission.

a telecommuting program necessitates commitment on the part of all staffers concerned. Your "high" response takes you to the LI node.

3. At the LI node, you ask: "Do you have sufficient information to make a high-quality decision?" You answer "no" because you need to gather many facts before you can decide whether a telecommuting program will work for the division. Your "no" response takes you to node ST.

4. At the ST node, you ask: "Is the problem well structured?" You respond "no" because a telecommuting program involves many nuances, including determining what format the program will take. Your "no" answer takes you to node CP.

5. At the CP node, you ask: "If you were to make the decision by yourself, is it reasonably certain that your subordinate(s) would be committed to the decision?" You answer "yes" because you believe you have a cohesive team who will make a commitment to any rational decision from above. Your "yes" response takes you directly to the terminal node, CII. Your action plan, as defined in Table 6–1, is to share the decision with team members, obtain their ideas and suggestions, and so forth.

Now try Leadership Development Exercise 6–1 for additional practice with the Vroom–Yetton–Jago model.

Evidence and Opinion About the Model

Researchers and managers have reacted positively to the Vroom–Yetton–Jago model and its earlier versions. Managers who follow the step-by-step

---

LEADERSHIP DEVELOPMENT EXERCISE 6–1

Using a Decision Tree to Select an Appropriate Leadership Style

Directions: You are the president of a chain of ten deep-discount drug stores. Sales have increased 20 percent in the previous year, but profits are down by 110 percent. You have actually lost money. One of the problems you see is that some of your discounts have been too deep and employee turnover has been too high. You are thinking about offering no salary increases next year in order to bring the chain back to profitability. You have four vice presidents reporting to you, all of whom have a financial stake in the business.

Take this problem through the Vroom–Yetton–Jago model by yourself. Next, meet in a group with classmates and discuss your conclusions about which decision-making style you reached. If group members disagree, discuss the answers given at each node to learn why you pursued different branches on the decision-making tree.

procedures of the model are likely to increase their decision-making effectiveness. The model also predicts accurately the type of decisions practicing managers make. Furthermore, managers who make decisions consistent with the model are more likely to be perceived as effective managers.[11]

The Vroom–Yetton–Jago model provides a valuable service to practicing managers and leaders. It prompts them to ask intelligent and perceptive questions about decision-making situations. Although the decision tree appears formidable at first glance, a person with answers to the eight diagnostic questions can work through it in fewer than ten minutes.

Despite the utility of the Vroom–Yetton–Jago model, it can be criticized on the same grounds as other contingency models. All of them are more about *management* than about leadership. Contingency theories and models provide supervisors and middle managers precise guidelines for selecting an appropriate leadership style. Yet they have little to do with inspiring and influencing others, and bringing about important changes.

SUMMARY

Contingency and situational leadership theories specify the factors that determine which style of leadership will achieve the best results in a given situation.

Fiedler's contingency theory states that the best style of leadership is determined by the situation in which the leader is working. Style, in Fiedler's theory, is measured by the least preferred coworker (LPC) scale. You are relationship-motivated if you have a reasonably positive attitude toward your least preferred coworker. You are task-motivated if your attitude is negative, and you are socioindependent if your attitude is neutral. Situational control, or favorability, is measured by a combination of the quality of leader-member relations, the degree of task structure, and the leader's position power.

The key proposition of Fiedler's theory is the leader-match concept: in situations of high control or low control, leaders with a task-motivated style are the most effective. In a situation of moderate control, a relationship-motivated style works best. In a high-control situation, a socioindependent style is best.

The path-goal theory of leadership effectiveness specifies what the leader must do to achieve high productivity and morale in a given situation. Effective leaders clarify the paths to attaining goals, help group members progress along these paths, and remove barriers to goal attainment. Leaders must choose a style that best fits the two sets of contingency factors—the characteristics of the subordinates and the tasks. The four styles in path-goal theory are directive, supportive, participative, and achievement-oriented.

The situational leadership model (developed by Hersey and Blanchard) explains how to match leadership style to the readiness of group members.

The model classifies leadership style according to the relative amount of task and relationship behavior the leader engages in. The four styles are different combinations of task and relationship behavior, both rated as high versus low. *Readiness* refers both to ability and to willingness to accomplish a specific task. As group member readiness increases, a leader should rely more on relationship behavior and less on task behavior. When a group member becomes very ready, however, minimum task or relationship behavior is required.

According to the Vroom–Yetton–Jago decision-making model, leadership is a decision-making process. A leader examines certain factors in the situation to determine which decision-making style will be the most effective. The model identifies five decision-making styles: two autocratic, two consultative, and one group-centered. By answering a series of eight diagnostic questions in a decision tree, the manager follows the path to a terminal node, which recommends one of the five styles.

A general criticism made of contingency and situational leadership is that it concerns management rather than true leadership. The various models deal more with conducting transactions with group members than with inspiration and influence.

KEY TERMS

Contingency theory of leadership	Task behavior
Leader-match concept	Relationship behavior
Path-goal theory	Readiness
Situational leadership model	Vroom-Yetton-Jago model

GUIDELINES FOR ACTION AND SKILL DEVELOPMENT

1. To apply contingency and situational theory, a leader typically has to make choices between two related considerations. The first is to achieve the right balance between a task and relationship orientation. Unless there is strong evidence to the contrary, the leader should strive to emphasize both task and relationships. The second consideration is to choose a decision style at some place on the leadership continuum, from autocratic to democratic. A consultative decision-making style is called for when a decision is complex, technical accuracy is important, and group acceptance is necessary.

2. In relation to the Vroom–Yetton–Jago model, George R. H. Field has proposed a convenient rule of thumb for choosing the right leadership style: "If acceptance of a decision by subordinates is critical to effective implementation and it is reasonably certain that subordinates would

not accept autocratic decisions, but they share organizational goals (or decision quality is not important), use GII. Otherwise, use CII."[12]

DISCUSSION QUESTIONS AND ANSWERS

1. Some people argue, "Contingency leadership states that everything depends on the situation. This means that you can do what you want as a leader because there are no general rules." What is the fallacy of this point of view?

2. Following Fiedler's theory, how can a leader make the situation more favorable for himself or herself?

3. Assume that your natural leadership style is autocratic. Following the dictates of Fiedler's theory, how can you maintain your effectiveness as a leader?

4. What kind of personal payoffs might group members be seeking?

5. To which Leadership Grid style does the achievement-oriented style correspond the most closely?

6. How can a leader increase structure for team members?

7. According to the situational model of leadership, which style is likely to be the most effective for leading a strongly motivated group of software developers? Explain.

8. In what way does the situational model of leadership take an optimistic view of leadership ability?

9. One criticism of the Vroom–Yetton–Jago model is that practically all nonroutine decisions wind up requiring the consultative style or group style. How valid is this criticism?

10. Give the Vroom–Yetton–Jago model to an experienced leader. Obtain his or her opinion on its value, and be ready to discuss your findings in class.

LEADERSHIP CASE PROBLEM

A Hard Decision at Nucor

F. Kenneth Iverson, the chairman of Nucor Steel, has created what many believe to be the world's premier steelmaker. Since Iverson became president of Nucor in 1965, sales have climbed from just over $20 million to about $1.5 billion. As a result, Iverson is something of a cult figure in the international steel industry.

When asked to summarize the philosophy and style that underpins his company's success, Iverson replied: "You can probably summarize the underpinning in three or four principles. One is few management layers, which we believe in very, very strongly. The second is a minimum of staff people. That's reflected, of course, in the size of our corporate office, which has only 22 people. Our people out in the divisions are all aware of that. They feel more responsible because we don't have a lot of people here. The third factor is to push responsibilities down to the lowest possible level. And the fourth is the use of strong incentives that focus everyone on productivity and earnings."

According to Iverson, the company culture is egalitarian. At Nucor, an effort is made to eliminate the distinction between managers and individual contributors. Everybody has the same vacations, holidays, health care program. Iverson has also worked at eliminating status barriers by changing workers' hat colors.

Several years ago, Iverson read about a plant in Canada where all 400 employees wore the same color hard hat. He liked the idea, so he decided to eliminate Nucor's practice of assigning certain hat colors to certain job ranks. Iverson issued a memorandum saying that by a certain date everyone would wear the same color hard hat. There would be no more blue hats for line workers, for example, or white hats for supervisors.

Company personnel quickly told Iverson that he made a mistake, that in a steel mill you have to be able to spot the maintenance people quickly. So Iverson decided that maintenance workers would wear yellow hats and everyone else would wear green.

Some people were very unhappy with that decision. Iverson received letters from supervisors saying you can't do this to me. To a supervisor, a white hat is the supervisor's authority. As one supervisor put it, "I put my hat on the back shelf of my car when I go home and everybody knows I am a supervisor at Nucor."

Iverson reacted to these letters, and decided to give the issue of color-coded hard hats some careful thought.

1. Did Iverson do anything wrong in passing his hat-color edict?

2. Based on the evidence in the case, how would you characterize Iverson's leadership style? Use more than one approach to categorizing leadership style.

3. How should Iverson resolve this problem?

Source: Based on facts reported in "Hot Steel and Good Common Sense," *Management Review,* August 1992, pp. 25–27.

LEADERSHIP EXERCISE

The Hard-Hat Decision

Choose which leadership decision-making style F. Kenneth Iverson should have used in arriving at a decision about color-coded hats for company personnel. With information from the case problem, use the Vroom–Yetton–Jago decision tree to reach your conclusion. You will have to use your best guess about the characteristics and attitudes of key staff members at Nucor. If class time permits, make this a small-group project.

Power, Politics, and Leadership

*S*ara Penwalt, director of sales and marketing, heard during the Monday morning staff meeting that the president planned to lay off 10 percent of the work force. To minimize bickering over which departments would have to streamline the most, the president ordered across-the-board cuts. Each major function would have to lay off 10 percent of its employees. Penwalt scheduled a meeting with the president later that day to fight this proposal.

Penwalt argued that eliminating 10 percent of people in her division would be counterproductive. "How can we lay off people who are producing sales and providing customer service?" she argued. "If you proceed with your cuts, you can have my resignation first." Penwalt got her way. The president agreed to eliminate only substandard performers from the sales and marketing group. Deeper cuts would then be made in other divisions within the company.

To exercise influence a leader must have *power*, the potential or ability to influence decisions and control resources. Sara Penwalt had the power to influence the president's decision because she controlled an important resource: the sales and marketing department, which attracted and retained customers. She also knew the president was unlikely to fire her because he had supported her decisions many times previously.

To acquire and retain power, a leader must often skillfully use politics. No matter how meritorious a leader's ideas for constructive change, without political backing those ideas will not be implemented.

As used here, the term **organizational politics** refers to informal approaches to gaining power through means other than merit or luck. Politics are played to achieve power, either directly or indirectly. The power may be achieved in such diverse ways as being promoted, receiving a larger budget or other resources, obtaining more resources for one's work group, or being exempt from undesirable assignments.

The definition of organizational politics here is nonevaluative, except that we shall draw a distinction between ethical and unethical political behavior. Many other writers regard organizational politics as emphasizing self-interest at the expense of others, or engaging in mysterious activities. Two researchers, for example, said "Politics are the observable, but often covert, actions by which executives enhance their power to influence a decision."[1]

This chapter covers the nature of power, the ways leaders acquire power and empower others, and the use and control of organizational politics. Chapter 8 continues the discussion of organizational politics by examining influence tactics.

SOURCES AND TYPES OF POWER

Organizational power can be derived from many sources, as shown in Table 7–1. How a person obtains power depends to a large extent on the type of power he or she seeks. Therefore, to understand the mechanics of acquiring power, one must also understand what types of power exist and the sources

TABLE 7–1 Types or Sources of Power

1. Power granted by the organization (position power)

2. Power stemming from characteristics of the person (personal power)

3. Power stemming from ownership

4. Power stemming from providing resources

5. Power derived from capitalizing upon opportunity

6. Power stemming from managing critical problems

7. Power stemming from being close to power

and origins of these types of power. The seven types or sources of power listed in Table 7–1 are described in the following sections.

Position Power

Power is frequently classified according to whether it stems from the organization or the individual.[2] Four of these bases of power—legitimate power, reward power, coercive power, and information power—stem from the organization, that is, from the person's position in the organization.

Legitimate Power.   Power granted by the organization is called **legitimate power.** People at the highest levels in the organization have more power than do people below them. However, organizational culture helps establish the limits to anyone's power. Newly appointed executives, for example, are often frustrated with how long it takes to affect major change. A chief financial officer (CFO) recruited to improve the profitability of a telecommunications firm noted: "The company has been downsizing for three years. We have more office space and manufacturing capacity than we need. Yet whenever I introduce the topic of selling off real estate to cut costs, I get a cold reception."

Reward Power.   The authority to give employees rewards for compliance is referred to as **reward power.** If a vice president of operations can directly reward supervisors with cash bonuses for achieving quality targets, this manager will exert considerable power. Of course, leaders can use reward power effectively only when they have meaningful rewards at their disposal.

Coercive Power.   **Coercive power** is the power to punish for noncompliance; it is based on fear. A common coercive tactic is for an executive to demote a subordinate manager if he or she does not comply with the executive's plans for change. Coercive power is limited, in that punishment and fear achieve mixed results as motivators. The leader who relies heavily on coercive power runs the constant threat of being ousted from power.

Information Power.   **Information power** is power stemming from formal control over information people need to do their work.[3] A sales manager who controls the leads from customer inquiries holds considerable power. As the branch manager of a real estate agency put it: "Ever since the leads were mailed directly to me, I get oodles of cooperation from my agents. Before that they would treat me as if I were simply the office manager."

Personal Power

Three sources of power stem from characteristics or behaviors of the power actor: expert power, referent power, and prestige power. All are classified as **personal power,** because they are derived from the person rather than from the organization. Expert power and referent power contribute to charisma.

Expert power is the ability to influence others through specialized knowledge, skills, or abilities, as does a marketing manager who is adept at identifying new markets. Referent power is the ability to influence others through desirable traits and characteristics.

Another important form of personal power is **prestige power,** the power stemming from one's status and reputation.[4] A manager who has accumulated important business successes acquires prestige power. Executive recruiters, for example, identify executives who could readily be placed in key CEO positions because of their excellent track record. Members of this elite group include Paul G. Stern, former chairman of Northern Telecom, Craig R. Barrett, operations chief at Intel Corp., Cinda A. Hallman, chief information officer at Du Pont, Judy C. Lewent, chief financial officer at Merck & Co., and Roger T. Servison, a retailing marketing executive at Fidelity Investments.

According to a new analysis, personal power is **leadership power,** the exercise of position power. To make effective use of position power, the leader should have such characteristics as integrity, initiative, the desire to lead, communication skills, and emotional security.[5] Outstanding leaders such as John Purcell at Dean Witter and Carol Bartz at Autodesk (both described previously) exercise leadership power.

Leadership Self-Assessment Exercise 7–1 on page 146 provides a sampling of the specific behaviors associated with five of the sources of power: three kinds of position power and two kinds of personal power.

Power Stemming from Ownership

Executive leaders accrue power in their capacity as agents acting on behalf of shareholders. The strength of ownership power depends on how closely he or she is linked to shareholders and board members. A leader's ownership power is also associated with how much money he or she has invested in the firm.[6] An executive who is a major shareholder is much less likely to be fired by the board than one without an equity stake. The New Golden Rule applies: The person who holds the gold, rules.

Power from Providing Resources

A broad way to view power sources is from the **resource dependence perspective.** According to this perspective, the organization requires a continuing flow of human resources, money, customers and clients, technological inputs, and materials to continue to function. Organizational subunits or individuals who can provide these key resources accrue power.[7]

An important consequence of resource-related power is that when leaders start losing their power to control resources, their power declines. A case in point is Donald Trump. When his vast holdings were generating a positive cash flow and his image was one of extraordinary power, he found many willing investors. The name *Trump* on a property escalated its value. As his cash-flow position worsened, however, Trump found it difficult to

LEADERSHIP
SELF-ASSESSMENT
EXERCISE 7–1   **Rating a Manager's Power**

Directions: If you currently have a supervisor or can clearly recall one from the past, rate him or her. Circle the appropriate number of your answer, using the following scale: 5 = strongly agree, 4 = agree, 3 = neither agree nor disagree, 2 = disagree, 1 = strongly disagree. (The actual scale presents the items in random order. They are classified here according to the power source for your convenience.)

My manager can (or former manager could) . . .	Strongly Agree				Strongly Disagree
Reward Power					
1. increase my pay level.	5	4	3	2	1
2. influence my getting a pay raise.	5	4	3	2	1
3. provide me with specific benefits.	5	4	3	2	1
4. influence my getting a promotion.	5	4	3	2	1
Coercive Power					
5. give me undesirable job assignments.	5	4	3	2	1
6. make my work difficult for me.	5	4	3	2	1
7. make things unpleasant here.	5	4	3	2	1
8. make being at work distasteful.	5	4	3	2	1
Legitimate Power					
9. make me feel that I have commitments to meet	5	4	3	2	1
10. make me feel like I should satisfy my job requirements	5	4	3	2	1
11. give me the feeling that I have responsibilities to fulfill.	5	4	3	2	1
12. make me recognize that I have tasks to accomplish.	5	4	3	2	1
Expert Power					
13. give me good technical suggestions.	5	4	3	2	1
14. share with me his or her considerable experience and/or training.	5	4	3	2	1

15. provide me with sound job-related
    advice.   5   4   3   2   1

16. provide me with needed technical
    knowledge.   5   4   3   2   1

Referent Power

17. make me feel valued.   5   4   3   2   1

18. make me feel that he or she approves
    of me.   5   4   3   2   1

19. make me feel personally accepted.   5   4   3   2   1

20. make me feel important.   5   4   3   2   1

Total score: _____

Scoring and interpretation: Add all the circled numbers to calculate your total score. You can make a tentative interpretation of the score as follows:

    90+:   high power
    70–89:   moderate power
    below 70:   low power

Also, see if you rated your manager much higher on one type of power than the others.

Source: Adapted from "Development and Application of New Scales to Measure the French and Raven (1959) Bases of Social Power," by Thomas R. Hinkin and Chester A. Schriescheim, *Journal of Applied Psychology,* August 1989, p. 567. Copyright 1989 by the American Psychological Association. Adapted by permission.

find investment groups willing to buy his properties at near the asking price.[8] Yet by mid-1993, Trump's cash-flow position improved again and investors showed renewed interest.

Power from Capitalizing on Opportunity

Power can be derived from being at the right place at the right time and taking the appropriate action. A person also needs to have the right resources to capitalize on the opportunity.[9] It pays to be "where the action is" in order to gain power through capitalizing on opportunity. For example, the best opportunities in a diversified company lie in one of its growth divisions.

Leaders can escalate their power by meeting the needs of the time. William Rothschild has identified four types of leaders, each of whom exercises the most power when his or her type matches the times. A *risktaker* is a visionary, such as Bill Gates of Microsoft, who starts the business. A *caretaker* institutionalizes the business so it can run smoothly. Quite often the care-taker is a key executive hired by a risktaker to manage the business profes-sionally. An *undertaker* phases down a failed business and is sometimes hired after a company has declared bankruptcy. *Surgeon leaders* are analyti-cal and objective with no ties to the past. Nothing is sacred to them, so they can surgically remove unprofitable lines of business even if the business is a sentimental favorite. A surgeon leader accrues the most power when a large business has become overweight, complacent, and slow.

Jack Welch of General Electric is a legendary surgeon leader. He had the courage to trade GE's RCA consumer electronics division for medical sys-tems. In 1993 Welch sold GE's aerospace business to Martin Marietta. By carefully crafting a "new" General Electric, Jack Welch has become an enor-mously powerful leader.[10]

Power Stemming from Managing Critical Problems

A simple but compelling theory has been developed to explain why some organizational units are more powerful than others. The **strategic contin-gency theory** of power suggests that units best able to cope with the firm's critical problems and uncertainties acquire relatively large amounts of power.[11] The theory implies, for example, that when an organization faces substantial lawsuits, the legal department will gain power and influence over organizational decisions. The sudden power and influence of the legal department is based on its exclusive ability to handle the particular problem of lawsuits.

Another important aspect of the strategic contingency theory concerns the power a subunit acquires by virtue of its centrality. **Centrality** is the extent to which a unit's activities are linked into the system of organiza-tional activities. A unit has high centrality when it is an important and inte-gral part of the work done by another unit. The second unit is therefore dependent on the first subunit. A sales department would have high cen-trality, whereas an employee credit union would have low centrality.

Power Stemming from Being Close to Power

The closer a person is to power, the greater the power he or she exerts. Like-wise, the higher a unit reports in a firm's hierarchy, the more power it pos-sesses. In practice, this means that a leader in charge of a department reporting to the president has more power than a department reporting to a vice president. Leaders in search of more power typically maneuver toward a higher-reporting position in the organization. Many managers of quality assurance now report at a higher organizational level than previously. Part of this enhanced power can be attributed to the increasing attention organi-zations are paying to quality as part of their strategy.

DEVELOPING A PLAN FOR INCREASING POWER

Leaders and others intent on increasing their power are advised to develop a plan, much like an officeseeker develops a plan to win political office. The plan should include six key steps:

1. *Establish goals for the political behavior to achieve.* Political behavior should be geared toward important goals such as getting promoted, receiving a raise, or being transferred from a manager who gives very little recognition. Implementation of the plan will be based on the type of power being sought. A person who seeks power derived from centrality would seek employment in a major line department such as marketing or manufacturing, whereas a person who seeks power through ownership might have to start a small business and work toward achieving substantial growth.

2. *Evaluate the campaign's cost-effectiveness.* Before selecting a political tactic, one should assess any potential costs of using it against potential benefits. The costs of influencing others can exceed the benefits derived from exerting influence. An example would be an attempt to discredit a respected executive.

3. *Identify the true power.* To plan a political campaign properly, it is necessary to identify the true power holders in the organization. At times the true power holder may be outranked by a less powerful person, such as an assistant vice president who is a major stockholder. Subtle questioning of experienced workers can sometimes identify the true power.

4. *Conduct a power analysis of powerful people.* After identifying the powerful players in the organization, one should determine how much power each possesses. For example, a powerful manager can make many decisions without having to confer with a superior. Someone who has received a series of rapid promotions is clearly someone with power.

5. *Size up the manager.* Because organizational politics begins with creating a favorable impression on the boss, it is important to understand his or her preferences and values. For example, what is the manager's most pressing problem? What does he or she regard as good performance? How much time does he or she like to spend conferring with team members?

6. *Analyze what type of politics senior management plays.* Top-level political behavior often serves as an appropriate model for political tactics played below. For example, top managers might underplay their power by dressing casually or having a minimum number of assistants. An employee who seeks to look and act powerful by dressing formally and by requesting two personal assistants could fall into immediate disfavor.

TACTICS FOR BECOMING AN EMPOWERING LEADER

A leader's power and influence increase when he or she shares power with others. A partial explanation for this paradox is that as team members receive more power, they can accomplish more. And because the manager shares credit for their accomplishments, he or she becomes more powerful. A truly powerful leader, then, makes team members feel powerful and able to accomplish tasks on their own.[12] To empower others is thus to be perceived as an influential person. Almost any form of participative management and shared decision making can be regarded as empowerment. In addition, specific empowering practices have been identified that enhance a manager's ability to be influential.

Empowering Practices

The practices that foster empowerment described here supplement standard approaches to participative management such as conferring with team members before reaching a decision. Many of them are based on direct observations of successful executives, including a study by Jay Conger.[13]

Providing a Positive Emotional Atmosphere.   Conger identified an unusual empowering practice: executives providing emotional support to team members, especially through play or drama. For example, every few months several executives would hold a day-long event devoted to confidence building. Among the activities were inspirational speeches and films about mountain climbing. The message conveyed in such activities is that the person featured is finding extraordinary satisfaction in work, and is performing superbly.

Providing a positive emotional atmosphere contributes to empowerment indirectly by helping group members develop greater self-confidence. As their self-confidence grows, they are more willing to assume the responsibilities required of an empowered worker.

Rewarding and Encouraging in Visible and Personal Ways.   The majority of executives in the Conger study rewarded the achievements of team members by praising them and by giving them rewards in visible and confidence-building ways. For example, one executive established the "I Make a Difference Club." Each year staff members who have performed exceptionally well are invited to a company dinner in which they are inaugurated into this exclusive club.

Expressing Confidence.   The empowering leaders in the study invested considerable time expressing their confidence in team members' abilities. They did so daily in speeches, at meetings, and even during chance encounters in the hallways. The Leader in Action essay describes an executive who expresses extreme confidence in workers.

Fostering Initiative and Responsibility.   A leader can empower team members simply by fostering greater initiative and responsibility in their

LEADER
IN
ACTION

Dennis K. Pawley of Chrysler Corp.

Dennis Pawley says that teamwork is the key to rejuvenating cash-hungry Chrysler Corp. One time he walked out of a plant meeting with the terse comment, "You're wasting my time." It had become clear to Pawley that plant managers had drawn up a business plan without union input. President Robert A. Lutz says, "Dennis is fundamentally changing our manufacturing culture by empowering the people to do what they know they can do."

Pawley is the key person in implementing a more efficient manufacturing system. It involves designers, plant engineers, and production managers working in teams under one budget to design easily assembled autos. To reverse years of autocratic decision making, Pawley spends hours walking the plant floors. He encourages worker input and demands greater accountability.

Pawley learned some of his empowerment techniques from the Japanese. Prior to working for Chrysler, he was the top manufacturing executive at the U.S. division of Mazda Motor Corporation.

Source: Based on facts in "Dennis Pawley: Improving Chrysler's Japanese Accent," *Business Week,* April 20, 1992, p. 55.

assignments. For example, one bank executive transformed what had been a constricted branch manager's job into a branch "president" role. Managers were then evaluated on the basis of deposits because they had control over them. After the transformation, branch managers were allowed to stay with one branch rather than being rotated every three years.

Building on Success.   Empowering executives often introduce organizational change by starting small. If the change proves successful in the pilot run, it then proceeds on a larger scale. For example, a new technology might be introduced in one plant rather than throughout the organization. In Conger's study, the managers who launched such new projects successfully reported feelings of self-efficacy (the self-perception of effectiveness).

Praising Initiative.   To reinforce empowerment, leaders praise workers who take risks and display initiatives that lead to success. They also recognize workers who make honest and thoughtful efforts yet fall short of achieving worthwhile results.

Practicing SuperLeadership

Encouraging team members to practice self-leadership is the heart of empowerment. When employees lead themselves, they feel empowered. At W. L. Gore and Associates, a manufacturer of insulated material including GORE-TEX®, a popular buzzword is *unmanagement*—no bosses or managers but many leaders. One example of unmanagement takes place during salary reviews. Each associate's (employee's) salary is periodically reviewed by a compensation team drawn from individuals at the associate's work site. Each associate has a sponsor who acts as his or her advocate during the reviews. The sponsor gathers data about the associate's performance by speaking to internal and external customers.

Leadership Skill-Building Exercise 7–1 gives you an opportunity to assess your readiness to be an empowering leader. The quiz is based on attitudes, behaviors, and skills characteristics of empowering managers.

FACTORS THAT CONTRIBUTE TO POLITICAL BEHAVIOR

People want power for many different reasons, which is why political behavior is so widespread in organizations. By definition, politics is used to acquire power. A number of individual and organizational factors contribute to political behavior, as outlined in Table 7–2.

Pyramid-Shaped Organization Structure

Organizations have been described as political structures that operate by distributing authority and setting the stage for the exercise of power.[14] The very shape of large organizations is the most fundamental reason why organizational members are motivated toward political behavior. A pyramid concentrates power at the top. Only so much power is therefore available to distribute among the many people who would like more of it. Each successive

TABLE 7–2 Factors Contributing to Political Behavior in Organizations

1. Pyramid-shaped organization structure
2. Subjective standards of performance
3. Environmental uncertainty and turbulence
4. Emotional insecurity
5. Machiavellian tendencies
6. Disagreements that prevent rational decision making

LEADERSHIP SKILL-BUILDING EXERCISE 7–1   Becoming an Empowering Manager

Directions: To empower employees successfully, the leader has to convey appropriate attitudes and develop effective interpersonal skills. To the best of your ability, indicate which skills and attitudes you now have, and which ones require further development.

Empowering Attitude or Behavior	*Can Do Now*	*Would Need to Develop*
1. Believe in team members' ability to be successful	____	____
2. Have patience with people and give them time to learn	____	____
3. Provide team members with direction and structure	____	____
4. Teach team members new skills in small, incremental steps so they can easily learn those skills	____	____
5. Ask team members questions that challenge them to think in new ways	____	____
6. Share information with team members, sometimes just to build rapport	____	____
7. Give team members timely feedback and encourage them throughout the learning process	____	____
8. Offer team members alternative ways of doing things	____	____
9. Exhibit a sense of humor and demonstrate care for workers as people	____	____
10. Focus on team members' results and acknowledge their personal improvement	____	____

layer on the organization chart has less power than does the layer above. At the very bottom of the organization, workers have virtually no power.

In one study, every member of the top management team in eight microcomputer firms was asked about decision making and politics. The finding suggested that a pyramid-shaped structure fosters politics. According to the study, politics arises from power centralization (the consequence of a pyramid). Furthermore, autocratic executives (those who prefer to centralize power) engage in politics and generate political behavior among their team members.[15]

A pyramid-shaped organization creates competition for the limited resource of high-level positions. Competition for other limited resources also breeds political behavior. As Gregory Moorhead and Ricky W. Griffin note, whenever resources are scarce, some people will fail to attain what they want or deserve. Consequently, they may behave politically as a means of inflating their share of resources.[16]

Recognizing that budgets were tight, a director of training predicted dire consequences if her request for funding a training program were denied. She told top management, "If we are not fully funded, the board of directors will be very unhappy. We will not be able to make the quality improvements the board wants."

Subjective Standards of Performance

People often resort to organizational politics because they do not believe that the organization has an objective and fair way of judging their performance and suitability for promotion. Similarly, when managers have no objective way of differentiating effective people from the less effective, they will resort to favoritism. The adage "It's not what you know but who you know" applies to organizations that lack clear-cut standards of performance.

Environmental Uncertainty and Turbulence

When people, or the organizational subunits they represent, operate in an unstable and unpredictable environment, they tend to behave politically. They rely on organizational politics to create a favorable impression because uncertainty makes it difficult to determine what they should really be accomplishing.

The uncertainty, turbulence, and insecurity created by corporate downsizings is a major contributor to office politics. Many people believe intuitively that favoritism plays a major role in deciding who will survive the downsizing. In response to this perception, organizational members attempt to ingratiate themselves with influential people.

Emotional Insecurity

Some people resort to political maneuvers to ingratiate themselves with superiors because they lack confidence in their talents and skills. As an extreme example, a pension fund manager who had directed the firm toward investments with an annualized 35 percent return does not have to be overly political because of confidence in his or her capabilities. A person's choice of political strategy may indicate emotional insecurity. For instance, an insecure person might laugh loudly at every humorous comment the boss makes.

Machiavellian Tendencies

Some people engage in political behavior because they want to manipulate others, sometimes for their own personal advantage. The term *Machiavellianism* traces back to Niccolo Machiavelli (1469–1527), an Italian political philosopher and statesman. His most famous work, *The Prince*, describes how a leader may acquire and maintain power. Machiavelli's ideal prince was an amoral, manipulating tyrant who was able to unify Italy.

Research conducted by Gerald Biberman provided the evidence for the relationship between Machiavellianism and political behavior. He found a high correlation between scores on a test of Machiavellian attitudes and an organizational politics scale.[17] An updated version of this scale is presented in Leadership Self-Assessment Exercise 7–2. Recent research also demonstrates that people with a strong disposition to dominate other people are more likely to seek power and feel powerful in an organizational setting. Marshall Schminke used a computer-based experimental job simulation to study the effects of a need for dominance on perceived power. Structural characteristics of the job were held constant, and the success or failure of individuals on job performance was varied. People with a high need to dominate perceived themselves to be more powerful independent of their job success.[18]

LEADERSHIP SELF-ASSESSMENT EXERCISE 7–2   The Organizational Politics Questionnaire

Directions: Answer each question "mostly agree" or "mostly disagree," even if it is difficult for you to decide which alternative best describes your opinion.

	Mostly Agree	Mostly Disagree
1. The boss is always right.	____	____
2. It is wise to flatter important people.	____	____
3. If you do somebody a favor, remember to cash in on it.	____	____
4. Given the opportunity, I would cultivate friendships with powerful people.	____	____

5. I would be willing to say nice things about a rival in order to get that person transferred from my department. ___ ___

6. If it would help me get ahead, I would take credit for someone else's work. ___ ___

7. Given the chance, I would offer to help my boss build some shelves for his or her den. ___ ___

8. I laugh heartily at my boss's jokes, even if I do not think they are funny. ___ ___

9. Dressing for success is silly. Wear clothing to work that you find to be the most comfortable. ___ ___

10. Never waste lunch time by having lunch with somebody who can't help you solve a problem or gain advantage. ___ ___

11. I think using memos to zap somebody for his or her mistakes is a good idea (especially if you want to show that person up). ___ ___

12. If somebody higher up in the organization offends you, let that person know about it. ___ ___

13. Honesty is the best policy in practically all cases. ___ ___

14. Power for its own sake is one of life's most precious commodities. ___ ___

15. If I had a legitimate gripe against my employer, I would air my views publicly (such as writing a letter to the editor of a local newspaper). ___ ___

16. I would invite my boss to a party at my home, even if I didn't like him or her. ___ ___

17. An effective way to impress people is to tell them what they want to hear. ___ ___

18. Having a high school or skyscraper named after me would be an incredible thrill. ___ ___

19. Hard work and good performance are usually sufficient for career success. ___ ___

20. Even if I made only a minor contribution to a project, I would get my name listed as being associated with that project. ___ ___

21. I would never publicly correct mistakes
    made by the boss. —— ——

22. I would never use my personal contacts in
    order to gain a promotion. —— ——

23. If you happen to dislike a person who
    receives a big promotion in your firm,
    don't bother sending that person a
    congratulatory note. —— ——

24. I would never openly criticize a powerful
    executive in my organization. —— ——

25. I would stay in the office late just to
    impress my boss. —— ——

Scoring and Interpretation: Give yourself a plus one for each answer
that agrees with the keyed answer. Each question that receives a score of
plus one shows a tendency toward playing organizational politics. The
scoring key is as follows:

1. Mostly agree	10. Mostly agree	18. Mostly agree
2. Mostly agree	11. Mostly agree	19. Mostly disagree
3. Mostly agree	12. Mostly disagree	20. Mostly agree
4. Mostly agree	13. Mostly disagree	21. Mostly agree
5. Mostly agree	14. Mostly agree	22. Mostly disagree
6. Mostly agree	15. Mostly disagree	23. Mostly disagree
7. Mostly agree	16. Mostly agree	24. Mostly agree
8. Mostly agree	17. Mostly agree	25. Mostly agree
9. Mostly disagree		

Based on a sample of 750 men and women managers, professionals, administrators, sales representatives, and business owners,* the mean score is 10.

1–7:	below-average tendency to play office politics
8–12:	average tendency to play office politics
13 and above:	above-average tendency to play office politics; strong need for power.

---

*Andrew J. DuBrin, "Career Maturity, Organizational Rank, and Political Behavior Tendencies: A Correlational Analysis of Organizational Politics and Career Experience," *Psychological Reports,* Vol. 63, 1988, pp. 531–537; DuBrin, "Sex Differences in Endorsement of Influence Tactics and Political Behavior Tendencies," *Journal of Business and Psychology,* Fall 1989, pp. 3–14.

Disagreement over Major Issues

Many executives attempt to use rational criteria when making major decisions, but rational decision making is constrained by major disagreements over employees' preferences and theories of what the organization should be doing. Unless strategy and goals are shared among key organizational members, political motivation is inevitable in organizational decision making. Jeffrey Pfeffer analyzes this contributor to organizational politics in this manner:

> In some ways the relative weighting of the various demands and criteria must be determined. Since there is no way of rationalizing away the dissensus, political strength within the coalition comes to determine which criteria and whose preferences are to prevail.[19]

An example of disagreement over major issues leading to political behavior took place at a savings bank. Substantial inner turmoil occurred because of power struggles between the consumer loans and home mortgage departments. Both departments saw themselves as the most important future thrust of the bank. Representatives of both groups often diverted marketing and customer service efforts while they waged their internal power struggles.

POLITICAL TACTICS AND STRATEGIES

To make effective use of organizational politics, leaders must be aware of specific political tactics and strategies. To identify and explain the majority of political tactics would require years of study and observation. Leaders so frequently need support for their programs that they search for innovative types of political behaviors. Furthermore, new tactics continue to emerge as the workplace becomes increasingly competitive. Let's look at a representative group of political tactics and strategies, categorized as to whether they are ethical or unethical. (Several of the influence tactics described in Chapter 8, such as ingratiation, might also be considered political behaviors.)

Ethical Political Tactics and Strategies

So far we have discussed organizational politics without pinpointing specific tactics and strategies. This section describes a sampling of ethical political behaviors divided into three related groups: tactics and strategies aimed directly at (1) gaining power, (2) building relationships with superiors and coworkers, and (3) avoiding political blunders. All of these approaches help the leader gain or retain power. They also help the leader cope with the fact that organizations are not entirely rational. In the words of Gerald R. Ferris and Thomas R. King, "Politics is what takes place between the perfect workings of the rational model (efficiency) and the messiness of human interaction. The greater the gap, the more political behavior becomes necessary."[20]

Strategies and Tactics Aimed Directly at Gaining Power. All political tactics are aimed at acquiring and maintaining power, even the power to avoid a difficult assignment. Here are six techniques aimed directly at gaining power.

1. *Develop power contacts.* After powerful people have been identified, alliances with them must be established. Cultivating friendly, cooperative relationships with powerful organizational members and outsiders can make the leader's cause much easier to advance. These contacts can benefit a person by supporting his or her ideas in meetings and other public forums. One way to develop these contacts is to be more social, for example, throwing parties and inviting powerful people and their guests. Some organizations and some bosses frown on social familiarity, however. And power-holders receive many invitations, so they might not be available.

2. *Control vital information.* Power accrues to those who control vital information, as indicated in the discussion of personal power. Many former government or military officials have found power niches for themselves in industry after leaving the public payroll. Frequently such individuals are hired as the Washington representative of a firm that does business with the government. The vital information they control is knowledge of whom to contact to shorten some of the complicated procedures in getting government contracts approved. The Clinton administration has attempted to decrease this blatant use of vital information by establishing a lag time between departure from a government post and assumption of certain types of jobs.

3. *Keep informed.* In addition to controlling vital information, it is politically important to keep informed. Management consultant Eugene Schmuckler writes that we are all aware of the significance of having our name removed from a memo distribution list. Even if the information is not accurate, being able to tap into the corporate grapevine is power-enhancing. Successful leaders develop a pipeline to help them keep abreast, or ahead, of developments within the firm. For this reason, a politically astute individual befriends the president's assistant. No other source offers the potential of information as does the executive administrative assistant.[21]

4. *Control lines of communication.* Related to controlling information is controlling lines of communication, particularly access to key people. Administrative assistants and staff assistants frequently control an executive's calendar. Both insiders and outsiders must curry favor with the *conduit* in order to see the important executive. The administrative assistant can also control how quickly the executive responds to telephone and fax messages.

5. *Bring in outside experts.* To help legitimate their positions, executives will often hire a consultant to conduct a study or cast an opinion. Consciously or unconsciously, many consultants are hesitant to "bite the hand that feeds them." A consultant will therefore often support the executive's position. In turn, the executive will use the consultant's findings to prove that he or she is right. This tactic might be considered ethical because the executive believes he or she is obtaining an objective opinion.

6. *Make a quick showing.* A display of dramatic results can help gain acceptance for one's efforts or those of the group.[22] Once a person has impressed management with his or her ability to solve that first problem, that person can look forward to working on problems that will bring greater power. For instance, the manager of a systems analysis group volunteered to take on a mundane assignment of reducing paperwork in the accounts payable department. Within two weeks, paperwork was reduced 75 percent through electronic information storage and retrieval. The group next received a series of plum assignments without having to volunteer.

Strategies and Tactics Aimed at Building Relationships.   Much of organizational politics involves building positive relationships with network members who can be helpful now or later. This network includes superiors, subordinates, other lower-ranking people, coworkers, external customers, and suppliers. The following are several representative strategies and tactics:[23]

1. *Display loyalty.* A loyal worker is valued because organizations prosper more with loyal than with disloyal employees. Blind loyalty—the belief that the organization cannot make a mistake—is not called for; most rational organizations welcome constructive criticism. An obvious form of loyalty to the organization is longevity. The average chief executive of the nation's largest firms has spent 22.5 years with the firm. In some companies, 90 percent of the senior staff is promoted from within.[24]

2. *Manage the impression you make.* Impression management includes behaviors directed at enhancing one's image by drawing attention to oneself. Often the attention of others is directed toward superficial aspects of the self, such as clothing and appearance. Impression management also includes telling people about your success or implying that you are an "insider." Displaying good manners and business etiquette has received renewed attention as a key part of impression management.

3. *Ask satisfied customers to contact your boss.* A favorable comment by a customer receives considerable weight because customer satisfaction is a top corporate priority. If a customer says something nice, the comment will carry more weight than one from a coworker or subordinate. The reason is that coworkers and subordinates might praise a person for political reasons. Customers' motivation is assumed to be pure because they have little concern about pleasing suppliers.

4. *Be courteous, pleasant, and positive.* According to employment specialist Robert Half, courteous, pleasant, and positive people are the first to be hired and the last to be fired (assuming they are also technically qualified).[25]

5. *Ask advice.* Asking advice on work-related topics builds relationships with other employees. Asking another person for advice—someone whose job does not require giving it—will usually be perceived as a compliment. Asking advice transmits a message of trust in the other person's judgment. The accompanying Leader in Action insert illustrates the effective use of asking advice.

LEADER
IN
ACTION

Felicia Anderson, Bank Manager and Input Seeker

Felicia Anderson was brought in from another bank to be the manager of small business loans for a bank in Indianapolis. The three previous incumbents had lasted fewer than two years. Each was transferred to another position because of poor investment decisions. Because the bank executives thought poorly of the performance of the small business loan department, morale was low and turnover was high.

Anderson recognized she was moving into a sensitive situation. Her mandate was to improve performance of the unit as quickly as possible without creating any additional morale problems. She wanted to implement certain changes, but she decided to move slowly. She scheduled full-hour interviews with all seventeen members of the department. During these meetings, Anderson expressed considerable interest in learning about each worker's job responsibilities. Furthermore, she asked each person how the unit could make better loans and how morale could be improved.

Anderson took four of the best suggestions offered by the group and added several of her own. Immediate support was found for these new procedures. As the suggestions for improvement proved to be effective, top management at the bank was willing to give the department more resources. One of Anderson's suggestions for improving the performance of loans was to actively solicit loans to small businesses with good track records. A bank representative called on these firms and offered to lend them money for expansion. In the past, the bank had relied heavily on startup firms seeking funds to open a business.

Avoiding Political Blunders.   A strategy for retaining power is to refrain from making power-eroding blunders. Committing these politically insensitive acts can also prevent one from attaining power. Several leading blunders are described next.

1. *Criticizing the boss in a public forum.* The oldest saw in human relations is to "praise in public and criticize in private." Yet in the passion of the moment, we may still surrender to an irresistible impulse to criticize the boss publicly. In the early days of President Bill Clinton's administration, Senator Richard Shelby (D-Ala.) crossed Clinton publicly by criticizing his economic plan. Clinton promptly yanked federal money from a Huntsville, Alabama project.

2. *Bypassing the boss.* Protocol is still highly valued in a hierarchical organization. Going around the boss to resolve a problem is therefore hazardous. You

might be able to accomplish the bypass but your career could be damaged and your recourses limited. Courts upheld an oil company's dismissal of a manager because the manager had repeatedly ignored the chain of command. The manager would go over his superior's head, directly to the president.[26]

3. *Declining an offer from top management.* Turning down top management, especially more than once, is a political blunder. You thus have to balance sensibly managing your time against the blunder of refusing a request from top management. An increasing number of managers and professionals today decline promotional opportunities when the new job requires geographic relocation. For these people, family and lifestyle preferences are more important than gaining political advantage on the job.

4. *Burning your bridges.* A potent political blunder is to create ill will among former employers or people who have helped you in the past. The most common type of bridge burning occurs when a person departs from an organization. A person who leaves involuntarily is especially apt to express anger toward those responsible for the dismissal. Venting your anger may give a temporary boost to your mental health, but it can be detrimental in the long run.

Unethical Political Tactics and Strategies

Any technique of gaining power can be devious if practiced in the extreme. A person who supports a boss by feeding him or her insider information that could affect the price of company stock is being devious. Some approaches are unequivocally unethical, such as those described next. In the long range they erode a leader's effectiveness by lowering his or her credibility. Devious tactics might even result in lawsuits against the leader, the organization, or both.

Back Stabbing.   The ubiquitous back stab requires that you pretend to be nice, but all the while plan someone's demise. A frequent form of back stabbing is to initiate a conversation with a rival about the weaknesses of a common boss, encouraging negative commentary and making careful mental notes of what the person says. When these comments are passed along to the boss, the rival appears disloyal and foolish.

Embrace-or-Demolish.   The ancient strategy of "embrace or demolish" suggests that you remove from the premises rivals who suffered past hurts through your efforts; otherwise the wounded rivals might retaliate at a vulnerable moment. This kind of strategy is common after a hostile takeover; many executives lose their jobs because they opposed the takeover.

Setting a Person Up for Failure.   The object of a setup is to place a person in a position where he or she will either fail outright or look ineffective. For example, an executive whom the CEO dislikes might be given responsibility for a troubled division whose market is rapidly collapsing. The newly assigned division president cannot stop the decline and is then fired for poor performance.

Divide and Rule.   An ancient military and governmental strategy, this tactic is sometimes used in business. The object is to have subordinates fight among themselves, therefore yielding the balance of power to another person. If team members are not aligned with each other, there is an improved chance that they will align with a common superior. One way of getting subordinates to fight with each other is to place them in intense competition for resources—for example, asking them to prove why their budget is more worthy than the budget requested by rivals.

EXERCISING CONTROL OVER DYSFUNCTIONAL POLITICS

Carried to excess, organizational politics can hurt an organization and its members. Too much politicking can result in wasted time and effort, thereby lowering productivity. For example, a highly political environment was said to contribute to IBM's decline under the leadership of former CEO John Akers. It was politically unwise for top executives to suggest that the company deemphasize mainframe computers. (The market had shifted away from mainframes and toward smaller computers.) The human consequences of excessive politics can also be substantial; examples are lowered morale and the loss of people who intensely dislike office politics. Leaders are therefore advised to combat political behavior when it is excessive and dysfunctional.

In a comprehensive strategy to control politics, organizational leaders must be aware of its causes and techniques. For example, during a downsizing the CEO can be on the alert for instances of back stabbing and transparent attempts to please him or her. Open communications also can constrain the impact of political behavior.[27] For instance, open communication can let everyone know the basis for allocating resources, thus reducing the amount of politicking.

Setting good examples at the top of the organization can help reduce the frequency and intensity of organizational politics. When leaders are nonpolitical in their actions, they demonstrate in subtle ways that political behavior is not welcome. It may be helpful for the leader to announce during a staff meeting that devious political behavior is undesirable and unprofessional.

Finally, politics can sometimes be constrained by a threat to discuss questionable information in a public forum. People who practice devious politics usually want to operate secretly and privately. They are willing to drop hints and innuendoes and make direct derogatory comments about someone else, provided they will not be identified as the source. An effective way of stopping the discrediting of others is to offer to discuss the topic publicly.[28] The person attempting to pass on the questionable information will usually back down and make a statement closer to the truth.

SUMMARY

To acquire and retain power, a leader must skillfully use organizational politics—informal approaches to gaining power through means other than merit or luck. Organizational power is derived from many sources, including position power (legitimate, reward, coercive, and information) and personal power (expert, reference, and prestige). Power also stems from ownership, providing resources, capitalizing upon opportunity, and being close to power.

Leaders intent on increasing their power are advised to develop a plan. Such a plan includes setting a goal, measuring the cost-effectiveness of politicking, conducting a power analysis of powerful people, and analyzing what type of politics is played at the top. Certain actions can be taken to become an empowering leader. These include providing a positive emotional atmosphere, giving visible rewards, expressing confidence, fostering initiative and responsibility, building on success, and practicing SuperLeadership.

The quest for power causes political behavior. Specific contributing factors include the pyramidal shape of organizations, competition for limited resources, subjective performance standards, and environmental uncertainty. Emotional insecurity and Machiavellianism also contribute to political behavior.

To make effective use of organizational politics, leaders must be aware of specific political tactics and strategies. Ethical methods can be divided into those aimed directly at gaining power, building relationships, and avoiding political blunders. Unethical and devious tactics, such as the embrace-or-demolish strategy, constitute another category of political behavior.

Carried to an extreme, organizational politics can hurt an organization and its members. Being aware of the causes and types of political behavior can help leaders deal with the problem. Setting good examples of nonpolitical behavior is helpful, as is threatening to publicly expose devious politicking.

KEY TERMS

Organizational politics
Legitimate power
Reward power
Coercive power
Information power
Personal power

Prestige power
Leadership power
Resource dependence perspective
Strategic contingency theory
Centrality

GUIDELINES FOR ACTION AND SKILL DEVELOPMENT

The information presented throughout this chapter can be used by leaders to acquire and maintain power for the purpose of influencing people. Gary A. Yukl has prepared suggestions for using five standard power sources to gain commitment. An adaptation and abridgement of these suggestions is as follows:

1. Referent power will likely lead to commitment if the request is believed to be important to the leader. The leader must therefore enthusiastically convey the importance of the request.

2. Expert power will likely lead to commitment if the request is persuasive and group members share the leader's task goals. The leader is therefore advised to be persuasive and hold a group discussion about the relevance of task goals.

3. Legitimate power will possibly lead to commitment if the request is polite and very appropriate. The leader should therefore be mannerly and explain the appropriateness of the request.

4. Reward power possibly leads to commitment if rewards are used in a subtle, very personal way. The leader must therefore avoid the appearance of offering bribes.

5. Coercive power is very unlikely to lead to commitment, so another type of power should be used.[29]

DISCUSSION QUESTIONS AND ACTIVITIES

1. In what way might a highly ethical leader also be highly political?

2. Why is a knowledge of organizational politics particularly important when jobs are scarce?

3. How might you be able to acquire information power?

4. Empowerment has been criticized because it leaves no one in particular accountable for results. What is your opinion of this criticism?

5. How can you "build on success" in your own career?

6. To what extent do you think flat organization structures reduce the incidence of organizational politics?

7. Assume a leader received the maximum score of 25 on the organizational politics questionnaire. How would this affect his or her ability to lead?

8. Should a leader ask a group member's advice even if the leader already has made up his or her mind on the issue?

9. Of the various antidotes for dysfunctional politics described in this chapter, which one do you think is the most effective?

10. Read a current report about an organizational leader, and identify at least one political tactic he or she has used.

LEADERSHIP CASE PROBLEM

The Computerization Power Failure

Jerry Falvo was an information systems manager for a life insurance and financial services company. The firm planned to computerize all its operating systems. Such a sweeping change meant that 40 percent of the work force would have to learn new skills. Jerry thought that a program to help all employees become computer literate would be beneficial because they would become more versatile. He therefore developed a curriculum, gathered materials, and performed a cost-benefit analysis. He also surveyed 200 employees on their computer knowledge.

Armed with convincing information, Jerry secured approval from his boss to establish a training program. He then went to the director of corporate training to discuss obtaining instructors. Jerry was taken aback when the director said that her group was already aware of the need for expanded training. The director also said that the training department had already upgraded the course content of its computer literacy program.

After reviewing the training director's program, Jerry concluded that it was of low quality. After listening to Jerry's analysis, his boss ordered the training department to cooperate. The director agreed, as long as a pilot program proved Jerry's program to be worthwhile. Jerry enlisted the cooperation of a manager to volunteer his people for the pilot program. Only six out of a possible twenty-three showed up for the first class.

With such a poor turnout, Jerry's boss ordered the program terminated. He also gave Jerry a poor performance evaluation for having spent so much time on a failed effort.

1. What political mistakes did Jerry make?

2. How might Jerry have improved his program's chances of success?

3. What political behavior does it appear the training director used to hamper Jerry's program?

_____

Source: Based on information in William H. Fonvielle, *From Manager to Innovator: Using Information to Become an Idea Entrepreneur* (Trevose, Pa: Administrative Management Society Foundation, 1991).

LEADERSHIP EXERCISE

Classroom Politics

Gather in groups of about five students. Each group's task is to identify student political behaviors you have observed in this or other classes. Label the tactics you have observed, and indicate what you think the political actor hoped to achieve by the tactic. Also attempt to indicate what the political behavior achieved. Finally, summarize the leadership implications of what you have observed. If time permits, each team appoints a leader who presents the team's findings to the rest of the class.

Influence Tactics of Leaders

LEARNING OBJECTIVES

After studying this chapter, you should be able to

1. describe the relationship between power and influence.
2. identify a set of honest and ethical influence tactics.
3. identify a set of less honest and ethical influence tactics.
4. summarize some empirical research about the effectiveness of influence tactics.

Maria Chavez, a materials handling manager, was asked how her company came to be on Ford Motor Co.'s preferred supplier list. She explained, "The answer is simple. Joe Riordan was appointed the new manager of quality assurance. He convinced us that we could all do better in dozens of ways; that we had the potential to become a world-class supplier to top-quality firms. We were skeptical at first, but we accepted the challenge. Joe has been a great influence on us."

Joe Riordan fulfilled a leader's quintessential responsibility—he influenced group members to achieve a worthwhile goal. Leadership, as oft repeated, is an influence process. To become an effective leader, a person must therefore be aware of the specific tactics leaders use to influence others. Here we discuss a number of specific influence tactics, but other aspects of leadership also concern influence. Being charismatic, as described in Chapter 3, influences many people. Leaders influence others through power and politics, as described in Chapter 7. Furthermore, motivating and coaching skills, as described in Chapter 10, involve influencing others toward worthwhile ends.

The terms *influence* and *power* have understandable, everyday meanings yet present complexities to the scholar. The two terms are sometimes used interchangeably, whereas at other times power is said to create influence and vice versa. In this book, let's distinguish between power and influence as follows: **influence** is the ability to affect the behavior of others in a partic-ular direction,[1] whereas **power** is the potential or capacity to influence. Keep in mind, however, that recognizing power as the ability to influence others will not interfere with learning how to use influence tactics.

Leaders are influential only when they exercise power. A leader there-fore must acquire power to influence others. Assume that a worker is the informal leader among a group of quality technicians. The worker exerts a modicum of influence because of his talent, charm, and wit. Move the per-son into the position of vice president of quality assurance (more formal authority), and his or her influence will multiply.

This chapter presents some underlying theories, a description and explanation of influence tactics (both ethical and less ethical), and a sum-mary of research about the relative effectiveness of influence tactics.

A MODEL OF POWER AND INFLUENCE

The model shown in Figure 8–1 helps clarify the relationship between power and influence.[2] According to the model, possessing power alone is not sufficient for exercising influence. To exercise power, the leader must also use a variety of influence tactics. Among them might be rational per-suasion, bargaining, and the promise of exchanging favors. By using influ-ence tactics, the leader achieves certain outcomes, such as commitment to carry out the task. Nevertheless, using influence tactics does not guarantee the outcomes the leader intended. Instead, the outcomes are moderated (affected or shaped) by the leader's power and skills.

According to Gary Yukl, the success of an influence attempt can be defined by three anchor points on a continuum: commitment, compliance, and resistance. **Commitment** indicates the highest degree of success: the tar-get of the influence attempt is enthusiastic about carrying out the request and makes a full effort. An example would be a person who responded to the manager, "Yes, I will do everything in my power to achieve zero defects." **Compliance** means that the influence attempt is partially success-ful: the target person is apathetic (not overjoyed) about carrying out the request and makes only a modest effort. **Resistance** is an unsuccessful influ-ence attempt: the target is opposed to carrying out the request and finds ways either not to comply or to do a poor job.

The leader's power in this model stems generally from the person or from the position. Personal power includes charisma and expertise, whereas

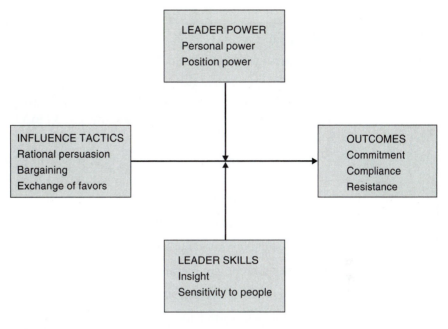

FIGURE 8–1

A Model of Power and Influence

Source: Gary Yukl, *Skills for Managers and Leaders: Text, Cases, and Exercises,* © 1990, p. 59. Reprinted by permission of Prentice-Hall, Englewood Cliffs, New Jersey.

position power can include formal authority and control over rewards and punishments. (Power is a major topic of the previous chapter.)

Leader skills enable the leader to implement the influence attempt successfully. For example, if the leader has good insight into people, he or she will choose an influence tactic appropriate to the situation. Many of the traits and behaviors described in Chapters 2 and 4 are directly related to leader skills. Among them are assertiveness, warmth, sensitivity to others, the ability to inspire others, and the ability to satisfy human needs.

Skills and power jointly moderate the effects of an influence attempt. For example, having expert power (or talent) and good insight into people (trait and skill) would combine to facilitate the success of an influence attempt.

The influence tactics shown in Figure 8–1 are the primary subject of this chapter. If a leader's primary role is to influence others, he or she needs effective influence tactics at his or her disposal. Leaders sometimes fail to achieve their objectives because they use too few influence tactics. For example, some leaders are unable or unwilling to use joking, kidding, and humor in general to influence others. Another problem is that they may be unaware that humor can be an effective influence tactic. Leadership Self-Assessment Exercise 8–1 gives you an opportunity to think about which influence tactics you use.

LEADERSHIP _____
SELF-ASSESSMENT
EXERCISE 8–1   Survey of Influence Tactics

Directions: Indicate how frequently you use the influence tactics listed below. VI = very infrequently or never; I = infrequently; S = sometimes; F = frequently; VP = very frequently. The VI to VF categories correspond to a 1-to-5 scale.

	1 VI	2 I	3 S	4 F	5 VF
1. I am a team player.	__	__	__	__	__
2. I am personally charming.	__	__	__	__	__
3. I make a good personal appearance.	__	__	__	__	__
4. I manipulate the situation.	__	__	__	__	__
5. I manipulate people.	__	__	__	__	__
6. I am assertive (open and forthright in my demands).	__	__	__	__	__
7. I joke with or kid other people.	__	__	__	__	__
8. I exchange favors with the other person.	__	__	__	__	__
9. I promise to reward the person.	__	__	__	__	__
10. I threaten to punish the person.	__	__	__	__	__
11. I get the other person to like me.	__	__	__	__	__
12. I make an appeal to logic or reason.	__	__	__	__	__
13. I form an alliance with the other person.	__	__	__	__	__
14. I threaten to go over the person's head to the boss.	__	__	__	__	__
15. I compliment the other person.	__	__	__	__	__
16. I offer to compromise with the other person.	__	__	__	__	__

Interpretation: The more of the above tactics you use frequently or very frequently, the more influential you probably are. You might also want to compare your scores to normative data. Listed below are the mean scores on each tactic for a group of 523 working adults (292 men and 231 women). The sample was composed of mostly managers and professionals. You will recall that the scale runs from 1 for *very infrequently* to 5 for *very frequently.*

Influence Tactic	Men	Women
1. Team play	4.1	4.2
2. Charm	3.3	3.5
3. Appearance	3.3	3.5
4. Manipulation of situation	3.1	2.7*
5. Manipulation of person	2.6	2.3*
6. Assertiveness	3.9	3.9
7. Joking or kidding	3.7	3.5
8. Exchange of favors	2.9	3.0
9. Promise of reward	2.5	2.2*
10. Threat of punishment	1.8	1.5*
11. Ingratiation	3.2	3.2
12. Logic or reason	4.3	4.1*
13. Alliances	3.3	3.5
14. Threat of appeal	1.5	1.6
15. Compliments	3.6	3.5
16. Compromise	3.4	3.5

Suggestions for skill development: In comparing your profile to the norms, it could be apparent that you are neglecting to use, or are overusing, one or more influence tactics. For example, being a team player is used "frequently" by men and women. If you are not using team play to influence others, you could be at a competitive disadvantage. Observe also that both men and women make "very infrequent" use of threats of appeal. If you are making threats of appeal very frequently, you could be perceived as using an unacceptable influence tactic.

---

*Differences between the means is significant at or beyond the 1 percent level of significance.
Source: Andrew J. DuBrin, "Sex and Gender Differences in Tactics of Influence," *Psychological Reports,* Vol. 68, 1991, pp. 635–646.

DESCRIPTION AND EXPLANATION OF INFLUENCE TACTICS

Influence tactics are often viewed from an ethical perspective. Following this perspective, the influence tactics described here are classified into those that are essentially ethical and honest versus those that are essentially manipulative and dishonest. (The tactics described in this chapter include, but extend beyond, those listed in Self-Assessment Exercise 8–1.)

Several guidelines, or ethical screens, have been developed to help the influence agent decide whether a given act is ethical or unethical. The center for Business Ethics at Bentley College has developed six questions to evaluate the ethics of a specific decision. Before engaging in a particular influence act or political tactic, a person should seek answers to the following questions:

- *Is it right?* (based on absolute principles of moral rights)
- *Is it fair?* (based on absolute principles of justice)
- *Who gets hurt?* (the fewer the better)
- *Would you be comfortable if the details of your decision or actions were made public in the media or through electronic mail?* (based on the principle of disclosure)
- *What would you tell your child, sibling, or young relative to do?* (based on the principle of reversibility)
- *How does it smell?* (based on common sense and intuition)[3]

The categorization of the influence tactics presented here is far from absolute. Except for the extremes, most of the tactics could conceivably be placed in either category, depending on how they are used. For example, the tactic "joking and kidding" can be either good-spirited or mean-spirited. Joking and kidding could therefore be classified as "essentially ethical" or "essentially manipulative."

Essentially Ethical and Honest Tactics

This section describes essentially ethical and honest tactics and strategies for influencing others, outlined in Table 8–1. Used with tact, diplomacy and good intent, these strategies can facilitate getting others to join you in accomplishing a worthwhile objective. Because these influence tactics vary in complexity, they also vary with respect to how much time is required to develop them.

Leading by Example.   A simple but effective way of influencing group members is **leading by example,** or leading by acting as a positive role model. The ideal approach to leading by example is to be a "do as I say and do" manager—that is, one whose actions and words are consistent. Also, actions and words confirm, support, and often clarify each other. For example, if the firm has a dress code and the manager explains the code and dresses accordingly, he or she provides a role model that is consistent in words and actions. The action of following the dress code provides an example that supports and clarifies the words used in the dress code.[4]

Rational Persuasion.   The traditional way of influencing people through rational persuasion is still an important tactic. Rational persuasion involves using logical arguments and factual evidence to convince another person

TABLE 8–1 Essentially Ethical and Honest Influence Tactics

1. Leading by example

2. Rational persuasion

3. Developing a reputation as a subject matter expert (SME)

4. Exchanging favors and bargaining

5. Developing a network of resource persons

6. Legitimating a request

7. Inspirational appeal and emotional display

8. Consultation

9. Forming coalitions

10. Team play

that a proposal or request is workable and likely to result in goal attainment.[5] Assertiveness combined with careful research is necessary to make rational persuasion an effective tactic. It is likely to be most effective with people who are intelligent and rational. Chief executive officers typically use rational persuasion to convince their boards that an undertaking, such as product diversification, is mandatory.

Developing a Reputation as a Subject Matter Expert. Becoming a subject matter expert (SME) on a topic of importance to the organization is an effective strategy for gaining influence. Being an SME can be considered a subset of rational persuasion. A series of interviews conducted by Bernard Keys and Thomas Case support this observation. Managers who possess expert knowledge in a relevant field and who continually build on that knowledge can get others to help them get work accomplished.[6]

Exchanging Favors and Bargaining. Offering to exchange favors if another person will help you achieve a work goal is another standard influence tactic. By making an exchange, you strike a bargain with the other party. The exchange often translates into being willing to reciprocate at a later date. The exchange might also be promising a share of the benefits if the other person helps you accomplish a task. For example, you might promise to place a person's name on a report to top management if that person helps analyze the data and prepare the tables.

Another perspective on exchange and bargaining is that you are building a favor bank. In other words, you do favors for people today with the expectation that you can make a withdrawal from the favor bank when needed. A human resources manager took the initiative to help a colleague in another company recruit a physically disabled compensation analyst.

Several months later the same human resources professional called on the colleague to nominate her for office in their professional society.

Robert Dilenschneider, the CEO of the worldwide public relations firm of Hill and Knowlton, describes how middle managers can build favor banks: "At any level, it's a matter of knowing who needs you and whom you need. You should build good will. If you are a middle manager, look around you. You interact with a money specialist, with a lawyer, with a variety of operations people. Use them and let them use you."[7]

Developing a Network of Resource Persons.   Networking is an important strategy for career management, including becoming an influential person. The ability to establish a network and call on support when needed helps a manager or professional exert influence. A branch bank manager used his network of resource persons when he needed additional space for his operation. He felt that part of providing the right leadership was to expand the operation physically.

> My strategy was to convince my immediate superior that the current facilities were too small to not only manage the current volume of business, but too small to allow us to increase our market share in a rapidly growing area. First, I persuaded my manager to visit the branch more often, especially when the branch was very busy. I also solicited my accountant's help to provide statistical reports on a regular basis that communicated the amount of overall growth in the area, as well as the growth of our competitors. These reports showed that our market share had increased.
>
> I then asked my superior to visit with me as I called on several prospects in the area. This would let him know the types of potential business in the area. During this time I kept pushing to increase all levels of business at the branch.
>
> Finally, I encouraged key bank customers to say favorable things about my branch when they visited with my senior managers. Eventually my boss got behind my proposal. We were able to build an addition to the building which allowed me to add several new employees.[8]

Legitimating a Request.   To legitimate is to verify that an influence attempt is within your scope of authority. Another aspect of legitimating is to show that your request is consistent with organizational policies, practices, and expectations of professional people. Making legitimate requests is an effective influence tactic because most workers are willing to comply with regulations. A team leader can thus exert influence with a statement such as this one: "Top management wants a 25 percent reduction in customer complaints by next year. I'm therefore urging everybody to patch up any customer problem he or she can find." According to research conducted by Gary Yukl, behavior intended to establish the legitimacy of a request includes the following:

Providing evidence of prior precedent.

Showing consistency with organizational policies that are involved in the type of request being made.

Showing consistency with the duties and responsibilities of the person's position or role expectations.

Indicating that the request has been endorsed by higher management or by the person's boss.[9]

Inspirational Appeal and Emotional Display. A leader is supposed to inspire others, so it follows that making an inspirational appeal is an important influence tactic. As Jeffrey Pfeffer notes, "Executives and others seeking to exercise influence in organizations often develop skill in displaying, or not displaying, their feelings in a strategic fashion."[10] An inspirational appeal usually involves an emotional display by the leader. It also involves appealing to group members' emotions.

In 1983, the Gary Works of U.S. Steel (a division of USX) was threatened with extinction. Major customers such as General Electric, Westinghouse, and General Motors were on the verge of eliminating the Gary plant as a steel supplier. To help turn around this crisis situation, Thomas Usher, president of U.S. Steel, made an emotional appeal. He asked the steelworkers how long they were going to put up with being insulted for their shoddy quality, their high costs, and their smug attitude toward customers. Usher's emotionally charged appeal helped start a process of constructive change that brought success to the Gary Works.

For an emotional appeal to be effective, the influence agent must understand the values, motives, and goals of the influence target. The U.S. Steel executive believed that the once-proud steelworkers still had some pride. An emotional appeal will also be more effective when the leader displays emotion. Indicators of emotion include talking about feelings, raising and lowering voice tone, showing moist eyes or a few tears, and pounding a table. As described in Chapter 3, charismatic leadership relies heavily on making inspirational appeals.

Consultation. Consulting with others before making a decision is both a leadership style and an influence technique. The influence target becomes more motivated to follow the agent's request because the target is involved in the decision-making process. Yukl explains that consultation is most effective as an influence tactic when the objectives of the person being influenced are consistent with those of the leader.[11]

An example of such goal congruity took place in a major U.S. corporation. The company had decided to shrink its pool of suppliers to form closer partnerships with a smaller number of high-quality vendors. As a way of influencing others to follow this direction, a manufacturing vice president told his staff, "Our strategy is to reduce dealing with so many suppliers to improve quality and reduce costs. Let me know how we should implement this strategy." The vice president's influence attempt met with excellent reception, partially because the staff members also wanted a more streamlined set of vendor relationships.

Forming Coalitions.   At times it is difficult to influence an individual or group by acting alone. A leader will then have to form coalitions, or alliances, with others to create the necessary clout. A **coalition** is a specific arrangement of parties working together to combine their power. Coalition formation works as an influence tactic because, to quote an old adage, "there is power in numbers." Coalitions in business are a numbers game—the more people you can get on your side, the better.

The more powerful the leader, the less need exists for coalition formation. Yet there are times when even a powerful leader needs an extraordinary amount of power to accomplish a major goal. Recall that John Sculley formed the Magic Six coalition to help shape the future of telecommunications.

Team Play.   Influencing others by being a good team player is an important strategy for getting work accomplished. Refer to Leadership Self-Assessment Exercise 8–1. Observe that team play, along with logic or reason, was the influence tactic most frequently chosen by men and women. Another study of influence tactics compared frequency of use among seven influence tactics. Men and women endorsed team play more frequently than the other six tactics (personal charm, manipulation, personal appearance, assertiveness, exchange of favors, and upward appeal).[12]

Chapter 9 provides more information about teamwork, and you can apply much of this information to yourself. The tactic recommended for now is to emphasize that you are part of the team rather than a solo performer. A critical part of achieving this end is to emphasize "we" rather than "I" when talking about work accomplishments. A convenient way of emphasizing the "we" concept is to share credit with coworkers for your good suggestions and achievements. When you receive a compliment, explain that the group deserves most of the credit. This emphasis on teamwork will enhance your ability to influence others because you will be regarded as a team player.

The accompanying Leader in Action profile describes a manager who successfully uses ethical and honest influence tactics. As you read the description, attempt to identify several of her tactics.

Essentially Dishonest and Unethical Tactics

The tactics to be described in this section are less than forthright and ethical, yet they vary in intensity with respect to dishonesty. Most people would consider the first four influence strategies presented here as unethical and devious, yet they might regard the last five tactics as still within the bounds of acceptable ethics, even though less than fully candid. The tactics in question are outlined in Figure 8–2.

Deliberate Machiavellianism.   Almost 500 years ago, Niccolo Machiavelli advised that princes must be strong, ruthless, and cynical leaders because

LEADER IN ACTION

Jan Thompson, Marketing Vice President at Mazda

Jan Thompson has become the highest-ranking woman in the male-dominated business of auto sales. As the marketing vice president for the Mazda Division of Mazda Motors of America Inc., she is playing by her own rules. Whereas most automakers direct their marketing efforts at men, Thompson focuses on women. "Women are now buying by default, because nobody is reaching out to them," she says.

Part of Thompson's strategy is to appeal to buyers who consider themselves outside the mainstream and who are willing to pay more money to satisfy their tastes. Thompson has deliberately avoided the engine-racing, macho image conveyed by most U.S. auto companies. Rather, she has chosen ads that make a personal appeal, including the nostalgic ads that introduced the Miata.

After twenty years of selling cars, Thompson can sound like a grizzled veteran. Mazda dealers love her ability to speak their often colloquial language. Thompson believes that by learning the game from the inside out she can more confidently break the rules.

After years of experience at both Chrysler and Toyota, Thompson joined Mazda. She eliminated the ad campaign that referred to the vague "Mazda Way." The new theme she endorsed was "It just feels right." An auto market researcher says, "Jan Thompson has really been the visionary at Mazda."

Thompson, who received an MBA from the University of Detroit, says she has never felt out of place in her career. She gets along fine playing golf and schmoozing with men. Yet she believes strongly that carmakers were wrong to assume that a focus on women buyers would tarnish their brand image. Thompson introduced sponsorship of high-profile women's events such as the Mazda LPGA golf champions and the Mazda Tennis Classic. Then came the Mazda Golf Clinics for Executive Women. The clinics teach golf as a business networking tool and simultaneously build goodwill for Mazda among affluent women.

A stockbroker manager who attended one of these clinics currently drives a Saab, but she is toying with the idea of buying a Mazda. "People do business with people they feel comfortable with," she says.

Source: Based on information in Larry Armstrong, "Women Power at Mazda," *Business Week,* September 21, 1992, p. 84.

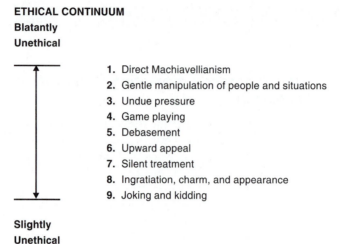

ETHICAL CONTINUUM
Blatantly
Unethical

1. Direct Machiavellianism
2. Gentle manipulation of people and situations
3. Undue pressure
4. Game playing
5. Debasement
6. Upward appeal
7. Silent treatment
8. Ingratiation, charm, and appearance
9. Joking and kidding

FIGURE 8–2

Essentially Dishonest and Unethical Influence Tactics

Slightly
Unethical

people are self-centered and self-serving. People in the workplace who ruthlessly manipulate others have therefore come to be called **Machiavellians.** They tend to initiate actions with others and control the interactions. Machiavellians regularly practice deception, bluff, and other manipulative tactics.[13]

A current example of deliberate Machiavellianism is the practice of forcing managerial and professional employees into working many extra hours of uncompensated overtime. The employees are told that if they refuse to work extra hours they will be fired. Because jobs in some categories are scarce, the employees comply. The person profiled in the next Leader in Action essay would be perceived by many as Machiavellian.

Gentle Manipulation of People and Situations.   Some people attempting to influence others are manipulative but to a lesser extent than an outright Machiavellian. By making untrue statements, or faking certain behaviors, they gain the compliance of another person. For example, a leader might imply that if a colleague supports his position in an intergroup conflict, the person *might* be recommended for promotion. A widely used manipulative approach is the **bandwagon technique** in which one does something simply because others are doing likewise. An example is a manager who informs the vice president that she wants an enlarged budget for attendance at quality seminars because "all other companies are doing it."

Undue Pressure.   Effective leaders regularly use motivational techniques such as rewards and mild punishments. Yet when rewards become bribes for compliance, and threats of punishment become severe, the target person is subjected to undue pressure or coercion. An example of a bribe by a manager might be, "If you can work 80 hours on this project this week, I'll

LEADER
IN
ACTION

Paul Kazarian, Former Sunbeam Chairman

Paul Kazarian, the 37-year-old chairman of Sunbeam, was attending a consumer products trade show. Late that night, a company director entered Kazarian's hotel room and fired him, despite his excellent business performance. Kazarian was perplexed by his firing, but Sunbeam employees and outside contacts could understand why.

The chairman had developed the reputation of intentionally abusing and humiliating employees, suppliers, and people with whom he negotiated. So many employees complained of Kazarian's insensitivity and hostility that the board conducted an independent investigation of his handling of people. The results showed that the chairman was so hostile that he could no longer provide effective leadership at Sunbeam.

Kazarian, an investment banker, came into power during a hostile takeover. Executives who knew him said he was far better with numbers than with people. One former executive says Kazarian's comments to people were often "obscene, vulgar, and haranguing. Every other word was the F word." During one negotiation session involving the takeover, Kazarian spit a cigar butt on the floor and nearly came to blows with an attorney.

Kazarian defends his blunt, intimidating style in this way: "You don't change a company in bankruptcy without making a few waves. I wasn't there to be a polite manager. I was there to create value for shareholders." Because Kazarian was not fired for poor performance, he will receive five years of compensation worth approximately $8.75 million.

Source: Based on facts in "How to Lose Friends and Influence No One," *Business Week,* January 25, 1993, pp. 42–43.

recommend you for the highest pay grade." Several specific behaviors labeled coercive in a research study were as follows:

I demand that she do it.

I yell at her until she does it.

I criticize her for not doing it.

I curse at her until she does it.

I threaten her with something if she doesn't do it.[14]

Game Playing.   Leaders, as well as others, often play games in order to influence others. A **game** in this context is a repeated series of exchanges between people that seems plausible but has a hidden agenda or purpose. Influence is exerted in a game because the person whom the game is played against is made to feel humble.

Blemish is an example of a simple game often used by managers to keep team members in line. All that is required is for the leader to find some flaw in every assignment completed by team members. The game-playing boss stays one up with comments such as "You did a great job on that report except in your conclusion. It just didn't seem to fit the body of the report."

One-time transactions between the influence agent and the influence target sometimes resemble a game. One such tactic is the door-in-the-face technique. The person attempting to exert influence makes a major request which will most likely be rejected. Shortly thereafter comes a more modest request, which was really intended in the first place.[15] In rejecting the first request, the target person may feel guilty and thus be responsive to a future request. For example, a security manager wanted a larger budget for cellular telephones and pagers for her group. At the time the company was carefully controlling expenditures. The security manager approached her manager and requested authorization for new office space for her staff. Her budget request was rejected quickly. She returned two weeks later with a request for an increased cellular telephone and paging system budget to compensate for the denial of new offices. Her request was granted within one week.

Debasement.   A subtle manipulative tactic is **debasement,** demeaning or insulting oneself to control the behavior of another person. For example, the security manager just mentioned might say, "I realize our department just contributes to overhead, but we do need more cellular telephones and pagers to get our job done." Specific debasing tactics revealed by research include the following:

> I allow myself to be debased so she'll do it.
>
> I lower myself so she'll do it.
>
> I act humble so she'll do it.[16]

Upward Appeal.   In **upward appeal,** the leader exerts influence on a team member by getting a person with more formal authority to do the influencing. An example: "I sent the guy to my boss when he wouldn't listen to me. That fixed him." More than occasional use of upward appeal weakens the leader's stature in the eyes of group members and superiors, thus eroding his or her effectiveness.

Leaders can apply upward appeals in other ways. A leader might attempt to persuade another staff member that his or her request is approved by higher management. The target of the influence event is thus supposed to grant acceptance automatically. Or the leader can request higher management's assistance in gaining another person's compliance with the request. The influence target thus feels pressured.[17]

Silent Treatment. A leader uses the **silent treatment** through saying nothing, sulking, or other forms of passivity until the influence target complies. Research questionnaire items related to sulking are as follows:

> I don't respond to him until he does it.
>
> I ignore him until he does it.
>
> I am silent until he agrees to do it.
>
> I refuse to do something he likes until he does it.[18]

Ingratiation, Charm, and Appearance. Getting somebody else to like you can be considered a mildly manipulative influence tactic—particularly if you do not like the other person. Ingratiating tactics identified in a study about influence tactics included the following:

> Made him or her feel important. (For example, "Only you have the brains and talent to do this.")
>
> Acted very humbly toward him or her while making my request.
>
> Praised him or her.
>
> Sympathized with him or her about the added problems that my request caused.
>
> Waited until he or she appeared in a receptive mood before asking.
>
> Asked in a polite way.
>
> Pretended I was letting him or her decide to do what I wanted. (Acted in a pseudo-democratic manner.)[19]

Another way of being ingratiating is through charm and appearance. Charm contributes to ingratiation because many people like a charming person. Being charming includes such behaviors as complimenting others profusely, expressing thanks, and displaying impeccable etiquette. Appearance in the context here means dressing professionally and fashionably. In the survey referred to in the self-assessment exercise, men gave both charm and appearance a frequency rating of 3.3 on a 1-to-5 scale. Women gave charm and appearance frequency ratings insignificantly different from those given by men.

Joking and Kidding. Good-natured kidding is especially effective when a straightforward statement might be interpreted as harsh criticism. Joking or kidding can thus get the message across and lower the risk that the influence target will be angry with the influence agent. Joking and kidding might be interpreted either as dishonest or as extraordinarily tactful because the criticizer softens the full blow of the criticism. A vice president of manufacturing successfully used joking and kidding to influence his team to improve quality. After examining what he thought were low-quality components for the company's power tools, he commented "I appreciate your effort, but I'm afraid you misinterpreted my message. I wanted you to produce a component we could use as a positive model of quality. You went out of your way to produce a negative model. Otherwise you did a great job."

Leadership Skill-Building Exercise 8–1 will help you recognize several of the influence tactics described in this chapter. Another tactic, assertiveness, is mentioned in the exercise but was described previously.

A STUDY OF THE EFFECTIVENESS OF INFLUENCE TACTICS

Influence tactics are a major component of leadership. Research about their relative effectiveness is therefore worth noting. A recent study by Gary Yukl and J. Bruce Tracey provides insights about the relative effectiveness of influence tactics.[20] One hundred and twenty managers participated in the study, along with 526 subordinates, 543 peers, and 128 superiors, who also rated the managers' use of influence tactics. The proportion of men and women in the study is unknown because respondents were not asked to reveal demographic information. (Some people prefer to remain anonymous in such studies.) Half the managers worked for manufacturing companies, and half worked for service companies.

The people who worked with the managers completed a questionnaire to identify which of nine influence tactics the managers used. Defined for the participants, the tactics were as follows:

1. Rational persuasion
2. Inspirational appeal
3. Consultation
4. Ingratiation
5. Exchange
6. Personal appeal
7. Coalition
8. Legitimating
9. Pressure

Another question asked how many influence attempts by the agent resulted in complete commitment by the target respondent. The seven response choices were (1) None of them; (2) A few of them; (3) Some (less than half); (4) About half of them; (5) More than half of them; (6) Most of them; and (7) All of them. Respondents were also asked to rate the overall effectiveness of the manager in carrying out his or her job responsibilities. The item had nine response choices, ranging from the least effective manager I have ever known (1) to the most effective manager I have ever known (9).

LEADERSHIP SKILL-BUILDING EXERCISE 8–1 Identifying Influence Tactics

Directions: After reading each tactic listed here, label it as being mostly an example of one of the following: I = Ingratiation; E = Exchange of Favors; R = Rationality; A = Assertiveness; U = Upward Appeal.

Tactic	Code
1. I sympathized with the person about the added problems that my request caused.	___
2. I offered to help if the person would do what I wanted.	___
3. I set a time deadline for the person to do what I asked.	___
4. I obtained the informal support of higher-ups.	___
5. I used logic to convince him or her.	___
6. I made a formal appeal to higher levels to back up my request.	___
7. I had a showdown in which I confronted the person head-on.	___
8. I offered to make a personal sacrifice if the person would do what I wanted (for example, work late or harder).	___
9. I made him or her feel good about me before making my request.	___
10. I explained the reasons for my request.	___

Answers:

1. I	6. U
2. E	7. A
3. A	8. E
4. U	9. I
5. R	10. R

Source: Based on information in Chester A. Schriescheim and Timothy R. Hinkin, "Influence Tactics Used by Subordinates: A Theoretical and Empirical Analysis and Refinement of the Kipnis, Schmidt, and Wilkinson Subscales," *Journal of Applied Psychology,* June 1990, p. 246.

The results suggested that the most effective tactics were rational persuasion, inspirational appeal, and consultation. (An effective tactic was one that led to task commitment, and that was used by managers who were perceived to be effective by the various raters.) In contrast, the least effective were pressure, coalition, and appealing to legitimate authority (legitimating). Ingratiation and exchange were moderately effective for influencing team members and peers. The same tactics, however, were not effective for influencing superiors.

Inspirational appeal, ingratiation, and pressure were used primarily in a downward direction. Personal appeal, exchange, and legitimating were used primarily in a lateral direction. It was also found that coalitions were used most in lateral and upward directions, and that rational persuasion was used most in an upward direction.

The researchers concluded that some tactics are more likely to be successful. Yet they caution that the results do not imply that these tactics will always result in task commitment. The outcome of a specific influence attempt is determined by factors in addition to influence attempts, such as the target's motivation and the organizational culture. Also, any tactic can trigger target resistance if it is not appropriate for the situation or if it is applied unskillfully. Tact, diplomacy, and insight are required for effective application of influence tactics.

SUMMARY

To become an effective leader, a person must be aware of specific influence tactics. Influence is the ability to affect the behavior of others in a particular direction. Power, in contrast, is the potential or capacity to influence. A model presented here indicates that to exercise influence the leader must possess power and use a variety of influence tactics. These tactics lead to outcomes such as commitment, but the outcomes are moderated by the leader's power and skills. Influence attempts can lead to commitment, compliance, or resistance.

Influence tactics are often viewed from an ethical perspective. Some tactics are clearly ethical, but some others are clearly unethical. Used with tact, diplomacy, and good intent, ethical influence tactics can be quite effective. The essentially ethical tactics described here include leading by example, rational persuasion, developing a reputation as an expert, exchanging of favors and bargaining, developing a network of resource persons, and legitimating a request. Also included are inspirational appeal and emotional display, consultation, forming coalitions, and team play.

Essentially dishonest and unethical tactics presented here were divided here into two groups: clearly unethical and borderline. The more clearly unethical and devious tactics are deliberate Machiavellianism, gentle manipulation of people and situations, undue pressure, and game playing. The five borderline influence tactics are debasing oneself to gain advantage; upward appeal; silent treatment; ingratiation, charm, and appearance; and joking and kidding (hardly devious at all).

A study of influence tactics concluded that the most effective were rational persuasion, inspirational appeal, and consultation. The least effective were pressure, coalition, and appealing to legitimate authority. Certain tactics are more effective for exerting influence upward, whereas others are better suited for downward influence. For example, inspirational appeal, ingratiation, and exchange are moderately effective for influencing subordinates and peers. Yet the same tactics are not effective for influencing superiors.

KEY TERMS

Influence

Power

Commitment

Compliance

Resistance

Leading by example

Coalition

Machiavellians

Bandwagon technique

Game

Blemish

Debasement

Upward appeal

Silent treatment

GUIDELINES FOR ACTION AND SKILL DEVELOPMENT

A starting point in choosing influence tactics to help you lead others is to select those that fit your ethical code. For example, a person might say, "Being a team player and ingratiation fit my ethics but I can't use undue pressure."

Another major consideration is to choose the correct combination of influence tactics. You must choose these tactics carefully on the basis of the influence target and your objectives. For example, ingratiation and joking and kidding might not work well with superiors. Quite often it is best to begin with a gentle influence tactic, then strengthen your approach as needed. Keys and Case found that most first influence attempts by managers involved gentle approaches such as requests or logical persuasion. Later attempts included firmer tactics when the influence target was reluctant to comply.[21] (In days of old, this was referred to as tightening the thumb screws!)

A person must also choose influence tactics to fit the influence objectives. Kipnis and his associates have observed that managers should not rely on a single influence tactic, such as assertiveness, to achieve both organizational and personal objectives. It may be appropriate to insist that one's boss be mindful of cost overruns. It is inappropriate, however, to insist that one be granted time off to golf with network members.[22]

Good communication skills are required to implement influence tactics. As Keys and Case note, "Managers who choose rational ideas based on the needs of the target, wrap them with a blanket of humor or anecdotes, and cast them in the language of the person to be influenced, are much more likely to see their influence objectives achieved."[23]

DISCUSSION QUESTIONS AND ACTIVITIES

1. Explain how leader skills moderate the use of influence tactics (see Figure 8–1).

2. Which of the tactics described in this chapter help explain the widespread use by leaders of person-to-person meetings when they want to accomplish a major objective?

3. Identify two exchanges of favors you have seen or can envision on the job.

4. If a leader's job is to influence others, why does the term *influence peddling* have such negative connotations?

5. Describe an example of how a leader might manipulate a situation in order to influence a team member.

6. Interpret the significant differences found among the data presented in Leadership Self-Assessment Exercise 8–1.

7. At what stage in a leader's career should he or she begin building a network of resource persons?

8. Which of the influence tactics described in this chapter is a charismatic leader the most likely to use? Explain.

9. Identify two influence tactics used by Jan Thompson, the Mazda marketing vice president.

10. Explain how a leader can use debasement to influence a team member.

LEADERSHIP CASE PROBLEM

The Tough-Minded Hank Greenberg

Maurice Raymond Greenberg, the chairman of the American International Group, Inc., smiled as he concluded the deal to form the Russian-American Investment Bank. Boris N. Yeltsin, the Russian president, cordially shook hands with Greenberg. The new partnership plans to infuse Western investment into the cash-poor Russian energy and real estate industries.

In his 24 years as CEO, Greenberg (nicknamed "Hank," after the famous Detroit Tiger slugger) has successfully networked and bargained with chiefs of state around the world. In the process, the American International Group (AIG) has become a potent financial force in 130 countries. AIG is also a highly profitable insurance company.

At one time considered the *enfant terrible* of the insurance industry, Greenberg in his late sixties is making more deals than ever. He has turned his insurance business into a global financial-services growth company. AIG is involved in businesses as diverse as aircraft leasing, trading foreign currencies, and interest-rate swaps. ("Swaps" are hedging instruments that permit financial institutions to exchange interest payments.) Greenberg's drive toward diversification has moved AIG into a multitude of deals. For example, in 1990 his firm paid $1.26 billion in cash and stock to buy the major aircraft leasing group, International Lease Finance Corporation.

Greenberg hates surprises, so he stays tuned to gossip in his offices around the globe. Associates describe Greenberg as demanding, profane, and intimidating. He is known in the insurance business as a one-person Lloyd's of London. One insurance analyst said Greenberg "will take on some of the grungiest risks around." He is also acknowledged worldwide as one of the sharpest insurance underwriters.

Greenberg's putdowns of colleagues, competitors, regulators, and even customers have become an industry legend. In sizing up a major competitor, Greenberg recently said, "They don't break down their foreign earnings because they don't have any. They all want to do what we're doing. But no other underwriter in the world comes remotely close."

Internally, Greenberg is known to practice the "I-am-the-law" leadership style. "There's only one royal highness around here," says Thomas R. Tizzio, AIG's president and property and casualty director. Greenberg insists that staff members be ready at all times, midnight included, to answer his inquiries and handle customer problems. Greenberg's office is lined with photos of himself and world leaders.

Throughout his life, Greenberg has been energetic and risk seeking. As an army attorney, he angered his commander by winning a string of acquittals for the soldiers he defended. Greenberg obtained his first insurance job after chastising a manager for the behavior of his arrogant personnel manager. According to one close friend of Greenberg's, "He doesn't mince any words, and a lot of them are four-letter ones."

In addition to being a relentless cost-cutter, Greenberg is regarded as one of Wall Street's sharpest bargainers. Observers contend that AIG is very reluctant to pay major claims, and that a tough legal battle is required to settle a complex claim.

1. Which influence tactics does Hank Greenberg favor?

2. How would you characterize Greenberg's leadership style?

3. What mistakes as a leader do you believe Greenberg might be making?

4. How would you like to report directly to Greenberg?

Source: Based on information in William Glasgall, "Mr. Risk," *Business Week,* December 7, 1992, pp. 104–109.

LEADERSHIP EXERCISE

Influence Tactics

Divide the class into small teams. Each group assigns one leadership influence tactic to each team member. During the next week or so, each team member takes the opportunity to practice the assigned influence tactic in a work or personal setting. Hold a group discussion with the same people after the influence attempts have been practiced. Report back the following information: (1) under what circumstances the influence tactic was attempted; (2) how the influence target reacted; and (3) what results, both positive and negative, were achieved.

Developing Teamwork

LEARNING OBJECTIVES

After studying this chapter, you should be able to

1. present an overview of the advantages and disadvantages of working in groups.
2. list and describe leader behaviors and attitudes that foster teamwork.
3. describe how the leader-member exchange model contributes to an understanding of teamwork.

---

*A*sked how she achieves such good teamwork among the various departments in her HMO (health maintenance organization), chief administrator Allison Hoffman replied: "Now and then we get the various department heads together for an 'anything goes' meeting. We challenge each other as to how each department, and each department head, could be an even better asset to other departments. On occasion, a few feelings get hurt. But on balance, the result is that we work better as a team."

As implied by the preceding anecdote, modern organizations require leaders to build effective teams. Strong teamwork is required for such activities as group problem solving and achieving total quality. Unless group members are working together smoothly and sharing information about mistakes and areas for improvement, quality targets are unlikely to be met. Developing teamwork is such an important leadership role that team building is said to differentiate successful from unsuccessful leaders.[1]

A challenge faced by leaders—and others studying the subject of teamwork—is that the words *team* and *teamwork* are overused. For some, *team* is simply another term for a group. In the context of leadership, however, a team is characterized by common commitment. A team accomplishes many *collective work products* in addition to individual results. The term *teamwork* is sometimes used as a catchall phrase for any work conducted by a group within the organization. As used here, **teamwork** is an understanding and commitment to group goals on the part of all team members.[2] Robert H. Waterman, Jr., has identified a teamwork pattern whose presence suggests that true teamwork will be achieved. The **teamwork pattern** is a situation in which constructive candor is valued, and collaboration is not an end but a means to goal attainment. The leader enlists everyone as needed, and commitment is an obvious consequence.[3]

Although the distinction between a group and a team may have some validity, it is difficult to cast aside the practice of using the terms *group* and *team* interchangeably. For example, a customer service team is still a *team* even if teamwork is poor.

As background for this chapter, let's look briefly at the advantages and disadvantages of working in groups. The central focus of this chapter is a description of specific leader behavior and attitudes that foster teamwork. We also examine outdoor training, a widely-used method of teamwork development. In addition, we summarize a leadership theory that provides some insights into how teamwork emerges within a work group.

ADVANTAGES AND DISADVANTAGES OF GROUP WORK AND TEAMWORK

Groups have always been the building blocks of organizations. Yet as Peter F. Drucker and others have noted, groups and teams have recently grown in importance as a fundamental unit of organization structure.[4] In an attempt to adapt to rapidly changing environments, many work organizations have granted teams increased autonomy and flexibility. Cross-functional teams have been formed in many firms to achieve a broader perspective on problem solving, and simultaneously to help downplay intergroup rivalries. Teams are also asked to span traditional boundaries by working more closely with groups from other disciplines. Furthermore, teams are often required to work more closely with customers and suppliers.

The increased acceptance of teams suggests that group work offers many advantages. Nevertheless, it is useful to specify several of these advantages and also examine the potential problems of groups.

Advantages of Group Work and Teamwork

Group work and group decision making offer several advantages over individual effort. If several knowledgeable people are brought into the decision-making process, a number of worthwhile possibilities may be uncovered. It is also possible to achieve synergy, whereby the group's total output exceeds the sum of each individual's contribution. For example, it would be a rare person working alone who could build an automobile. Group decision making is helpful in gaining acceptance and commitment, as described in the context of the Vroom–Yetton–Jago model in Chapter 6.

Group members often evaluate each other's thinking, so the team is likely to avoid major errors. The information systems manager in one company was formulating plans to install a computer network that would make electronic mail feasible. Shortly before a contract was signed with a vendor, one of the committee members asked, "Are you sure the PCs we have throughout the company have sufficient memory to run that system?" A quick review of equipment revealed that they did not. The electronic mail system had to be postponed until the PCs were upgraded.

Working in groups also enhances many members' job satisfaction. Being a member of a work group makes it possible to satisfy more needs than if one worked alone. Among these needs are needs for affiliation, security, self-esteem, and self-fulfillment. For example, playing a key role in a successful team effort can be fulfilling because of the job challenge and the recognition.

Disadvantages of Group Activity

Group activity has some potential disadvantages for both organizations and individuals. A major problem is that members face pressure to conform to group standards of performance and conduct. Some work groups might ostracize a person who is much more productive than his or her coworkers. Shirking of individual responsibility is another problem frequently noted in groups. Unless work is assigned carefully to each group member, an under-motivated person can often squeeze by without contributing his or her fair share to a group effort.

Social loafing is the psychological term for shirking individual responsibility in a group setting. The social loafer risks being ostracized by the group but may be willing to pay the price rather than work hard. Loafing of this type is sometimes found in groups such as committees and project teams. Many students who have worked on team projects have encountered a social loafer.

At their worst, groups foster conflict on the job. People within the work group often bicker about such matters as doing a fair share of the undesirable tasks within the department. Cohesive work groups can also become xenophobic (fearful of outsiders); that is, they may grow to dislike other groups and enter into conflict with them. A marketing group might devote considerable effort into showing up the finance group because the latter often puts financial brakes on marketing activities.

A well-publicized disadvantage of group decision making is **group-think,** a deterioration of mental efficiency, reality testing, and moral judgment in the interest of group solidarity. Simply put, groupthink is an extreme form of consensus. The group atmosphere values getting along more than getting things done. The group thinks as a unit, believes it is impervious to outside criticism, and begins to have illusions about its own invincibility. As a consequence, the group loses its own powers of critical analysis.[5]

Groupthink took place at one of the failed savings and loan associations. The senior management group voted themselves extraordinary salaries and bought art collections that they frequently borrowed for personal use. In addition, they purchased a corporate jet to fly around the country looking for investments, and to take vacations for themselves and their families. Not one of the savings and loan association executives expressed a dissenting opinion.

LEADER BEHAVIOR AND ATTITUDES THAT FOSTER TEAMWORK

Sometimes a leader's inspiring personality alone can foster teamwork. Yet inspirational leaders, as well as less charismatic ones, can encourage teamwork through certain behaviors and attitudes. Table 9–1 lists the teamwork-enhancing behaviors that are described in the following pages. (The suggestions for becoming an empowering leader offered in Chapter 8 also contribute to teamwork, but less directly.)

Defining the Team's Mission

A starting point in developing teamwork is to specify the team's mission. The mission should contain a specific goal, purpose, and philosophical tone. Here are two examples:

"To plan and implement new total quality approaches to enhance our quality image and bolster our competitive edge."

"To enhance our expert systems capability so we can provide decision makers throughout the organization with an advanced decision-making tool."

The leader can specify the mission when the team is first formed or at any other time. Developing a mission for a long-standing team breathes new life into its activities. Being committed to a mission improves teamwork, as does the process of formulating a mission. The dialogue necessary for developing a clearly articulated mission establishes a climate in which team members can express feelings, ideas, and opinions. Participative leadership is required in developing a mission, as in most other ways of enhancing teamwork.

TABLE 9–1 Leader Behavior and Attitudes That Foster Teamwork

1. Defining the team's mission

2. Developing a norm of teamwork

3. Emphasizing pride in being outstanding

4. Serving as a model of teamwork

5. Using a consensus leadership style

6. Designing systems and structures to overcome the "we–they" attitude

7. Establishing urgency, demanding performance standards, and providing direction

8. Emphasizing group recognition

9. Challenging the group regularly with fresh facts and information

10. Encouraging competition with another group

11. Encouraging the use of jargon

12. Initiating ritual and ceremony

13. Soliciting feedback on team effectiveness

14. Minimizing micromanagement

Developing a Norm of Teamwork

A major strategy for teamwork development is to promote the attitude among group members that working together effectively is an expected standard of conduct. Developing a norm of teamwork will be difficult for a leader when a strong culture of individualism exists within the firm. Yet the leader can otherwise make progress toward establishing a teamwork norm. Some leaders encourage team members to treat each other as if they were customers, thus encouraging cooperative behavior and politeness. The leader can also foster the norm of teamwork by explicitly stating its desirability. The manager of a group of financial analysts used the following comments, with good results, to promote teamwork:

> My manager is concerned that we are not pulling together as a cohesive team. I do see some merit in her argument. We are performing quite well as a group of individuals. Yet I see a need for an improved united effort in our group. We need to share ideas more frequently and to touch base with each other. It would also help if we picked each other's brains more frequently. From now on when I evaluate performance, I'm going to give as much weight to group effort as I do to individual contribution.

The leader can also communicate the norm of teamwork by making frequent use of words and phrases that support teamwork. Emphasizing the words *team members* or *teammates*, and deemphasizing the words *subordinates* and *employees*, helps communicate the norm of teamwork. Group incentives are typically used to substitute for, rather than replace, individual incentives.

Normative statements about teamwork by influential team members are also useful in reinforcing the norm of teamwork. A team member might say to coworkers, for example: "I'm glad this project is a joint effort. I know that's what earns us merit points around here."

Emphasizing Pride in Being Outstanding

A standard way to build team spirit, if not teamwork, is to help the group realize why it should be proud of its accomplishments. William A. Cohen argues that most groups are particularly good at some task. The leader should help the group identify that task or characteristic, and promote it as a key strength. A shipping department, for example, might have the best on-time shipping record in the region. Or a claims processing unit might have the least overpayments in an insurance company.[6] To try your hand at being an outstanding team, do Leadership Skill-Building Exercise 9–1.

Serving as a Model of Teamwork

A powerful way for a leader to foster teamwork is to be a positive model of team play. And one way to exemplify teamwork is to reveal important information about ideas and attitudes relevant to the group's work. As a result

---

LEADERSHIP SKILL-BUILDING EXERCISE 9–1   Shelters for the Homeless

This exercise should take about one hour; it can be done inside or outside of class. Organize the class into teams of about six people. Each team takes on the assignment of formulating plans for building temporary shelters for the homeless. The dwellings you plan to build, for example, might be two-room cottages with electricity and indoor plumbing. During the time allotted to the task, formulate plans for going ahead with Shelters for the Homeless. Consider dividing up work by assigning certain roles to each team member. Sketch out tentative answers to the following questions: (1) How will you obtain funding for your venture? (2) Which homeless people will you help? (3) Where will your shelters be? (4) Who will do the actual construction?

After your plan is completed, evaluate the quality of the teamwork that took place within the group. Search the chapter for techniques you might have used to improve it.

of this behavior, team members may follow suit. A leader's self-disclosure fosters teamwork because it leads to shared perceptions and concerns.[7]

Interacting extensively with team members serves as a model of teamwork because it illustrates the mechanism by which team development takes place—frequent informal communication. While interacting with team members, the team leader can emphasize that he or she is a team member. For example, he or she might say, "Remember the deadline. We must all have the proposal in the mail by Thursday." A less team-member-oriented statement would be, "Remember the deadline. I need the proposals in the mail by Thursday."[8]

Using a Consensus Leadership Style

Teamwork is enhanced when a leader practices consensus decision making. Contributing input to important decisions helps group members feel that they are valuable team members. Consensus decision making also leads to an exchange of ideas within the group, including supporting and refining each other's suggestions. As a result, the feeling of working jointly on problems is enhanced.

The Japanese approach to human resource management is embedded in the philosophy of teamwork and group harmony. To help achieve such harmony, many Japanese managers use consensus leadership. When all group members contribute to and finally support a decision, teamwork is enhanced. Because each person has contributed important input, he or she is less likely to be in conflict with other group members. The accompanying Leader in Action vignette illustrates how practicing consensus leadership can foster teamwork. Recognize, however, that consensus decision making alone does not create good teamwork. Many of the other ingredients described here must also be included to bring about a cohesive team effort.

Overcoming the "We–They" Attitude

The "we–they" attitude is a major deterrent to teamwork because one group regards the other as an adversary. Such attitudes can pit line versus staff, marketing versus manufacturing, field versus headquarters, and so on. A bold leadership act is to design structures and systems that lessen physical barriers that encourage the "we–they" attitude. A number of years back Roger Schipke, a senior executive in General Electric's appliance division, accomplished such a feat. The appliance division had been organized into so many small segments that artificial walls had been created among them.

To lessen the problem, Schipke designed an organization structure that would foster teamwork and strike a balance between short- and long-range thinking. The various functions were combined into four major operating units. The production and sales divisions were considered "Now Organizations." Technology and marketing were considered "Future Organizations."

LEADER IN ACTION

Rod Canion, Consensus Leader

Joseph ("Rod") Canion founded Compaq Computer Corporation in 1982, and he remained as the CEO of the highly successful firm for ten years. (The board of directors replaced Canion in 1992 because he did not believe Compaq had to compete directly with low-priced competitors.) From the beginning, Canion practiced consensus leadership, using teamwork to get the job done. During Canion's tenure, groups of managers and employees made all major decisions jointly.

Canion believes strongly in teamwork, and he rejects the idea of executive privilege. To emphasize his egalitarian attitudes, Canion occupied a small, inconspicuous office at Compaq. He explains how he practices consensus leadership: "We use a team of people to come to critical decisions. The consensus aspect has to do with striving to get them all to agree. You have a number of people who are very qualified and represent different backgrounds and disciplines.

"You need to get them to focus on an issue with the right attitude. They are not trying to win their own position, but are contributing to the best possible solution. That gives you the ability to get to a better answer than any one individual could working alone."

As Canion sees it, the leader contributes to the consensus process by helping the group keep on course. If the group is blocked on reaching a decision, the leader can get the group to try an alternate plan.

Canion has a favorite example of consensus leadership: Compaq had to choose whether to introduce a laptop or a desktop computer to the market because the company lacked the resources to introduce both. Canion favored moving ahead with the laptop, yet he listened carefully to a market researcher, who concluded that the short-term market for laptops was limited. The group achieved consensus on going ahead with the desktop computer. Later, when the market for laptops had increased, Compaq entered the market successfully.

Source: Based on facts in Danny Turner, "Consensus Builder: Teamwork Tips to Make Your Company Soar," *Success,* October 1990, pp. 43–45.

Each pair of organizations was placed in a situation where they had to work together. To further foster teamwork, managers from the top to the bottom of the organization were allowed to choose their own teams. The combination of working with other units, as well as self-selection of team members, fostered teamwork.

To break down barriers further, Schipke had identifying signs taken down from the factories. Instead of Dishwasher, Range, Laundry, and Refrigeration, the buildings became 1, 2, 3, and 4.[9] One limitation to this technique, however, is that in many situations, the numbers would become synonyms for the older product groups.

Establishing Urgency and Demanding Performance Standards

As management consultants, Jon R. Katzenbach and Douglas K. Smith have studied work teams in many organizations. They have observed that team members need to believe that the team has urgent, constructive purposes. Team members also want to have a list of explicit expectations. The more urgent and relevant the rationale, the more likely the team will achieve its potential. A customer service team was told that further growth for the corporation would be impossible without major improvements in providing service to customers. Energized by this information, the team met the challenge.[10]

Emphasizing Group Recognition

Giving rewards for group accomplishment reinforces teamwork because people receive rewards for what they have achieved collaboratively. The recognition accompanying the reward should emphasize the team's value to the organization rather than the individual. Recognition promotes team identity by enabling the team to take pride in its contributions and progress. The following are examples of team recognition:

- A display wall for team activities such as certificates of accomplishment, schedules, and miscellaneous announcements
- Team logos on items such as identifying T-shirts, athletic caps, mugs, jackets, key rings, and business cards
- Celebrations to mark milestones such as first-time activities, cost savings, and safety records
- Equipment painted in team colors
- Athletic team events such as softball, volleyball, and bowling
- Team-of-the-Month award, with gifts from the organization to team members or to the entire team

As the team evolves, some individuals will be more worthy of recognition than others. Rather than denying the reality of individual effort, the team might present an award to an outstanding performer.[11] Consultant Gerald Graham suggests that recognizing an outstanding performer is likely to build teamwork. He defines a good performer as a person who works quickly and accurately and who gets along with others.[12]

Challenging the Group

A leader can enhance teamwork by feeding the team valid facts and information that motivate team members to work together to modify the status quo. According to Katzenbach and Smith, new information prompts the team to redefine and enrich its understanding of the challenge it is facing. As a result, the team is likely to focus on a common purpose, set clearer goals, and work together more smoothly. Feeding the group relevant facts and information is also valuable because it helps combat groupthink.

A quality improvement team in a manufacturing plant recognized the high cost of poor quality. Nevertheless, they did not know what to do next until they researched the different types of defects and established the price on each one. In contrast, teams err when they assume that all the information they need exists within the group.[13]

Encouraging Group Competition

One of the best-known methods of encouraging teamwork is rallying the support of the group against a real or imagined threat from the outside. Beating the competition makes more sense when the competition is outside your organization. When the enemy is within, the team spirit within may become detrimental to the overall organization, and we–they problems may arise.

When encouraging competition with another group, the leader should encourage rivalry, not intense competition that might lead to unethical business practices. One factor contributing to the success of the Saturn automobile is the rivalry created with competitive brands. One of the marketing executives asked his staff several times, "How much longer are you going to take the insult that Americans can't make a world-class car in the low-price range? The Japanese are great automakers, but I know you people from Tennessee can be just as good." Observe that the executive encouraged rivalry with a formidable opponent but did not bash the competition.

Encouraging the Use of Jargon

An analysis by Lee G. Bolman and Terrence E. Deal suggests that the symbolic and ritualistic framework of a group contributes heavily to teamwork. An important part of this framework is a specialized language that fosters cohesion and commitment. In essence, this specialized language is in-group jargon. The jargon creates a bond among team members and sets the group apart from outsiders. It also reinforces unique values and beliefs, thus contributing to corporation culture. Jargon also allows team members to communicate easily, with few misunderstandings.

Bolman and Deal analyzed reports contained in Tracy Kidder's book about the computer industry, *The Soul of a New Machine* (Little, Brown, 1981).

The Eagle Group outperformed all other Data General divisions to produce a new, state-of-the-art computer. Here is some of the jargon the highly cohesive Eagle Group used:

A kludge: something to be avoided such as a machine with loose wire held together with duct tape.

A canard: anything false.

Give me a core dump: tell me your thoughts.

A stack overflow: an engineer's memory compartments are suffering from communication overload.[14]

The accompanying Team in Action vignette illustrates the colorful, jargon-laden speech of an organization known for its teamwork.

Initiating Ritual and Ceremony

According to Bolman and Deal, another way to enhance teamwork is to initiate ritual and ceremony. Ritual and ceremony afford opportunities for reinforcing values, revitalizing spirit, and bonding workers to one another and the team. An example would be holding a team dinner whenever the group achieves a major milestone, such as making a winning bid on a major contract. Leadership in Data General's Eagle Group encouraged ritual and ceremony from the beginning of the project. Bolman and Deal provide an example:

Eagle's leaders met regularly, including a meeting every Friday afternoon. But their meetings dealt more with symbols, gossip, and play than substance and decisions. Friday afternoon was a traditional time for winding down and relaxing. Honoring such a tradition was all the more important for a group whose members often worked all week and then all weekend.[15]

Soliciting Feedback on Team Effectiveness

Yet another approach to building teamwork is for the leader to systematically collect feedback on how well the team is working together. After rating its performance as a team, the team can discuss areas for improvement. Working together in this manner enhances cooperation. Edward Glassman recommends that after a meeting, each member rate on a scale of 1 to 10 (with 10 the highest) the performance of the leader and the team in several key areas, including the following:

1. Was participation in the discussion equally balanced among all members?
2. Were your opinions and thoughts solicited by the team?
3. Do you feel you influenced the final outcome?
4. Do you feel others influenced the final product?
5. Do you feel the final outcomes were creative?[16]

*TEAM
IN
ACTION*

A Technical Group at Microsoft Corp.

Microsoft organization members, headed by the charismatic Bill Gates, are known for their cohesiveness and team spirit. Part of the organizational culture is to learn and use *Microspeak,* as sampled in the following representative comments made by a software development team within the firm.

Person A: "He's very bandwidth."

Person B: "Bill sent me some wicked flame mail."

Person C: "Your idea has no granularity."

Person D: "She's hardcore about spreadsheets."

Person E: "He went nonlinear on me."

Person F: "That's the most random thing I've ever heard."

Translation:

Bandwidth: a measure of a person's intelligence, much like IQ.

Flame mail: hypercritical, emotional, and inflammatory electronic mail, often containing vulgarisms.

Granularity: fineness of detail.

Hardcore: serious about work.

Nonlinear: out of control, angry.

Random: illogical.

Source: "Microsoft: Bill Gates' Baby Is on Top of the World. Can It Stay There?" *Business Week,* February 24, 1992, p. 63.

Meeting participants can also be asked to write a one-sentence comment about their ratings. They discuss the feedback at the next meeting, with the anticipation of bringing about constructive change and stronger team spirit.[17]

Many methods of building teamwork have now been described. Leadership Skill-Building Exercise 9–2 is a tool for diagnosing the extent of teamwork within a group.

Minimizing Micromanagement

A strategic perspective on encouraging teamwork is for the leader to minimize **micromanagement,** the close monitoring of most aspects of group member activities. To be a good team leader, the manager must give group

LEADERSHIP
SKILL-BUILDING
EXERCISE 9–2   The Teamwork Checklist

Directions: This checklist serves as an informal guide to diagnosing teamwork. Base your answers on whatever experience you have in leading a team, at work or outside of work. Indicate whether your team has (or had) the following characteristics:

	Mostly Yes	Mostly No
1. Clearly defined goals and expectations	____	____
2. Clearly established roles and responsibilities	____	____
3. Well-documented guidelines of behavior and ground rules	____	____
4. Open communication in an atmosphere of trust and mutual respect	____	____
5. Continuous learning and training in appropriate skills	____	____
6. Higher management's patience and support	____	____
7. Rewards tied to individual as well as team results	____	____
8. Desire to improve and innovate continuously	____	____

Scoring and interpretation: The larger the number of statements answered *mostly yes,* the more likely good teamwork is present, thus contributing to productivity. The answers will serve as discussion points among team members for improving teamwork and group effectiveness. Negative responses to the statements can be used as suggestions for taking action to improve teamwork in your group.

Source: Based on material from *The Adventures of a Self-Managing Team* by M. Kelly. Copyright © 1991 by Pfeiffer & Company, San Diego, CA. Used with permission.

members ample opportunity to manage their own activities. Avoiding micromanagement is a core ingredient to employee empowerment because empowered workers are given considerable latitude to manage their own activities.[18] Research has shown that leaders of self-managing teams encourage self-reinforcement, self-goal setting, self-criticism, self-observation/evaluation, self-expectation, and rehearsal (mental review of upcoming events).[19]

OUTDOOR TRAINING AND TEAM DEVELOPMENT

Cognitive information about strategies and tactics for improving teamwork is potentially valuable. The person reading such information can selectively apply the concepts, observe the consequences, and then fine-tune his or her approach. Another approach to developing teamwork is to participate in experiential activities.

One popular experiential approach to building teamwork and leadership skills is outdoor training. Wilderness training is closely associated with outdoor training, except that the setting is likely to be much rougher—perhaps in the frozen tundra of northernmost Minnesota. Some forms of outdoor training take place in city parks.

Both outdoor and wilderness training are forms of learning by doing. Participants are supposed to acquire leadership and teamwork skills by confronting physical challenges and exceeding their self-imposed limitations.

Features of Outdoor Training Programs

Program participants are placed in a demanding outdoor environment. Of significance, they have to rely on skills they did not realize they had, and each other, to complete the program. The emphasis is on building not only teamwork but also self-confidence for leadership. Sometimes lectures on leadership, self-confidence, and teamwork precede the outdoor activity.

Outward Bound is the best known and largest of outdoor training programs. The program offers more than 500 courses in wilderness areas in twenty states and provinces. The courses typically run from three days to four weeks; one course in North Carolina lasts eighty-eight days. Worldwide, Outward Bound runs about forty-eight schools on five continents, with a total annual enrollment of about 28,000.

The Outward Bound Professional Development Program is geared to organizational leaders because it emphasizes teamwork, leadership, and risk taking. The wilderness is the classroom, and the instructors draw analogies between each outdoor activity and the workplace. Among the courses offered are dogsledding, skiing and winter camping, desert backpacking, canoe expeditioning, sailing, sea kayaking, alpine mountaineering, mountain backpacking and horsetrailing, and cycling.

Rope activities are typical of outdoor training. Participants are attached to a secure pulley with ropes, then climb up a ladder and jump off to another spot. Sometimes the rope is extended between two trees. Another activity is a "trust fall," in which each person takes a turn standing on a platform and falling backwards into the arms of coworkers. The trust fall can also be done on ground level.[20]

Outdoor training enhances teamwork by helping participants examine the process of getting things done through working with people. Participants practice their communication skills in exercises such as rappeling down a cliff by issuing precise instructions to each other about how to scale the cliff safely.

At the same time they have to learn to trust each other more because survival appears to depend on trust. The accompanying Leaders in Action vignette provides more details about how outdoor training is used for team building.

Evaluation of Outdoor Training for Team Development

Many outdoor trainers and participants believe strongly that they derived substantial personal benefits from outdoor training. Among the most important are developing greater self-confidence, appreciating hidden strengths,

LEADERS IN ACTION

Electronics Company Staff at Outward Bound

The chief operating officer of TCI West Inc., an electronics firm, wanted key personnel to develop into a smooth team. He chose Outward Bound training because he hoped to break down communication barriers and put all participants on equal footing. The first TCI representatives were sent to a course on orienteering in the Nevada desert. Among these people were top managers, marketing directors, and five manager trainees. The group learned rappeling, rock climbing, and first aid. They hiked through hot desert days and awakened to temperatures of 5°F (–15°C). They cooked meals, pitched tents, rationed water, and taught each other outdoor techniques.

Another TCI group participated in an Outward Bound river program. One exercise that incorporates team building, leadership, and communication skills required participants to intentionally flip a raft over in deep water. Next they had to return it to the upright position and then help each other back into the raft.

Developing trust is another critical aspect of Outward Bound. Participants must trust the commands that are shouted from the person leading the raft through swirling rapids. They must trust the lead person's sense of direction while hiking through the desert. Most of all they must trust the person belaying the rappel that will save them from serious injury or death in case of a fall. (A belay is a mountain-climbing hold to secure the rope.)

Among the lessons learned are that getting help from others is not always a sign of weakness, that it's all right not to be perfect, and that most fears can be put in proper perspective.

Source: Based on facts in Sally Howe, "TCI West Trains Outdoors," *Personnel Journal,* June 1991, pp. 58–59.

and learning to work better with people. Strong proponents of outdoor training believe that those who do not appreciate the training simply do not understand it. Many training directors also have positive attitudes toward outdoor training. They believe that a work team who experiences outdoor training will work more cooperatively back at the office.

Many people have legitimate reservations about outdoor training, however. Although outdoor trainers claim almost no accidents occur, a threat to health and life does exist. (To help minimize casualties, participants usually need medical clearance.) Another concern is that the teamwork learned in outdoor training does not spill over into the job environment. As Jay Conger explains, the workplace is a different environment from the wilderness. And real workplace teams tend to gain and lose their members rapidly as teammates are transferred, promoted, terminated, or quit. This mobility often negates all the team-building efforts that take place in the wilderness experience. Another problem is that when teams return to work, they often revert to noncollaborative behavior.[21]

One way to facilitate the transfer of training from outdoors to the office is to hold debriefing and follow-up sessions. Debriefing takes place at the end of outdoor training. The participants review what they learned and discuss how they will apply their lessons to the job. Follow-up sessions can then be held periodically to describe progress in applying the insights learned during outdoor training.

THE LEADER-MEMBER EXCHANGE MODEL: A PARTIAL EXPLANATION OF TEAMWORK

Research and theory about the development of teamwork lag far behind research and theory about many other aspects of leadership. Nevertheless, the leader-member exchange model, developed by George Graen and associates, helps explain why one subgroup in a unit is part of a cohesive team and another subgroup is excluded.[22] The **leader-member exchange model** (also called the **vertical dyad linkage model**) proposes that leaders develop unique working relationships with subordinates. By so doing, they create in-groups and out-groups. The in-groups become part of a smoothly functioning team headed by the formal leader. Out-group members are less likely to experience good teamwork. Figure 9–1 depicts the major concept of the leader-member exchange model.

Graen and his associates argue that leaders do not typically use the same leadership style in dealing with all group members. Instead, they treat each member somewhat differently. According to the model, each linkage (relationship) that exists between the leader and one team member probably differs in quality. With some group members the leader has a good relationship; with others, a poor relationship. Each of these pairs of relationships, or dyads, must be judged in terms of whether a group member is "in" or "out" with the leader.

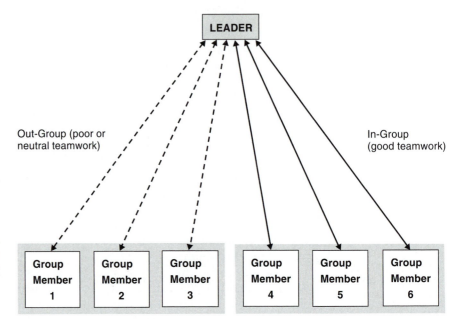

FIGURE 9–1

The Leader-Member Exchange Model

Source: Adapted from Gregory Moorhead and Ricky W. Griffin, *Organizational Behavior: Managing People and Organizations,* p. 273. Copyright © 1992 by Houghton Mifflin Company. Adapted with permission.

Members of the in-group are invited to participate in important decision making, given added responsibility, and are privy to interesting gossip. Members of the out-group are managed according to the requirements of their employment contract. They receive little warmth, inspiration, or encouragement. Robert Vecchio explains that an in-group member is elevated to the unofficial role of trusted assistant.[23] An out-group member is treated much like a hired hand. In-group members tend to achieve a higher level of performance, commitment, and satisfaction than do out-group members. Furthermore, they are less likely to quit.

The in-group versus out-group membership also includes an element of reciprocity or exchange. The leader grants more favors to the in-group member, who in turn works harder to please the leader. As a result, the leader then feels justified in granting the in-group member more resources, such as a larger salary increase or a larger budget.

Being part of the in-group can facilitate a member's future promotional opportunities. Unfortunately, choices about who becomes an in-group or out-group member are sometimes based on factors unrelated to job performance. Leaders sometimes form bonds with group members who participate in golf with them, or who belong to the same ethnic, religious, or racial group, or who are the same sex.

The leader's first impression of a group member's competency plays an important role in placing the group member into the in-group or out-group. Another key linking factor is whether the leader and team member have positive or negative chemistry. We can assume that group members who make effective use of influence and political tactics increase their chances of becoming a member of the in-group.

A recent study seems to confirm that first impressions make a difference. The researchers gathered ratings of six aspects of the manager–group member dyad. One measure was the group members' perceived similarity with the leader. For example, "My supervisor and I are alike in a number of ways." A second measure was feelings about the manager, such as "I like my supervisor very much as a friend." A third rating dealt directly with the member's view of the leader-member exchange (LMX). An example is "I can count on my supervisor to 'bail me out,' even at his or her expense, when I really need it."

A fourth rating measured the leader expectation of the member, such as "I think my new employee will be an excellent employee." A fifth rating measured leader liking of the member, such as "I like my subordinate very much as a person." A sixth rating was the leader's view of the LMX, including a rating of the statement, "I would be willing to 'bail out' my subordinate, even at my own expense, if he or she really needed it."

Results showed that the initial leader expectations of members and member expectations of the leader were good predictors of the leader-member exchanges at two weeks and at six weeks. Member expectations of the leader also accurately predicted member assessments of the quality of the leader-member exchange at six months. An important interpretation of these results is that the leader-member exchange is formed in the first several days of the relationship.[24] As the adage states, "You have only one chance to make a first impression."

In summary, the leader-member exchange model provides a partial explanation of teamwork development. Members of the in-group work smoothly together and with the leader because they feel privileged. Being a member of the out-group may not diminish teamwork, but it certainly does not make a positive contribution.

SUMMARY

Leaders are required to build teamwork because it is needed for such key activities as group problem solving and achieving total quality. Teamwork is an understanding and commitment to group goals on the part of all group members. Group work and group decision making offer several advantages, including the possibility of synergy and catching major errors. Working in groups often enhances job satisfaction, and many personal needs can be satisfied. Group activitiy has some potential disadvantages, including pressures toward conformity, social loafing, the breeding of conflict, and groupthink.

A wide range of leader behaviors and attitudes contributes directly to teamwork: (1) defining the team's mission; (2) developing a norm of teamwork; (3) emphasizing pride in being outstanding; (4) serving as a model of teamwork; (5) using a consensus leadership style; (6) designing systems and structures to overcome the "we–they" attitude; (7) establishing urgency, demanding performance standards, and providing direction; (8) emphasizing group (rather than individual) recognition; (9) challenging the group regularly with fresh facts and information; (10) encouraging competition with another group; (11) encouraging the use of jargon; (12) initiating ritual and ceremony; (13) soliciting feedback on team effectiveness; and (14) minimizing micromanagement.

In outdoor training, a popular experiential approach to building teamwork and leadership skills, emphasis is placed on building self-confidence. Outdoor training enhances teamwork by helping participants examine the process of getting things done collaboratively. The Outward Bound Professional Development Program is particularly geared toward organization leaders. Opinion about the effectiveness of outdoor training for developing teamwork and leadership skills is mixed. Concern has been expressed that the skills learned in the field do not carry over to the workplace.

The leader-exchange model helps explain why one subgroup in a work unit is part of a cohesive team and another unit is excluded. According to the model, leaders develop unique working relationships with subordinates. As a result, in-groups and out-groups are created. Members of the in-group tend to perform better, have higher satisfaction, and exhibit more teamwork. The leader's first impression of a group member's competency plays an important role in placing that person into the in-group or the out-group.

KEY TERMS

Teamwork	Micromanagement
Teamwork pattern	Leader-member exchange model
Social loafing	(or Vertical dyad linkage
Groupthink	model)

GUIDELINES FOR ACTION AND SKILL DEVELOPMENT

Management consultant Robert J. Waterman, Jr., offers many suggestions for strengthening teamwork throughout the organization. Among those not already described in this chapter are the following:

1. *Hire people who both qualify for the job and fit into the culture.* Too many like-minded team players could create problems. Nevertheless, attempt to hire the best people for your business, not necessarily any business.

2. *Destroy at least one "we–they" barrier a year.* Encourage your team to be loyal to broader groups than your own. People have the capacity to

identify with at least several larger groups than their own, including the division and region.

3. *Use training programs to build relationships.* When people are being trained and retrained, they are also forging new cross-organization bonds.

4. *Share the facts.* Sharing information engenders trust, and trust is a major contributor to teamwork. Sharing facts is also a way of sharing power.

5. *Come down hard on political infighting.* Political squabbles hamper teamwork, so it is advisable to confront team members who continually engage in conflict with each other.

6. *Do not tolerate lack of integrity or of trustworthy behavior.* An atmosphere low in trust breeds negative politics and poor cooperation. Confront instances of low trustworthiness.[25]

DISCUSSION QUESTIONS AND ACTIVITIES

1. How should the mission of the team be linked to the mission of the organization?

2. Identify several *collective work products* forthcoming from any group you have worked in.

3. What similarity do you see between being a leader who develops teamwork, and a *team manager* in the context of the Leadership Grid®?

4. Identify and describe any team you been a member of, or know about otherwise, that has a strong norm of teamwork.

5. How do the suggestions for developing teamwork presented in this chapter relate to achieving high quality?

6. What forces for and against being a good team player are embedded in the American culture?

7. What evidence of a "we–they" attitude have you observed or read about in the workplace?

8. How effective are team symbols such as athletic caps and coffee mugs in building teamwork among managers and professionals?

9. You have probably been told many times to minimize jargon in speech and writing to enhance communication—yet this chapter advocated jargon for teamwork. How do you reconcile the difference in both pieces of advice?

10. How can political skill help a person prevent being adversely affected by the leader-exchange model?

11. Find anybody who has experienced outdoor training. Find out what the person thought of the training, and share your findings with classmates.

LEADERSHIP CASE PROBLEM

The Unbalanced Team

Mercury Printing is one of the largest commercial printing companies in San Diego, California, with annual sales of $25 million. Two years ago, Alvero Velasquez, the vice president of marketing, reorganized the sales force. Previously the sales force had consisted of inside sales representatives (who took care of phone-in orders) and outside sales representatives (who called on accounts). The reorganization divided the outside sales force into two groups: direct sales and major accounts. The direct sales representatives were made responsible for small and medium-size customers. As before, they would service existing customers and prospect for new accounts.

Four of the people who were direct sales representatives were promoted to major account executives. The account executives would service the company's largest accounts, including prospecting for new business within those accounts. To promote teamwork and cooperation, Velasquez assigned group sales quotas to the account representatives. Collectively, their goal was to bring in sixteen new large accounts per month.

Because the sales quota was a group quota, the account representatives were supposed to work together on strategy for acquiring new accounts. If a particular account exec did not have the expertise to handle his or her customer's problems, another account executive was supposed to offer help. For example, Darcy Wentworth was the resident expert on printing packages and inserts for packages. If invited, Darcy would join another account representative to call on a customer with a complex request for package printing.

After the new sales organization had been in place eighteen months, Ann Osaka, an account executive, was having lunch with George Lewis, a production superintendent at Mercury Printing. "I've about had it," said Ann. "I'm tired of singlehandedly carrying the team."

"What do you mean you are singlehandedly carrying the team?" asked George.

"You're a trusted friend, George. So let me lay out the facts. Each month the group is supposed to bring in sixteen new sales. If we don't average those sixteen sales per month, we don't get our semiannual bonus. That represents about 25 percent of my salary. So a big chunk of my money comes from group effort.

"My average number of new accounts brought in for the last twelve months has been nine. And we are averaging about fourteen new sales per month. This translates into the other three account reps' averaging five sales among them. I'm carrying the group, but overall sales are still below quota. This means I didn't get my bonus last month.

"The other account execs are friendly and helpful in writing up proposals. But they just don't bring in their share of accounts."

George asked, "What does your boss say about this?"

"I've had several conversations with him about the problem. He tells me to be patient and to remember that the development of a fully balanced team requires time. He also tells me that I should develop a stronger team spirit. My problem is that I can't pay my bills with team spirit."

1. What does this case illustrate about teamwork?

2. What steps should Alvera Velasquez take, if any, to remedy the situation of unequal contribution of the account representatives?

3. What type of leadership input might help this situation?

4. To what extent are Ann Osaka's complaints justifiable?

LEADERSHIP EXERCISE

Learning Teamwork Through Ball Handling

The exercise to be described next is used to develop leadership, as well as to practice brainstorming.[26] If the class has twenty-five or fewer students, the entire class can participate. Otherwise, divide the class into groups of about fifteen people. One person in the group is handed a ball, who then hands it to the adjacent person, who hands it to the next, and so on, until everyone has had a chance with the ball. Each person tries to remember who gave him or her the ball, and who the ball was handed to. A timekeeper records how long the passing along of the ball takes.

The process begins all over again, with the goal of cutting the ball-passing time in half. The one rule is that the ball must touch everyone's hand. With each new round, the goal is to cut the time again by one-half. A point will be reached quickly where the team has only several seconds to pass the ball along to all the participants. Use brainstorming to find a way of reducing the time required for passing the ball to all the participants. (See page 366 for a suggested solution.)

Motivating and Coaching Skills

LEARNING OBJECTIVES

After studying this chapter, you should be able to

1. identify and describe leadership skills linked to the reinforcement theory of motivation.
2. identify and describe leadership skills linked to the expectancy theory of motivation.
3. explain how coaching can be a philosophy of leadership.
4. be ready to practice a number of coaching skills and techniques as the opportunity presents itself.

*W*hit Garson is a plant superintendent at a Chrysler minivan assembly plant in Windsor, Ontario. A visitor to his office inquired about a glass-encased whistle on a bookshelf adjacent to his desk. Garson replied, "The whistle is a constant reminder to me that a good leader has to be a good coach. You have to cheer people on when they are doing something right. When they make a mistake, you have to blow the whistle and show them how to improve. Even when they don't make a mistake, it helps to blow the whistle to show them how to reach new heights."

As the manager of a highly successful automotive plant just explained, effective leaders are outstanding motivators and coaches. They influence others in many of the ways previously described. In addition, they often use specific motivational and coaching skills. These techniques are important because not all leaders can influence others through formal authority or charisma and inspirational leadership alone. Face-to-face, day-by-day motivational skills are also important. As explained by Roger D. Evered and James C. Selman, good coaching is the essential feature of really effective management.[1]

In this chapter we approach motivation and coaching skills from four perspectives. We examine first how leaders make effective use of behavior modification; second, motivational skills and behaviors required from a comprehensive theory of motivation, expectancy theory; third, coaching as a leadership philosophy; and fourth, specific coaching skills that the leader can use to enhance performance.

BEHAVIOR MODIFICATION AND MOTIVATIONAL SKILLS

Behavior modification, a well-known system of motivation, is an attempt to change behavior by manipulating rewards and punishment. Behavior modification stems directly from reinforcement theory. Since many readers are already familiar with reinforcement theory and behavior modification (often shortened to "behavior mod"), we will limit our discussion to a brief summary of the basics of behavior modification, and focus instead on its leadership applications.

An underlying principle of behavior modification is the law of effect: behavior that leads to a positive consequence for the individual tends to be repeated; in contrast, behavior that leads to a negative consequence tends not to be repeated. Leaders typically emphasize linking behavior with positive consequences, such as expressing enthusiasm for a job well done.

Behavior Modification Strategies

The techniques of behavior modification apply to both learning and motivation; they can be divided into four strategies. *Positive reinforcement*, which rewards the right response, increases the probability that the behavior will be repeated. The phrase *increases the probability* means that positive reinforcement improves learning and motivation but is not 100 percent effective. The phrase *the right response* is also noteworthy. To use positive reinforcement properly, a reward is contingent upon the person doing something right. If the company achieves a high-quality award, the company president might recognize the accomplishment through a bonus to all. Authorizing a bonus for no particular reason might be pleasant, but it is not positive reinforcement.

Negative reinforcement is rewarding people by taking away an uncomfortable consequence of their behavior. It is the withdrawal or avoidance of a disliked consequence. A leader offers negative reinforcement when she or he says, "We have performed so well that the wage freeze will now be lifted." The undesirable consequence of a wage freeze was contingent upon performance above expectations. Be careful not to confuse negative reinforcement with punishment. Negative reinforcement is the opposite of punishment: it involves rewarding someone by removing a punishment or an uncomfortable situation.

Punishment is the presentation of an undesirable consequence, or the removal of a desirable consequence, because of unacceptable behavior. A leader or manager can punish a group member by demoting him or her for an ethical violation such as lying to a customer. Or the group member can be punished by losing the opportunity to attend an executive development program.

Extinction is decreasing the frequency of undesirable behavior by removing the desirable consequence of such behavior. Company leaders might use extinction by ceasing to pay employees for making frivolous cost-saving suggestions. Extinction is sometimes used to eliminate annoying behavior. Assume that a group member persists in telling ethnic jokes. The leader and the rest of the group can agree to ignore the jokes and thus extinguish the joke telling.

Rules for the Use of Behavior Modification

Behavior modification, often called OB Mod, frequently takes the form of a companywide program administered by the human resources department.[2] Our focus here is with leaders' day-by-day application of behavior mod, with an emphasis on positive reinforcement. The coaching role of a leader exemplifies the application of positive reinforcement. Although using rewards and punishments to motivate people seems straightforward, behavior modification requires a systematic approach. The rules presented here are specified from the standpoint of a leader or manager trying to motivate an individual or a group.[3]

Rule 1: Choose an appropriate reward or punishment. An appropriate reward or punishment is one that is (1) effective in motivating a given group member or group and (2) feasible from the company standpoint. If one reward does not work, try another. Feasible rewards include money, recognition, challenging new assignments, and status symbols such as a private work area. When positive motivators do not work, it may be necessary to use negative motivators (punishment).

It is generally best to use the mildest form of punishment that will motivate the person or group. For example, if a group member reads a newspaper during the day, the person might simply be told to put away the newspaper. Motivation enters the picture because the time not spent on reading the newspaper can now be invested in company work. If the mildest form of punishment does not work, a more severe negative motivator is selected. Written documentation placed in the person's personnel file is a more severe form of punishment than a mere mention of the problem.

Rule 2: Supply ample feedback. Behavior modification cannot work without frequent feedback to individuals and groups. Feedback can take the form of simply telling people when they have done something right or wrong. Brief paper or electronic messages are another form of feedback. Be aware, however, that many employees resent seeing a message with negative feedback flashed across their video display terminals.

Rule 3: Do not give everyone the same size reward. Average performance is encouraged when all forms of accomplishment receive the same reward. Say one group member makes substantial progress in providing input for a strategic plan. He or she should receive more recognition (or other reward) than a group member who makes only a minor contribution to the problem.

Rule 4: Schedule rewards intermittently. Rewards should not be given on every occasion for good performance. *Intermittent* rewards sustain desired behavior longer, and also slow the process of behavior fading away when it is not rewarded. If a person is rewarded for every instance of good performance, he or she is likely to keep up the level of performance until the reward comes, then slack off. Another problem is that a reward which is given continuously may lose its impact. A practical value of intermittent reinforcement is that it saves time. Few leaders have enough time to dispense rewards for every good deed forthcoming from team members.

Rule 5: Rewards and punishments should follow the behavior closely in time. For maximum effectiveness, people should be rewarded shortly after doing something right, and punished shortly after doing something wrong. A built-in feedback system, such as a computer program working or not working, capitalizes on this principle. Many effective leaders get in touch with people quickly to congratulate them on outstanding accomplishment.

Rule 6: Change the reward periodically. Rewards do not retain their effectiveness indefinitely. Team members lose interest in striving for a reward they have received many times in the past. This is particularly true of a repetitive statement such as "Nice job," or "Congratulations." Plaques for outstanding performance also lose their motivational appeal after a group receives many of them. It is helpful for the leader or manager to formulate a list of feasible rewards and try different ones from time to time.

EXPECTANCY THEORY AND MOTIVATIONAL SKILLS

Behavior modification is an effective, general-purpose method of motivating people in the workplace and elsewhere. Another familiar explanation of motivation, expectancy theory, is given special attention here for two important reasons. First, the theory is comprehensive because it incorporates features of other motivation theories, including behavior modification. Second, it offers the leader many guidelines for triggering and sustaining constructive effort from group members.

An Overview of Expectancy Theory

The **expectancy theory** of motivation is based on the premise that the amount of effort people expend depends on how much reward they expect to get in return. The theory is really a group of theories based on a rational-economic view of people.[4] In any given situation, people want to maximize gain and minimize loss. The theory assumes that people choose among alternatives by selecting the one they think they have the best chance of attaining. Furthermore, they choose the alternative that appears to have the biggest personal payoff. Given a choice, people select an assignment they think that they can handle and that will benefit them the most.

An example will help clarify the central thesis of expectancy theory. Gary, a 52-year-old middle manager, receives early retirement from a large business firm. Unable to find a comparable job in another corporation, he narrows his career alternatives to four choices: (1) accepting a low-paying, entry-level position in a retail store or factory, (2) starting his own manufacturing or service business, (3) purchasing a franchise business, and (4) becoming a management consultant in his field of expertise.

Gary automatically rejects the first choice because, although he knows he could perform the job, the payoffs seem so undesirable. He likes alternatives 2, 3, and 4 because all appear to have good potential payoffs. Gary rejects alternatives 2 and 4 because, although he thinks he could do the work, he questions whether he would earn enough money. Gary thus has high effort-to-performance expectancies for all four alternatives. Finally, Gary chooses to purchase a franchise because he thinks he could perform as required, and he has a hunch that a franchise will bring him sufficient income. (He also has the necessary $300,000 franchise fee!)

Basic Components of Expectancy Theory

All versions of expectancy theory have three major components: (1) effort-to-performance expectancies, (2) performance-outcome expectancies, and (3) valence of outcomes. Figure 10–1 presents a basic model of expectancy theory.

Effort-to-Performance Expectancy.   **Effort-to-performance expectancy** is the probability assigned by the individual that effort will lead to correct performance of the task. An important question people ask themselves before putting forth effort to accomplish a task is, "If I put in all this work, will I really get the job done properly?" Gary, the early-retired middle manager, for example, was confident that he could learn the proper skills to operate a franchise successfully. In addition, he was confident that his experience as a big-company middle manager would be an asset. Each behavior is associated in the individual's mind with a certain expectancy or subjective hunch of the probability of success.

Effort-to-performance expectancies range from 0 to 1.0, where 0 is no expectation of performing the task correctly and 1.0 signifies absolute faith in being able to perform the task properly. Expectancies thus influence whether a person will even strive to earn a reward. Self-confident people,

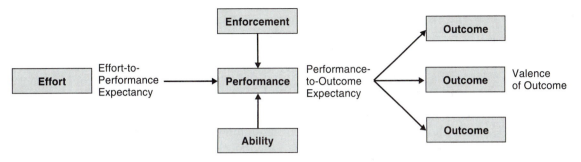

FIGURE 10–1

The Expectancy Theory of Motivation

Source: From Gregory Moorhead and Ricky W. Griffin, *Organizational Behavior*, 3rd ed., p. 161. Copyright © by Houghton Mifflin Company. Used with permission.

such as Gary, have higher expectancies than do less self-confident people. Being well trained increase a person's subjective hunch that he or she can perform the task.

Figure 10–1 suggests that performance is considered a joint function of effort, environment, and ability. Although a person's effort contributes greatly to performance, he or she must also have a supportive environment. The franchise environment, for example, may offer the right technology, equipment, advertising, and advice to help make the business successful. Furthermore, ability is very important. Without proper ability, no matter how hard one tries, good performance will not be forthcoming. Even an inspiring leader must offer people the right training so they can perform well.

Performance-to-Outcome Expectancy.   **Performance-to-outcome expectancy** is the probability assigned by the individual that performance will lead to certain outcomes. An **outcome** is anything that might stem from performance, such as a reward. (A performance-to-outcome expectancy is also called an **instrumentality** because it is instrumental in attaining a desired outcome.) When people engage in a particular behavior, they do so with the intention of achieving a desired outcome or reward.

Performance-to-outcome expectancies also range from 0 to 1.0, where 0 is no chance of receiving the desired reward, and 1.0 is a belief that the reward is certain to follow. For example: "I know for sure if I invest my money in a certificate of deposit, I will earn the specified interest." Gary, the new franchise owner, perhaps had a .75 hunch that if he followed the franchise plan he would earn a satisfactory income.

The performance portion of effort-to-performance expectancy is a first-level outcome. It is rooted in the job itself. If people work hard, they expect to accomplish such outcomes as producing goods, supplying a service, or achieving quality. Performance-to-outcome expectancies, on the other hand, deal with second-level outcomes—the rewards associated with performing. A performance-to-outcome expectancy can also be regarded as a hunch that a first-level outcome will lead to a second-level outcome. For example, you might have a strong belief that if you produce high-quality work, you will receive recognition from the organization.

Valence.   **Valence** is the worth or attractiveness of an outcome. As shown in Figure 10–1, each work situation has multiple outcomes. Each outcome has a valence of its own. Potential second-level outcomes for a successful franchise operator include high income, an opportunity to purchase another franchise from the same company, and a feeling of independence.

Valences range from −100 to +100 in the version of expectancy theory presented here. (The usual method of placing valences on a −1.00 to +1.00 scale does not do justice to the true differences in preferences.) A valence of +100 means that a person intensely desires an outcome. A valence of −100 means that a person is strongly motivated to avoid an outcome such as being fired or declaring bankruptcy. A valence of zero signifies indifference to an outcome and is therefore of no use as a motivator.

According to expectancy theory, three conditions must be present for motivation to occur. First, the effort-to-performance expectancy must be reasonably high. The person must believe that effort will lead to task accomplishment. Second, the performance-to-outcome expectancy must also be reasonably high. Few people will be willing to work hard if no reward (either external or internal) is forthcoming. Third, the sum of all the valences must be positive for the person to work hard. If the sum of all the valences is negative, the person will probably work hard to avoid the outcome. Most performances lead to both negative and positive outcomes. If Gary, the laid-off manager, becomes a successful franchise operator, he may earn a high income. Yet he may also have to work seventy hours per week, thus creating conflicts with his personal life.

A seeming contradiction in expectancy theory requires explanation. Some people will engage in behaviors with low performance-to-outcome expectancies, such as trying to invent a successful new product or win a lottery. The compensating factor is the large valences attached to the second-level outcomes associated with these accomplishments. The payoffs from introducing a successful new product or winning a lottery are so great that people are willing to take a long shot.

Leadership Skills and Behaviors Associated with Expectancy Theory

Expectancy theory has many implications for leaders and managers with respect to motivating others.[5] Some of these implications would also stem from other motivational theories, and they fit good management practice in general. As you read each implication, reflect on how you might apply the skill or behavior during a leadership assignment.

1. *Determine what levels and kinds of performance are needed to achieve organizational goals.* Motivating others proceeds best when workers have a clear understanding of what needs to be accomplished. At the same time, the leader should make sure that the desired levels of performance are possible. For example, sales quotas might be set too high because the market is already saturated with a particular product or service.

2. *Train and encourage people.* Leaders should give group members the necessary training and encouragement to be confident they can perform the required task. (We will return to the encouragement aspect of leadership in the discussion of coaching.) Some group members who appear to be poorly motivated simply lack the right skills and self-confidence.

3. *Make explicit the link between rewards and performance.* Group members should be reassured that if they perform the job up to standard, they will receive the promised reward.

4. *Make sure the rewards are large enough.* Some rewards fail to motivate people because although they are the right kind, they are not in the right amount. The promise of a large salary increase might be motivational, but a 1 percent increase will probably have little motivational thrust for most workers.

5. *Explain the meaning and implications of second-level outcomes.* It is helpful for employees to understand the value of certain outcomes, such as receiving a favorable performance appraisal. (For example, it could lead to a salary increase, assignment to a high-status task force, or promotion.)

6. *Understand individual differences in valences.* To motivate group members effectively, leaders must recognize individual differences or preferences for rewards. An attempt should be made to offer workers rewards to which they attach a high valence. One employee might value a high-adventure assignment; another might attach a high valence to a routine, tranquil assignment. Cross-cultural differences in valences may also occur. For example, many (but not all) Asian workers prefer not to be singled out for recognition in front of the group. According to their cultural values, receiving recognition in front of the group is insensitive and embarrassing. Leadership Skill-Building Exercise 10–1 on page 218 deals further with the challenge of estimating valences.

7. *Use the Pygmalion effect to increase effort-to-performance expectancies.* By communicating confidence that group members can perform at a high level, they will gradually raise their levels of expectation. (As described in Chapter 4, this phenomenon is called the Pygmalion Effect.) As the levels of expectation increase, so will performance. The high expectations thus become a self-fulfilling prophecy.

8. *Make sure the system is equitable for everyone.* Workers who achieve the same level of performance should receive comparable rewards. Similarly, workers who fail to attain certain levels of performance should receive comparable punishment.

LEADERSHIP
SKILL-BUILDING
EXERCISE 10–1 **Estimating Valences for Applying Expectancy Theory**

Directions: A major challenge in applying expectancy theory is estimating what valence attaches to possible outcomes. A leader or manager also has to be aware of the potential rewards or punishment in a given work situation. Listed below are a group of rewards and punishments, along with a space for rating the reward or punishment on a scale of –100 to +100. Work with about six teammates, with each person rating all the rewards and punishments.

Potential Outcome	**Rating (–100 to +100)**
1. Promotion to vice president	___
2. One-step promotion	___
3. Above-average performance rating	___
4. Top-category performance rating	___
5. $5,000 performance bonus	___
6. $1,000 performance bonus	___
7. $50 gift certificate	___
8. Employee-of-the-month plaque	___
9. Note of appreciation placed in file	___
10. Luncheon with boss at good restaurant	___
11. Lunch with boss in company cafeteria	___
12. Challenging new assignment	___
13. Allowed to do more of preferred task	___
14. Allowed to purchase software of choice	___
15. Assigned new equipment for own use	___
16. Private corner office with great view	___
17. Assigned a full-time administrative assistant	___
18. Documentation of poor performance	___
19. Being fired	___
20. Being fired and put on industry "bad-list"	___
21. Demoted one step	___

22. Demoted to entry-level position   ____

23. Being ridiculed in front of others   ____

24. Being suspended without pay   ____

25. Being transferred to undesirable location   ____

After completing the ratings, discuss the following issues:

1. Which rewards and punishments received the most varied ratings?
2. Which rewards and punishments received similar ratings?

Another analytical approach would be to compute the means and standard deviations of the valences for each outcome. Each class member could then compare his or her own valence ratings with the class norm. To add to the database, each student might bring back two sets of ratings from employed people outside of class.

To apply this technique to the job, modify the above form to fit the outcomes available in your situation. Explain to team members that you are attempting to do a better job of rewarding and disciplining, and that you need their input. The ratings made by team members might provide fruitful discussion for a staff meeting.

COACHING AS A LEADERSHIP PHILOSOPHY

As mentioned at the outset of this chapter, effective leaders who deal directly with people are good coaches. The coaching demands are much less rigorous for leaders who have little face-to-face contact with organization members. Among such leaders would be financial dealmakers, chairpersons of the board, and high-ranking government officials. The chairperson of the board is not expected to coach the board members, and the president of the United States does not coach cabinet members.

The quality of the relationship between the coach and the person coached distinguishes coaching from other forms of leader-member interactions. The person being coached trusts the leader's judgment and experience and will listen to advice and suggestions. Similarly, the coach believes in the capacity of the group member to learn and profit from his or her advice. The coach is a trusted superior, and the person being coached is a trusted subordinate. Several of the points made here about coaching as a philosophy of management present more details about the quality of the relationship between the coach and the team member.

Roger D. Evered and James C. Selman regard coaching as a paradigm shift from traditional management, which focuses heavily on control, order, and compliance. Coaching, in contrast, focuses on uncovering actions that enable people to contribute more fully and productively. Furthermore, people feel less alienated than when working under the control model.[6] Coaching is also seen as a partnership for achieving results. At the same time, it represents a commitment to collaborating in accomplishing new possibilities rather than holding on to old structures. Figure 10–2 depicts coaching as a philosophy of management.

When coaching is elevated to a philosophy of leadership, it becomes more complex than a handy technique leaders and managers use to rev up and sustain performance. Evered and Selman have observed a number of characteristics of coaching that contribute to its close relationships with leadership.[7]

Coaching is a comprehensive and distinctive way of being linked to others in the organization. The type of relationship inherent in coaching facilitates the accomplishments of coaching. Mentoring is one example of this unique relationship. Protégés are inspired to greater achievement partially because of the quality of their relationship with their mentors. More will be said about mentoring in Chapter 15, which covers leadership development.

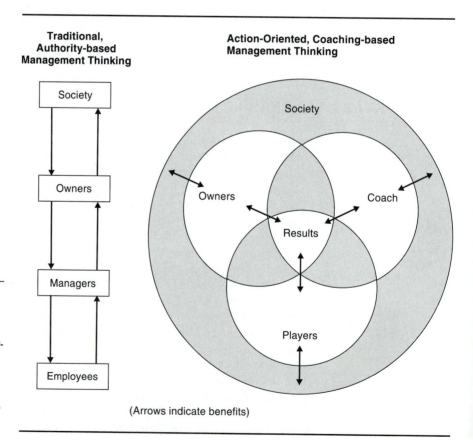

FIGURE 10–2

Coaching Versus the Traditional Way of Thinking about Management

Source: Reprinted, by permission of the publisher, from *Organizational Dynamics,* Autumn 1989, © 1989, American Management Association, New York. All rights reserved.

Coaching in the workplace might ordinarily be explained as the "art of management." Because of the uniqueness of a coaching relationship, the person being coached is better motivated to accomplish goals for the good of the organization. Unfortunately, coaching is not ordinarily understood as a way of working and relating in most firms. As a result, most management development programs do not give enough attention to developing the skills and qualities of effective coaching.

Coaching is often overlooked by virtue of a cultural blind spot that emphasizes control-and-order rather than the development of people. A good leader/coach is more concerned about developing team members than controlling their behavior. Recognize also that coaching is a two-way process, suggesting that to be a great coach one needs formidable team members. The people coached must also be good listeners, open to suggestions, and eager to develop.

Coaching produces results only through the process of communication. The actions of coaches are found in the messages they send both verbally and nonverbally, and in their listening and noticing. During the game on the athletic field or in the workplace, coaches influence action by how they listen and what they say.

Coaching is a dyad—that is, it cannot exist without at least two participants, the same as leader/group member, or director/actor. The interaction of the two personalities influences the coaching outcome. Some leaders, for example, can successfully coach certain people but not others. An executive vice president of finance was highly regarded as a good coach. Yet a newly appointed special assistant asked to be transferred after she worked for him for several months. The explanation she offered was, "My working relationship with Marty (the executive vice president) is just flat."

Coaching requires a high degree of interpersonal risk and trust on the part of both people in the relationship. The coach might give the person being coached wrong advice. Or the person being coached might reject the coach's encouragement. Think of the risk involved when a basketball player ask the coach for advice on how to correct a shot that is not working well. As a result of the coaching, the player might shoot more poorly, to the embarrassment of both. Similarly, an organizational leader might coach a team member in a direction that backfires—for example, by resulting in even fewer sales than before.

An important advantage of coaching is that it generates new possibilities for action and facilitates breakthroughs in performance. A vice president might say to a lower-ranking manager, "Had you thought of getting your people more involved in setting objectives? If you did, you might find greater commitment and follow through." The middle manager begins to involve managers more in setting objectives, and performance does increase. Coaching has achieved substantial results.

Coaching requires the transformation of traditional models of management, organization, work, and society. A coaching philosophy calls for a more dynamic organization based to a large extent on relationship, commitment, purpose, and results. In contrast, the very traditional organization is based more on role, hierarchical position, and authority.

Despite all the exalted statements made about coaching as a philosophy of leadership, it is still useful to specify a few concrete contributions of coaching. One advantage is higher motivation. An effective coach keeps up the spirit and administers praise and recognition frequently. Good coaching also leads to personal development. Group members are encouraged to cross-train and serve as backups for each other. Good coaching also improves group performance. The effective coach makes team members aware of one another's skills and how these skills can contribute to attaining the group's goals.[8]

The accompanying Leader in Action box describes an athletic coach who also gives motivational speeches to business groups. In addition, he provides inspiration for a business of his own.

LEADER IN ACTION

Rick Pitino, Kentucky Wildcats Head Coach

The Kentucky Wildcats men's basketball team reached the final four of the NCAA basketball tournament at the end of the 1992–93 season. Head coach Rick Pitino had helped inspire his team to another glorious year. Several years back, however, the mood was somber in Lexington, Kentucky, home of the Wildcats. The NCAA was investigating the team for alleged recruiting violations. As a result, the team received a two-year suspension from tournament competition. They were also excluded from national television. Top players from the team transferred to basketball programs at other universities.

Enter newly hired coach Rick Pitino. Among his credits were three coaching jobs in which he turned losers into winners. Pitino was confident he could restore the Kentucky team to its past glory. By his second year, Pitino had achieved his goal. The team won twenty-two games and lost only six.

A balance of a systematic basketball technique and a spontaneous optimism that spreads to others makes Pitino a winner. Shortly after taking over as head coach of the demoralized Wildcats, Pitino challenged the team with these words: "They say you don't have enough talent, that it will take me five or six years to get a winning program here, but I don't believe that. You stick with me. I guarantee you that you'll be better than what you expect and what people expect."

Pitino believes that a successful team reflects the personality of the coach. He emphasizes hard work, but he thinks that hard work alone is not sufficient for winning. You must get people to enjoy working hard. People will work hard if they are motivated by knowing *why* they are working hard.

Pitino emphasizes individual coaching and motivational sessions with his players. He says that every worker in an organization is motivated by something different. "As coach, as CEO, you must learn what makes each person act. You can motivate an entire team to perform on a certain night, but you've got to understand what motivates every individual." The leader must therefore get to know each team member.

Pitino also believes that the leader must be sincere and show care for people. Projecting a feeling that you are better than them will backfire. To be a winner, the coach continues, each player must feel great about himself and have very high self-esteem. You have to make sure that players do not feel negative about themselves.

Pitino is hired frequently as a motivational speaker by business firms. He believes that his style of coaching and motivating applies equally well to business. The way to motivate a sales representative, for example, is to tell him or her, "I know you've got the potential to get the job done." This is much better than threatening the sales rep with being fired if the quota is not reached.

Pitino also applied his coaching techniques to running a successful restaurant in Lexington, called Bravo Pitino. To begin, he hired top talent to run the restaurant. Pitino opened the restaurant believing that with a good product, the right ambiance, and an exciting concept, customers will flock to the door. When he attended staff meetings at the restaurant, he praised everyone from the dishwashers to the wait staff and the maitre d'. By 1993 Pitino sold the restaurant to concentrate on his other activities. But he left behind an inspired and winning organization.

Source: Based on facts reported in Michael Maren, "A Master Motivator Teaches You to Create Superstars," *Success*, April 1992, pp. 36–41.

COACHING SKILLS AND TECHNIQUES

Leaders and managers have varied aptitudes for coaching. One way to acquire coaching skill is to study basic principles and suggestions, and then practice them. Another way is to attend a training program for coaching that involves modeling (learning by imitation) and role playing. Here we examine a number of suggestions for coaching. If implemented with skill, the suggestions will improve the chances that coaching will lead to improved performance.

1. *Provide specific feedback.* To coach a group member toward higher levels of performance, the leader pinpoints what specific behavior, attitude, or skill requires improvement. A good coach might say, "I read the product-line expansion proposal you submitted. It's okay, but it falls short of your usual level of creativity. Each product you mentioned is already being carried by competitors. Have you thought about. . . ."

2. *Listen actively.* Listening is an essential ingredient in any coaching session. An active listener tries to grasp both facts and feelings. Observing the group member's nonverbal communication is another part of active listening. The leader must also be patient and not poised for a rebuttal to any difference of opinion between him or her and the group member.

Part of being a good listener is encouraging the person being coached to talk about his or her performance. Asking open-ended questions facilitates a flow of conversation. For example, ask: "How did you feel about the way you handled conflict with the marketing group yesterday?" A close-ended question covering the same issue would be "Do you think you could have done a better job of handling conflict with the marketing group yesterday?"

3. *Give emotional support.* By being helpful and constructive, the leader provides much-needed emotional support to the group member who is not performing at his or her best. A coaching session should not be an interrogation. An effective way of giving emotional support is to use positive rather than negative motivators. For example, the leader might say, "I liked some things you did yesterday, yet I have a few suggestions that might bring you closer to peak performance." The accompanying Leader-In-Action box describes a leader who emphasizes emotional support and a coaching philosophy.

4. *Reflect feelings.* The counseling professional is adept at reflecting feelings. To reflect feelings is to give a person immediate feedback on the feelings and emotions that he or she is expressing. Some reflection of feelings is recommended in a job situation. Too much reflection, however, is inappropriate because the work situation may begin to feel like a continuous counseling session. Reflection-of-feeling responses typically begins with "You feel. . . ." For example, assume that a groupmember says to the leader, "The workload is too much for me. I can't cope!" The manager then responds, "You feel overwhelmed right now."

Here is another example of reflection of feelings: An inventory-control analyst is asked why a report was late. She answers, "Those clods in manufacturing held me up again." The manager responds, "You are angry with manufacturing?" The inventory-control analyst, now feeling encouraged, might vent her anger about manufacturing. The manager's reflection of feelings communicates the fact that he or she understands the real problem. Because the analyst felt understood, she *might* be better motivated to improve.

5. *Reflect content or meaning.* Reflecting feelings deals with a person's emotions. Reflecting content or meaning deals with the person's intellectual or cognitive behavior. An effective way of reflecting meaning is to rephrase and summarize concisely what the group member is saying. A substandard per-

LEADER
IN
ACTION

Sam Rivera of Fel-Pro Inc.

Ten years ago Sam Rivera was promoted to assistant foreman at Fel-Pro Inc., an auto-parts maker based in Skokie, Illinois. He made up his mind early he was going to become a manager who cared about people. For Rivera, caring about people meant things such as giving production worker Edwin Carrera three days of emergency leave so he and his son could meet with Fel-Pro's on-site psychologist. The production worker needed help in removing his son from Chicago's Latino gang culture.

Caring about people also meant finding another job for Pedro Hernandez, who wasn't able to operate a forklift truck, the job he was hired for. Sensing that the 45-year-old Hernandez would have a difficult time finding employment elsewhere, Rivera found him an assignment as a press-punch operator. Hernandez is now one of Fel-Pro's best punch-press operators.

Rivera attempts to place himself in the employee's shoes. He also gives workers ample flexibility and discretion. "As long as the job gets done, that's the bottom line," he says. According to Rivera and Fel-Pro top management, Rivera's unit exceeds objectives 95 percent of the time. Company management believes that Rivera's leadership style motivates workers to extend themselves. Carrera was so grateful that Rivera gave him time to help his son that he found a way to repay the company. In his spare time he developed a way to increase machine productivity and safety that the company found valuable enough to implement.

Rivera says that his leadership philosophy stems from his poor childhood in Puerto Rico. "I know what people have to do to survive," he says. Rivera's manager, Ricky Justus, believes that if Rivera has a limitation it is that he hates to turn down special requests and to discipline people. Rivera agrees, but adds: "I'd rather be soft than hard, because hard people are hated and can't accomplish anything."

Source: Based on facts as reported in Ann Therese Palmer, "An Easygoing Boss—And a Master Motivator," *Business Week*, June 28, 1993, p. 84.

former might say, "The reason I've fallen so far behind is that our company has turned into a bureaucratic nightmare. We're being hit right and left with forms to fill out for quality improvement. My computer has twenty-five messages waiting to be read." You might respond, "You're falling so far behind because you have so many forms and messages that require attention." The group member might then respond something like, "That's exactly what I mean. I'm glad you understand my problem."

6. *Give some constructive advice.* Too much advice-giving interferes with two-way communication, yet some advice can elevate performance. The manager should assist the group member in answering the question, "What can I do about this problem?"[9] Advice in the form of a question or suppositional statement is often effective. One example is, "Could the root of your problem be insufficient planning?" A direct statement—such as "The root of your problem is obviously insufficient planning"—often makes people resentful and defensive. By responding to a question, the person being coached is likely to feel more involved in making improvements.

7. *Allow for modeling of desired performance and behavior.* An effective coaching technique is to show the group member by example what constitutes the desired behavior. Assume that a manager has been dealing with making statements to customers that stretch the truth, such as falsely saying that the product met a zero-defects standard. In coaching him, the manager's boss might allow the manager to observe how she handles a similar situation with a customer. The manager's boss might telephone a customer and say, "You have been inquiring about whether we have adopted a zero-defects standard for our laser printers. Right now we are doing our best to produce error-free products. Yet, so far we do not have a formal zero-defects program. We stand by our printers and will fix any defect at no cost to you."

8. *Gain a commitment to change.* Unless the leader receives a commitment from the team member to carry through with the proposed solution to a problem, the team member may not attain higher performance. An experienced manager/coach develops an intuitive feel for when employees are serious about performance improvement. Two clues that commitment to change is lacking are (1) overagreeing about the need for change, and (2) agreeing to change without display of emotion.

Leadership Self-Assessment Exercise 10–1 will help you think through the development you might need to be an effective coach.

SUMMARY

Effective leaders are outstanding motivators and coaches. Behavior modification is a widely used motivational strategy. Its key principle is the law of effect: behavior that leads to a positive effect tends to be repeated, and the opposite is also true. The basic behavior modification strategies are positive reinforcement, negative reinforcement, punishment, and extinction.

Rules for the effective use of behavior modification include the following: (1) choose an appropriate reward or punishment; (2) supply ample feedback; (3) do not give everyone the same reward; (4) schedule rewards intermittently; and (5) change rewards periodically.

The expectancy theory of motivation is useful for developing motivational skills because it is comprehensive, building on other explanations

LEADERSHIP _____
SELF-ASSESSMENT
EXERCISE 10–1 **Characteristics of an Effective Coach**

Directions: Below is a list of traits, attitudes, and behaviors characteristic of effective coaches. Indicate next to each trait, attitude, or behavior whether you need to develop along those lines (for example, whether you need to become more patient). Also, develop an action plan for improvement for each trait, attitude, or behavior that you need to develop. An example of an action plan for improving patience might be, "I'll ask people to tell me when I appear too impatient. I'll also try to develop self-control about my impatience."

Trait, Attitude, or Behavior	**Action Plan for Development**
1. Empathy (putting self in other person's shoes)	_____
2. Listening skill	_____
3. Insight into people	_____
4. Diplomacy and tact	_____
5. Patience toward people	_____
6. Concern for welfare of people	_____
7. Low hostility toward people	_____
8. Self-confidence and emotional security	_____
9. Noncompetitiveness with group members	_____
10. Enthusiasm for people	_____

Source: Adapted with permission from Andrew J. DuBrin, *Participant Guide to Module 10: Development of Subordinates,* p. 11. Copyright © 1985. Used by permission of Leadership Systems Corporation.

of motivation. Expectancy theory has three major components: effort-to-performance expectancies, performance-to-outcome expectancies, and valence of outcomes.

Effort-to-performance expectancy is the probability assigned by the individual that effort will lead to performing the task correctly. Performance-to-outcome expectancy is the probability assigned by the individual that performance will lead to certain outcomes. (An outcome is anything that might stem from performance, such as a reward.) Performance is a first-level outcome because it is rooted in the job itself. Performance-to-outcome expectancies deal with second-level outcomes—the rewards associated with performing.

Valence is the worth or attractiveness of an outcome. Each work situation has multiple outcomes, and each outcome has a valence of its own. Valences range from –100 to +100 in the version of expectancy theory presented here. Zero valences reflect indifference and therefore are not motivational. Very high valences help explain why some people will persist in efforts despite a low probability of payoff.

Expectancy theory has implications and provides guidelines for leaders, including the following: (1) determine necessary performance levels; (2) train and encourage people; (3) make explicit the link between rewards and performance; (4) make sure the rewards are large enough; (5) explain the meaning and implications of second-level outcomes; (6) understand individual differences in valences; (7) use the Pygmalion effect to increase effort-to-performance expectancies; (8) ensure that the system is equitable for everyone.

Coaching can also be regarded as a paradigm shift from traditional management, which focuses heavily on control, order, and compliance. As such, coaching is a partnership for achieving results. Several characteristics of coaching contribute to its close relationship with leadership. Coaching is a comprehensive and distinctive way of being linked to others in the organization. Coaching is also a two-way process, suggesting that being a great coach requires having a talented team. Coaching requires a high degree of interpersonal risk and trust on the part of both people in the relationship. Also, coaching requires the transformation of traditional models of management, organization, work, and society.

Coaching can be improved in the following ways: (1) by providing specific feedback; (2) by listening actively; (3) by giving emotional support; (4) by reflecting feelings; (5) by reflecting content or meaning; (6) by giving some constructive advice; (7) by allowing for modeling of desired performance and behavior; and (8) by gaining a commitment to change.

KEY TERMS

Behavior modification	Outcome
Expectancy theory	Instrumentality
Effort-to-performance expectancy	Valence
Performance-to-outcome expectancy	

GUIDELINES FOR ACTION AND SKILL DEVELOPMENT

We have seen many suggestions for incorporating coaching into leadership. Gerald M. Sturman recommends that a leader should also engage in career coaching with team members. If executed properly, career coaching benefits the group member, the manager, and the organization. Career management, in Sturman's view, is the process by which individuals take responsibility for developing their ability to expand their contribution to the organization. The following five-point guide, AIM . . . CM, suggests that a career coach should aim employees at career management.

1. *Assess.* Encourage group members to assess their strengths and weaknesses, and provide feedback of your own. Suggest that group members also obtain feedback from others.

2. *Investigate.* Has the group member investigated all the needs and opportunities his or her organizational unit and the total organization have to offer?

3. *Match.* Group members should match their preferences and self-assessments with the organizational opportunities available.

4. *Choose.* Upon careful examination of the match between capabilities and preferences versus opportunities, have group members chosen feasible targets?

5. *Manage.* Encourage group members to formulate a career development plan that can lead to the achievement of their goals.[10]

DISCUSSION QUESTIONS AND ACTIVITIES

1. Based on your own experiences, how important do you think coaching is for effective management and leadership?

2. In what way is expectancy theory related to microeconomics?

3. What is your effort-to-performance expectancy with respect to the grade you hope to achieve in this course? Your performance-to-outcome expectancy? Explain.

4. Identify several outcomes you expect from occupying a leadership position. What valences do you attach to them?

5. How can the influence exerted by a charismatic and transformational leader tie in with expectancy theory?

6. Explain how you could apply Leadership Skill-Building Exercise 10–1 to motivate group members more effectively.

7. Why is coaching supposed to be a departure from traditional management philosophy?

8. Many other big-name athletic coaches besides Rick Pitino are hired by business organizations to give motivational speeches. Do you think athletic coaches are qualified to advise business leaders about motivation?

9. Some people contend career coaching by managers is an invasion of privacy. What is your reaction to this contention?

10. Ask a manager to describe the amount of coaching he or she does on the job. Be prepared to report your findings back to class.

LEADERSHIP CASE PROBLEM

The Financial Services Coach

Jennifer Falcone is an account representative (stockbroker) at a branch office of an established financial services firm. Her manager, Derek Anderson, is concerned that Jennifer is 25 percent below quota in sales of a new index mutual fund offered by the company. Derek sets up an appointment with Jennifer to spur her to achieve quota. The conversation proceeds, in part, in this manner:

ANDERSON: My most important responsibility is to help team members work up to their potential. I wanted to get together with you today to see if there is any way I can help you.

During the last quarter you were 25 percent below quota in your sales of our new index fund. That displeases me and top management because our margin of profit on this fund is very high.

FALCONE: I know I'm under quota. But I can't help it. It's just tough these days pushing an index fund. Our clients are getting very conservative, and they don't want to jump into a new product they don't understand.

ANDERSON: Why don't your clients understand the new index fund?

FALCONE: It's a new fund, so they don't understand it. The information I send them is pretty complicated for a layperson.

ANDERSON: What steps could you take to make this fund easier for our clients and prospects to understand?

FALCONE: Maybe I could work up a thirty-second presentation that would give a nice overview of an index fund. This would enable me to make a quick pitch over the phone.

ANDERSON: Now you're making good sense. But I'm disappointed that an intelligent person like you didn't think of that before. Do you have a self-confidence problem when it comes to making quota on a new product?

FALCONE: I never thought I had a self-confidence problem until today's session with you.

ANDERSON: Whether or not you have a self-confidence problem, you can earn a lot more commissions by selling more of the new index fund.

1. Identify the strengths in Anderson's coaching technique.

2. Identify the areas for improvement in Anderson's coaching technique.

3. In what way does Anderson's motivational technique correspond to the effective use of expectancy theory?

LEADERSHIP ROLE PLAY

The Financial Services Coach Role Play

Three months later, Derek Anderson calls Jennifer Falcone into his office to discuss her progress in selling the new index fund. Jennifer is now within 2 percent of making quota, and Derek wants to motivate her to surpass quota. One person plays the role of Derek, the other Jennifer. Derek is confident Jennifer can do even better, but Jennifer feels that Derek is unappreciative of the substantial progress she has made.

Before assuming the role of Jennifer, imagine how you would feel if you thought your immediate superior was unappreciative of your progress. Assert your feelings in your discussion with Derek. Before assuming the role of Derek, review the suggestions in this chapter about motivating and coaching skills.

Class members not participating in the role play observe the action, and then provide constructive feedback—in their best coaching style!

Creative Problem Solving and Leadership

LEARNING OBJECTIVE

After studying this chapter, you should be able to
1. identify the steps in the creative process.
2. identify characteristics of creative leaders.
3. be prepared to overcome traditional thinking in order to become more creative.
4. describe both organizational and individual approaches to enhance creative problem solving.
5. recognize how the leader can establish an atmosphere that fosters creativity.

---

*M*ichael Eisner of Walt Disney Company explains, "Every CEO has to spend an enormous amount of time shuffling papers. The question is how much of your time can you leave free to think about ideas. To me the pursuit of ideas is the only thing that really matters. You can always find capable people to do almost anything else."[1]

Eisner's words emphasize dramatically that creative problem solving is an important requirement for effective leadership. Leaders of lesser rank than CEOs also have to be creative because leadership at every level involves seeing new possibilities.

The role of a creative leader is to bring into existence ideas and things that did not exist previously, or that existed in a different form. Leaders are not bound by current solutions to problems. Instead, they create images of other possibilities. For example, a leader might move a firm into an additional business or start a new department that offers another service.[2]

This chapter emphasizes creativity development for the leader. It also explains the nature of creativity and creative people and examines the leader's role in establishing an atmosphere conducive to creativity among group members.

STEPS IN THE CREATIVE PROCESS

An important part of becoming more creative involves understanding the stages involved in **creativity,** which is generally defined as the production of novel and useful ideas. A recent attempt has been made to understand creativity more specifically as it pertains to the workplace. As defined by Richard Woodman, John Sawyer, and Ricky Griffin, **organizational creativity** is the "creation of a valuable, useful new product, service, idea, procedure, or process by individuals working together in a complex social system."[3]

An old but well-accepted model of creativity can be applied to organizations. This model divides creative thinking into five stages,[4] as shown in Figure 11–1. Step 1 is *opportunity or problem recognition:* a person discovers that a new opportunity exists or a problem needs resolution. Thirty years ago an entrepreneurial leader, Robert Cowan, recognized a new opportunity and asked, "Why do business meetings have to be conducted in person? Why can't they connect through television images?"[5]

Step 2 is *immersion.* The individual concentrates on the problem and becomes immersed in it. He or she will recall and collect information that seems relevant, dreaming up alternatives without refining or evaluating

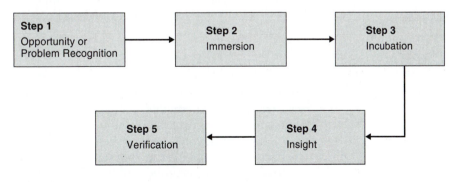

FIGURE 11–1

Steps in the Creative Process

them. Cowan grabbed every fact he could about teleconferencing. At one point he helped NASA and the University of Alaska produce the first video-conference by satellite. Cowan synthesized all his information into a book about teleconferencing.

Step 3 is *incubation*. The person keeps the assembled information in mind for a while. He or she does not appear to be working on the problem actively, yet the subconscious mind takes over. While the information is simmering, it is being arranged into meaningful new patterns. Cowan did not actively pursue his business videoconferencing idea for several years.

Step 4 is *insight*. The problem-conquering solution flashes into the person's mind at an unexpected time, such as on the verge of sleep, during a shower, or while running. Insight is also called the *Aha! experience:* all of a sudden something clicks. At one point Cowan suddenly thought of forming a teleconferencing business to exploit the potential of his idea.

Step 5 is *verification and application*. The individual sets out to prove that the creative solution has merit. Verification procedures include gathering supporting evidence, logical persuasion, and experimenting with new ideas. Application requires tenacity because most novel ideas are first rejected as being impractical. When banks refused to finance Cowan's startup business, Cowan and his wife raised $45,000 from friends and obtained a second mortgage on their house. Cowan did start his business, but he faced financial trouble. With his company on the verge of folding, Charles Schwab, the brokerage firm, hired Cowan's company to connect its 100 branch offices.

Note that the end product of Cowan's creative thinking was a business possibility rather than an invention. Nevertheless, businesspeople typically follow the same five steps of creative thought that inventors do. Even though creativity usually follows the same steps, it is not a mechanical process that can be turned on and off. Much of creativity is intricately woven into a person's intellect and personality. Furthermore, creativity varies among individuals; creative people themselves have peaks and valleys in their creativity.[6]

CHARACTERISTICS OF CREATIVE LEADERS

Creative leaders, as with creative workers of all types, are different in many ways from their less creative counterparts. As stated by Robert Kreitner and Angelo Kinicki, creative people often march to the beat of a different drummer.[7] They are devoted to their fields and enjoy intellectual stimulation. Creative leaders challenge the status quo, which leads them to seek improvements. The creative leader often observes, "There must be a better way." (Robert Cowan, for example, thought there must be a better way of conducting meetings that would not require many people to travel to a distant location.) Above all, creative people are mentally flexible, which allows them to overcome the traditional way of looking at problems.

The characteristics of creative people, including creative leaders, can be grouped into four areas: knowledge, intellectual abilities, personality, and social habits and upbringing.[8] These characteristics are described below and highlighted in Figure 11–2. Before studying this list, compare your thinking to that of creative people by doing the self-assessment exercise on page 236.

Knowledge

Creative problem solving requires a broad background of information, including facts and observations. Knowledge is the storehouse of building blocks for generating and combining ideas. This is particularly true because creativity often takes the form of combining two or more existing things in a new and different way. For example, a personal digital assistant is a combination of a personal computer, fax machine, and cellular telephone.

Knowledge
Knowledgeable about wide range information

Intellectual Abilities
Highly intelligent
Intellectually curious
Able to think divergently

Personality
Nonconformist
Self-confident
Thrill seeking
Energetic
Persistent

Social Habits and Upbringing
Sociable
People-loving
Experienced rough childhood

FIGURE 11–2

Characteristics of Creative Leaders

LEADERSHIP
SELF-ASSESSMENT
EXERCISE 11–1   The Creative Personality Test

Directions: Describe each of the following statements as "mostly true" or "mostly false."

	Mostly True	Mostly False
1. It is generally a waste of time to read articles and books outside my immediate field of interest.	___	___
2. I frequently have the urge to suggest ways of improving products and services I use.	___	___
3. Reading fiction and visiting art museums are time wasters.	___	___
4. I am a person of very strong convictions. What is right is right; what is wrong is wrong.	___	___
5. I enjoy it when my boss hands me vague instructions.	___	___
6. Making order out of chaos is actually fun.	___	___
7. Only under extraordinary circumstances would I deviate from my To Do list (or other ways in which I plan my day).	___	___
8. Taking a different route to work is fun, even if it takes longer.	___	___
9. Rules and regulations should not be taken too seriously. Most rules can be broken under unusual circumstances.	___	___
10. Playing with a new idea is fun even if it doesn't benefit me in the end.	___	___
11. Some of my best ideas have come from building on the ideas of others.	___	___
12. In writing, I try to avoid the use of unusual words and word combinations.	___	___
13. I frequently jot down improvements in the job I would like to make in the future.	___	___

14. I prefer to avoid high-technology devices as much as possible. ____ ____

15. I prefer writing personal notes or poems to loved ones rather than relying on greeting cards. ____ ____

16. At one time or another in my life I have enjoyed doing puzzles. ____ ____

17. If your thinking is clear, you will find the one best solution to a problem. ____ ____

18. It is best to interact with coworkers who think much like you. ____ ____

19. Detective work would have some appeal to me. ____ ____

20. Tight controls over people and money are necessary to run a successful organization. ____ ____

Scoring and interpretation: Give yourself a +1 for each answer in the creative direction for each statement, indicated as follows:

1. Mostly false	8. Mostly true	15. Mostly true
2. Mostly true	9. Mostly true	16. Mostly true
3. Mostly false	10. Mostly true	17. Mostly false
4. Mostly false	11. Mostly true	18. Mostly false
5. Mostly true	12. Mostly false	19. Mostly true
6. Mostly true	13. Mostly true	20. Mostly false
7. Mostly false	14. Mostly false	Total ____

Extremely high or low scores are the most meaningful. A score of 15 or more suggests that your personality and attitudes are similar to those of creative people, including creative leaders. A score of 8 or less suggests that you are more of an intellectual conformist at present. Don't be discouraged. Most people can develop in the direction of becoming more creative.

How does your score compare to your self-evaluation of your creativity? We suggest you also obtain feedback on your creativity from somebody familiar with your thinking and your work.

Intellectual Abilities

Intellectual abilities comprise cognitive abilities such as general intelligence and abstract reasoning. Creative problem solvers tend to be bright rather than brilliant. Extraordinarily high intelligence is not required to be creative, yet creative people are good at generating alternative solutions to problems in a short period of time. Creative people also maintain a youthful curiosity throughout their lives, and the curiosity is not centered just on their own field of expertise. Instead, their range of interests encompasses many areas of knowledge, and they are enthusiastic about puzzling problems. Creative people are also open and responsive to others' feelings and emotions.

Creative people show an identifiable intellectual style, being able to think divergently. They are able to expand the number of alternatives to a problem, thus moving away from a single solution. Yet the creative thinker also knows when it is time to narrow the number of useful solutions. For example, the divergent thinker might think of twenty-seven ways to reduce costs. Yet at some point he or she will have to move toward choosing the best of several cost-cutting approaches.

Personality

The emotional and other nonintellectual aspects of a person heavily influence creative problem solving. Creative people tend to have a positive self-image without being blindly self-confident. Because they are self-confident, creative people are able to cope with criticism of their ideas. They can tolerate the isolation necessary for developing ideas. Talking to others is a good source of ideas, yet at some point the creative problem solver has to work alone and concentrate.

Creative people are frequently nonconformists and do not need strong approval from the group. Many creative problem-solvers are thrill seekers, who find that developing imaginative solutions to problems is a source of thrills. Creative people are also persistent, which is especially important for the verification and application stage of creative thinking. Selling a creative idea to the right people requires considerable follow-up. Finally, creative people enjoy dealing with ambiguity and chaos. Less creative people become quickly frustrated when task descriptions are unclear and disorder exists.

Teresa M. Amabile studied research and development (R&D) scientists to obtain their viewpoint of the personality requirements for creativity. These scientists consistently identified the traits of persistence, curiosity, energy, and intellectual honesty as being important for creativity.[9] A number of other studies have shown that highly creative people tend to have an internal locus of control.[10] When creative people are faced with a difficult problem, they therefore are likely to believe that they have the internal resources to find a creative solution.

Social Habits and Upbringing

Contrary to their stereotype, most creative people are not introverted loners or nerds. Many, especially those who become leaders, enjoy interacting with people and exchanging ideas. The majority of creative adults lacked a smooth and predictable environment during childhood. Family upheavals caused by financial problems, family feuds, and divorce are common occurrences. During their childhood, many people who became creative adults sought escape from family turmoil by pursuing ideas.

OVERCOMING TRADITIONAL THINKING AS A CREATIVITY STRATEGY

A unifying theme runs through all forms of creativity training and suggestions for creativity improvement: creative problem solving requires an ability to overcome traditional thinking. The concept of *traditional thinking* is relative, but it generally refers to a standard and frequent way of finding a solution to a problem. A nontraditional solution to a problem is thus a modal or most frequent solution. For example, traditional thinking suggests that to increase revenue a retail store should conduct a sale. Creative thinking would point toward other solutions. Border's Book Stores, a chain of upscale book stores, increased revenues substantially by starting to offer audiotapes and CDs, and by opening cafés in their stores.

The creative person looks at problems in a new light and transcends conventional thinking about them. For many years, banks were unable to solve the problem of how to decrease the cost of customer withdrawals. They already knew how to decrease the cost of customer deposits: night deposit devices enabled customers to deposit cash into a safe. Customers gained access with a key and deposited money into a mailbox-style drop. An inventor from outside the banking industry asked the right question: "Why not find a way to allow customers to deposit and withdraw money automatically?" This seminal thought led to the invention of the automatic teller machine (ATM).

The central task in becoming creative is to break down rigid thinking that blocks new ideas.[11] A conventional-thinking leader might accept the long-standing policy that spending more than $5,000 requires three levels of approval. A creative leader might ask, "Why do we need three levels of approval for spending $5,000? If we trust people enough to make them managers, why can't they have budget authorization to spend at least $10,000?"

Overcoming traditional thinking is so important to creative thinking that the process has been characterized in several different ways. Listed next are six concepts of creative thinking, which have much in common and can be considered variations of the same theme. Distinguishing among these concepts is not nearly as important as recognizing that they all carry the same message: creative thinking requires nontraditional thinking.

1. *A creative person thinks outside the box.* A *box* in this sense is a category that confines and restricts thinking. Many executives have saved millions of company dollars by thinking outside the box, in this case abandoning the notion that headquarters must be located in a major city. Leadership Skill-Building Exercise 11-1 offers you an opportunity to "think outside the box."

2. *People who are not creative suffer from "hardening of the categories."* A noncreative person thinks categorically: "Only men can climb telephone poles"; "Only women can work in child care centers as caregivers."

3. *To be creative, one must develop new paradigms.* A paradigm is a model or framework. An example of a quality-inhibiting paradigm is that suppliers should be treated shabbily because they need the company more than the company needs them. In reality, creative companies form partnerships of mutual respect with suppliers.

4. *Creativity requires overcoming traditional mental sets.* A **traditional mental set** is a conventional way of looking at things and placing them in familiar categories. One traditional mental set is that the only way to sell new automobiles is for commission salespeople to haggle with customers. Marketing executives at Saturn Automobile Company, however, overcame this traditional mental set. Casually dressed, salaried sales persons at Saturn dealerships help customers purchase cars at sticker price only. Owing in part to this creative sales strategy, up until 1994 Saturn was unable to produce enough cars to meet demand. At that point, competition became intense.

5. *Creative people overcome conventional wisdom.* Traditional mental sets can also be regarded as conventional wisdom. Robert Cowan overcame the con-

---

LEADERSHIP _____
SKILL-BUILDING
EXERCISE 11–1 Thinking Outside the Box

Directions: Many people suffer from *functional fixedness,* in the sense that they can think of only one (or a fixed) function for an object, such as using a frying pan only for cooking. Visualize a table with three objects on top: a crayon, a box containing six thumbtacks, and a book of matches. Your problem is to explain how a candle can be mounted on the wall behind the table.

If you, or you and your team members, can think of a way to mount the candle on the wall, you are skillful at thinking outside the box, or overcoming functional fixedness. The solution to the problem appears on page 368.

For additional practice in overcoming functional fixedness, think of ten uses for a safety pin, a razor blade, a brick, and a wine bottle.

ventional wisdom that small businesses would never be interested in conducting conferences by video. The Leader in Action box below describes another entrepreneurial leader who rejected conventional thinking.

6. *Creative people engage in lateral thinking in addition to vertical thinking.* **Vertical thinking** is an analytical, logical, process that results in few answers.[12] The vertical, or critical, thinker is looking for the one best solution to a problem, much like solving an equation. In contrast, **lateral thinking** spreads out to find many different solutions to a problem. The vertical-thinking leader attempts to find the best possible return on investment in financial terms only. The lateral, or creative, thinking leader might say, "A financial return on investment is desirable. But let's not restrict our thinking. Customer loyalty, quality, being a good corporate citizen, and job satisfaction are also important returns on investment."

*LEADER
IN
ACTION*

Lyle Berman of Grand Casinos, Inc.

Critics scoffed at the thought of opening a gambling casino in the middle of a Native American reservation. Many said that it would be impossible to build a thriving establishment in a destitute economy. People demand glitz and glamour in a casino setting. Other critics complained that Native Americans would be harmed by legal gambling. Despite these challenges, Lyle Berman opened his first casino on the Mille Lacs Indian Reservation, approximately 70 miles north of Minneapolis.

In less than one year of operation, Grand Casinos, Inc. generated $56.3 million in revenues and $11.2 million in profits. Everyone on the reservation who wanted a job found one. By 1993 the Mille Lacs band of Ojibwa had financed $10 million in civic improvements, including new schools and a water treatment plant, through profits from gaming. Between the original casino and another one in Hinckley, Minnesota, about 600 Native Americans are employed by Berman's company. Marvin Hanson, a Chippewa who is a Grand Casino vice president, said, "The quality of life, the pride of the reservation, has really changed. Gaming filled a void. It makes people feel good about the reservation they belong to."

Source: As reported in Anna Esaki-Smith and Michael Warshaw, "Creating the Future," *Success*, January/February 1993, p. 34; Chet Lunner, "Indian Gaming Faces Showdown," Gannet News Service, April 18, 1993.

LEADERS
IN
ACTION

Cyndi Weiss and Diane Castellani of the Fit Company

The Fit Company, run by Cyndi Weiss and Diane Castellani, is capitalizing on an increasing interest in the development of wellness programs for employees. By installing fitness centers, companies hope to reduce health costs and absenteeism. Humanitarian considerations are also a factor. The Fit Company offers companies expertise in fitness and nutrition and establishing wellness programs.

Weiss and Castellani, both former aerobics instructors, opened their business in 1986 after attending a national fitness conference and conducting local research. The two business founders began by offering two exercise classes a week in a company basement. At that time, local businesspeople did not take them seriously. They currently teach about seventy exercise classes a week at large and small companies in their area. In addition, Weiss, who is a registered dietitian, offers brief nutrition courses.

To launch their venture, Weiss and Castellani tried various techniques to help sell their concept. They were frustrated by the results of cold calls to human resources people, many of whom did not give top priority to fitness. The partners then broadened their thinking about the right people to speak to about fitness and wellness. As a result, they called on company nurses or medical staff concerned about expanding fitness programs. Besides making the right contact, they also learned to gear presentations to potential client needs, rather than to Fit Company's interests.

Source: Kathleen Driscoll, "Marketing Flexibility Helps Fitness Firm Stay Healthy," *Rochester (New York) Democrat and Chronicle/Times Union,* April 19, 1993, p. 6.

The Leader in Action essay above presents a small-business example of lateral thinking. To clarify this concept further, see Figure 11–3, which presents more details about the difference between vertical and lateral thinking.

ORGANIZATIONAL METHODS TO ENHANCE CREATIVE PROBLEM SOLVING

To enhance creative problem solving, the majority of organizations regularly engage in brainstorming. Many others also maintain suggestion programs

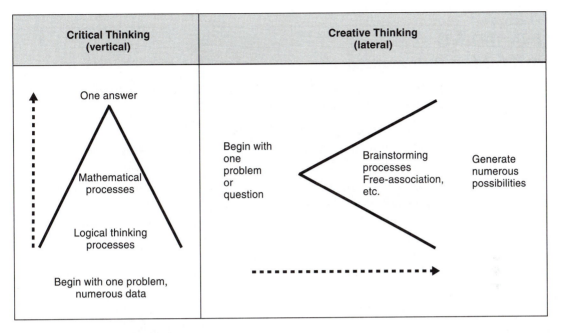

FIGURE 11–3

Vertical and Lateral Thinking

Source: Robert E. Quinn, Sue R. Faerman, Michael P. Thompson, and Michael R. McGrath, *Becoming a Master Manager: A Competency Framework*, p. 250. Copyright © 1990. Reprinted by permission of John Wiley & Sons, Inc.

to solicit creative ideas from employees, with cash awards for employees whose creative ideas are approved by the suggestions committee. Here we describe brainstorming and other creativity-enhancing methods. Programs of this nature are applied to actual problems, while at the same time they provide an opportunity to improve creative thinking.

The leader has a dual role in implementing creative problem-solving techniques. He or she facilitates group interaction and also provides a fair share of creative output. The four creativity-enhancing, problem-solving techniques described here are brainstorming, the pet-peeve technique, the forced-association method, and the excursion method.

Brainstorming

The best-known method for creativity improvement is brainstorming, which most of you have already done at some point. As a refresher, do Leadership Skill-Building Exercise 11–2 on page 244, which presents rules and guidelines for brainstorming.

LEADERSHIP _____
SKILL-BUILDING
EXERCISE 11–2 **Brainstorming**

Directions: First study the rules for brainstorming to refresh your memory. Then do the brainstorming exercise.

1. The ideal group size is five to seven people.

2. The expression of ideas should be spontaneous. All suggestions are welcome, even if they seem outlandish or outrageous.

3. Quantity and variety are important. The greater the number of ideas, the greater the likelihood of a breakthrough idea.

4. Group members should encourage combination and improvement of ideas. This process is called piggybacking or hitchhiking.

5. One person serves as the secretary and records ideas, writing them on a chalkboard or flipchart, or inputting them on a computer.

6. In many instances, a moderator can help keep the session on track by preventing one or two members from dominating the session. If the moderator takes notes, a secretary is not needed.

7. The session should not be overstructured; rules should not be followed too rigidly. Brainstorming is a spontaneous process.

Organize into groups to brainstorm one of the following problems:

1. How can a leader get more respect from group members?

2. How can a leader cut costs yet still maintain a productive and satisfied group?

3. For what useful purposes can a leader apply brainstorming?

A key aspect of brainstorming is that all ideas can be stepping-stones and triggers for new and more useful ideas. Any idea might lead to other associations and connections. Thus, during the idea-generating part of brainstorming, potential solutions are not criticized or evaluated in any way, so spontaneity is encouraged. The idea for an antitheft device for automobiles, The Club, is reported to have stemmed from brainstorming. One marketing person suggested that cars should have a portable steering wheel the driver could remove after the car is parked. Somebody else suggested that the steering wheel be made inoperative, which led to the idea of an ultra-strong bar to lock the steering wheel in place. The Club, and its imitators, have become highly successful products; a version of The Club has been developed for securing doors.

The Pet-Peeve Technique

An important part of quality leadership is for organizational units to find ways to continuously improve their service to external and internal customers. The **pet-peeve technique** is a method of brainstorming, in which a group identifies all the possible complaints others might have about the group's organizational unit.[13] Through brainstorming, group members develop a list of complaints from any people who interact with their group. Sources of complaints include inside customers, outside customers, competitors, and suppliers.

Group members can prepare for the meeting by soliciting feedback on themselves from the various target groups. In keeping with the informal, breezy style of the pet-peeve group, feedback should be gathered informally. Rather than approaching target groups with a survey, members might tell others about the upcoming pet-peeve session, and then ask, "What complaints can you contribute?"

During the no-holds-barred brainstorming session, group members throw in some imaginary and some humorous complaints. Humorous complaints are especially important, for humor requires creative thinking. After all complaints have been aired, the group can process the information during a later session, at which they can draw up action plans to remedy the most serious problems.

A pet-peeve session in the human resources department of a small electronic appliance company generated the following complaints:

"A lot of people wonder what we are doing. They think we just fill out forms and create work for ourselves."

"Some line managers think our job is to find good reasons why they shouldn't hire their best job candidates."

"A lot of employees think we're the corporate ax carriers. We tell line management who to fire and whose job to eliminate."

"They call us the happiness people. They think our purpose is to keep everybody happy and create a big happy family."

"Job candidates from the outside think our job is to shred resumes. They think we throw away 90 percent of the resumes that arrive at the company."

As a result of these penetrating, albeit exaggerated, self-criticisms, the human resources department developed an effective action plan. The department leader arranged brief meetings with units throughout the organization to discuss their role, and to answer questions.

The Forced-Association Technique

A widely used method of releasing creativity is the **forced-association technique**, in which individuals or groups solve a problem by making associations between the properties of two objects. An individual (working alone or in a group) selects a word at random from a dictionary. Next, the person (or group) lists all the properties and attributes of this word.

Assume you randomly chose the word *pickle*. Among its attributes are "tasty," "green," "oblong," and "moderately priced." You then force-fit these properties and attributes to the problem you are facing. If you were trying to improve sunglasses, for example, making them "green" and "moderately priced" could be useful. The forced association is supposed to help solve the problem. A link is found between the properties of the random object and the properties of the problem object. An additional, supposedly true, example will help clarify this abstract process. A pharmaceutical company was investigating new ways of delivering medicine. In a forced-association session, someone picked *time bomb* from the dictionary. One of the key properties to emerge from the session was "slow release," which ultimately led to the development of "time capsules," medicine capsules that deliver medicine to the body over a period of time instead of all at once.[14]

The Excursion Method

The forced-association technique has many spinoffs. One of them is the **excursion method,** in which the problem solver makes word associations that relate to the problem. For instance, the leader of a company safety and health group wanted to increase the group's visibility. During a problem-solving meeting, team members were asked to "take an excursion with" (or free associate to) the word *visibility.*

Among the word associations were "big," "tall," "bright-colored," "shining light," "no fog," "sunny day," "media coverage," and "television." An indirect but powerful link between the word *television* and the problem flashed in the group leader's mind: What about becoming more visible by making a videotape showcasing the group? Copies of the videotape could then be sent to executives around the company, who could watch it at their leisure. Perhaps they could also encourage their staff members to watch the video.

The group ultimately prepared a videotape that explained the safety and health group's mission and some of its accomplishments. The video, in turn, led to more exposure such as coverage in the company newsletter.

Evaluation of Creativity Training

Very little research has been conducted to directly measure the results of creativity training. Research on creativity training, however, has provided useful insights into favorable conditions for such training. For creativity training to be effective, the environment and culture must be appropriate.[15] As an extreme example, creativity training will not help a person who is in a job setting where innovation is shunned. (More will be said about the right atmosphere for training toward the end of this chapter.)

A team of researchers trained manufacturing engineers to develop positive attitudes toward divergent (or lateral) thinking. The researchers found that training of work groups prompted far superior carryover to the job than did training of individuals. A work group trained in divergent thinking thus seems to lead to social support of such thinking.[16] If the group were not favorably disposed toward divergent thinking, it would not receive sufficient reinforcement to be sustained.

SELF-HELP TECHNIQUES TO ENHANCE CREATIVE PROBLEM SOLVING

Leaders and others who want to solve problems more creatively can find hundreds of methods at their disposal. All of these methods aim to increase mental flexibility. A representative group of six strategies and specific techniques for enhancing creative problem solving are presented below and outlined in Table 11–1. These strategies and techniques support and supplement the organizational programs described previously. An underlying contribution of these techniques is that they facilitate intuitive thinking. Intuition is not a mechanical process that can be learned directly, yet a person can develop the mental flexibility that enhances intuition.

Practicing Creativity-Enhancing Exercises

An established way to sharpen creative thinking is to regularly engage in activities that encourage flexible thinking. If you enjoy photography, put yourself on assignment to take a photograph illustrating a theme. You might, for example, take photographs illustrating the proper use of your company's product. Puzzles of all types are useful in stretching your imagination; many creative people regularly do crossword puzzles. Another mind stretcher is to force yourself to write jokes around a given theme. Can you create a joke about the creativity of a leader? One such joke follows:

TABLE 11–1   Self-Help Techniques

1. Practice creativity-enhancing exercises.
2. Stay alert to opportunities.
3. Maintain an enthusiastic attitude.
4. Speak to lead users.
5. Maintain an idea notebook.
6. Play the role of explorer, artist, and judge.

A quality assurance manager in an electronics firm rushed into the director of manufacturing's office. "We've got a terrible problem," he said. "Seventy-five percent of those new ink-jet printers produce blurry images. If we don't fix the problem right away, we won't be able to ship any orders, and the product will fail."

The director of manufacturing arose from his desk cluttered with puzzles and new wave gadgets. With a bored expression, he replied: "Sorry, I can't help you. I'm into innovation, not operations."

Leadership Skill-Building Exercise 11–3 gives you an opportunity to practice creative thinking. Doing exercises of this nature enhances creative problem-solving.

Staying Alert to Opportunities

The ability to spot opportunities that other people overlook characterizes creative leaders. Opportunity seeking is associated with entrepreneurial leadership because the entrepreneur might build an organization around an unmet consumer need. About a decade ago a man observed that most people had messy closets that were cramped for space. He built a successful company, California Closets, around this basic need. A leader within an organization can also be on the alert for an opportunity to bring about constructive change. A good example is the human resources manager at Digital Equipment Corp., who provided leadership within the company for recognizing the rights of gay and lesbian employees.

The Leader in Action box on page 250 describes an opportunity-seeking leader who combined an entrepreneurial interest with exercising social responsibility.

Maintaining an Enthusiastic Attitude

The managerial leader faces a major hurdle in becoming a creative problem solver. He or she must resolve the conflict between being judicial and imaginative. In many work situations, being judicial (or judgmental) is necessary. Situations calling for judicial thinking include reviewing proposed expenditures and inspecting products for quality or safety defects. Imaginative thinking is involved when searching for creative alternatives. Alex F. Osburn, a former advertising executive and the originator of brainstorming, notes how judgment and imagination are often in conflict:

> The fact that moods won't mix largely explains why the judicial and the creative tend to clash. The right mood for judicial thinking is largely negative. "What's wrong with this?. . . . No this won't work." Such reflexes are right and proper when trying to judge.
>
> In contrast, our creative thinking calls for a positive attitude. We have to be hopeful. We need enthusiasm. We have to encourage ourselves to the point of self-confidence. We have to beware of perfectionism lest it be abortive.[17]

LEADERSHIP _____

SKILL-BUILDING

EXERCISE 11–3 **Word Hints to Creativity**

Directions: Find a fourth word that is related to the other three words in each row. *Example:*

| poke | go | molasses | ____ |

The answer is *slow*: slow-poke, go slow, and slow as molasses. Now try these words:

1. surprise	line	birthday	____
2. base	snow	dance	____
3. rat	blue	cottage	____
4. nap	litter	call	____
5. golf	foot	country	____
6. house	weary	ape	____
7. tiger	plate	news	____
8. painting	bowl	nail	____
9. jump	sea	priest	____
10. maple	beet	loaf	____
11. oak	show	plan	____
12. light	village	golf	____
13. merry	out	up	____
14. jelly	green	kidney	____
15. bulb	house	lamp	____

Scoring: Answers appear on page 368. If you were able to think of the "correct" word, or another plausible one, for ten or more of these words, your score compares favorably to that of creative individuals. More important than the score is the fact that you acquired some practice in making remote associations—a characteristic talent of creative people.

_____

Source: This word hints test, developed by Eugene Raudsepp, is updated and adapted from "Ideas: Test Your Creativity," *Nation's Business* (June 1965), p. 80.

The action step is therefore to project oneself into a positive frame of mind when attempting to be creative. The same principle applies when attempting to be creative about a judicial task. For instance, a leader might be faced with the task of looking for creative ways to cut costs. The manager would then have to think positively about thinking negatively!

LEADER
IN
ACTION

John Bryant, Urban Rebuilder

South Central Los Angeles was hard hit by riot damage in July 1992. The looting and burning followed a controversial verdict that acquitted four police officers of violating the civil rights of a crime suspect, Rodney King. With the fires still smoldering, John Bryant, a former TV teen actor, organized a bus tour of the worst-hit areas for two dozen bank and thrift executives.

Two weeks later Bryant stood in front of a burned-out pharmacy and announced plans to rebuild the store with bank loans from some of the executives in the tour. On another day, Bryant joined with several of Los Angeles' most powerful black leaders for a meeting with Peter Ueberroth, the head of the post-riot rebuilding program.

Bryant is the chief of a fledgling financial services firm, Bryant Groups Cos. The firm has been involved in helping finance dozens of damaged businesses. Tom Bradley, then the mayor of Los Angeles, hired Bryant to provide consulting services for minority entrepreneurs. Bryant plans eventually to sell entrepreneur starter kits to people in low-income areas.

To implement his vision, Bryant has created a nonprofit organization, Operation Hope. But he also anticipates many profit-making opportunities in the future. Bryant says, "There is nothing wrong with doing well from doing good."

Source: Based on John R. Emshwiller, "Former TV Actor Stars as Entrepreneur," *The Wall Street Journal,* July 10, 1992, p. B1.

Speaking to Lead Users

Part of a leader's role is to furnish breakthrough ideas. To obtain such an idea, consultant David Israel-Rosen suggests that you talk to lead users of your product or service. A lead user is a person at the leading edge of the industry. In a few years most of your other customers will be doing business in the same manner. Lead users constantly improve products to match them with new opportunities. Rosen thinks that many companies discourage customers from modifying products through such means as voiding warranties because of the modification. An example would be a customer adding a new feature to a machine.

According to Rosen, leading-edge users have produced inventions like the electron microscope, CAD-CAM engineering systems, and a host of consumer products. Another application of the leading-edge technique is to look for someone who does what you do but has a larger stake.[18] If you want to make durable tires, for example, investigate what type of tires airplane manufacturers use; they have a considerable stake in tires that don't pop under heavy pressure.

Maintaining and Using an Idea Notebook

It is difficult to capitalize on creative ideas unless you keep a careful record of them. A creative idea trusted to memory may become forgotten in the press of everyday business. An important suggestion kept on your daily planner may become obscured. Creative ideas can lead to breakthroughs for your group and your career, so they deserve the dignity of a separate notebook or computer file. The cautious or forgetful person is advised to keep two copies of the idea book or computer file: one at home and one in the office.

Playing the Role of Explorer, Artist, Judge, and Lawyer

Another creativity-improvement method incorporates many of the preceding methods. Say you want to enhance your creativity on the job. This method calls for you to adopt four roles in your thinking.[19] First, be an *explorer.* Speak to people in different fields and get ideas that can bring about innovations for your group. For example, if you manage a telecommunications group, speak to salespeople and manufacturing specialists.

Second, be an *artist* by stretching your imagination. Strive to spend about 5 percent of your day asking what-if questions. For example, the leader of a telecommunications group might ask, "What if some new research suggests that the extensive use of telecommunications devices is associated with high rates of cancer?" Also remember to challenge the commonly perceived rules in your field. A bank manager, for example, challenged why customers needed their cancelled checks returned each month. The questioning led to a new bank practice: returning cancelled checks only if the customer pays an additional fee.

Third, know when to be a *judge.* After developing some imaginative ideas, at some point you have to evaluate them. Do not be so critical that you discourage your own imaginative thinking. Be critical enough, however, so that you don't try to implement weak ideas. A managing partner in an established law firm formulated a plan for opening two storefront branches that would offer legal services to the public at low prices. The branches would advertise on radio, television, and in newspapers. After thinking through her plan for several weeks, however, she dropped the idea. She decided that the storefront branches would most likely divert clients away from the parent firm, rather than create a new market.

Fourth, achieve results with your creative thinking by playing the role of *lawyer.* Negotiate and find ways to implement your ideas within your field or place of work. The explorer, artist, and judge stages of creative thought might take only a short time to develop a creative idea. Yet you may spend months or even years getting your breakthrough idea implemented. For example, many tax-preparation firms now give clients instant refunds in the amount of their anticipated tax refunds. It took a manager in a large tax-preparation firm a long time to convince top management of the merits of the idea.

ESTABLISHING A CLIMATE FOR CREATIVE THINKING

Leaders need to develop creative ideas of their own to improve productivity, quality, and satisfaction. Establishing a climate conducive to creative problem solving among team members is another requirement of effective leadership. The most influential step a leader can take to bring about creative problem solving is to develop a permissive atmosphere that encourages people to think freely. At the same time, group members must feel that they will not be penalized for making honest mistakes. Employees must receive positive feedback and an occasional tangible reward for making innovative suggestions.

A study of research and development scientists conducted by Teresa M. Amabile and S. S. Gryskiewicz supports the importance of a permissive atmosphere for enhancing creativity. The researchers interviewed 120 R&D scientists, asking each of them to provide information about two critical incidents: one illustrating high creativity and one illustrating low creativity. In describing incidents of high creativity, about 74 percent of the scientists mentioned freedom to decide what to do and how to do one's work; freedom from constraints; and an open atmosphere.[20]

A maverick manager, as proposed by Donald W. Blohwiak, is precisely the type of leader who fosters creative problem solving among team members. Such a manager actively encourages group members to "color outside the lines" (which is similar to thinking outside the box). Maverick managers also seek ways to do new things and new ways to do old things.[21] At Xerox Corp., a leader who qualifies as a maverick manager challenged his team to simplify the company's billing system. Many customers received multiple bills from Xerox each month. The manager welcomed all suggestions. Finally the accounts receivable department agreed upon procedures that enormously simplified the paperwork for customers.

Another strategy for enhancing creativity among team members is for the leader to avoid behavior and attitudes that block creativity. One such creativity blocker is an authoritarian—that is, inflexible and close-minded—attitude. Similarly, an attitude of *functional fixedness* will discourage creativity.[22] (Here the term *functional fixedness* refers to the belief that there is only one way to do something.) The manager should encourage team members to do things better and differently.

A final organizational condition favoring creativity is the presence of peers and managers who can act as role models.[23] Organizational creativity is thus self-perpetuating. As the leader brings more creative people into an organization, other people will be stimulated to think creatively.

SUMMARY

A creative leader brings forth ideas or things that did not exist previously, or existed in a different form. The creative process has been divided into five steps: opportunity or problem recognition; immersion (the individual becomes immersed in the idea); incubation (the idea simmers); insight (a solution surfaces); verification and application (the person supports and implements the idea).

Creative people have distinguishing characteristics, which fall into four categories: knowledge, intellectual abilities, personality, and social habits and upbringing. They possess extensive knowledge, good intellectual skills, intellectual curiosity, and a wide range of interests. Personality attributes of creative people include a positive self-image, tolerance for isolation, non-conformity, and the ability to tolerate ambiguity and chaos. Creative people also enjoy interacting with others. Many creative adults faced family problems during childhood.

A major strategy for becoming creative is to overcome traditional thinking, or a traditional mental set. Also, it is necessary to break down rigid thinking that blocks new ideas. A related idea is that creative people engage in lateral thinking in addition to vertical thinking. Lateral thinking seeks many different answers to problems, whereas vertical thinking looks for the one best answer.

Organizations enhance creative thinking through brainstorming and suggestion systems. A spinoff of brainstorming is the pet-peeve technique, in which a group of people think of all the possible complaints others might have about their unit. Another technique to facilitate creative thinking requires forced associations between the properties of two objects. A similar technique, the excursion method, requires the problem solver to make word associations that relate to the problem. For creativity training to be effective, the environment and culture must be appropriate.

Self-help techniques to enhance creative problem solving described here are (1) practicing creativity-enhancing exercises, (2) staying alert to opportunities, (3) maintaining enthusiasm, (4) speaking to lead users (customers who make advanced uses of the product), (5) maintaining an idea notebook, and (6) playing the roles of explorer, artist, judge, and lawyer.

Establishing a climate conducive to creative problem solving among team members is another requirement of effective leadership. A permissive atmosphere that encourages people to think freely facilitates creative problem solving. A maverick manager makes a contribution to creative thinking by encouraging group members to "color outside the lines."

KEY TERMS

Creativity

Organizational creativity

Traditional mental set

Vertical thinking

Lateral thinking

Pet-peeve technique

Forced-association technique

Excursion method

GUIDELINES FOR ACTION AND SKILL DEVELOPMENT

To encourage creative problem solving among team members, the leader should avoid certain *creativity dampeners*, as implied in the chapter. Gareth Morgan has identified seven of these dampeners, as follows:

1. Expressing attitudes that preserve the status quo by using such cliches as "Don't rock the boat"; "Don't make waves"; and "If it ain't broke don't fix it"

2. Policing team members by every device imaginable

3. Saying yes to new ideas but not doing anything about them

4. Being the exclusive spokesperson for everything in the area of responsibility

5. Putting every idea through formal channels

6. Responding to most suggestions for change with a pained look and saying, "But that will cost *money*"

7. Promoting the "not-invented-here" syndrome (if the manager did not invent it, the manager will not consider it)[24]

DISCUSSION QUESTIONS AND ACTIVITIES

1. Do you believe it is important for a leader to be a creative problem solver? Explain.

2. How might a person use information about the five stages of creative thought to become a more creative problem solver?

3. What evidence can you present that creative people are not typically nerds?

4. In what way does your present program of study contribute to your ability to solve problems creatively?

5. Why does requiring group approval sometimes inhibit creativity?

6. How might a leader help group members overcome traditional thinking?

7. Give an example of how you, or somebody you know, have thought "outside the box."

8. What type of problem faced by a leader might require vertical thinking? Lateral thinking?

9. At what level in the organization are people the most likely to use the forced-association technique to arrive at creative solutions to problems?

10. Speak to the most creative person you know in any field, and find out if he or she uses any specific creativity-enhancing technique. Be prepared to bring your findings back to class.

LEADERSHIP CASE PROBLEM

The Ship-Jumping Engineer

During his twenty-three years with IBM, Andrew R. Heller established a reputation as one of the company's most brilliant engineers. Despite his creativity, many people wondered how he lasted at IBM until his departure in 1989. In contrast to the usual IBM attire, Heller wore a beard, cowboy boots, and bolo tie. He quickly fixed ailing projects, but he would often insult the intelligence of executives before he began his fixup.

After leaving IBM, Heller began a company of his own, HaL Computer Systems Inc. (Hal is the name of the computer in the film *2001: A Space Odyssey;* the letters H, A, and L precede the letters I, B, and M in the alphabet.) Heller's company targets IBM's main customer base, large firms who use mainframe computers.

Heller believes that many of his ideas and ambitions were thwarted by working for a large firm. Heller's falling out with IBM began when he was given the opportunity to design a new entry into the burgeoning engineer-workstation market. Heller apparently was too successful in his undertaking. Company executives thought that the machines might siphon off sales of IBM's mainframes, so they took the division away from him. Heller left shortly thereafter to start his own business. By 1990, when IBM was fully committed to the workstation market, competitors had already captured much of the market.

Heller is building computer systems that he thinks are more powerful than those made by IBM. His machines range in size from desktop to mainframe, and are all aimed at the heavy-use applications still dominated by mainframes.

1. What messages about creativity do you glean from Heller's story?

2. What lesson should IBM learn from Heller's departure? (Or do you think Heller might be classified as a disgruntled former employee?)

3. What messages about power and politics are in Heller's story?

4. How unusual is it for a creative person like Heller to leave a large firm and begin another company?

Source: Based on information in "A Gallery of Risk Takers," *Business Week/Reinventing America 1992,* pp. 188–189.

LEADERSHIP EXERCISE

The Pet-Peeve Technique

Review the description of the pet-peeve technique given in the text. Break into groups of about five contributors each. Each group assumes the role of an organizational unit. (Pick one that is familiar to the group, either through direct contact or through second-hand knowledge. For example, you might assume the role of the auditing group of an accounting firm, the financial aid office at your school, or the service department of an automobile dealer.) Generate a number of real and imagined criticisms of your group. Take the two most serious criticisms and develop an action plan to move your group to a higher plane.

Communication and Conflict Resolution Skills

LEARNING OBJECTIVES

After studying this chapter, you should be able to

1. explain why good communication skills contribute to effective leadership.
2. describe the basics of inspirational and emotion-provoking communication.
3. describe the elements of supportive communication.
4. be sensitive to the importance of overcoming cross-cultural barriers to communication.
5. identify basic approaches to resolving conflict and negotiating.

*J*ack Welch, the oft-quoted CEO of General Electric Co., once said, "Leaders inspire people with clear visions of how things can be done better. Some managers, on the other hand, muddle things with pointless complexity and detail. They equate it with sophistication, with sounding smarter than anyone else. They inspire no one."[1] Welch's comment succinctly points to the relationship between communication skills and leadership effectiveness: effective communication skills contribute to inspirational leadership.

Chapter 3 described how charismatic leaders are masterful oral communicators. This chapter expands upon this theme and also covers the contribution of nonverbal, written, and supportive communication. Furthermore, it describes how the ability to overcome cross-cultural communication barriers enhances leadership effectiveness. Finally, the chapter presents conflict resolution skills, because leaders spend some of their time resolving conflicts.

RESEARCH EVIDENCE ABOUT COMMUNICATION AND LEADERSHIP EFFECTIVENESS

Research evidence supports accumulated wisdom that effective leaders are also effective communicators. Based on his synthesis of studies, Bernard M. Bass found substantial evidence of a positive relationship between competence in communicating and satisfactory leadership and management performance. An interview study of 200 successful organizational leaders indicated that they had similar communication patterns. The leaders expanded their thinking regularly by actively soliciting new ideas and feedback from others. Furthermore, they continuously sought fresh information. They possessed the persuasive skills necessary to convince others of the quality of their ideas.[2]

An earlier study showed that high quality in oral communication skills facilitated leadership effectiveness. The subjects were 231 editorial workers and their 15 assistant managers, whose work involved abstracting technical publications. Two leadership behaviors studied were explicitness in giving instruction, and frequency of communication about job-related matters. Explicitness in communication correlated significantly (.57) with group members' satisfaction with supervisory leadership. Frequency of communication, however, was not significantly related (.19) to satisfaction.[3]

Research has also been conducted about the contribution of nonverbal behavior to leadership effectiveness. One study suggested that when nonverbal messages contradict verbal messages, the listener tends to place more reliance on the nonverbal messages. A manager who talks about wanting to empower employees but looks bored during the discussion will be regarded as insincere and manipulative. To be effective, the leader must synchronize verbal and nonverbal behavior.[4]

Fred Luthans, Richard M. Hodgetts, and Stuart A. Rosenkrantz observed 178 managers as they carried out their day-by-day activities. They found that about 44 percent of the managers' activities were devoted to routine communication—exchanging routine information and processing paperwork. An important conclusion was that communication activity made the biggest relative contribution to effectiveness, measured in terms of performance and satisfaction. The other activity categories were networking, traditional management, and human resource management.[5]

To focus your thinking on your communication effectiveness, complete Leadership Self-Assessment Exercise 12–1.

INSPIRATIONAL AND POWERFUL COMMUNICATION

Information about communicating persuasively and effectively is extensive. Here we focus on suggestions for creating the high-impact communication that contributes to effective leadership. Both formal and informal leaders

LEADERSHIP
SELF-ASSESSMENT
EXERCISE 12–1 A Test of Communication Effectiveness

The following scale consists of opposite descriptions of communication style. Between each pair is a 7-to-1 scale. Assess your communication style in terms of each pair of descriptions and circle the appropriate number. If you are not currently working as a manager, imagine how the situation would be based on your other work or social experience with people.

I think my communication with people who report to me:

Increases my credibility	7 6 5 4 3 2 1	Decreases my credibility
Is precise	7 6 5 4 3 2 1	Is imprecise
Is clear	7 6 5 4 3 2 1	Is unclear
Answers more questions than it raises	7 6 5 4 3 2 1	Raises more questions than it answers
Is effective	7 6 5 4 3 2 1	Is ineffective
Is competent	7 6 5 4 3 2 1	Is incompetent
Is productive	7 6 5 4 3 2 1	Is unproductive
Gets the results I want	7 6 5 4 3 2 1	Does not get the results I want
Is impressive	7 6 5 4 3 2 1	Is unimpressive
Creates a positive image of me	7 6 5 4 3 2 1	Creates a negative image of me
Is good	7 6 5 4 3 2 1	Is bad
Is skillful	7 6 5 4 3 2 1	Is unskillful
Is relaxed	7 6 5 4 3 2 1	Is strained
Is self-rewarding	7 6 5 4 3 2 1	Is not self-rewarding
Does not embarrass me	7 6 5 4 3 2 1	Does embarrass me

Total score _____ To find your total score, add the numbers you circled.

Interpretation: If your total score is 81 or above, you have analyzed yourself as a very effective communicator. If your total score is 59–80, you have analyzed yourself as an effective communicator. If your total score is 37–58, you have analyzed yourself as an ineffective communicator. If your total score is 15–46, you have analyzed yourself as a very ineffective communicator.

To increase the accuracy of your self-evaluation, ask another person to evaluate your on-the-job communication by taking this test. Many of the ideas contained in this chapter, and in books and articles about communication skills, will help you improve your communication effectiveness.

Source: Adapted from Lyle Sussman and Paul D. Krivnos, *Communication for Supervisors and Managers,* 1979, pp. 10–12. Used by permission of Mayfield Publishing.

must be persuasive and dynamic communicators. Effective communication often helps informal leaders be selected for formal leadership positions. Suggestions for becoming an inspirational and emotion-provoking communicator can be divided into two categories: (1) speaking and writing, and (2) nonverbal communication.

Speaking and Writing

Most of you are already familiar with the basics of effective spoken and written communication. Yet the basics—such as writing and speaking clearly, maintaining eye contact, and not mumbling—are only starting points. The majority of effective leaders have an extra snap or panache in their communication style. The same energy and excitement is reflected in both speaking and writing. James M. Kouzes and Barry Z. Posner underscore the importance of colorful language in communicating a vision (one of the leader's most important functions), in these words:

Language is among the most powerful methods for expressing a vision. Successful leaders use metaphors and figures of speech; they give examples, tell stories, and relate anecdotes; they draw word pictures; and they offer quotations and recite slogans.[6]

Group members and other constituents have more exposure to the spoken word of leaders. Nevertheless, with the increased use of electronic mail and printed memos, the written word exerts considerable influence. Suggestions for dynamic and persuasive oral and written communication are presented below and outlined in Table 12–1. Before studying them, reread the speech by Martin Luther King, Jr. on page 76.

Use Heavy-Impact, Embellishing Language. Certain words used in the proper context give power and force to your speech. Used comfortably, naturally, and sincerely, these words can help you project the image of a self-confident person with leadership ability or potential. A mortgage officer at a bank made the following progress report to her manager:

TABLE 12–1 Suggestions for Inspirational Speaking and Writing

1. Use heavy-impact, embellishing language.
2. Use emotion-provoking words.
3. Know exactly what you want.
4. Back up conclusions with data.
5. Minimize junk words and vocalized pauses.
6. Avoid or minimize common language errors.
7. Sell group members on the benefits of your suggestions.
8. Gear your message to the listener.
9. Explore the reasons for people's objections.
10. Frontload your message.
11. Write crisp, clear memos, letters, and reports.

> It's important that I fill you in on my recent activities. This bank's strategic plan is to get into the next generation of financial marketing. I've bought into the strategy, and it's working. Instead of simply selling commercial mortgages, I'm heavily into relationship banking. I've been building long-term symbiotic relations with some very big potential clients.
>
> So far, the short-term results I've achieved have been modest. But the long-term results could be mind boggling. We may soon become the dominant supplier of financial services to a key player in commercial real estate.

The mortgage officer frames her accomplishments and progress in buzz words of interest to top management. She talks about supporting the corporate strategy, relationship banking, outstanding long-term results, and her company becoming a dominant supplier. Using powerful and upbeat language of this type enhances her leadership image. Yet if she had taken the embellishment too far, she might have appeared deceptive and devious.

Use Emotion-Provoking Words.   An expert persuasive tactic is to sprinkle your speech with emotion-provoking—and therefore powerful—words. Emotion-provoking words bring forth images of exciting events. Examples of emotion-provoking and powerful words include *"outclassing* the competition," *"bonding* with customers," *"surpassing* previous profits," *"capturing* customer loyalty," and *"rebounding* from a downturn." It also helps to use words and phrases that connote power. Those now in vogue include *learning organization, virtual organization,* and *total customer satisfaction.* Leadership Skill-Building Exercise 12–1 illustrates one organizational leader's selective use of emotion-provoking words.

LEADERSHIP
SKILL-BUILDING
EXERCISE 12–1 Identifying Emotion-Provoking Words and Phrases

Directions: Identify the emotion-provoking words and phrases in the following excerpt from an interview with Thomas J. Usher, president of the U.S. Steel Group of USX Corporation, in which he expresses his views on the importance of quality in manufacturing. Compare your observations to those of other members of your class or study group. Also see the suggested answers to this exercise on page 370.

Twenty years ago, in basic industries like steel, the terms "quality-driven" and "customer-driven" often were viewed more as trendy slogans than as daily blueprints for competitive success. But that viewpoint simply doesn't fly any more.

Today quality has become a given—you're expected to have good quality as a basic element of being in business. The question in business today is how to get at quality. How is quality defined? And does it make a competitive difference?

U.S. Steel is being turned around by building employee teams, empowering hourly workers, and giving everyone in the company a sense of purpose. We encourage worker involvement and worker innovation in a culture geared toward satisfying customers with the best steel products possible.

While we still have a long way to go, we're proud of where we stand and how far we've come on quality and efficiency. We don't take a back seat to the Japanese, Koreans, Germans, or anybody else. We continue to work on changing our culture to embrace quality. Suggestions and ideas flow between all levels of the organization. We've changed the way we think. We're becoming a purpose- and vision-driven company.

Source: Excerpted from "Thomas J. Usher: The 1993 William D. Gasser Distinguished Lectureship in Business" (Rochester Institute of Technology, College of Business brochure), March 16, 1993.

Know Exactly What You Want. Your chances of selling an idea increase to the extent that you have clarified the idea in your own mind. The clearer and more committed you are at the outset of a selling or negotiating session, the stronger you are as a persuader. This is one of the many reasons why a leader with a vision is persuasive. In addition to knowing what you want, it is helpful to develop fallback positions. Consider what you might do if you cannot convince the other side to accept your first proposal. If plan A does not work, shift to plan B, then to plan C.[7]

Back Up Conclusions with Data.   You will be more persuasive if you support your spoken and written presentations with solid data. One approach to obtaining data is to collect it yourself—for example, by conducting a telephone survey of your customers or group members. The sales manager of an office supply company wanted to begin a delivery service for his many small customers, such as dental and real-estate offices. He telephoned a generous sampling of these accounts and found they would be willing to pay a premium price if delivery were included. The sales manager used these data to support his argument, thus convincing the company owner to approve the plan. He thus exercised leadership in providing a new service.

Published sources also provide convincing data for arguments. Supporting data for hundreds of arguments can be found in the business pages of newspapers, business magazines and newspapers, and electronic data retrieval services. The *Statistical Abstract of the United States,* published annually, is an inexpensive yet trusted reference for thousands of arguments.

Relying too much on research has a potential disadvantage, though. Being too dependent on data could suggest that you have little faith in your intuition. For example, you might convey a weak impression if, when asked your opinion, you respond, "I can't answer until I collect some data." Leaders are generally decisive.

An important issue, then, is for the leader to find the right balance between relying on data versus intuition alone when communicating an important point. One authority makes this observation:

> An effective leader does not willfully ignore relevant and available data just for the sake of looking decisive. Instead, he or she incorporates tentative conclusions based upon relevant data into a decisive action which may of necessity go beyond the available data.[8]

Minimize Junk Words and Vocalized Pauses.   Using colorful, powerful words enhances the perception that you are self-confident and have leadership qualities. Also, minimize the use of words and phrases that dilute the impact of your speech, such as "like," "you know," "you know what I mean," "he goes," (to mean he says), and "uhhhhhhh." Such junk words and vocalized pauses convey the impression of low self-confidence—especially in a professional setting—and detract from a sharp communication image.

An effective way to decrease the use of these extraneous words is to tape-record your side of a phone conversation and then play it back. (The latest voice mail systems enable the message sender to replay his or her message immediately.) Many people aren't aware that they use extraneous words until they hear recordings of their speech.

Avoid or Minimize Common Language Errors.   A good leader should be sure always to write and speak with grammatic precision to give the impression of being articulate and well-informed, thereby enhancing his or her leadership stature. Here are two examples of common language errors: "Just between you and I" is wrong; "just between you and me" is correct. *Irregardless* is a nonword; *regardless* is correct.

Another very common error is using the plural pronoun *they* to refer to a singular antecedent. For example, "The systems analyst said that *they* cannot help us" is incorrect. "The systems analyst said *she* cannot help us" is correct. Using *they* to refer to a singular antecedent has become so common in the English language that many people no longer make the distinction between singular and plural.[9] Some of these errors are subtle and are made so frequently that many people don't realize they're wrong—but again, avoiding grammatical errors may enhance a person's leadership stature.

When in doubt about a potential language error, consult a large dictionary. An authoritative guide for the leader (and anyone else) who chooses to use English accurately is *The Elements of Style* by William Strunk and E. B. White.[10]

Sell Group Members on the Benefits of Your Suggestions.   Leaders are constrained by the willingness of group members to take action on their suggestions and initiatives. As a consequence, the leader must explain to group members how they can benefit from what he or she proposes. From the standpoint of expectancy theory, the leader attempts to increase the performance-to-outcome expectancies. In Tom Usher's situation, U.S. Steel employees were told that if they became part of the company quality movement, their job security would be enhanced. At the same time, Usher and other company executives held out a threat: employees who could not accept the new way of doing business—such as being more responsive to customers—would lose their jobs.

Gear Your Message to the Listener.   An axiom of persuasive communication is that a speaker must adapt the message to the listener's interests and motivations. The company president visiting a manufacturing plant will receive careful attention—and build support—when he says that jobs will not be outsourced to another country. The same company president will receive the support of stockholders when he emphasizes how cost reductions will boost earnings per share and enlarge dividends.

Stephen P. Robbins, in his review of the evidence, concludes that the average intelligence level of the group is a key contingency factor in designing a persuasive message. People with high intelligence tend to be more influenced by messages based on strong, logical arguments. Bright people are also more likely to reject messages based on flawed logic.[11]

Explore the Reasons for People's Objections.   An important part of selling a product or an idea is to explore the reasons why the receiver is objecting to the message. After the objections are on the table, they can sometimes be overcome. The owner of a microelectronics company informed her staff that she had received an attractive offer to sell the company. Two of the key people, who were also major stockholders, said they would not consider selling their shares to a new owner. When the owner asked why, the objectors were concerned that they would lose their jobs after the takeover. The owner listened patiently. She then explained that she would demand job security for key staff members before agreeing to the sale.

Selling others on the benefit of a message capitalizes on the fact that many people act on the basis of self-interest. They want to know what's in it for them before they will buy an idea, product, or service, or move in a particular direction.

Frontload Your Message. A persuasive speaker or writer places key ideas at the beginning of a conversation, memo, paragraph, or sentence.[12] Frontloaded messages are particularly important for leaders because people expect leaders to be forceful communicators. A frontloaded and powerful message might be "Cost reduction must be our immediate priority," which emphasizes that cost reduction is the major subject. It is clearly much more to the point than, for example, "All of us must reduce costs immediately."

One way to make sure messages are frontloaded is to use the active voice, making sure the subject of the sentence is doing the acting, not being acted upon. Compare the active (and frontloaded) message, "Loyal workers should not take vacations during a company crisis" to the passive (non-frontloaded) message "Vacations should not be taken by loyal company workers during a crisis."

Write Crisp, Clear Memos, Letters, and Reports. According to Michael Mercer, high achievers write more effective reports than do their less highly achieving counterparts. Mercer examined the business writing (memos, letters, and reports) of both high achievers and low achievers. He observed that high achievers' writing was distinctive in that it had more active verbs than passive verbs, more subheadings and subtitles, and shorter paragraphs.[13]

Nonverbal Communication

Effective leaders are masterful nonverbal as well as verbal communicators. Nonverbal communication is important because leadership involves emotion that words alone cannot communicate convincingly. A major component of the emotional impact of a message is communicated non-verbally—perhaps up to 90 percent.[14] The classic study behind this observation has been misinterpreted to mean that 90 percent of communication is nonverbal. If this were true, facts, figures, and logic would make a minor contribution to communication, and acting skill would be much more important for getting across one's point of view.

A self-confident leader not only speaks and writes with assurance but also projects confidence through body position, gestures, and manner of speech. Not everybody interprets the same body language and other nonverbal signals uniformly, but some aspects of nonverbal behavior project a self-confident, leadership image in many situations.[15]

- Using an erect posture when walking, standing, or sitting. Slouching and slumping are almost universally interpreted as an indicator of low self-confidence.

- Standing up straight during a confrontation. Cowering is interpreted as a sign of low self-confidence and poor leadership qualities.

- Patting other people on the back, nodding slightly while patting.

- Standing with toes pointing outward rather than inward. Outward-pointing toes are usually perceived as indicators of superior status, whereas inward-pointing toes are perceived to indicate inferiority.

- Speaking at a moderate pace, with a loud, confident tone. People lacking in self-confidence tend to speak too rapidly or very slowly.

- Smiling frequently in a relaxed, natural-appearing manner.

- Maintaining eye contact with those around you.

A general approach to using nonverbal behavior that projects confidence is to have a goal of appearing self-confident and powerful. This type of auto-suggestion makes many of the behaviors seem automatic. For example, if you say, "I am going to display leadership qualities in this meeting," you will have moved an important step toward appearing confident.

Clothing, dress, and appearance are means of nonverbal communication as well. Many wardrobe consultants offer specific advice for projecting a powerful image, befitting a leader. The leader or prospective leader is therefore advised to pay some attention to suggestions for projecting a "power" appearance. Table 12–2 provides such suggestions.

What constitutes a "power presence" is also influenced not only by the organizational culture but by the culture in general. At a software development company, for example, powerful people might dress more casually than at an investment banking firm. Your verbal and nonverbal language, however, contributes more to your leadership image than clothing, providing you dress acceptably.

SUPPORTIVE COMMUNICATION

Communicating powerfully and inspirationally facilitates influencing and inspiring people. A more mellow type of communication is needed to implement the people-oriented aspects of a leader's role. A leader who uses supportive communication nurtures group members and brings out their best. Instead of dazzling them with a power presence, the leader is low key and interested in the other person's agenda. **Supportive communication** is a communication style that delivers the message accurately and that supports or enhances the relationship between the two parties. The process has eight principles or characteristics that have emerged from the work of many researchers.[16] They are described below and outlined in Table 12–3.

TABLE 12–2   Power Presence Wardrobes

Basic Power Presence Wardrobe for Men	
Suit	Conservative; two-button with narrow lapels, or double-breasted; slope shoulders; navy or gray; solid pinstripe or shadow plaid
Tie	Clean, distinct patterns in dominant colors such as gold, olive, or dark blue
Shoes	Basic lace-up, tassel loafers, or wingtips; black, brown, or oxblood; well shined and in good condition
Shirts	Solid white, medium blue, or blue striped with white collar; regular cuffs or French cuffs; 100 percent cotton; narrow pointed, round, or buttondown collars
Accessories	Gold pen; solid-color, leather briefcase; gold watch of simple elegance
Hair	Short haircut with no sideburns or beard

Basic Power Presence Wardrobe for Women	
Suit	Conservative; navy, gray, black, burgundy, or brown; pinstripe or solid
Dress	Coat style with the look of the suit with white collar and cuffs; one-piece, solid color, accented with necklace or scarf
Shoes	Plain pumps with medium-high heels in solid color (black, navy, brown, gray, or burgundy): well-shined and in good condition
Accessories	Gold pen; solid-color, leather briefcase; gold watch of simple elegance
Hair	Short or medium length and away from the face

Source: Camille Livingston, "How to Establish a Power Presence," *Business Week's Guide to Careers,* Fall/Winter 1983, p. 69; John T. Molloy, "Executive Style," *Success,* September 1986, p. 49; Diane Hofsess, "Neckware That Screams 'I'm a Wimp' Bothers Tie Reader," *Detroit News* syndicated story, January 2, 1992; Interview with Jeff Tomkinson of Jos. A. Bank Clothiers, April 1993.

TABLE 12–3   Principles and Characteristics of Supportive Communication

1. Problem-oriented, not person-oriented

2. Descriptive, not evaluative

3. Based on congruence, not incongruence

4. Focused on validating, rather than invalidating, people

5. Specific, not global

6. Conjunctive, not disjunctive

7. Owned, not disowned

8. Requires listening as well as sending messages

1. *Supportive communication is problem-oriented, not person-oriented.* Effective leaders and managers focus more on the problem than on the person when communicating with group members. Most people are more receptive to a discussion of what can be done to change a work method than to change them. Many people might readily agree that more alternative solutions to a problem are needed. Fewer people are willing to accept the message "You need to be more creative."

A helpful adjunct to problem-oriented communication is for the leader or manager to encourage the other person to participate in a solution to the problem. In the example at hand, the leader might say, "Perhaps you can find a method that will generate more alternative solutions to the problem."

2. *Supportive communication is descriptive, not evaluative.* A closely related principle is that when a person's worth is being evaluated, he or she often becomes defensive. If a leader says to a group member, "You are a low-quality performer," the person will probably become defensive. The descriptive form of communication—for example, "I found errors in your last two reports that created problems"—allows the person to separate the errors from himself or herself. A supervisor's "I message" ("I found errors") is less accusatory than the "you message" ("You are a low-quality performer").

3. *Supportive communication is based on congruence, not incongruence.* A superior form of communication is **congruence,** the matching of verbal and nonverbal communication to what the sender is thinking and feeling. The leader is more credible when his or her nonverbal signals mesh with spoken words. A chief executive officer might say to his staff, "I'm no longer concerned about the firm having to declare bankruptcy. Sales have improved substantially and our costs are way down." If at the same time, the CEO is fidgeting and has a sickly, upset appearance, the message will not be convincing. In this case the leader's message doesn't fit; it is *incongruent.* If the CEO delivers the same message with a smile and a relaxed manner, his credibility will increase.

4. *Supportive communication validates rather than invalidates people.* Validating communication accepts the presence, uniqueness, and importance of the other person. Whether or not the person's ideas are totally accepted, he or she is acknowledged. During a meeting, the manager of internal auditing said to a recently hired auditor, "Your suggestion of bonus pay for auditors when they have to stay away from home more than two weekends has some merit. We can't act on your suggestion now, but please bring it up again in a future meeting." The young auditor felt encouraged to make other suggestions in the future. An invalidating communication would have been for the manager to flat out ignore the auditor, or to make a snide comment such as "Your naiveté is showing. Nobody with much business experience would make such a bad suggestion."

The accompanying Leader in Action box describes the attitudes of an executive who believed strongly in validating other people. He also engaged in supportive communication in general.

LEADER IN ACTION

Frederick C. Crawford, Former Chairman of TRW

In 1958 Frederick C. Crawford retired as chairman of the board of TRW, a company he had helped build into an internationally prominent manufacturing and engineering corporation. Known as an excellent public speaker, Crawford was interviewed in 1991 at age 100. Asked which communications technique proved to be the most effective, he replied:

"The most effective thing in influencing an employee's faith in the company was the mass meetings. They were emotional. Here were five thousand people together, all looking in one direction, all thinking the same things, and they responded. The value of the mass meetings was that I was able to show employees that I had their interests at heart, as well as my own. I considered the employees to be friends. We were all friends in a venture that stressed always that the humblest job was just as important as the top job.

"I never left it to anybody else to speak at the mass meetings. The employees wanted to hear the top guy. That way you build up their trust."

Source: Excerpted and adapted from Davis Dyer, "A Voice of Experience: An Interview with TRW's Frederick C. Crawford," *Harvard Business Review,* November–December 1991, p. 122.

5. *Supportive communication is specific, not global.* As described in Chapter 10, most people benefit more from specific than from global, or general, feedback. To illustrate, the statement "We have terrible customer service" is too general to be very useful. A more useful statement would be "Our customer satisfaction ratings are down 25 percent from previous years": it is more specific and provides an improvement target.

6. *Supportive communication is conjunctive, not disjunctive.* **Conjunctive communication** is linked logically to previous messages, thus enhancing communication. **Disjunctive communication** is not linked to the preceding messages, resulting in impaired communication. Conjunctive communication makes it easier for group members and other constituents to follow the leader's thoughts. David A. Whetton and Kim S. Cameron explain that communication can be disjunctive in three ways: (1) people might have unequal opportunity to speak because of interruptions and simultaneous speaking; (2) lengthy pauses are disjunctive because listeners lose the speaker's train of thought; and (3) communication is perceived as disjunctive when one person controls the topics. Many leaders, as well as group members, fail to relate their comments to the topics introduced by others.[17]

7. *Supportive communication is owned, not disowned.* Effective communicators take responsibility for what they say and do not attribute the authority behind their ideas to another person. The effective leader might say, "I want everybody to work eight extra hours per week during this crisis." The less effective leader might say, "The company wants everybody to work overtime." Other ways of disowning communication include using statements such as "they say," or "everybody thinks." Using the word *I* indicates that you strongly believe what you are saying.

8. *Supportive communication requires listening as well as sending messages.* Truly supportive communication requires active listening (as described in the discussion of coaching). The relationship between two parties cannot be enhanced unless both listen to each other. Furthermore, leaders cannot identify problems unless they listen carefully to group members. Listening is a fundamental management and leadership skill.

OVERCOMING CROSS-CULTURAL COMMUNICATION BARRIERS

Another communication challenge facing leaders and managers is to overcome communication barriers created by dealing with people from different cultures and subcultures. In today's workplace, leaders communicate with people from other countries, and with a more diverse group of people in their own country. The latter is particularly true in culturally diverse countries such as the United States and Canada. Because of this workplace diversity, leaders who can manage a multicultural and cross-cultural work force are in strong demand.[18] Here are some guidelines for overcoming cross-cultural communication barriers.

1. *Be sensitive to the fact that cross-cultural communication barriers exist.* Awareness of these potential barriers is the first step in dealing with them. When dealing with a person of a different cultural background, solicit feedback to minimize cross-cultural barriers to communication. For example, investigate which type of praise and other rewards might be ineffective for a particular cultural group. In many instances, Asians newly arrived in the United States feel uncomfortable being praised in front of others, because in Asian cultures group performance is valued more than individual performance.

Being alert to cultural differences in values, attitudes, and etiquette will help you communicate more effectively with people from different cultures. Observe carefully the following cultural mistakes.

- Insisting on getting down to business quickly in most countries outside the United States. (In most countries, building a social relationship precedes closing a deal.)
- Misinterpreting "We'll consider it" as "Maybe" when spoken by a Japanese. (Japanese negotiators mean "No" when they say, "We'll consider it.")

- Misinterpreting "Yes" (*Hai*) during the course of conversation with a Japanese. (*Hai* only acknowledges that what has been said has been heard, and does not mean agreement.)

- Giving small gifts to Chinese when conducting business. (Chinese are offended by these gifts.)

- Not giving small gifts to Japanese when conducting business. (Japanese are offended by not receiving gifts.)

- Misinterpreting when a British boss says, "Perhaps you ought to think about this a little more" as an opportunity for you to revise your proposal. (In American terms the Englishman is saying, "Your proposal is worthless.")

- Thinking that a businessperson from England is unenthusiastic when he or she says, "Not too bad at all." (English people understate positive emotion.)

- Appearing in shirtsleeves at a business meeting in Germany. (Germans believe that a person is not exercising proper authority when he or she appears at a meeting in shirtsleeves.)

- Being overly rank-conscious in Scandinavian countries. (Scandinavians pay relatively little attention to a person's rung on the organizational ladder.)

- Appearing perturbed when somebody shows up late for a meeting in most countries outside the United States. (Time is much less valued outside the United States. Exceptions, however, include Germany and Scandinavia.)

- Pressuring an Asian job applicant or employee to brag about his or her accomplishments. (Boasting about his or her work achievements makes most Asians feel self-conscious. They prefer to let the record speak for itself.)

- Greeting a French customer or other business contact for the first time in a French-speaking country by saying, "Glad to meet you." (French is a polite language. It is preferable to say, "Glad to meet you, sir [or madame, or miss].)[19]

2. *Use straightforward language, and speak slowly and clearly.* When working with people who do not speak your language fluently, speak in an easy-to-understand manner. Minimize the use of idioms and analogies specific to your language. A systems analyst from New Delhi, India, left a performance review with her manager confused. The manager said, "I will be giving you more important assignments because I notice some good chemistry between us." The woman did not understand that *good chemistry* means *rapport,* and she did not ask for clarification because she did not want to appear uninformed.

Speaking slowly is also important because even people who read and write a second language at an expert level may have difficulty catching some nuances of conversation. Facing the person from another culture directly also improves communication because your facial expressions and lips contribute to comprehension. And remember, there is no need to speak much louder.

3. *When the situation is appropriate, speak in the language of the people from another culture.* Americans who can speak another language are at a competitive advantage when dealing with businesspeople who speak that language. The language skill, however, must be more advanced than speaking a few basic words and phrases. A new twist in knowing another language has surged recently: as more deaf people have been integrated into the work force, knowing American Sign Language can be a real advantage to a leader when some of his or her constituents are deaf.

4. *Observe cross-cultural differences in etiquette.* Violating rules of etiquette without explanation can erect immediate communication barriers. A major rule of etiquette is that in many countries people address each other by last name unless they have worked with each other for a long time. Letitia Baldridge recommends explaining the difference in custom to prevent misunderstanding. Imagine this scenario in which you are working with a man from Germany, and you are speaking:

> Herr Schultz, in my country by now I would be calling you Heinrich and you would be calling me Charlie. Would you be comfortable with that? Because if you wouldn't, I would be glad to call you Herr Schultz until you tell me it's time to call you Heinrich.[20]

5. *Do not be diverted by style, accent, grammar, or personal appearance.* Although these superficial factors are all related to business success, they are difficult to interpret when judging a person from another culture. It is therefore better to judge the merits of the statement or behavior.[21] A highly intelligent worker from another culture may still be learning English and thus make basic mistakes. He or she might also not have yet developed a sensitivity to dress style in your culture.

6. *Be sensitive to differences in nonverbal communication.* A person from another culture may misinterpret nonverbal signals.[22] To use positive reinforcement, some managers will give a sideways hug to an employee or will touch the employee's arm. People from some cultures resent touching from workmates and will be offended. Koreans in particular dislike being touched by or touching others in a work setting.

A general way to understand cross-cultural differences in nonverbal communication is to recognize that some cultures emphasize nonverbal communication more than others. People from high-context cultures are more sensitive to the surrounding circumstances or context of an event. As a result, they make extensive use of nonverbal communication. Among these high-context cultures are Asians, Hispanics, and African Americans. People from low-context cultures pay less attention to the context of an event and therefore make less use of nonverbal communication. Among these low-context cultures are northern Europeans and Swiss. Anglo-Americans are from a medium-context culture.[23] Many new members of the work force are from high-context cultures. Leaders from medium-context cultures must therefore learn to be extra responsive to nonverbal communication.

THE LEADER'S ROLE IN RESOLVING CONFLICT AND NEGOTIATING

Leaders, as well as most managers, spend considerable time resolving conflict and negotiating. An extensive description of conflict resolution is more appropriate for the study of managerial skills rather than leadership skills because it has more to do with establishing equilibrium than helping the firm or an organizational unit reach new heights. Here we focus on a basic framework for understanding conflict resolution styles, and a few suggestions for negotiating.

Conflict Management Styles

As shown in Figure 12–1, Kenneth Thomas identified five major styles of conflict management: competitive, accommodative, sharing, collaborative, and avoidant. Each style is based on a combination of satisfying one's own concerns (assertiveness) and satisfying the concerns of others (cooperativeness).[24]

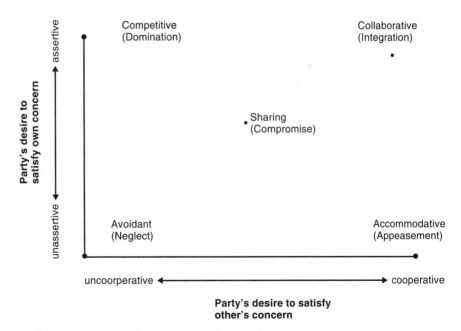

FIGURE 12–1

Conflict-Handling Styles According to the Degree of Cooperation and Assertiveness

Source: Marvin D. Dunnette, ed., *Handbook of Industrial and Organizational Psychology,* p. 900 (Rand McNally). Copyright © 1976. Used by permission of Marvin D. Dunnette.

Competitive Style.   The competitive style is a desire to win one's own concerns at the expense of the other party, or to dominate. A person with a competitive orientation is likely to engage in win-lose power struggles.

Accommodative Style.   The accommodative style favors appeasement, or satisfying the other's concerns without taking care of one's own. People with this orientation may be generous or self-sacrificing just to maintain a relationship. An irate customer might be accommodated with a full refund, "just to shut him (or her) up." The intent of such accommodation might also be to retain the customer's loyalty.

Sharing Style.   The sharing style is halfway between domination and appeasement. Sharers prefer moderate but incomplete satisfaction for both parties, which results in a compromise. The term *splitting the difference* reflects this orientation, and is commonly used in such activities as purchasing a house or car.

Collaborative Style.   In contrast to the other styles, the collaborative style reflects a desire to fully satisfy the desire of both parties. It is based on the underlying philosophy of the **win-win approach to conflict resolution,** the belief that after conflict has been resolved both sides should gain something of value. The user of win-win approaches is genuinely concerned about arriving at a settlement that meets the needs of both parties, or at least does not badly damage the welfare of the other side. When collaborative approaches to resolving conflict are used, the relationships among the parties are built on and improved.

The collaborative style is the approach an effective leader is most likely to use because the outcome leads to increased productivity and satisfaction. The accompanying Leader in Action vignette illustrates this approach to conflict resolution.

Avoidant Style.   The avoider combines lack of cooperation and un-assertiveness. He or she is indifferent to the concerns of either party. The person may actually be withdrawing from the conflict or be relying upon fate. An example of an avoider is a manager who stays out of a conflict between two team members, leaving them to resolve their own differences.

Negotiating and Bargaining

Conflicts can be considered situations calling for negotiating and bargaining—that is, conferring with another person in order to resolve a problem. When you are trying to negotiate a fair salary for yourself, you are simultaneously trying to resolve a conflict. At first the demands of both parties may seem incompatible, but through negotiation a salary may emerge that satisfies both parties (as described earlier). Here are some negotiation techniques leaders may need at their disposal.

LEADER IN ACTION

Elizabeth Elton, Product Manager

Elizabeth Elton is a product manager for a pharmaceutical company. One of the products under her responsibility is zinc oxide ointment, which facilitates the healing of rashes, cuts, and abrasions. In the last several years conflict over this product has arisen between manufacturing and sales.

Although the entire company has adopted a system of total quality management (TQM), so far it has been implemented more directly in manufacturing. The head of the unit that manufactures zinc oxide ointment proudly claims that defects have been virtually eliminated in the product. The sales director is proud of manufacturing's accomplishments in achieving total quality. Nevertheless, he maintains that the high product quality has led to a high manufacturing cost. In turn, the high cost has made it difficult to offer substantial discounts to distributors.

The head of sales has presented convincing data that the company product lost substantial sales to house brands of zinc oxide. In retail outlets, the house brands are placed adjacent to the company brand, making it easy for the consumer to purchase by price.

Frequent mention was made in staff meetings of the struggle of having to produce a top-quality product that competes against lower-priced brands of acceptable quality. Elton stepped into the conflict by working closely with manufacturing and sales to arrive at a mutually agreeable solution to resolving the conflict. She told the two unit heads that she agreed strongly with both of them—both quality *and* price are important. Elton then suggested that manufacturing should strive for total quality, but at a price consumers are willing to pay. She also suggested that the sales manager should not abandon the idea that many consumers are willing to pay a slight premium for a name-brand pharmaceutical product.

The manufacturing group responded by finding a way to decrease the manufacturing cost 15 percent without a measurable impact on quality. The sales group then aggressively pushed the sales theme of total quality and brand-name reliability, at a small price differential. Sales returned to a satisfactory level, and the manufacturing group was comfortable that the company did not slip backwards in offering a quality product.

Begin with a Plausible Demand or Offer.   Most people believe that compromise and allowing room for negotiation includes beginning with an extreme demand or offer. The theory is that the final compromise will be closer to the true demand or offer than if the negotiation were opposed more realistically. But a plausible demand is better because it reflects good-faith bargaining. Also, if a third party has to resolve the conflict, a plausible demand or offer will receive more sympathy than an implausible one.

Focus on Interests, Not Position.   Rather than clinging to specific negotiating points, one should keep overall interests in mind and try to satisfy them. Remember that the true object of negotiation is to satisfy the underlying interest of both sides.

Here is how this strategy works: Your manager asks you to submit a proposal for increasing productivity. You see it as an opportunity to acquire an additional staff member. When you submit your ideas, you learn that management is really thinking about additional computerization, not additional staff. Instead of insisting on hiring a new worker, be flexible. Ask to be included in the decision making for acquiring an additional computer. You will reduce your workload (your true interest), and you may enjoy such secondary benefits as having helped the company increase productivity.[25]

Be Sensitive to International Differences in Negotiating Style.   A challenge facing the multicultural leader is how to negotiate successfully with people from other cultures. Frank L. Acuff notes that Americans often have a no-nonsense approach to negotiation. Certain key attitudes underlie the American approach to negotiation, including:

"Tell it like it is."

"What's the bottom line?"

"Let's get it out."

A problem with this type of frankness and seeming impatience is that people from other cultures may interpret such remarks as rudeness. The adverse interpretation, in turn, may lead to a failed negotiation. Acuff gives a case example: "It is unlikely in Mexico or Japan that the other side is going to answer yes or no to any question. You will have to discern answers to questions through the context of what is being said rather than from the more obvious direct cues that U.S. negotiators use."[26] By sizing up what constitutes an effective negotiating style, the negotiator stands a reasonable chance of achieving a collaborative solution.

SUMMARY

Systematic observation and empirical research support the idea that effective leaders are also effective communicators. Substantial evidence exists of a positive relationship between competence in communication and leadership performance. Nonverbal communication skill is also important for leadership effectiveness.

Inspirational and powerful communication helps leaders carry out their roles. Suggestions for inspirational and powerful speaking and writing include the following: use heavy-impact, embellishing language; use power words; know exactly what you want; back up conclusions with data; minimize junk words and vocalized pauses; avoid or minimize common language errors; and sell group members on the benefits of your suggestions. It is also important to gear your message to the listener, explore the reasons for people's objections, frontload your message, and write crisp and clear memos, letters, and reports.

Skill can also be developed in using nonverbal communications that connote power, being in control, forcefulness, and self-confidence. Among the suggestions are to stand erect, speak at a moderate pace with a loud, clear tone, and smile frequently in a relaxed manner.

Supportive communication enhances communication between two people and therefore contributes to leadership effectiveness. The process has identifiable principles and characteristics. Supportive communication is (1) problem-oriented, not person-oriented, (2) descriptive, not evaluative, (3) based on congruence, not incongruence, (4) focused on validating rather than invalidating people, (5) specific, not global, (6) conjunctive, not disjunctive, (7) owned, not disowned, and (8) characterized by intense listening.

Overcoming communication barriers created by dealing with people from different cultures is another leadership and management challenge. Guidelines for overcoming cross-cultural communication barriers include the following: (1) Be sensitive to the existence of cross-cultural barriers. (2) Use straightforward language, and speak slowly and clearly. (3) When appropriate, speak in the language of the people from another culture. (4) Observe cross-cultural differences in etiquette. (5) Do not be diverted by differences in style, grammar, accent, or personal appearance. (6) Be sensitive to differences in nonverbal communication.

KEY TERMS

Supportive communication
Congruence
Conjunctive communication

Disjunctive communication
Win-win approach to conflict
  resolution

GUIDELINES FOR ACTION AND SKILL DEVELOPMENT

Gay Lumsden and Donald Lumsden recommend a specific communications improvement program that can supplement the suggestions already made in this chapter.

1. *Seek congruity with your messages.* The information and feelings you communicate should be consistent with the verbal and nonverbal messages you use to send them.

2. *Ask for feedback from family, friends, coworkers, and managers.* Ask people who are familiar with your communications style about the congruence between your verbal and nonverbal messages.

3. *Observe others' responses.* Watch for positive, negative, and comprehending responses from others. Question how well your messages are received.

4. *Observe a videotape of yourself.* Obtain a videotape of yourself in daily conversation or making a presentation. Scrutinize your strengths and areas for development. Look for ways to appear more powerful and inspiring. Be particularly alert to voice quality, junk words, and weak expressions.

5. *Decide what to change.* Identify specific verbal and nonverbal behaviors you think you should change to enhance your communication effectiveness. Follow up by practicing the new or modified behaviors.[27]

DISCUSSION QUESTIONS AND ACTIVITIES

1. Now that you have studied this chapter, what are you going to do differently to improve your communication effectiveness as a leader?

2. A team of researchers found that powerful people use more expletives and profanity in their speech than do others. Do you think this finding is valid? Why?

3. Find a model of a powerful written message by a leader. Bring the information back to class.

4. Videotape a powerful spoken message delivered by a leader. If time and equipment permit, share your videotape with classmates.

5. How can you determine if a given word is truly a "power word"?

6. Executive leaders in some large business corporations use videotapes of themselves to deliver important messages to large numbers of employees. From a leadership standpoint, what are the advantages and disadvantages of this means of communication?

7. Suppose a leader has to deliver a message to employees about downsizing. Under these circumstances, how can the leader capitalize on the principle of selling group members on the benefits of the suggestions?

8. A wardrobe consultant recently suggested that people who aspire to executive leadership positions should invest $12,000 in a new

wardrobe. Do you see a good return on investment of this $12,000 for yourself?

9. Which leadership styles do you think most closely conform to supportive communication?

10. Assume a CEO is giving a pep talk to the entire company, and that about 10 percent of the employees speak limited English. How should the CEO adapt his motivational talk to overcome any potential cross-cultural communication barriers?

LEADERSHIP CASE PROBLEM

Tough Day at Southern Tel

Chet Rivera, CEO at Southern Tel, thanked the human resources director for introducing him as the keynote speaker at the annual manager's meeting. Rivera began his presentation by talking about the progress the company had made during the last five years. He explained that the profits and return on investment were solid enough to satisfy the majority of stockholders. He then leaned forward, held onto the lectern, and cleared his throat before continuing. Rivera quickly moved to the core of his presentation, in these words:

"But don't let our satisfactory financial progress make you complacent. We are treading water in an era when we must be splashing toward new records. Ever since the telephone industry has become deregulated, the competition is tougher than ever.

"Unshackle yourself from the Southern Tel of old. We are a company that has reinvented itself. We intend to lead the pack, not follow. We are forging our way into new technologies. We seek to maximize return on investment. Southern Tel has trimmed considerable fat, but we're still too bloated. We have a long way to go to sort out the doers of the future from the hangers on to the past.

"Those of you who can adapt to the new way of doing business in a competitive, deregulated world will have a job with us. Those of you whose thinking is not in line with our new corporate strategy will be asked to retire or find employment elsewhere. We have no place for the laggards, and for those who think in the past. Above all, we have no place for those managers who think we are doing customers a favor by providing them phone service.

"Be part of our new thinking or go find a compatible environment for yourself. I have no sympathy for those who lack commitment to our strategy, and for those who are not committed to excellence. Yet there will be a job for those of you who identify with the Southern Tel of today.

"I have allotted five minutes for questions and answers."

Hardly a sound could be heard in the auditorium at Southern Tel for two minutes. After those two minutes, a loud buzz arose as the managers talked to each other nervously in groups of two and three.

1. What aspects of Rivera's talk contain inspirational language?

2. What aspects of Rivera's talk contain powerful language?

3. How would you evaluate Rivera's talk as a form of supportive communication?

LEADERSHIP EXERCISE

Feedback on Verbal and Nonverbal Behavior

Ten volunteers have one week to prepare a three-minute presentation on a course-related subject of their choice. The presentations could include such far-reaching topics as "The Importance of the North American Free Trade Agreement," or "My Goals and Dreams." The class members who observe the presentations prepare feedback slips on 3 x 5 cards, describing how well the speakers communicated powerfully and inspirationally. One card per speaker is usually sufficient. Notations should be made for both verbal and nonverbal feedback.

Emphasis should be placed on positive feedback and constructive suggestions. Students pass the feedback cards along to the speakers. The cards can be anonymous to encourage frankness, but they should not be mean-spirited.

International and Culturally Diverse Aspects of Leadership

LEARNING OBJECTIVES

After studying this chapter, you should be able to

1. explain the potential competitive advantage from leading and managing diversity.
2. describe how cross-cultural factors influence leadership practice.
3. summarize characteristics and behaviors important for leading diverse groups.
4. pinpoint leadership initiatives to enhance valuing diversity.
5. outline a plan for developing the multicultural organization.
6. outline a plan for achieving leadership diversity within the organization.

*J*eanne Engel, the vice president of a machine shop in Toronto, Ontario (Canada), told the company president, "Wish me luck. I'm headed off to Montreal. I'm trying to get some subcontract business from Chrysler of Canada. Business is approaching overcapacity for them, and we're hurting. I've been speaking French every chance I've had for the last two weeks. I want to be prepared for my meeting with Girard Balfour, the plant manager I'll be dealing with. "

"Jeanne, is that really necessary?" asked Max Fairbanks, the machine shop owner. "All businesspeople in Quebec speak English fluently."

"*Absolument*" said Engel. "Yet even if Monsieur Balfour speaks English perfectly, remember one fact. I'm selling, not buying. I'm trying to please, not be pleased."

281

The exchange between Jeanne Engel and her boss presents an important message about cross-cultural relations and influence in today's world. Engel knows through both experience and intuition that speaking the language of a person from another culture can give one a competitive edge—especially when selling. In a broader sense, Engel demonstrates that sensitivity to, and an appreciation of, cultural diversity improves working relationships.

The modern leader must be multicultural because corporate success, profit, and growth depend increasingly on the management of a diverse work force.[1] For example, the average age of the American worker is increasing, and white males now constitute less than 50 percent of the work force. An increasing number of new entrants to the work force are women and people of color, as shown in Figure 13–1. The diversity umbrella in the work force encompasses such groups as men, women, people of color, white people, able-bodied people, the physically disabled, gay males, lesbians, the old, the young, married people with children, unmarried people with children, and single parents. These groups want their leaders and coworkers to treat them with respect, dignity, fairness, and sensitivity.

Not only is the work force becoming more diverse, but business has become increasingly global. Small and medium-size firms, as well as corporate giants, are increasingly dependent on trade with other countries. An estimated 10 to 15 percent of jobs in the United States depend on imports or exports. Furthermore, most manufactured goods contain components from more than one country.

This chapter's approach to cultural diversity both within and across countries emphasizes the leadership perspective. Key topics include the

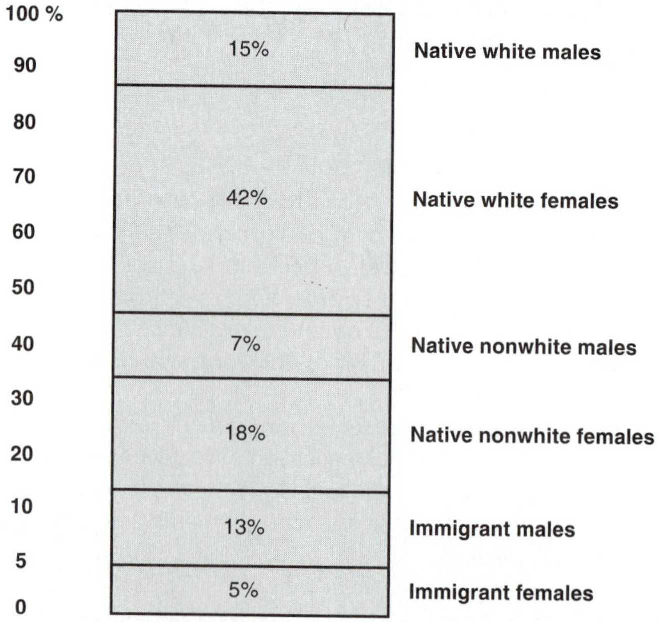

FIGURE 13–1

Projected New Entrants to the Work Force in the Year 2000

Source: Hudson Institute, Indianapolis, IN.

15%	Native white males
42%	Native white females
7%	Native nonwhite males
18%	Native nonwhite females
13%	Immigrant males
5%	Immigrant females

competitive advantage of managing for diversity, cultural factors influencing leadership practices, and the attributes of leaders important for leading diverse groups. The chapter also discusses organizational approaches leaders can take to enhance valuing diversity, developing the multicultural organization, and creating a more diverse group of leaders. The underlying theme is that effective leadership of diverse people requires a sensitivity to and enjoyment of cultural differences.

THE COMPETITIVE ADVANTAGE OF MANAGING FOR DIVERSITY

The social responsibility goals of leaders and their organizations support the importance of providing adequately for members of the diverse work force. The many spheres of activity that managing for diversity encompasses are shown in Figure 13–2. According to Taylor H. Cox and Stacy Blake, managing

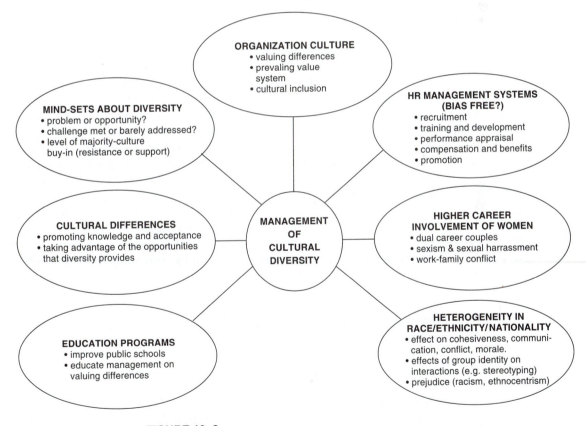

FIGURE 13–2

Spheres of Activity in the Management of Cultural Diversity

Source: Taylor H. Cox and Stacy Blake, "Managing for Cultural Diversity: Implications for Organizational Competitiveness," *Academy of Management Executive*, August 1991, p. 46. Used by permission.

for diversity also brings a competitive advantage to the firm. Their conclusions are based on their own analysis and the experiences of business observers.[2]

An important cost argument can be presented for providing effective leadership to the management of diversity. As organizations become more diverse, the cost of managing diversity poorly will increase. Turnover and absenteeism are often higher among women and racioethnic minorities than for white males. Job satisfaction is also lower for minorities, even among those with MBA degrees. More effective management of diversity may increase job satisfaction of diverse groups, thus decreasing turnover and absenteeism and their associated costs. At one point, Ortho Pharmaceutical Corporation estimated its accumulated savings to be $500,000, primarily from reduced turnover among women and ethnic minorities.[3]

Companies with a favorable record in managing diversity are at a distinct advantage in recruiting and retaining talented people. Those companies with a favorable reputation for welcoming diversity attract the strongest job candidates among women and racioethnic minorities.

Managing diversity well also offers a marketing advantage. A representational work force facilitates selling goods and services. A key factor is that a multicultural group of decision makers may be at an advantage in reaching a multicultural market. For example, Avon Corporation faced low profitability in its inner-city markets. The company then gave African American and Hispanic managers considerable authority over these markets. Soon the inner-city markets became highly profitable for Avon. Another marketing advantage is that many people from these same groups may prefer to buy from a company with a good reputation for managing diversity.

Heterogeneity in the work force may also offer a company a creativity advantage. Creative solutions to problems are more likely to be reached when a diverse group attacks a problem. A study of organizational innovation suggested that innovative companies had above-average records on reducing racism, sexism, and classism. In addition, they tended to employ more women and other minorities than did less innovative companies.[4]

Closely related to the creativity advantage, managing diversity well has the potential to improve problem solving and decision making. Decision quality appears to be best when the group is neither excessively homogeneous nor overly heterogeneous. With a culturally diverse group present, there is less likelihood of groupthink. (Groupthink, as you will recall, occurs when a group tries so hard to be cohesive that it loses its faculty for critical self-analysis.)

Managing diversity can also offer the advantage of system flexibility. Cox and Taylor argue that bilingual people have higher levels of divergent thinking and cognitive flexibility. Both characteristics enhance flexible thinking. Another argument is that managing diversity fosters less standardization of policies and procedures, leading to more fluidity and adaptability.

The accompanying Leader in Action box describes a manager whose efforts contribute to managing diversity. Her initiatives make it easier for employees with different lifestyles to balance work and family demands.

LEADER IN ACTION

Sharon Allred Decker of Duke Power

In 1990, Duke Power Co. in Charlotte, N.C., asked Sharon Allred Decker to build a centralized customer service department highly responsive to customer needs. Decker designed and implemented a round-the-clock customer service center. But she also realized that the company had to be more responsive to the different lifestyles of Duke Power's 500 employees.

Decker's goal was to create an environment in which the employees could better balance work and family demands. She convinced top management not only to build a fitness center, but also to join forces with two other large employers to build a child-care center.

Another problem Decker recognized was that employees disliked swing shifts: working days one week, evenings the next, and nights the next. She devised 22 separate schedules for employees to bid on yearly, based on seniority. The schedules eliminate swing shifts, thus facilitating child and elder care arrangements. Her plan allows the Duke Power customer service staff—75 percent of whom are women—to trade shifts with each other without approval from *coaches* (the company term for supervisor).

Decker's centralized service center has paid tangible benefits to the company. The manager-to-employee ratio has shrunk from 1 to 12 to 1 to 20. Turnover is running 12 percent annually, in comparison to a national average of about 40 percent for telephone call service centers. Most of the Duke Power employees who leave the center transfer somewhere within the utility.

Decker summarizes her leadership philosophy succinctly: "As I treat my team, that's how they're going to treat the customer."

Source: Based on facts in Chuck Hawkins, "We Had to Recognize That People Have Lives," *Business Week*, June 28, 1993, p. 88; interview with Duke Power representative, July 1994.

CULTURAL FACTORS INFLUENCING LEADERSHIP PRACTICE

To influence, motivate, and inspire culturally diverse people, the leader must be aware of overt and subtle cultural differences. Such culturally based differences are generalizations, but they function as starting points in the leader's attempt to lead a person from another culture. For example, many Asians are self-conscious about being praised in front of the group because they feel that individual attention clashes with their desire to maintain group harmony. A manager might refrain from praising the group as a whole until he or she understands an Asian group member's preferences.

The manager is likely to find that many Asians welcome praise in front of peers, especially when working outside their homeland.

Here we examine three topics that help a leader learn how to manage in a culturally diverse workplace: (1) understanding key dimensions of differences in cultural values; (2) applying a motivational model across cultural groups; and (3) choosing the most appropriate leadership style for a national group.

Key Dimensions of Differences in Cultural Values

One way to understand how national cultures differ is to examine their values. Here we examine seven different values and how selected nationalities relate to them. Geert Hofstede identified the first five value dimensions in research spanning eighteen years, involving over 160,000 people from over sixty countries.[5] The qualitative research of Arvind V. Phatak identified the other two values.[6] A summary of these values is described next, and outlined in Figure 13–3.

1. *Individualism/Collectivism.* At one end of the continuum is **individualism**, a mental set in which people see themselves first as individuals and believe their own interests and values take priority. **Collectivism**, at the other end of the continuum, is a feeling that the group and society receive top priority. Members of a society that value individualism are more concerned with their careers than with the good of the firm. Members of a society who value collectivism, on the other hand, are typically more concerned with the organization than with themselves. Individualistic cultures

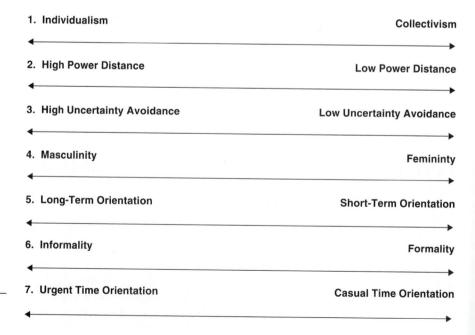

1. **Individualism**   **Collectivism**

2. **High Power Distance**   **Low Power Distance**

3. **High Uncertainty Avoidance**   **Low Uncertainty Avoidance**

4. **Masculinity**   **Femininty**

5. **Long-Term Orientation**   **Short-Term Orientation**

6. **Informality**   **Formality**

FIGURE 13–3

Dimensions of Individual Values

7. **Urgent Time Orientation**   **Casual Time Orientation**

include the United States, Canada, and Great Britain; collectivistic cultures include Japan, Hong Kong, Mexico, and Greece.

2. *Power Distance.* The extent to which employees accept the idea that members of an organization have different levels of power is referred to as **power distance**. In a high-power-distance culture the boss makes many decisions simply because he or she is boss, and group members readily comply. In a low-power-distance culture, employees do not readily recognize a power hierarchy. They accept directions only when they think the boss is right or when they feel threatened. High-power-distance cultures include France, Spain, Japan, and Mexico. Low-power-distance cultures include the United States, Israel, Germany, and Ireland.

3. *Uncertainty Avoidance.* People who accept the unknown, and tolerate risk and unconventional behavior, are said to have low **uncertainty avoidance**. In other words, these people are not afraid to face the unknown. A society ranked high in uncertainty avoidance contains a majority of people who want predictable and certain futures. Low-uncertainty-avoidance cultures include the United States, Canada, and Australia. At the other end of the continuum, workers in Israel, Japan, Italy, and Argentina value certainty and predictability more highly.

4. *Masculinity/Femininity.* The terms *masculinity* and *femininity* are now considered sexist in relation to work. Nevertheless, Hofstede used the terms to refer to the useful distinction between materialism versus concern for personal welfare. In this context, **masculinity** refers to an emphasis on assertiveness and the acquisition of money and material objects, and a deemphasis on caring for others. At the other end of the continuum is **femininity**, which refers to an emphasis on personal relationships, concern for others, and a high quality of life. "Masculine" countries include Japan and Italy, whereas "feminine" cultures include Sweden and Denmark.

5. *Long-Term Orientation/Short-Term Orientation.* Workers from a culture with a **long-term orientation** maintain a long-range perspective, thus being thrifty and not demanding quick returns on their investments. A **short-term orientation** is characterized by a demand for immediate results, and a propensity not to save. Pacific Rim countries are noted for their long-term orientation. In contrast, the cultures of the United States and Canada are characterized by a more short-term orientation.

6. *Formality/Informality.* A country that values **formality** attaches considerable importance to tradition, ceremony, social rules, and rank. In contrast, **informality** refers to a casual attitude toward tradition, ceremony, social rules, and rank. Workers in Latin American countries highly value formality, such as lavish public receptions and processions. American and Canadian workers are much more informal.

7. *Urgent Time Orientation/Casual Time Orientation.* Long- and short-term orientations focus mostly on planning and investment. Another time-related value dimension is how much importance a person attaches to time. People with an **urgent time orientation** perceive time as a scarce resource and tend to be impatient. People with a **casual time orientation** view time

as an unlimited and unending resource and tend to be patient. Americans are noted for their urgent time orientation. They frequently impose deadlines and are eager to "get down to business." Asians and Middle Easterners, in contrast, are patient negotiators. In fact, businesspersons in the Middle East are known to allow a business meeting to run over while another visitor waits outside the office.

How might a manager use information about cultural differences in values to become a more effective leader? A starting point would be to recognize that a person's national values might influence his or her behavior. Assume a leader wants to influence a person with a low-power-distance orientation to strive for peak performance. The "low-power" person will not spring into action just because the boss makes the suggestion. Instead, the leader needs to patiently explain the personal payoffs of achieving peak performance. Another example is a leader who wants to improve quality and therefore hires people who value collectivism. A backup tactic would be to counsel people who value individualism on the merits of collective action, and thereby achieve high quality. Leadership Skill-Building Exercise 13–1 will help you think about how values can moderate (or influence) work performance.

Applying a Motivational Theory Across Cultural Groups

As we have seen, motivating people is a major leadership function. What would happen, then, if we were to apply a motivation theory to various cultural groups? Let's take another look at the expectancy theory of motivation, which provides detailed guidelines for leaders. Doing so will illustrate the principle that some aspects of motivation theory apply across cultures, whereas other aspects most be modified. Two aspects of expectancy theory are especially important for understanding cross-cultural differences in motivation: perception of individual control over the environment, and appropriateness of rewards.

Environmental Control.   As analyzed by Nancy J. Adler, expectancy theories depend on the extent to which workers believe they have control over the outcome of their efforts, and how much faith they have in leaders to deliver rewards.[7] The assumption that workers believe they have control over their own fate may be culturally dependent. In countries where individualism dominates, employees may believe more strongly that they can influence performance and outcomes. In collectivist societies, such as Taiwan and Japan, the ties between the individual and the organization have a moral component. In the United States and similar cultures, many people believe that "where there is a will, there is a way."

Adler argues that people in individualistic societies become committed to organizations for quite different reasons than people in collectivist societies. An employee in an individualistic culture (such as the United States, Canada, or Germany) is more likely to ask, "What's in it for me?" before

LEADERSHIP
SKILL-BUILDING
EXERCISE 13–1 **Charting Your Cultural Value Profile**

Directions: For each of the seven value dimensions, circle the number that most accurately fits your standing on the dimension. For example, if you perceive yourself to be "highly concerned for others," circle the 7 on the fourth dimension.

1. Individualism   Collectivism

    1   2   3   4   5   6   7

2. High Power Distance   Low Power Distance

    1   2   3   4   5   6   7

3. High Uncertainty Avoidance   Low Uncertainty Avoidance

    1   2   3   4   5   6   7

4. Materialism (masculinity)   Concern for Others (femininity)

    1   2   3   4   5   6   7

5. Long-Term Orientation   Short-Term Orientation

    1   2   3   4   5   6   7

6. Informality   Formality

    1   2   3   4   5   6   7

7. Urgent Time Orientation   Casual Time Orientation

    1   2   3   4   5   6   7

Scoring and Interpretation: After circling one number for each dimension, use a felt-tip pen to connect the circles, thus giving you a *profile of cultural values*. Do not be concerned if your marker cuts through the names of the dimensions. Compare your profile to others in class. Should time allow, develop a class profile by computing the class average for each of the seven points and then connecting the points. If the sample size is large enough, compare the cultural value profiles of Westerners and Easterners.

One possible link to leadership development is to hypothesize which type of profile would be the most responsive, and which would be the least responsive to your leadership.

responding to a motivational thrust. Employees with collectivistic values commit themselves to the organization more because of ties with managers and coworkers than because of intrinsic job factors or individual incentives.

Despite the cultural generalization, the leader must be alert to individual and subcultural differences. Many Japanese workers are becoming less loyal to their employers and thus more self-centered and eager for individual recognition. Workers from rural areas in the United States are much more collectivist than their counterparts from large cities. One of the many reasons Saturn Motors located its plant in Tennessee is the presence of a more harmonious and loyal work force.

Appropriateness of Rewards.   Expectancy theories are universal because the motivator must search for rewards that have valence for individual employees. Leaders themselves must analyze the type and level of rewards that have the highest valence for individuals. The appropriateness of rewards is most strongly tied to individual differences, yet cultural differences are also important. A classic study by David Sirota and M. J. Greenwood investigated the work goals of 19,000 employees in a multinational electrical equipment manufacturer.[8] (Goals are related to rewards because people are motivated to achieve rewards that enable them to achieve their goals.) Results were reported for twenty-five countries with a minimum of forty employees.

The five most important goals related to achievement. Next in importance were the immediate environment, general aspects of the organization, and employment conditions such as compensation and work hours. Many significant differences in goal importance were found among the various countries. Workers from English-speaking countries, for example, placed more emphasis on individual achievement and less emphasis on job security. In the current era, job security would probably have a much higher valence because of the decrease in full-time, permanent jobs in many countries. Table 13–1 presents a sampling of cultural differences in goal preferences.

Many American managers have mistakenly assumed that a reward with a high valence among American workers will also have high valence among workers from other cultures. In one situation, raising the salary of a particu-

TABLE 13–1   A Sampling of Cross-Cultural Differences in Work Goals

1. English-speaking countries attached more importance to individual achievement and less to job security.

2. French-speaking countries gave greater importance to job security and somewhat less to challenging work.

3. Northern European countries placed less importance on getting ahead and work recognition, but more emphasis on job accomplishment. Furthermore, they showed more concern for the welfare of others and less for the organization as a whole.

4. Germany placed very high emphasis on getting ahead, and high emphasis on job security and employee benefits.

5. Japan deemphasized advancement and autonomy but emphasized good working conditions and a congenial working environment.

Source: Based on information presented in David Sirota and M. J. Greenwood, "Understanding Your Overseas Workforce," *Harvard Business Review*, January–February 1971, pp. 53–60.

lar group of Mexican workers motivated them to work fewer rather than more hours. A spokesperson for the Mexican workers said, "We can now make enough money to live and enjoy life in less time than previously. Now, we do not have to work so many hours."[9]

Choosing the Most Appropriate Leadership Style for a National Group

Another way to understand how culture influences leadership is to examine whether certain leadership styles fit certain national cultures best. Based on the discussion so far, we would expect the authoritarian style of leadership to be effective in countries such as India, where people have high respect for authority. Robert Kreitner synthesized two related studies to develop an international contingency model of leadership.[10] Based on the path-goal styles of leadership, the model presents general guidelines, rather than infallible rules, for international managers.

According to the model, as shown in Table 13–2, national culture determines which leadership style will be acceptable in a given culture. Observe

TABLE 13–2 An International Contingency Model of Leadership Based on Culturally Appropriate Path-Goal Leadership Styles

Country	Directive	Supportive	Participative	Achievement-oriented
Australia		X	X	X
Brazil	X		X	
Canada		X	X	X
France	X		X	
Germany		X	X	X
Great Britain		X	X	X
Hong Kong	X	X	X	X
India	X		X	X
Italy	X	X	X	
Japan	X	X	X	
Philippines	X	X	X	X
Sweden			X	X
Taiwan	X	X	X	
United States		X	X	X

Source: Robert Kreitner, *Management*, 5th ed. (Boston: Houghton Mifflin, 1992), p. 647. Kreitner's sources were Carl A. Rodrigues, "The Situation and National Culture as Contingencies for Leadership Behavior: Two Conceptual Models," in S. Benjamin Prasad (ed.), *Advances in International Comparative Management,* Vol. 5 (Greenwich, Conn.: JAI Press, 1990), pp. 51–68; and Geert Hofstede and Michael Harris Bond, "The Confucius Connection: From Cultural Roots to Economic Growth," *Organizational Dynamics,* Spring 1988, pp. 4–21.

that the participative style is considered acceptable in all the countries studied, and that the directive leadership is evaluated as the least acceptable style for the countries studied. Hong Kong and the Philippines are the two countries most receptive to a variety of leadership styles, probably owing to their rich cultural diversity. Kreitner observes that international managers require a full range of leadership styles in a culturally diverse world.

The international contingency model of leadership is valuable because it urges the leader to think about which style will work best in a given country. One concern about the model is that it underestimates the appropriateness of the directive leadership style in many situations in certain countries. As described in Chapter 5, many directive (authoritarian) leaders achieve good results without damaging morale.

CULTURAL SENSITIVITY

Some managers are more effective at leading diverse groups than others, depending on their characteristics and behaviors. The traits and behaviors described in Chapters 2, 3, and 4 would equip a person to lead diverse groups, but cultural sensitivity is also essential for inspiring people from cultures other than one's own. Leaders, as well as others, attempting to influence a person from a foreign country, must be alert to possible cultural differences. Thus the leader must be willing to acquire knowledge about local customs and learn to speak the native language at least passably.

A cross-cultural leader must be patient, adaptable, flexible, and willing to listen and learn. All these characteristics are part of **cultural sensitivity**, an awareness of and a willingness to investigate the reasons why people of another culture act as they do.[11] A person with cultural sensitivity will recognize certain nuances in customs that will help build better relationships with people in his or her "adopted" cultures. Table 13–3 presents a sampling of appropriate and less appropriate behaviors in a variety of countries. (These are suggestions, not absolute rules.)

Sensitivity is the most important characteristic for leading people from other cultures because cultural stereotypes rarely provide entirely reliable guides in dealing with others. An American manager, for example, might expect Asian group members to accept his or her directives immediately because Asians are known to defer to authority. Nevertheless, an individual Asian might need considerable convincing before accepting authority.

Another aspect of cultural sensitivity for cross-cultural leaders is to pay close attention to foreign business practices. Lester Thurow contends that when Americans ignore international developments, they lose out as business partners. He explains that Americans need to keep their egos in check. Cultures steeped in centuries-long traditions are seldom inspired or persuaded by a Wall Street smile. "The rest of the world is not panting to

TABLE 13–3   Protocol Do's and Don'ts

Country	Do's	Don'ts
Great Britain	DO hold your fork (tines pointed down) in the left hand and your knife in the right hand throughout the meal.	DON'T ask personal questions. The British protect their privacy.
	DO say please and thank you—often.	DON'T gossip about royalty.
France	DO be punctual for appointments.	DON'T expect to complete any work during the French two-hour lunch.
	DO shake hands (a short, quick pump) when greeting, being introduced, and leaving. Only close friends kiss cheeks.	DON'T try to do business during August—*les vacances* (vacation time).
Italy	DO write business correspondence in Italian for priority attention.	DON'T eat too much pasta, as it is not the main course.
	DO make appointments between 10 a.m. and 11 a.m., or after 3 p.m.	DON'T hand out business cards freely. Italians use them infrequently.
Spain	DO write business correspondence in English, unless your Spanish is impeccable.	DON'T expect punctuality. Your appointments will arrive 20–30 minutes late.
	DO take business lunches at 2:30 p.m. and dinner at 9 p.m. or 10 p.m. Be prepared to dine until midnight, or later if chatter flows.	DON'T make the American sign for "okay" with your thumb and forefinger. In Spain, this is vulgar.

Source: Dorothy Manning of International Business Protocol, cited in Heidi J. LaFleche, "When in Rome," *TWA Ambassador*, October 1990, p. 69.

become a little America," reports Thurow. With the consolidation of the European Common Market and the rapid expansion of the Pacific Rim, America's attitude of being number one is becoming obsolete.[12]

Cultural sensitivity is enhanced by diversity training (or valuing differences training) as well as simply learning to listen carefully and observe. Another way to develop cultural sensitivity is to acquire broad experience in working in different countries, as illustrated in the Leader in Action box on page 294.

LEADER
IN
ACTION

Barry Romeril, Transnational Leader

Barry D. Romeril, age 49, is an executive whose entire career has been with international business corporations. In 1993, he was elected executive vice president and chief financial officer of Xerox Corp. Romeril had been group finance director for British Telecommunications plc for the previous five years. Romeril's areas of responsibility include control, treasury, tax and audit, and business development and strategy. He also is a member of the Xerox corporate office.

Originally from Jersey in the Channel Islands, Romeril is a British citizen. He graduated with honors from Oxford University in 1966 with a degree in economics. During his university career, he spent time teaching in India as part of a voluntary service program. He also taught for an additional year after graduation. Romeril began his professional career as a senior economist for Moscow Nardony Bank, and later worked for Iraq Petroleum Co., spending two years in Qatar. He then spent three years with BTR inc. and BTR plc, and fourteen years with Imperial Chemical Industries plc. His assignments for the two British firms included two tours in the United Sates before joining British Telcom in 1988.

A work associate said of Romeril, "Barry is a man for all seasons. He's a distinguished fellow but he can relate as well to a street peasant as to royalty."

Source: Adapted from William Patalon III, "New Xerox CFO Is an International Expert," *Rochester (New York) Democrat & Chronicle*, April 29, 1993; comments with work associate obtained separately.

LEADERSHIP INITIATIVES

For organizations to value diversity, top management must be committed to it as well. The commitment is clearest when valuing diversity is embedded in organizational strategy. A true diversity strategy should encourage all employees to contribute their unique talents, skills, and expertise to the organizations's operations, independent of race, gender, ethnic background, and any other definable difference. Organizational leaders sometimes formulate strategy with the input of a wide range of organizational members. In addition, leaders should take the initiative to assure that dozens of other activities are implemented to support the diversity strategy.

Four hundred human resource professionals responded to a survey to determine the kinds of diversity policies that existed in their organizations. The firms included manufacturers, service firms, retailers and wholesalers, government agencies, health care providers, and educational institutions. In the firms studied, certain employee groups represented current and future priorities for accommodating special needs. Minority and women represented the highest priority groups; disabled and older employees represented the next priority; functionally illiterate employees received the lowest priority.[13] As shown in Table 13–4, the diversity policies and programs were divided into four categories: building a diversity culture, educational initiatives, career support, and accommodating special needs.

A diversity policy not shown in Table 13–4 is developing an employee base to match the customer base. For example, if 20 percent of a company's

TABLE 13–4   Managing Diversity Policies within a Variety of Private and Public Employers

Policy/Program	% Policy Exists	% Need Policy/ *Need to Do More
Building a Valuing-Diversity Culture		
Discussion groups to promote tolerance and understanding	49.9	75.1*
Diversity training for supervisors	38.0	74.5
Efforts to change corporate culture to value differences	37.0	61.4
Team building for diverse groups that must work together	35.3	68.8
Diversity task force to recommend policy changes where needed	34.6	44.9
Holding managers accountable for increasing diversity in managerial ranks	32.7	65.5
Awareness training to reduce prejudice	11.6	26.2
Educational Initiatives		
Incentives for younger workers to complete their education	65.5	72.7
Basic education classes (Reading, Math)	29.8	57.1
Classes in English for non-English-speaking employees	21.4	64.8
Career Support		
Minority internships	58.1	62.2
Networking among minority groups	41.7	70.3
Programs to steer women and minorities into "pivotal" jobs— key positions critical to rapid advancement	25.7	61.8
Specific goals to diversify middle and upper management	27.7	57.1
Accommodating Special Needs		
Scheduled days off to accommodate religious preferences	58.2	40.5
Policies to hire retirees for temporary assignments	45.1	51.6
Day-care arrangements or benefits	24.5	48.8
Work-at-home arrangements	19.5	32.7
Job redesign to accommodate disabled employees	17.3	49.4
Translation of written materials (manuals, newsletters) into several languages	12.6	21.0

Source: Benson Rosen and Kay Lovelace, "Piecing Together the Diversity Puzzle," *HRMagazine*, June 1991, p. 82. Reprinted with the permission of *HRMagazine*, published by the Society for Human Resource Management, Alexandria, VA.

athletic shoes are sold to young African American males, then about 20 percent of the employees should be young African American males. Digital Equipment Corporation was the first business firm to strive to achieve this balance. As described in the accompanying Leader in Action insert, Kinney Shoe is another firm attempting to match the employee base with the customer base.

LEADER IN ACTION

Bob Jacinto, Director of Fair Employment Practice

Nearly 4,000 Kinney Shoe stores sell footwear, athletic footwear, and accessories to culturally diverse clientele. Kinney's policy is that equal employment opportunity is the right thing to do within the retail environment. The company implements the policy through education: it provides its executives and store managers with the information they need to make the best hiring decisions. Sometimes the information may help a store manager overcome a preconceived idea that a person's accent reflects his or her intelligence. Or a manager might be coached about how to recruit and retain the best talent in huge unemployment and high minority areas such as Detroit.

Bob Jacinto, director of the Office of Fair Employment Practice, says, "We stress that talent is color- and gender-blind and color-neutral. We're trying to create a better sensitivity among our supervisors about the issues and challenges women and minorities face in pursuing their careers.

"We must teach our managers to understand the challenges these new workers face and develop the skills to remove barriers. If we can do that, we'll attract more of this work force."

As part of his leadership role, Jacinto conducts eight-hour seminars for Kinney Shoe executives and store managers. He implements the Valuing Diversity program developed by Griggs Productions. The program focuses on managing people in the workplace who have different cultural backgrounds. One feature of the program is to study how different individuals react to different work situations. In one situation, a supervisor publicly praises a Native American worker, unaware that public praise is likely to embarrass a Native American.

The director of human resources at Kinney emphasizes that today's retail environment needs a diverse work force to service a diverse customer base. Jacinto says he is shocked that so few other retailers have attempted to match their work force composition to the makeup of their customer base. He concludes, "I say, good we have the advantage here."

Source: Based on facts in Joyce E. Santora, "Kinney Shoe Steps into Diversity," *Personnel Journal*, September 1991, pp. 72–77.

DEVELOPING THE MULTICULTURAL ORGANIZATION

The leadership initiatives just reviewed strongly contribute to valuing diversity. An even more comprehensive strategy is to establish a **multicultural organization**. Such a firm values cultural diversity and is willing to encourage and even capitalize on such diversity. Developing a multicultural organization helps achieve the potential benefits of valuing diversity described previously. In addition, the multicultural organization helps avoid problems stemming from diversity such as increased turnover, interpersonal conflict, and communication breakdowns.[14]

According to Taylor Cox, Jr., the multicultural organization has six key characteristics, all requiring effective leadership to achieve. These characteristics are shown in Figure 13–4 and summarized next.

1. *Creating pluralism.* In a pluralistic organization, both minority and majority group members are influential in creating behavioral norms, values, and policies; Kinney Shoes exemplifies such an organization. Valuing diversity training is a major technique for achieving pluralism. Another useful technique is to encourage employees to be conversant in a second language spoken by many coworkers, customers, or both.

2. *Creating full structural integration.* The objective of full structural integration is a zero correlation between culture-group identity and job status—that is, no one should be assigned to a specific job just because of his or her ethnicity or gender. One approach to achieving full structural integration is

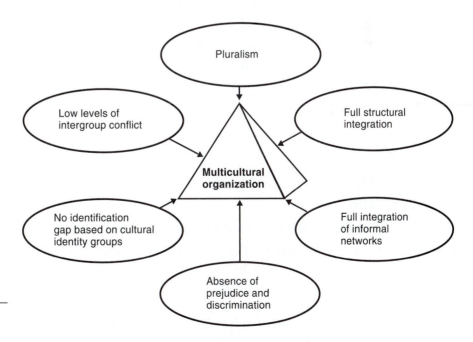

FIGURE 13–4

The Multicultural Organization

to upgrade the education of minority group members where needed. Affirmative action programs and career development programs also help achieve integration. The firm's performance appraisal and reward systems should reinforce the importance of effectively managing for diversity. Employers linking pay to performance on diversity management objectives include Baxter Health Care, Amtrak, Merck & Co., and Coca-Cola.

3. *Creating integration of informal networks.* Minorities are often excluded from informal networks, making it difficult for them to achieve career advancement. Several things can help integrate informal networks: company-sponsored mentoring programs that target minorities; company-sponsored social events that minorities are encouraged to attend; and the creation of minority associations and support groups within an organization, provided they do not foster a "minority-versus-majority" attitude. The Xerox Corp.'s Hispanic Professional Association is a positive example of a minority association within a company.

4. *Creating a bias-free organization.* Bias and prejudice create discrimination, so organizational efforts to reduce bias help prevent discrimination. Northern Telecom, for example, offers a sixteen-hour program designed to help employees identify and modify cultural biases and prejudices. Some companies create task forces that monitor organizational policy and practices for evidence of unfairness.

5. *Organizational identification.* In a multicultural organization, there is a zero correlation between the cultural identity group and levels of organizational identification. This would mean, for example, that Asians would identify as strongly with the organization as would white males. All the techniques mentioned in the other five steps help foster such strong identification.

6. *Minimizing intergroup conflict.* To achieve a multicultural organization, conflict must be at healthy levels. Cox believes the most effective approach to minimizing conflict among cultural groups is to collect and share data about sensitive issues. Corning Incorporated, for example, collected data to help white males understand that diversity programs had not adversely affected their promotion rates.

Leadership Skill-Building Exercise 13–2 gives you an opportunity to examine your attitudes toward valuing diversity.

LEADERSHIP SKILL-BUILDING EXERCISE 13–2 How Much Do I Value Diversity?

Directions: Rate yourself on your responses to the statements below. Use a scale of 1 to 5 to rate how strongly you agree with the statements, 1 being for low agreement, and 5 being high.

1. I regularly assess my strenghts and weaknesses and consciously work towards my goals.

2. I am interested in the ideas of people who do not think as I think, and I respect their opinions even when I disagree with them.

3. Some of my friends or associates are different from me in age, race, gender, physical abilities, economic status, and education.

4. If I were at a party with people outside of my own group, I would go out of my way to meet them.

5. I do not need to understand everything going on around me. I tolerate ambiguity.

6. I am able to change course quickly. I readily change my plans or expectations to adapt to a new situation.

7. I recognize that I am a product of my upbringing and my way is not the only way.

8. I am patient and flexible. I can accept different ways of getting a job done as long as the results are good.

9. I am always asking questions, reading, exploring. I am curious about new things, people, and places.

10. I am interested in human dynamics and often find myself thinking, "what's really going on here?"

11. I can see two sides on most issues.

12. I have made mistakes and I have learned from them.

13. In an unfamiliar situation, I watch and listen before acting.

14. I listen carefully.

15. When I am lost, I ask for directions.

16. When I don't understand what someone is saying, I ask for clarification.

17. I sincerely do not want to offend others.

18. I like people and accept them as they are.

19. I am sensitive to the feelings of others and observe their reactions when I am talking.

20. I am aware of my prejudices and consciously try to control my assumptions about people.

Scoring: Total your answers. If your score is 80 or above, you probably value diversity and are able to manage people who are different from yourself—but you certainly have room for improvement. If your score is below 50 you probably experience much difficulty managing diversity and could benefit from further training.

***

Source: Teacher's Trainer's Guide, *Valuing Diversity*®, Part I, "Managing Differences." Used by permission of Griggs Productions, San Francisco, CA.

ACHIEVING LEADERSHIP DIVERSITY

To achieve a multicultural organization, firms must also practice **leadership diversity**, the presence of a culturally heterogeneous cadre of leaders. Many global firms based in the United States have already achieved leadership diversity with respect to ethnicity. Among these international executives are the following:

Peter van Cuylenburg, the British president and chief operating officer of NeXT, Inc.

Fritz Ammann, the Swiss president and chief executive officer of Esprit de Corps.

H. Onno Ruding, the Netherlands-born vice chairman of Citicorp

Jean-Paul Valles, the French vice chairman of Pfizer, Inc.

Eckhard Pfeiffer, the German president and chief executive officer of Compaq Computer[15]

Ethnicity is but one aspect of diversity, as emphasized by the research of Ann M. Morrison. Based on interviews with over 200 managers at sixteen exemplary organizations, she has identified the best practices for encouraging the advancement of the new leaders: white women and people of color.[16] Morrison provides five steps an organization can follow to achieve leadership diversity.

Step 1: Discover and rediscover diversity problems in the organization. The first step should analyze barriers to achieving diversity goals. A cross-section of women and minority-group employees should be interviewed. Interviews should be conducted periodically to demonstrate that achieving leadership diversity is not a one-time program.

Step 2: Strengthen top-management commitment. The same axiom of organizational improvement surfaces again. Without top-management commitment, long-lasting changes are unlikely to occur.

Step 3: Choose solutions to fit a balanced strategy. Bringing about leadership diversity requires sensitivity and tact. For example, top management might have to deal with the puzzlement and anger of a middle-aged, white male who wonders why a woman of color with half his seniority is becoming his boss! The key principles underlying Morrison's guidelines are flexibility, patience, training, and communication.

Step 4: Demand results and revisit the goals. Objective standards must be established to evaluate the diversity results. Morrison goes beyond quantifying human resource decisions, such as how many people in which demographic group get promoted. Human resource decisions must also be tied to productivity factors, such as evaluating the effectiveness of the new leaders. Unless the new leader group is composed of highly competent people, the leadership diversity program will invite skepticism.

Step 5: Use building blocks to maintain momentum. Although step 5 is a summary of the entire leadership diversity program, it has a theme of its own. Each successful outcome in the program makes the next step easier. At one manufacturer, a Latino woman became the vice president of marketing. Her initiatives improved sales. Shortly thereafter managers throughout the company were much more receptive to identifying more women and minority group members as future leaders.[17]

SUMMARY

The modern leader must be multicultural because corporate success, profit, and growth depend increasingly on the management of a diverse work force. Managing for diversity brings a competitive advantage to the firm in several ways. Costs may be lower because minorities and women become more satisfied. A marketing advantage accrues because a representational work force facilitates selling goods and services. A heterogeneous group of workers may be more creative and may improve problem solving and decision making. A more diverse work force may also be more flexible, leading to system flexibility.

To influence, motivate, and inspire culturally diverse people, the leader must be aware of overt and subtle cultural differences. Differences in cultural values help explain differences among people. Seven of these values are as follows: degree of individualism or collectivism; power distance (how much the power hierarchy is accepted); uncertainty avoidance; masculinity versus femininity (materialism and aggressiveness versus concern for others); long-term versus short-term orientation; degree of formality; time orientation.

Understanding differences in cultural groups is important for applying motivational techniques. For example, when applying expectancy theory, we must recognize that cultures differ in how much control they perceive to have over the environment. Also, appropriate rewards (those with high valence) have to be selected for various cultural groups.

Another way to understand how culture influences leadership is to examine how certain leadership styles fit certain national cultures. An international contingency model of leadership based on path-goal styles helps fit styles to culture. Its most general finding is that the participative model will at least be acceptable in all the countries studied.

Cultural sensitivity is essential for inspiring people from different cultures. Part of this sensitivity is the leader's willingness to acquire knowledge about local customs and learn to speak the native language. A person with cultural sensitivity will recognize certain nuances in customs that help build better relationships with people from other cultures. Paying close attention to foreign business practices is another important aspect of cultural sensitivity.

Top-management commitment to valuing diversity is clearest when valuing diversity is embedded in organizational strategy. Specific leadership initiatives for valuing diversity can be divided into four categories: building a diversity culture, educational initiatives, career support, and accommodating special needs. It is also important to develop an employee base to match the customer base.

A comprehensive strategy for valuing diversity is to establish a multicultural organization. Such a firm values cultural diversity and is willing to encourage such diversity. A multicultural organization has six key characteristics: pluralism; full structural integration; full integration of informal networks; absence of prejudice and discrimination; organizational identification among all workers; and low levels of intergroup conflict.

To achieve a multicultural organization, the firms must also practice leadership diversity—the presence of a culturally heterogeneous cadre of leaders. A five-step approach has been proposed to achieve leadership diversity. It includes identifying diversity problems, strengthening top management commitment, choosing solutions to fit a balanced strategy, demanding good results and revisiting the goals, and using building blocks to maintain momentum.

KEY TERMS

Individualism	Formality
Collectivism	Informality
Power distance	Urgent time orientation
Uncertainty avoidance	Casual time orientation
Masculinity	Cultural sensitivity
Femininity	Multicultural organization
Long-term orientation	Leadership diversity
Short-term orientation	

GUIDELINES FOR ACTION AND SKILL DEVELOPMENT

Conducting diversity training is an important part of developing a multicultural organization. Such training often involves exercises in which employees candidly reveal their stereotypes about ethnic and racial groups and women. The point of these revelations is to raise awareness about possible prejudices. At a diversity training session conducted at the grocery chain Lucky Stores, a company official took notes of people's comments, such as "black women are aggressive" and "women cry more." An employee discovered these notes and speculated that prejudice within the company was preventing women and minorities from being promoted.

Employees then sued the grocery chain for intentional discrimination, and the judge authorized the employees to submit the workshop notes as evidence. Lucky Stores was found guilty. Although the judge's ruling was not based exclusively on the notes, they did contribute to the guilty verdict.[18]

Attorney Kirby Wilcox advises that employers cannot be unduly cautious. If they do not conduct diversity training, they might be in violation of equal-employment opportunity statutes. To prevent diversity training from backfiring, companies should make sure information about negative stereotypes does not get into the wrong hands. Better yet, no records of negative stereotypes should be retained.

Diversity trainer Perry Thomas protects his clients by destroying the flipcharts on which comments are recorded. He says that he tells the group that the characteristics noted are garbage. After that he discards the garbage.[19]

DISCUSSION QUESTIONS AND ACTIVITIES

1. Since the U.S. work force is becoming increasingly Hispanic, should managers all be required to speak and read Spanish?
2. How does managing for diversity really help a firm financially?
3. How does a culturally heterogeneous staff contribute to the leader's ability to make effective decisions?
4. Would it be fair for a sales manager to exclude a sales candidate because the candidate was raised in a country with a "casual time orientation"?
5. Assume that you are the leader of a culturally diverse group. How might you learn which rewards will have the highest valence for the particular subgroups?
6. How does the aphorism "When in Rome, do as the Romans do" relate to cultural sensitivity?
7. Why are work-at-home arrangements considered part of managing diversity?
8. What tasteful steps might a company take to demonstrate to the public that it is a multicultural organization?
9. Assume that a company is conducting a search for a new president. An employee group demands that the new president be a minority group member or woman. How should the board of directors react to the request?
10. Find an article or book, or interview a business leader, to help you answer the question, "How can I prepare myself to become a leader in a multicultural organization?"

LEADERSHIP CASE PROBLEM ▧

"We're Working in Chicago, Not Stockholm"

It was 9:30 one Tuesday morning. Naomi Green, the manager of collections at Oakdale Street Bank and Trust, was planning her day and getting ready for a staff meeting at 11 that morning. Into her office walked Sven Olsen—again without a prior appointment. Feeling a little taken aback, Naomi asked, "How can I help you, Sven?"

Olsen replied, "I need you to do something for me right away. I'm leaving this afternoon for a trip to Springfield. One of our delinquent accounts is still too far behind schedule. Phone calls and faxes haven't worked. I need to make an in-person visit."

"If that's what needs to be done," responded Green. "Go ahead and make the trip. I assume you will be gone just one night."

"Please let me finish," said Olsen. "You have to authorize me a cash advance. I'm out of cash. I'll need about $350 to cover everything.

"Also, so long as I'm here, we might as well schedule my next performance review. I want to know how big my raise will be so I can make

some plans with my wife to buy a new Volvo."

"Okay, Sven, I'll sign your advance voucher. And I can give you next Friday at 3 P.M. for the performance review. But quite frankly I don't like the demanding tone in your voice. You act as if I work for you, not the other way around."

"I don't think it matters who's the boss," said Olsen. "We're supposed to work as a team to get the job done. Back in Sweden, that's the way it goes. Maybe you Americans get a little uptight."

"Sven, you and I will have to talk some more when I'm not so busy. I appreciate Scandinavian management as much as you do. But we're working in Chicago, not Stockholm."

1. What does this case problem reveal about managing cultural diversity?

2. What cultural value is Sven Olsen expressing?

3. Evaluate the extent of Naomi Green's cultural sensitivity.

4. What, if anything, should Green do about the different perceptions she and Olsen have about the role and authority of the leader?

LEADERSHIP EXERCISE

The Diversity Circle

Some diversity trainers use the *diversity circle* exercise to help workers appreciate diversity and overcome misperceptions. The exercise adapts well for classroom use. Form a group of about ten students. Arrange your chairs into a circle, and put one additional chair in the center of the circle. A "diverse" group member volunteers to sit in the center chair and become the first "awareness subject." Because most people are diverse in some way, most people are eligible to occupy the center chair.

The person in the center tells the others how he or she has felt about being diverse or different and how people have reacted to his or her diversity. For example, an Inuit described how fellow workers were hesitant to ask him out for a beer, worrying whether he could handle alcohol.

The "awareness subject" then moves back with the group, and they all discuss his or her perceptions. An important subject to approach is whether this person has been the recipient of negative prejudice in the past or simply has misperceived people's attitudes and comments.

Another volunteer then moves to the center of the circle; the exercise continues until everyone has had a turn in the center.

Leadership of Quality and Technology

OBJECTIVES

After studying this chapter, you should be able to

1. describe key leadership practices related to achieving total quality management (TQM) at the organizational level.
2. describe key leadership practices related to achieving total quality management (TQM) at the team level.
3. summarize the leader's contribution to helping an organization conform to the Baldrige Award criteria for high quality.
4. describe key leadership practices for fostering high technology.

---

*H*CR, a United States health care and research firm, is attempting to modernize health care in the Republic of Tatarstan, part of the Russian Federation. The company has reached an agreement with several Tatarstan entrepreneurs to form a new company to provide health care services. Louise Woerner, chairman and chief executive officer of HCR, said the new company will draw on her firm's expertise in developing such services as home health care. Woerner spearheaded the new venture both to expand HCR and to increase the quality of health care in Tatarstan.[1]

As illustrated by the HCR venture, an underlying theme throughout our study of leadership is that the leader's efforts should enhance quality. In this chapter we look more specifically at the leader's contribution to **total quality management (TQM),** a management system for improving performance throughout the firm by maximizing customer satisfaction and making continuous improvements based on extensive employee involvement. Consistent with the purpose of this book, we will examine what role the leader plays in moving the organization toward total quality.

The leader's contribution to stimulating the use of high technology is related to his or her role in enhancing quality. An important link exists between quality and high technology: the effective use of technology improves quality. This chapter describes how leaders inspire and influence their constituents to embrace high technology.

LEADERSHIP PRACTICES THAT FOSTER TOTAL QUALITY MANAGEMENT

Under a system of total quality management, employees at all levels contribute input to quality improvement. Workers receive training in problem-solving techniques to enhance their ability to identify and rectify conditions that might create customer dissatisfaction. Workers also learn how to prevent quality problems. Despite this heavy worker involvement, leaders still play a crucial role in creating and maintaining the right climate for achieving high quality.

Most of you are already familiar with TQM principles. As a review, do Leadership Skill-Building Exercise 14–1, which presents a current overview of the principles, prepared by leading quality expert Richard J. Schonberger. The exercise will refresh your thinking on the subject and offer new insights.

LEADERSHIP SKILL-BUILDING EXERCISE 14–1 Principles of Total Quality Management

Directions: Next to each TQM principle, circle AF (already familiar) or MS (more study required).

General

1. Get to know the next and final customer.	AF	MS
2. Get to know the direct competition, and world-class leaders (whether competitors or not).	AF	MS
3. Dedicate to continual, rapid improvement in quality, response time, flexibility, and cost.	AF	MS
4. Achieve unified purpose via extensive sharing of information and involvement in planning and implementation of change.	AF	MS

Design and Organization

5. Cut the number of components or operations and number of suppliers to a few good ones.	AF	MS

6. Organize resources into chains of customers, each chain mostly self-contained and focused on a product or customer "family."   AF   MS

Operations

7. Cut flow time, distance, inventory, and space along the chain of customers.   AF   MS

8. Cut setup, changeover, get-ready, and startup time.   AF   MS

9. Operate at the customer's rate of use (or a smoothed representation of it).   AF   MS

Human Resource Development

10. Continually invest in human resources through cross-training (for mastery), education, job switching, and multi-year, cross-career reassignments; and improved, health, safety, and security.   AF   MS

11. Develop operator-owners of products, processes, and outcomes via broadened ownerlike reward and recognition.   AF   MS

Quality and Process Improvement

12. Make it easier to produce or provide the product without mishap or process variation.   AF   MS

13. Record and *own* quality, process, and mishap data at the workplace.   AF   MS

14. Ensure that front-line associates get first chance at process improvement—before staff experts.   AF   MS

Accounting and Control

15. Cut transactions and reporting; control courses and measure performance at the source, not via periodic cost reports.   AF   MS

Capacity

16. Maintain/improve present resources and human work before thinking about new equipment and automation.   AF   MS

17. Automate incrementally when process variability cannot otherwise be reduced.   AF   MS

Marketing and Sales

19. Market and sell your firm's increasing customer-oriented capabilities and competencies.   AF   MS

Source: Adapted from Richard J. Schonberger, "Is Strategy Strategic? Impact of Total Quality Management on Strategy," *Academy of Management Executive,* August 1992, p. 83. Used by permission.

Let's now examine some of the myriad ways leaders foster total quality management. For convenience, the principles and techniques are divided into those primarily concerned with the total organization, and those directed at the team and individual level.

Organizationwide Principles and Practices

At its best, total quality management is a transformation in the way an organization manages. Management's energies are focused on the continuous improvement of operations, functions, and especially work processes.[2] It therefore follows that many TQM leadership principles and practices are strategic and organization-level.

Demonstrating Top-Level Commitment.   Top-management commitment is the most important contributor to the successful implementation of any quality improvement effort. Demonstrating such commitment is therefore a primary leadership principle for achieving total quality management. Many quality experts maintain that TQM must be a top-down process, integrated into the corporate culture.[3] Executive leaders must allocate resources to prevent as well as repair quality problems. Quality must be included in the organization strategy, and every manager and organizational unit must be responsible for quality.

Workers throughout the organization must perceive the quest for quality as a top-management commitment. Executive leaders should therefore talk about quality frequently, for example, by giving speeches on the topic and asking questions about quality at every staff meeting. The Leader in Action box on page 310 illustrates how commitment by an organizational leader facilitates total quality throughout the organization.

Building Quality into the Mission Statement.   A firm's **mission statement** indicates the general field in which the firm operates, along with the its purpose, values, and direction. A mission statement relates to leadership because it is a clear and compelling statement of the firm's future direction. When quality is incorporated into the mission statement, workers have another strong reminder of the importance of quality. According to consultant David L. Calfee, well-crafted mission statements provide inspiration and information to employees.[4]

Mission statements can be inspiring because they present an uplifting, idealized version of what the firm can accomplish, such as making a unique contribution to the markets served. The information provided in a mission statement includes statements of (1) what businesses the company will be in down the road, (2) the company objectives, and (3) the sources of the organization's competitive strength and advantage. Several mission statements that directly or indirectly mention quality are presented here. Visualize yourself as an employee working for the companies identified. Would these mission statements inspire you toward high-quality work?

LEADER
IN
ACTION

Horst Schulze of Ritz Carlton

Several years ago, the Ritz Carlton Hotel Co. initiated TQM. President and CEO Horst Schulze told his staff that the Ritz Carlton was lucky to be considered the leader in the luxury hotel field. The hotel chain's high ranking could be attributed to the fact that the competition was even worse.

Schulze took personal responsibility for directing the company's effort toward achieving 100 percent guest satisfaction. When a new hotel is ready to open, Schulze and other executives spend a week there showing new employees the proper way to interact with guests. The corporate director of quality, Patrick Mene, says, "It sends a strong message to employees when the CEO takes time to show a dishwasher how to greet and make small talk with guests."

Mene believes that the involvement of Schulze and other hotel executives was an important reason the Ritz Carlton received the Baldrige Award for quality in 1992. "Providing thick towels and offering customers an extensive array of luxuries is easy, compared with providing genuinely caring, highly personalized service," says Mene. Furthermore, he believes that the personal involvement of company leaders has made the personalized service possible.

Source: Based on information in Shari Caudron, "Keys to Starting a TQM Program," *Personnel Journal,* February 1993, p. 29.

■ Lockheed: Our mission is to meet the needs of our United States and foreign customers with high-quality products and services and, in so doing, produce superior returns for our shareholders and foster growth and achievement for our employees.

■ The Boeing Co.: Our long-range mission is to be the number-one aerospace company in the world, and among the premier industrial firms, as measured by quality, profitability, and growth.

■ Ben & Jerry's Homemade Inc.: To make, distribute, and sell the finest quality of all-natural ice cream and related products in a wide variety of innovative flavors made from Vermont dairy products.

■ McDonald's Corp.: To satisfy the world's appetite for good food, well-served, at a price people can afford.

Creating a Corporate Culture of Quality.   A mission statement contributes substantially to creating a corporate culture of quality. This is important because significant quality improvement requires an upheaval of the corporate culture. If the corporate culture does not embody quality, any quality improvement efforts will probably be shallow and short-lived. As Karen Pennar observes, "If the process is half-hearted or poorly planned, quality will become simply another fashionable word in the executive's lexicon or yet another trendy promotion vehicle for new goods."[5] World-class quality leaders such as Xerox, Saturn, Motorola, and Waterman (manufacturer of writing instruments) operate in a culture of quality.

Continuous improvement as a way of life is one of the dominant values in a corporate culture of quality. The quest for continuous improvement is closely associated with **kaizen,** a philosophy of gradual improvement in personal and work life. Companies use *kaizen* to program themselves with positive thinking so that small improvement takes place everyday.

Kaizen is a long-term gradual improvement, involving a series of small, sometimes imperceptible changes. The spirit of *kaizen* improves quality because it prompts employees to stay alert for possible small improvements. Workers are also encouraged to look for things that are not quite right but are not yet full-blown problems.

Doing Leadership Skill-Building Exercise 14–2 will give you additional insights into the nature of a corporate culture that favors quality. You can also use the instrument contained in the exercise as a diagnostic tool.

Empowering and Involving Employees. To achieve total quality management, leaders must empower employees to fix and prevent problems. Equally important, group members have to accept the authority and become involved in the improvement process. Empowerment is one of the key principles supporting the Leadership Through Quality program at Xerox Corp. The quality improvement process revitalized the company and allowed it to compete successfully against Japanese manufacturers of photocopiers.

Empowerment is valuable because it may release creative energy. A relevant example took place at Advance Circuits of Hopkins, Minnesota. A team eliminated pinhole defects in circuit-board film after discovering that a smaller darkroom eliminated many airborne particles that cause defects.[6]

Spearheading Financial Rewards for Quality. Many total quality management advocates believe that achieving high quality is self-rewarding. According to this viewpoint, financial rewards for achieving high quality become superfluous and may even take the focus away from quality and toward money. Although achieving high quality is intrinsically rewarding, the contribution of financial rewards to sustaining high quality cannot be dismissed. Leaders can strengthen the impact of TQM by championing a link between quality performance and pay.

Patricia Zingheim and Jay R. Schuster have studied the relationship between achieving high quality and financial rewards.[7] As they see it, TQM requires a firm to form partnerships with its customers and suppliers. Such partnerships are unlikely to be formed unless one is also formed between

LEADERSHIP
SKILL-BUILDING
EXERCISE 14–2   Do You Have the Right Corporate Culture for TQM?

Directions: To evaluate whether your company has a culture ideally suited to total quality, check whether the description in the left-hand or right-hand column best describes your firm. Confer with another person who works for the same employer to increase the accuracy of your ratings. If you are not currently working, speak to someone who is employed and evaluate his or her company. It would be helpful to interview more than one person from the same organization.

TQM Companies	*Traditional Companies*
___ Driven by customer needs	___ Driven by company wants
___ Prevention of problems before they happen	___ Detection of problems after the fact
___ Nothing less than 100 percent will do	___ Established maximum acceptable levels of error, waste
___ Committed to quality at the source	___ Belief that inspection is key to quality
___ Cooperative, interdepartmental teams	___ Autonomous, independent departments
___ High employee participation—empowered work force	___ Top-down, management-directed work force
___ Long-term staying power a primary goal.	___ Short-term profit a primary goal.

Interpretation: Seven check marks in the left-hand column would indicate that the firm you have evaluated is probably a world-class quality company. Seven check marks in the right-hand column suggests that the company you have evaluated might be at a competitive disadvantage in a quality-conscious economy. Check marks to the right can also be used as indicators of a need for organizational improvement.

Source: "Total Quality Management: A Step-by-Step Guide to Making TQM Work for You," National Seminars brochure, 1992.

the employer and employees. A key component of the employer-employee partnership is economic. It therefore follows that employees will respond favorably to receiving high pay for achieving high quality.

Group variable pay is the specific system Zingheim and Schuster recommend to create a link between achieving TQM goals and financial rewards. Table 14–1 presents the rationale for the contribution of group variable pay over individual merit pay.

A successful application of linking pay to quality and productivity took place at Evarts Products Co. in Evart, Michigan. The company supplies automotive manufacturers with exterior signal lighting, high-mount stoplights, dashliners, and other products. To ameliorate low-quality and productivity problems, the company instituted a gainsharing program. Under such a program, employees as a group receive bonus pay for productivity improvements they originate and implement. During the first four years of the program, the company decreased its defect rate from 437 parts per 10,000 to two parts per 10,000.[8] Using data such as these, the leader can justify urging the organization to link pay to achieving high quality.

Team and Individual-Level Principles and Practices

The principles and practices just described take a broad approach by influencing everyone in the organization at the same time. In slight contrast, the leadership suggestions in this section emphasize influencing people at the group and individual level toward attaining high quality. Table 14–2 outlines these suggestions.

TABLE 14–1: Group Variable Pay versus Individual Pay as a Way of Linking Pay to Quality

Group Variable Pay	Individual Merit Pay
Rewards teamwork and collaboration	Can create internal competition for pay raises
Encourages communication	Can encourage withholding of information
Encourages group to improve systems	Encourages individuals to try to improve systems on their own, which is very difficult to accomplish
Makes quality outcome measures that are meaningful	Uses individual quality outcome measures, which are difficult to develop meaningfully
Encourages macro focus	Encourages micro focus
Increases flexibility, ability to respond to changing needs	Decreases flexibility
Requires re-earning each performance period	Becomes an annuity

Source: Adapted from Patricia K. Zingheim and Jay R. Schuster, "Linking Quality and Pay," *HRMagazine*, December 1992, p. 56. Reprinted with the permission of *HRMagazine*, published by the Society for Human Resource Management, Alexandria, VA.

TABLE 14–2   Improving Quality at the Group and Individual Level

1. Get group members immersed in quality.
2. Encourage staffers to look at the total quality experience.
3. Insist that group members figure out how to achieve extraordinary goals.
4. Encourage the measurement of quality.
5. Play the roles of advocate, facilitator, and cheerleader.
6. Be tolerant of mistakes attributed to risk taking.
7. Maintain personal contact with service operations.

Getting Group Members Immersed in Quality.   Quality consultant Oren Harari recommends that leaders do several things to immerse group members in quality: (1) get everyone in their sphere of influence reading and talking about innovative approaches to quality; (2) urge them to make commitments to innovative approaches to quality; (3) distribute challenging articles about quality; and (4) purchase multiple copies of outstanding books about quality for group members. Reading should be followed up with small group discussion, addressing such questions as the following:

- How do we as a firm (or organizational unit) stack up against the companies we just read about?
- After reading the article or book, what are our strengths, weaknesses, and opportunities?
- Where do we need to go? And what are our action plans for getting there?

One rationale for this leadership practice is symbolic. The leader's actions demonstrate a stronger commitment than do exhortations about quality. Another rationale is that with continuous action planning and follow-up, the leader creates a momentum toward total quality. At the same time he or she is contributing to a quality corporate culture.[9]

Encouraging Staffers to Look at the Total Quality Experience.   Quality improvement efforts frequently focus too narrowly on several measurable aspects of quality such as product reliability, cleanliness, or physical attractiveness. Yet customers typically rate quality on the basis of the total experience surrounding the purchase of goods or services. Oren Harari's research on the quality of coffee breaks illustrates the importance of the total quality experience. A diverse group of hoteliers concluded that a high-quality coffee break is characterized by timely availability of hot coffee, extras (pastry, fruit, bagels, etc.), attractive display, clean plates, and clean table covering.

Customers perceived the characteristics of a high-quality coffee break differently. They gave high ratings to hot coffee, a fast line, nearby and high-capacity rest rooms, nearby and numerous telephones, and ample space to chat. The customers evaluated the total quality experience of the coffee break, whereas the hoteliers focused too narrowly on the quality of coffee and food.[10]

The message for the leader is to help group members focus their attention on the customer's total quality experience, not just on the product. The accompanying Leader in Action box illustrates how a well-known company fashioned a comeback by broadening quality beyond technical aspects of the product.

LEADER IN ACTION

Richard Teerlink of Harley-Davidson

Richard Teerlink, the president of Harley-Davidson, believes strongly in a multifaceted approach to quality. In 1981, the motorcycle manufacturer's market share had fallen from a mid-1970s high of 70 percent to less than 25 percent. The company faced extinction, yet by 1990 the company's market share had surged back to 60 percent. In 1994, Harley-Davidson still held onto the same high market share. A major problem facing the company was how to produce enough motorcycles to meet demand.

Top leadership at Harley-Davidson fashioned the comeback through a multifaceted approach to quality. Managers made investments in technology and product design that significantly enhanced the motorcycle's dependability and styling. The company made improvements that would appeal to customers. Simultaneously, Harley-Davidson leaders focused on promotional quality. Advertising and promotion no longer presented the image of motorcyclists as tattooed roughnecks; rather, they portrayed them as individualists seeking a healthy outdoor experience.

Harley managers stayed in touch with customers and attempted to build a climate of trust. Many managers participated regularly in weekend riding rallies. A Harley Owners Group (H.O.G.) was created. With 140,000 members, it became the largest affinity group in the United States. Management also invested in distribution quality by such means as upgrading dealer education and training, and redesigning stores to fit the new Harley image. Teerlink commented during a speech that "Our goal is to have a mental tattoo."

Source: Based on facts in Leonard Berry and A. Parasuraman, "Prescriptions for a Service Quality Revolution in America," *Organizational Dynamics,* Spring 1992, p. 8.

Insisting That Group Members Determine How to Achieve Extraordinary Goals.   A bold quality-enhancing leadership practice is to establish extraordinarily difficult quality targets for group members, and then to insist that they find a way to attain them. Many companies have established one of two close-to-impossible goals: the zero-defects standard or the 6-Sigma quality standard. The *6-Sigma standard* refers to work that is 99.999997 percent error-free, allowing one defect per 3.4 million opportunities (see Figure 14–1). Extraordinary goals of this nature have helped propel Motorola and Federal Express toward the cutting edge of technology, reliability, internal efficiency, and responsiveness to customer needs.

According to Harari, the way for a leader to apply the extraordinary goal principle is to insist that workers attain the extraordinary goals, and then to confess that even he or she does not know how to achieve them. It is up to the group to choose the method for goal attainment. As a corollary, group members are then free to challenge any company rule or procedure that blocks the attainment of the extraordinary goal. For example, under some TQM systems people spend so much time filling out forms that it detracts from performing high-quality work. Coling Gilmore, an executive responsible for United Air Lines' quality efforts in engine repair and maintenance, explains how the extraordinary goal principle works:

> Tell people to increase quality by 5 percent or 10 percent and your message is basically, "Do what you've always done, but you'll just have to come to work earlier, skip lunch and concentrate more." That's foolish and gets you nowhere.

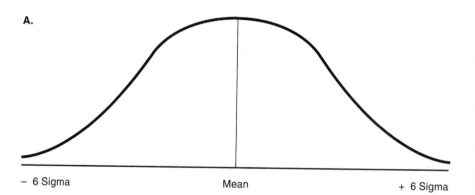

A.

− 6 Sigma   Mean   + 6 Sigma

B. 6 – Sigma translates into 99.999997% error free

C. 6 – Sigma = $\dfrac{\text{1 defect}}{\text{3.4 million opportunities}}$

FIGURE 14–1

The Meaning of the 6-Sigma Quality Standard

Note: *Sigma* is the Greek word for standard deviation.

But if you tell people you want increases of 70 percent or 80 percent, first they scream bloody murder but then they realize this goal is to challenge every step and every person in the current process, and if necessary, start from scratch.[11]

Encouraging the Measurement of Quality. An important leadership practice at the outset of a TQM process is to encourage people to assess the current level of quality. Furthermore, the leader should define the desired level of quality. Sometimes the company's missions, values, and vision statement provide a framework for evaluating current quality levels. After a company's vision has been identified clearly, managers can start to evaluate the status of quality. Some companies, including AT&T's Transmission Business Unit in Morristown, New Jersey, use the Baldrige Award criteria to help assess levels of quality throughout the organization.[12] The Baldrige Award process measures applicants in seven areas, as described later in this chapter.

Some industrial leaders tend to deemphasize using all the Baldrige criteria to measure quality because only one deals with customer satisfaction—the most important outcome of total quality management. In some circumstances it might therefore be more important for the leader to emphasize the last two measurements: quality results and customer satisfaction.

Playing the Roles of Advocate, Facilitator, and Cheerleader. According to Richard J. Schonberger, leaders can contribute heavily to total quality by functioning as visible advocates, facilitators, and cheerleaders. The "wandering-around leader" inspects wall charts and computer graphics tracking improvement efforts in every area for every process. Rapid improvements receive positive reinforcement. Slow improvements, stalls, and setbacks trigger on-the-spot discussions. Instead of assigning blame, the leader asks how he or she can help resolve the problem.

Acting in the role of advocate, facilitator, and cheerleader, the leader does not focus on a specific improvement goal. Instead, he or she focuses on the rate of improvement and obstacles in the way. In this way the wandering-around leader does not dig into the details that are more familiar to people closer to the job.[13] Although focusing on obstacles is helpful, we should remember that an important part of the leadership role *is* to set goals. Despite Schonberger's exhortation, most other quality experts support goal setting.

Tolerating Mistakes Attributed to Risk Taking. Accepting mistakes without getting angry is a straightforward yet high-impact leadership practice that enhances quality. Mistakes are inevitable if staffers attempt bold quality improvements. At one hotel the manager decided that the rooms would look more elegant if repainted with oil-based rather than the Latex-based paint so widely used. The repainted rooms did look elegant, but several guests complained that the fumes carried through the ventilation system. The manager's boss dismissed the problem as an understandable mistake when trying to upgrade quality.

Instead of finger pointing, the leader should help the employee resolve the problem that created the mistake.[14] Taking a "we" attitude about the problem will typically give the group member needed emotional support. (In the paint-fumes situation, painters were instructed to block the ventilation system in the room until the paint dried.)

Maintaining Personal Contact with Service Operations.   Leaders should visit service operations periodically. Not only do the visits demonstrate the leader's interest in customer service, but the leader obtains first-hand observations about needs for quality improvement. Many executive leaders make field inspections to understand what it is like to be a customer of their own firm. The Stouffer Hotel in Oak Brook, Illinois, assigns senior management a block of rooms to inspect thoroughly each month.

Chairman Richard Branson of Virgin Airways is another example of a leader who observes service operations directly. He travels economy class on his own airline to understand the customer experience personally.[15] (We suspect that Branson is so visible that he receives special attention from the flight attendants, unless he disguises himself.)

LEADERSHIP AND THE BALDRIGE AWARD

The quality movement in the United States if often associated with the Malcolm Baldrige National Quality Award. The award originated from the Malcolm Baldrige Quality Improvement Act of 1987. One objective of the award was to raise the consciousness of American business leaders about quality. The other was to provide a comprehensive framework for measuring the quality efforts undertaken by U.S. businesses. Awards are given annually in three categories: manufacturing, service, and small business.[16]

Baldrige award winners are chosen according to performance in seven major criteria, totaling 1,000 points. Leadership is 90 points, subdivided into senior executive leadership (45 points); management for quality (25 points); and public responsibility (20 points). The other six major categories are as follows: information and analysis, 80 points; strategic quality planning, 60 points; human resource utilization, 150 points; quality assurance of products and services, 140 points; quality results, 180 points; and customer satisfaction, 300 points.

Although leadership is but one award category, effective leadership is needed to help the organization perform well in the other six categories. Leadership Self-Assessment Exercise 14–1 presents the self-study diagnostic instrument used to evaluate the leadership criterion of the Baldrige Award.

The Leader in Action box on page 321 illustrates a senior executive's involvement in his company's pursuit of a Baldrige Award.

LEADERSHIP
SELF-ASSESSMENT
EXERCISE 14–1 The Leadership Criterion of the Baldrige Award

Directions: For each of the following questions, rate your organization on a scale of 0 to 10. If your organization does nothing in a particular area, rate it a 0. If your organization does a little, but nothing significant, you might rate it a 1 or a 2. If your organization has a moderate level of performance, you might rate it at 5. If the organization has excellent performance, you might rate it a 9 or a 10. Your point rating for each question should reflect how well your organization does in that particular area. A person would have to be closely familiar with a firm to make accurate ratings. If you do not have sufficient information to evaluate a firm, speculate about a firm you patronize, such as a retail store or a utility.

Leadership (90 possible points)

The Leadership Category examines senior executives' *personal* leadership and involvement in creating and sustaining a customer focus and clear and visible quality values. Examined also is how the quality values are integrated into the company's management system and reflected in the way the company addresses public responsibilities.

1. Do senior executives provide leadership through visible involvement in quality-related activities such as creating a customer focus, creating quality values, planning for quality, recognizing employee contributions, and communicating quality values outside the company?

    Not at All   Completely
    0   1   2   3   4   5   6   7   8   9   10

2. Has senior management created clearly defined quality values and communicated those values both internal and external to the company?

    Not at All   Completely
    0   1   2   3   4   5   6   7   8   9   10

3. Do the personal actions of senior management demonstrate, communicate, and reinforce a customer focus and quality values?

    Not at All   Completely
    0   1   2   3   4   5   6   7   8   9   10

4. Are senior executives evaluated on the effectiveness of their leadership and involvement in creating customer-focused quality values?

Not at All   Completely
0   1   2   3   4   5   6   7   8   9   10

5. Are the company's quality values and customer focus cascaded through the organization so that all employees understand how their job contributes to each?

Not at All   Completely
0   1   2   3   4   5   6   7   8   9   10

6. Does the company's organization structure effectively and efficiently enhance the attainment of the company's customer, quality, innovation, and cycle time objectives?

Not at All   Completely
0   1   2   3   4   5   6   7   8   9   10

7. Does management assist in the design and review of work unit quality plans and take action when nonconformance occurs?

Not at All   Completely
0   1   2   3   4   5   6   7   8   9   10

8. Does management establish key indicators to evaluate and improve awareness and use of quality values at all levels of management?

Not at All   Completely
0   1   2   3   4   5   6   7   8   9   10

9. Does the company explicitly include in its quality policies, practices, and values public responsibility issues such as business ethics, public health and safety, environmental protection, and waste management?

Not at All   Completely
0   1   2   3   4   5   6   7   8   9   10

The higher an organization scores on this self-assessment, the closer it is to qualifying as a contender for a Baldrige Award on the leadership dimension. Outside evaluators eventually rate the award candidates on these criteria.

Source: Adapted from the Malcolm Baldrige National Quality Award criteria distributed by the National Institute of Standards and Technology, Washington, D.C.

LEADER
IN
ACTION

Arden C. Sims of Globe Metallurgical Inc.

According to CEO Arden C. Sims, Globe Metallurgical first decided to pursue a quality program in 1985. At that time the Baldrige Award did not exist, and there were no prescribed quality criteria. When the company won the award in 1988, it reflected major quality initiatives already taken by the company. To compete in an international marketplace, the company had to offer high-quality products at low cost. After this goal was established, top management communicated the goals of quality to every employee.

To demonstrate a commitment to quality, Globe initiated a profit-sharing program for all employees and promised to respond to all quality-related questions within twenty-four hours. Sims also made a personal commitment to eliminate layoffs and to discuss Globe's financial performance with small groups of employees. In addition, the company trained suppliers and gave them the materials they needed to meet its high-quality standards.

Despite the major commitment to quality by top management and employees, achieving total quality was slow and frustrating. Sometimes when the company thought it was ready to meet the toughest customer standards, it discovered that it had misinterpreted customer requirements. Sims reflects back on these incidents: "Nevertheless, we learned to value these audits as yardsticks to gauge the progress of our quality efforts."

Source: Based on facts reported in Arden C. Sims, "Does the Baldrige Award Really Work?" *Harvard Business Review,* January–February 1992, pp. 126–127.

LEADERSHIP PRACTICES FOR FOSTERING ADVANCED TECHNOLOGY

Another leadership challenge is to stimulate, encourage, and inspire appropriate use of advanced technology. As the term is used here, **technology** refers to all the tools and ideas available for extending the physical and mental reach of people.[17] Using a shopping cart to restock returned merchandise in a supermarket is an example of using low technology. Using computers to communicate with staffers at various locations around the world is an example of using advanced (or high) technology. Leadership Self-Assessment Exercise 14–2 will help you think through your attitudes toward advanced technology.

LEADERSHIP
SELF-ASSESSMENT
EXERCISE 14–2 Attitudes Toward Technology

Directions: Indicate your strength of agreement with each of the following statements: strongly disagree, SD; disagree, D; neutral, N; agree, A; strongly agree, SA.

	SD	D	N	A	SA
1. Few organizations can succeed without continually moving toward higher forms of technology.	(1)	(2)	(3)	(4)	(5)
2. I regularly use high-technology devices at home such as a camcorder, CD player, or personal computer.	(1)	(2)	(3)	(4)	(5)
3. When I use a personal computer or camcorder, I make frequent use of the advanced features.	(1)	(2)	(3)	(4)	(5)
4. I enjoy interacting with technical people.	(1)	(2)	(3)	(4)	(5)
5. Electronic gadgets in the workplace have contributed very little to productivity.	(5)	(4)	(3)	(2)	(1)
6. During a downsizing, the first place I would recommend for layoffs would be the research and development group.	(5)	(4)	(3)	(2)	(1)
7. The contribution of technology to society is overrated.	(5)	(4)	(3)	(2)	(1)
8. Placed in an executive position, I would keep a computer on my desk and use it regularly.	(1)	(2)	(3)	(4)	(5)
9. Most of the great business firms of the world are high-tech companies.	(1)	(2)	(3)	(4)	(5)
10. Most technical people are nerds.	(5)	(4)	(3)	(2)	(1)

Total score: ____

Scoring and interpretation: Find your total score by summing the point values for each question. A score of 40 to 50 suggests very positive attitudes toward technology and technical people. Scores of 20 to 39 suggest a somewhat neutral, detached attitude toward technology and technical people; scores of 10 to 19 suggest negative attitudes.

This quiz is linked to skill development. To lead an organization or subunit toward effective use of technology, you should have favorable attitudes toward technology and technical people. If you scored 19 or lower, you would need to become more interested in advanced technology to inspire others to make good use of it.

Choosing an Appropriate Technological Strategy

An executive leader of a company or a strategic business unit may have the authority to choose a technological strategy. Choosing the most appropriate strategy greatly influences the success of the organization or unit. Technology plays a major role in four business strategies,[18] as described next and outlined in Table 14–3.

First to Market.   Being first to market is an offensive strategy with high potential rewards but high risk. New entrepreneurial high-tech firms are likely to use this strategy, as are more progressive, established firms such as Hewlett-Packard. Sometimes the competitive advantage can be sustained through patents and proprietary knowledge. Creative marketing people may be required to stimulate demand. Classic first-to-market products include Polaroid's instant camera and the Sony Walkman.

Fast Follower and Overtaker.   After the pioneering firm has demonstrated that a market for the product exists, the fast follower swoops in with a similar product developed through innovative imitation. General Electric used the fast-follower strategy to enter the market for computer axial tomography (CAT) scanners. The original CAT scanner was developed by Electrical and Musical Industries (EMI) of the United Kingdom.

Cost Minimization.   With the cost minimization strategy, a company finds a way to reduce the cost of manufacturing a mass-produced product with standard features. Japanese and other Pacific Rim companies succeeded in overtaking the U.S. consumer electronics industry by becoming low-cost producers of high-tech devices.

TABLE 14–3   Technological Strategies Initiated by Leaders

1. First to market (Take this approach if you're a courageous entrepreneur.)

2. Fast follower and overtaker (If you can't be original, copy the industry leader.)

3. Cost minimization (Beat them on price while maintaining quality.)

4. Market niche (Find your place in the sun, carefully.)

Market Niche.   New high-tech ventures searching to develop a unique competence employ the market-niche strategy. To succeed, the market niche must be chosen carefully and adhered to rigorously. Michael Dell of Dell Computers found a marketing niche for a high-tech product by marketing good-quality computers through the mail.

Investing Heavily in Training

Leaders play a key role in fostering a high-technology environment by advocating a heavy investment in training. Continuous training is necessary to become and to remain a high-tech firm. Several years ago, Fred Smith, the founder of Federal Express, said, "The most significant strategic investment we are making right now is a massive training and retraining effort to adapt for the next generation of technology."[19] Part of "Fed Ex's" continuing success in a competitive market can be attributed to its sophisticated, high-tech package-routing system.

Using Automation to Assist Rather Than Replace People

A humanitarian and supportive leadership practice is to find ways for automation to assist rather than replace workers.[20] When this principle is followed, workers throughout the organization will be willing participants in automation. In contrast, when workers perceive automation as a threat, they will resist it. One example of helpful automation is the hand-held data input device. Many companies have provided field personnel with hand-held computers to send data back to the home office. Among these workers are meter readers and truckers. At a midwestern utility, the president said to workers:

> These new hand-held devices are not going to replace anybody. I never met a computer yet that was smarter than one of you. But these little devices are going to make it easier for you to reduce errors, thereby increasing profits and paychecks.

Creating an Environment Suitable for Gold-Collar Workers

Gold-collar workers are a breed of professionals who combine business knowledge with technical expertise. Such workers are especially valuable because they bridge the gap between the research laboratory and the current market. To attract and retain these intelligent and resourceful professionals, the leader has to establish the right atmosphere. The right climate includes intellectually stimulating work, intellectually stimulating coworkers, freedom to pursue ideas, moderate controls, and accountability for results. The accompanying Leader in Action box illustrates an ideal example of a gold-collar worker.

*LEADER
IN
ACTION*

Jill Shurtleff of Gillette Co.

The only female industrial designer in Gillette Co.'s shaving division, Jill Shurtleff exercises leadership through ideas for product innovation. Five years ago Shurtluff was asked to develop a new product for the women's shaving market. After personally trying a variety of women's shavers, Shurtleff concluded that all of them were ergonomically inadequate for women.

Shurtleff's radical solution was the Sensor for Women. Gillette sold 7.6 million in the first six months. Including blades, sales for 1993 were predicted to be $100 million, with a 60 percent market share. The design contributes to the razor's popularity. It resembles a bar of bath soap, with the razor head looking like the business-end of a vacuum cleaner.

Shurtleff investigated how women shave. She found that, unlike men, women do not shave in front of a well-lit mirror. Also, they shave more parts of their body. The Sensor for Women produces many fewer nicks and cuts than do the traditional razors for women. The flat handle on the Sensor is designed to align the cartridge with the hand. Shurtleff says her shaver design has "succeeded beyond my wildest dreams. It's any designer's fantasy."

In designing a new razor, Shurtleff competed against a legendary Gillette success story, the Sensor. The Sensor was first introduced in the United States and overseas in 1990 to replace the conventional razor. In its first year, 24 million Sensors were sold, along with 350 blade cartridges. Shurtleff proved she could create another success story for Gillette.

Source: Mark Maremont, "A New Equal Right: The Close Shave," *Business Week,* March 29, 1993, pp. 58–59; "We Had to Change the Playing Field," *Forbes,* February 4, 1991, pp. 82–86.

Establishing a Reward System for Innovation

Advances in technology are, by definition, innovations. To encourage a stream of innovations, company leadership must establish a reward system for creative contribution. Part of the reward system can be intrinsic, such as rewarding the innovator with additional exciting assignments. (Perhaps the industrial designer described previously can now be given the opportunity to develop a product that does not already exist.) Another intrinsic reward is to grant innovative people more freedom to pursue work of interest to them. More freedom means fewer controls in terms of tight budgets and accountability for short-term results.

Although creative people are motivated by intrinsic rewards, they also require extrinsic ones, such as salary increases and bonuses. Some companies offer innovators part of the profit stemming from their inventions or product innovations. Monsanto, for example, presents a $50,000 award each year to the scientist or team of scientists who brings about the biggest commercial success.[21]

The technology-minded leader thus influences the organization to establish rewards for innovation. He or she then influences the innovator directly through judicious use of these rewards.

SUMMARY

Another leadership challenge is to foster total quality management. Organizationwide principles for achieving TQM include the following: (1) demonstrating top-level commitment; (2) building quality into the mission statement; (3) creating a corporate culture of quality; (4) empowering and involving employees; (5) spearheading financial rewards for quality; (6) getting group members immersed in quality; (7) encouraging staffers to look at the total quality experience; (8) insisting that group members figure out how to achieve extraordinary goals; (9) encouraging the measurement of quality; (10) playing the roles of advocate, facilitator, and cheerleader; (11) tolerating mistakes attributed to risk taking; and (12) maintaining personal contact with service operations.

Another leadership challenge is to stimulate, encourage, and inspire appropriate use of advanced technology. Principles and practices for achieving this end are as follows: (1) choosing an appropriate technological strategy, such as being first to market or finding a market niche; (2) investing heavily in training; (3) using automation to assist rather than replace people, (4) creating an environment suitable for gold-collar workers; and (5) establishing a reward system for innovation.

KEY TERMS

Total quality management (TQM)	Technology
Mission statement	Gold-collar workers
Kaizen	

GUIDELINES FOR ACTION AND SKILL DEVELOPMENT

Many TQM efforts have failed, and the reasons for these failures follow a pattern. An important contribution is for the leader to make the organization aware of the potential pitfalls of total quality management. The leader can also exert influence over the total quality efforts to avoid these problems. Suggestions for avoiding TQM failure are as follows:[22]

1. Do not expect total quality management to make an immediate financial contribution. The mere implementation of total quality will not overcome financial problems unless the program is properly focused on company needs such as improving customer satisfaction or responding to increased competition.

2. Avoid the common mistake made in early stages of TQM: emphasizing processes (such as surveys and problem-solving techniques) instead of results. The most important result, of course, is improving quality. Among the process contributors are training, motivational programs, and benchmarking. A recommended course of action is to seek some short-term improvements in quality. These quick improvements enhance motivation for achieving additional good results.

3. Avoid creating a cumbersome total quality management bureaucracy. Too often companies build an orderly, predictable bureaucracy around quality improvement. Many people are hired into the TQM unit. Forms proliferate, an excessive number of meetings are held, and signoffs (written statements of agreement) proliferate.

4. Avoid quantifying and objectifying quality to the point that important generators of quality, such as passion and pride, are discounted or neglected. Dedicated professionalism is still the most important generator of high-quality goods and services.

5. Avoid attempting to accomplish too much too quickly. A firm embracing the total quality should focus on a few specific areas that need improvement (such as customer billing) rather than attempting to convert the organizational culture all at once.

DISCUSSION QUESTIONS AND ACTIVITIES

1. How does total quality management relate to employee empowerment?
2. What leadership style is well suited to total quality management?
3. Which style of leadership is poorly suited to total quality management?
4. Where does the leader's contribution fit into the principles of total quality management outlined in Leadership Skill-Building Exercise 14–1.
5. How can the leader prevent TQM from being a passing fad in his or her sphere of influence?
6. Give examples of several actions top management can engage in to demonstrate a commitment to total quality.

7. Find somebody who is aware of the mission statement of his or her employer; inquire about how much the person finds the statement to be inspirational. Be ready to report your findings back to class.

8. How can a leader affect the total quality experience of customers?

9. How ethical is it for a leader to encourage group members to set next-to-impossible quality standards?

10. How important is it for a leader in a high-technology company to regularly use a computer himself or herself?

LEADERSHIP CASE PROBLEM

Let the Chips Fall Where They May

Andrew S. Grove, the shirt-sleeved leader of Intel Corp., often throws his meetings with employees open to the floor. Intel is the most profitable of the world's leading manufacturers of integrated circuits, the tiny slices of silicon that run electronic devices. The company has been the dominant manufacturer of micro-processors for IBM-style personal computers. Intel's annual sales are close to $5 billion, with profits over $800 million.

CEO Grove likes to know directly what Intel people are thinking. At a plant meeting in Chandler, Arizona, employees were asking tough questions. Among them were: What is the company doing to stop rivals from taking away more business? How will Intel compete favorably with the extraordinary speed of Digital Equipment Corp.'s new Alpha chip? Is Intel running up against the same kind of problems as IBM and DEC? Grove responded by telling employees that their company is under competitive attack.

Cloners of Intel chips, led by Advanced Micro Devices, Inc. (AMD), are eroding the company's profits. Even IBM, Intel's premier customer, has formed a consortium with Apple Computer, Inc., and Motorola, Inc., to build microprocessors for desktop publishers. The competitive threats have raised doubts about how long Intel can sustain its typical operating margins of 18 to 25 percent.

Grove has developed a strategy to deal with the challenges facing his company. He is bringing lawsuits against cloners and reducing prices lower than ever. Also, Intel is advertising its chips on television. The revamped strategic vision now focuses more on the core microprocessor business. Grove is also developing closer contacts with hardware and software manufacturers.

Grove thinks that his most important new competitive strategy is to get new products to market rapidly. "Speed is the only weapon we have," he says.

1. What inferences can you draw about Andrew S. Grove's leadership approach?

2. How effective does Grove appear to be as a leader of a high-technology company?

3. What is your evaluation of Grove's business strategy to meet the deal with the competition?

4. Can you offer Grove any suggestions for providing the right leadership at this stage of his company?

Source: Robert D. Hof, "Inside Intel: It's Moving at Double-Time to Head off Competitors," *Business Week,* June 2, 1992, pp. 86–94; Richard Brandt, "For Intel, One Good Friend Isn't Enough," *Business Week,* March 1, 1993, pp. 86–87.

LEADERSHIP EXERCISE

Developing a Mission Statement

Working in small groups, develop a twenty-five-word mission statement for an organization of your choosing. Search for an organization most of the group members are familiar with, such as a well-known business firm, an athletic team, or your school. Make the mission statement inspiring, and include a reference to quality. Spend about thirty minutes on the project, recognizing that many firms consume about one-half day per week for one year to develop their mission statement. For ideas, refer back to the section titled, "Building Quality into the Mission Statement." Share your mission statement with the other groups in the class.

Leadership Development, Succession, and the Future

At the conclusion of a leadership development workshop, the counselor said to the materials-handling manager of a small manufacturing company: "The feedback we've collected on your impact as a leader is generally positive. Yet we do see some areas for growth. The positive theme is that you're an energetic guy whose enthusiasm is contagious. According to the group, you express yourself in a colorful way. Several of the people at the workshop said they would enjoy working for you."

"Well, what didn't they like about my leadership impact?" asked the manager nervously.

"A few of the people were concerned that you don't process feedback at a deep level," replied the counselor. "No doubt you listen to what people think of you, but you don't take it a step further. You don't take a deeper look at the way you operate. You don't ask if you should be operating in a profoundly different way. You neglect to ask whether you are working on the right problems."

The exchange between the leadership development counselor and the manager illustrates but one of many ways in which leaders attempt to improve their effectiveness. The information presented previously in this book also deals with enhancing leadership effectiveness. Each chapter has included information and activities designed to enhance present or future leadership effectiveness. This chapter describes the processes organizations use to develop present and future leaders. (It also describes an important part of leadership self-development.) Such activities and processes are typically referred to as leadership development, leadership training, or management development.

Leadership and management development are substantial activities. An estimated 22 percent of the $30 billion annual corporate training budget is invested in managers.[1] Perhaps 10 percent of this $6.6 billion is devoted to programs aimed specifically at developing leaders.

In addition to describing various approaches to leadership development, we also examine two related topics. Leadership succession is included here because an important part of leadership development is to become groomed for promotion. The text concludes with an overview of the substantial leadership challenges of the future. Leaders must develop to meet these challenges.

DEVELOPMENT THROUGH SELF-AWARENESS AND SELF-DISCIPLINE

Leadership development is often perceived in terms of education and training, job experience, and coaching. Nevertheless, self-help also contributes heavily to developing leadership capabilities. Self-help takes many forms including working on one's own to improve communication skills, to develop charisma, and to model effective leaders. Two major components of leadership self-development are self-awareness and self-discipline.

Leadership Development Through Self-Awareness

An important mechanism underlying self-development is **self-awareness**, insightfully processing feedback about oneself to improve personal effectiveness. For example, a managerial leader might observe that three key group members left her group over a six-month time span. The leader might defensively dismiss this fact with an analysis such as, "I guess we just don't pay well enough to keep good people." Her first analysis might be correct. With a self-awareness orientation, however, the leader would dig deeper for the reasons behind the turnover. She might ask herself, "Is there something in my leadership approach that creates turnover problems?" She might ask for exit-interview data to sharpen her perceptions about her leadership approach.

Chris Argyris has coined the terms "single-loop learning" and "double-loop learning" to differentiate between levels of self-awareness.[2] **Single-loop learning** occurs when learners seek minimum feedback that might substantially confront their basic ideas or actions. As with the example of the high-turnover leader, single-loop learners engage in defensive thinking. Argyris offers the example of a thermostat that automatically turns on the heat whenever the room temperature drops below 68 degrees Fahrenheit (20 degrees Celsius).

Double-loop learning is an in-depth type of learning that occurs when people use feedback to confront the validity of the goal or the values implicit in the situation. The leader mentioned above was engaged in double-loop learning when she questioned the efficacy of her leadership approach. To achieve double-loop learning one must minimize defensive thinking. Argyris explains that a double-loop learning thermostat would ask, "Why am I set at 68 degrees?" The thermostat would then ask whether another temperature might more economically achieve the goal of heating the room. Figure 15–1 illustrates the difference between single-loop and double-loop learning.

An important contribution of double-loop learning is that it enables the leader to learn and profit from setbacks. By interpreting the reason a setback occurred, the leader might do better the next time. Faced with a group

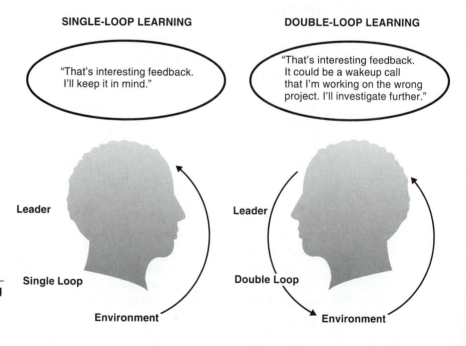

FIGURE 15–1

Single-Loop Learning versus Double-Loop Learning

in crisis, a leader might establish a vision of better days ahead for group members. The leader observes that the vision leads to no observable changes in performance and behavior. Perhaps the group was not ready for a vision. Encountering a comparable situation in the future, the leader might hold back on formulating a vision until the group is headed out of the crisis. Double-loop learning was shown by Louis Gerstner, the IBM chairman who previously held key leadership posts at two other major firms that faced financial troubles. When asked by analysts in 1993 why he had not yet formulated an Olympian strategy for IBM's future, Gerstner replied: "The last thing IBM needs right now is a vision. What it needs are tough-minded business strategies for each of its businesses."[3]

Leadership Development Through Self-Discipline

As with other types of personal development, leadership development requires considerable self-discipline. In the present context, *self-discipline* is mobilizing one's effort and energy to stay focused on attaining an important goal. Self-discipline is required for most forms of leadership development. Assume, for example, that a leader is convinced that active listening is an important leadership behavior. The leader reads about active listening and also attends a workshop on the subject. After the reading and workshop are completed, the leader will need to concentrate diligently in order to remember to listen actively. Self-discipline is particularly necessary because the pressures of everyday activities often divert a person's attention away from personal development.

Self-discipline plays an important role in the continuous monitoring of one's behavior to ensure that needed self-development occurs. After identifying a developmental need, it is necessary to periodically review if one is making the necessary improvements. Assume a person recognizes the developmental need to become a more colorful communicator as a way of enhancing charisma. The person would need self-discipline to make the conscious effort to communicate more colorfully when placed in an appropriate situation. Leadership Skill-Building Exercise 15–1 will help you identify your own developmental needs related to interpersonal relationships.

DEVELOPMENT THROUGH EDUCATION, EXPERIENCE, AND MENTORING

Much of leadership development takes place through means other than self-awareness and self-discipline, or leadership development programs. Leadership is such a comprehensive process that almost any life activity can help people prepare for a leadership role. The president and owner of a large residential and commercial heating and cooling company made the following comments:

LEADERSHIP SKILL-BUILDING EXERCISE 15–1 The Interpersonal Skills Checklist

Directions: Below are a number of specific aspects of behavior that suggest a person needs improvement in his or her interpersonal skills related to leadership and influence. Check each statement that is generally true for you. You can add to the reliability of this exercise by asking one or two other people who know you well to rate you. Then compare your self-analysis with their analysis of you.

Developmental Needs and Areas for Improvement

1. I'm too shy and reserved. _____

2. I bully and intimidate others too frequently. _____

3. I tell others what they want to hear rather than emphasizing the truth. _____

4. I have trouble expressing my feelings. _____

5. I make negative comments about group members too readily. _____

6. Very few people pay attention to the ideas I contribute during a meeting. _____

7. My personality isn't colorful enough. _____

8. People find me boring. _____

9. I pay too little attention to the meaning behind what team members and coworkers are saying. _____

10. It is very difficult for me to criticize others. _____

11. I'm too serious most of the time. _____

12. I avoid controversy in dealing with others. _____

13. I don't get my point across well. _____

14. It's difficult for me to make small talk with others. _____

15. I boast too much about my accomplishments. _____

16. I strive too much for individual recognition instead of looking to credit the team. _____

17. Self-confidence is my weak point. _____

18. My spoken messages are too bland. _____

19. My written messages are too bland. _____

20. I read people poorly.   ____

21. _____

 (Fill in your own statement.)   ____

Now that you (and perhaps one or two others) have identified specific behaviors that may require change, draw up an action plan. Describe briefly a plan of attack for bringing about the change you hope to achieve for each statement that is checked. Ideas might come from personal development books or human relations and leadership development workshops.[4] After formulating an action plan, you will need self-discipline for its successful implementation. For example, if you checked, "People find me boring" you might want to expand your fund of knowledge by extensive reading and by talking to dynamic people. You will then need the self-discipline to continue your quest for ideas and to incorporate some of these ideas into your conversation.

One of my best preparations for running a company came from my early days as a waiter. I learned how to handle difficult people and how to accept compliments. I also learned how to persuade people to make choices on the menu that gave them pleasure and increased the restaurant's profits. Those lessons are all important in running a $45 million business.

Three important life and work experiences that contribute to leadership development are education, experience as a leader, and mentoring. Let's look at the link between each of these three factors and leadership.

Education

Education generally refers to acquiring knowledge without concern about immediate application. If a potential leader studies mathematics, the logical reasoning acquired might someday help him or her solve a complex problem facing the organization. As a result, the leader's stature is enhanced. Formal education is positively correlated with achieving managerial and leadership positions. Furthermore, there is a positive relationship between amount of formal education and level of leadership position attained. Supporting data were described in Chapter 2.

Bernard M. Bass has concluded that educational credentials, demonstrated by degrees in engineering, law, or business administration, provide avenues to success in business leadership.[5] The correlation between education and leadership status, however, may not reflect causation. Many people get the opportunity to hold a business leadership position only *if* they have achieved a specified level of education. A more important issue than the statistical association between leadership and formal education is *how* education contributes to leadership effectiveness.

Most high-level leaders are intelligent, well-informed people who gather knowledge throughout their career. The knowledge that accrues from formal education and self-study, provides them with information for innovative problem solving. Being intellectually alert also contributes to exerting influence through logical persuasion.

Experience

On-the-job experience is an obvious contributor to leadership effectiveness. Without experience, knowledge cannot readily be converted into skills. For example, you will need experience to put into practice the appropriate influence tactics you studied in Chapter 8. Leadership experience also helps build skills and insights a person may not have formally studied. Here we look at two important aspects of experience: sources of experience and the importance of broad experience.

Sources of Experience.   The two major developmental factors in any work situation are work associates and the task itself.[6] Work associates can help a person develop in myriad ways. An immediate superior can be a positive or negative model of effective leadership. You might observe how your boss skillfully confronts a quality problem during a staff meeting. You observe carefully and plan to use a similar technique when it becomes necessary for you to confront a problem with a group. In contrast, assume that the boss's confrontational approach backfires—the group becomes defensive and recalcitrant. You have learned how *not* to confront. Members of upper management, peers, and reporting staff can also help a worker profit from experience. For example, by trial and error the worker might learn which type of praise is best for influencing others.

Work-related tasks can also contribute to leadership development because part of a leader's role is to be an effective and innovative problem solver. The most developmental tasks are more complex and ambiguous than a person has faced previously. Starting a new activity for a firm, such as establishing a dealer network, exemplifies a developmental experience. The accompanying Leader in Action box describes a manager who acquired experience in taking the initiative to help her organization cope with a serious problem.

Broad Experience.   Many aspects of leadership are situational. A sound approach to improving leadership effectiveness is therefore to gain managerial experience in different settings. An aspirant to executive leadership is well advised to gain management experience in at least two different organizational functions, such as marketing and operations. Daphna F. Raskas and Donald C. Hambrick use the term *multifunctional managerial development* to refer to the process of achieving broad experience. **Multifunctional managerial development** is an organization's intentional efforts to enhance the effectiveness of managers by giving them experience in multiple functions within the organization.[7]

LEADER
IN
ACTION

Tanya Bridges, Human Resources Manager

Tanya Bridges was working as a human resources manager in a company taken over by a larger food company. After the takeover, the edict was out to downsize the organization by 900 jobs, and to reduce general operating costs by 15 percent. Nobody's job was sacred. Instead of bemoaning her fate, Bridges surveyed the damage to the organization and then asked for an audience with the new vice president of human resources. She first presented him with an oral summary of her observations, followed by a written report. Bridges describes her presentation to management, and related events.

"I focused on the havoc downsizing was creating and what the company could do about it. I had done my homework by reading certain articles in human resources magazines. I explained to my boss that we had plenty of problems. Our photocopying costs were skyrocketing as hundreds of employees were updating their resumes. Important work was going unattended as people were chasing down job openings in other companies and calling personal contacts.

"I volunteered to head up a survivor assistance group that would help calm the people who were being asked to stay. First, we would have sessions with about thirty employees and one member of top management. He or she would explain when the cuts would end and how jobs would be changed. In the weeks following we would conduct voluntary group sessions with employees who wanted to express fears and concerns about their jobs.

"I presented evidence that survivors after a major downsizing often suffer guilt. They feel bad about being the lucky ones. We would have trained counselors from the employee assistance program to help with these sessions.

"I emphasized repeatedly that with a little time and effort, the company could stop the hemorrhaging in productivity and morale created by the downsizing. My efforts quickly received top management's attention and support. The president wrote me a note thanking me for providing leadership to an important program that would help make the combined company effective. My job became secure for now. I profited from the experience of helping a company cope with downsizing. Also, I felt an inner glow because I was really helping the employees in my company and their families."

As shown in Figure 15–2, the most modest level of commitment to multifunctional management development would be for managers merely to

FIGURE 15–2

Continuum of Practical Options for Multifunctional Managerial Development

Source: Reprinted, by permission of the publisher, from *Organizational Dynamics,* Autumn/1992, © 1992, American Management Association, New York. All rights reserved.

- **HIGH COMMITMENT**
- **Complete mobility across functions, i.e., "career maze"**
- **Temporary (six-month to two-year) assignments outside the person's "home function"**
- **Brief, orientational rotation through functions**
- **Exposure to other functions on task forces project teams**
- **Classroom education about other functions**
- **LOW COMMITMENT**

study other functions. Studying other functions, however, is quite useful because it provides a person with the necessary background to profit from experience. Participation in multifunctional task forces indicates more commitment to the acquisition of breadth.

The highest level of commitment is complete mobility across functions. Hewlett-Packard represents this approach through its *career maze* program. For example, an employee may begin in product design, and then move on to assignments in marketing, manufacturing, customer service, purchasing, human resources, and so forth. Employees judged to have leadership potential are the most likely to be offered the career maze.

Mentoring

Another experience-based way to develop leadership capability is to be coached by an experienced, knowledgeable leader. Quite often this person is a **mentor**, a more experienced person who develops a protégé's abilities through tutoring, coaching, guidance, and emotional support. The mentor is a trusted counselor and guide who is typically a person's manager. However, a mentor can also be a staff professional or coworker. An emotional tie exists between the protégé (or apprentice) and the mentor.

Mentoring is typically an informal relationship based on compatibility between two personalities. Nevertheless, several firms, including the Internal Revenue Service and IBM, have attempted formal matches between the mentor and the mentoree.[8] Sometimes the junior manager or professional is given a choice of mentors. The standard approach to finding a mentor is to make oneself visible through outstanding job performance and volunteering for assignments. Similar to other friendships, mentoring is based on a spark or chemical attraction between two people.

Mentors enhance the careers of protégés in many ways, such as recommending them for promotion and helping them establish valuable contacts. Of interest here is how a mentor can help you become a better leader. The mentor can serve as a model of effective (or sometimes ineffective) leadership. A high level of mentor involvement is to coach the apprentice on how he or she handles certain leadership assignments. The mentor is usually not physically present when the mentoree is practicing leadership. A substitute is for the mentoree to recap a leadership situation and ask for a critique. Wendy Lopez, who is the data processing manager for a payroll services firm, recounts a mentoring session with her boss about a leadership incident:

> I explained to Max [her mentor and the vice president of administration] that I had some trouble motivating my supervisors to pitch in with weekend work. We had received a surge of new clients because many firms had decided to downsize their own payroll departments. Our group was having trouble adjusting to the new workload. Instead of operations running smoothly, things were a little spastic. Although I tried to explain the importance of getting out the work, the supervisors were still dragging their heels a little.
>
> Max reviewed the incident with me. He told me that I might have helped the supervisors take a broader view of what this new business meant to the firm. Max felt I didn't communicate clearly enough how the future of our firm was at stake. He also suggested that I should have been more specific about how pitching in during an emergency would benefit the supervisors financially.
>
> With Max's coaching behind me, I did a much better job of enlisting cooperation the next time an emergency surfaced.

LEADERSHIP DEVELOPMENT PROGRAMS

A time-honored strategy for developing prospective, new, and practicing leaders is to enroll prospective leaders in leadership development programs. These programs typically focus on such topics as personal growth, leadership style, strategy formulation, influence, motivation, and persuasive communication. Outdoor and wilderness training, as described in Chapter 9, represents one important type of leadership training. Many management development programs are also aimed at leadership development. The difference, however, is that management development programs offer courses that cover hundreds of topics within the functions of planning, organizing, controlling, and leading. Table 15–1 lists a sample of leadership development programs.

Key Characteristics of a Leadership Development Program

Developing and training leaders is far more complex than merely sending aspiring leaders to a one-week seminar. The leadership development program has to be appropriately sponsored, carefully designed, and professionally executed. Marshall Whitmire and Philip R. Nienstedt have formulated such an approach to leadership development, as outlined in Table 15–2 and summarized below.[9]

1. *Involve executives and secure their sponsorship.* For a leadership training program to receive high priority, top executives must set the program's tone

TABLE 15–1   A Sampling of Leadership Development Programs Offered by Universities and Training and Development Firms

The Executive Program (four-week program for senior executives involved in the strategic management of their firms)

Executive Communication

How to Make Presentations with Confidence and Power

The Looking Glass (management simulation)

Team-Building Skills for Managers

Leadership and Team Development for Managerial Success

Outdoor Training

Developing Effective Leadership

Excellence in Leadership

Business Ethics and the Professional Manager

The Learning Organization: A New Approach to Leading Your Company

Note: Organizations offering such seminars and courses include the Michigan Business School, the Wharton School of the University of Pennsylvania, the American Management Association, and the Center for Creative Leadership.

and objectives. They should also sponsor implementation, as is done with the four-week executive program at General Electric.

2. *Target career transitions.* Managers at different levels should receive different types of leadership training. The Honeywell system, for example, targets training for current general managers, directors, and middle managers. Programs provide different leadership emphases for these three groups.

TABLE 15–2   Characteristics of a Comprehensive Leadership Development Program

1. Involve executives and secure their sponsorship

2. Target career transitions

3. Address current and future organizational needs

4. Use an appropriate model

5. Support individual improvement with diagnostic tools

6. Ensure practical and relevant content

7. Emphasize interpersonal relations and teamwork

8. Conclude with individual action plans

Source: Developed from information in Marshall Whitmire and Philip R. Nienstedt, "Lead Leaders into the '90s," *Personnel Journal,* May 1991, pp. 80–85.

General managers might have a workshop on vision setting and organizational change, whereas motivation and coaching might be a better fit for the other two groups.

3. *Address current and future organizational needs.* A company moving swiftly toward globalization would provide training on global leadership skills, such as developing the multicultural organization and adapting to rapid change.

4. *Use an appropriate model.* Leadership skills are often instilled better when taught in a solid conceptual framework. Several of the frameworks presented in this text are often used in leadership development, including the situational leadership model, SuperLeadership, and the Vroom–Yetton–Jago model.

5. *Support individual improvement with diagnostic tools.* Many leadership development programs include self-evaluation with the type of assessment instruments presented throughout this text. In addition to self-evaluation, other people who know the participant also complete the forms. In one program at the Center for Creative Leadership, about nine work associates complete an inventory on various dimensions of leadership for each participant. Particularly meaningful are significant discrepancies between self-perceptions and perception by others.

6. *Ensure practical and relevant content.* Many leadership development programs present participants with problems closely related to those found on the job. General Electric's action learning program features actual problems encountered at a GE business. As part of the program, participants' solutions are presented to GE executives.

7. *Emphasize interpersonal relationships and teamwork.* Many leadership development programs emphasize team building and outdoor training because leaders at every level must have good interpersonal and teamwork skills.

8. *Conclude with individual action plans.* In a high-quality leadership program, attendees must develop personalized action plans for improvement (such as those requested in Leadership Skill-Building Exercise 15–1). At Motorola, participants prepare a self-letter describing personal changes to which they are willing to commit.

Types of Leadership Development Programs

In practice, the various programs for developing leaders often overlap. For ease of comprehension, however, we'll divide these programs into four categories: personal growth; feedback on traits and style; developing conceptual skills; and simulations. Figure 15–3 places these types of leadership development programs on a continuum. As the figure shows, personal growth approaches are most clearly related to leadership development, whereas simulations overlap considerably with management development.

Personal Growth. Leadership development programs that focus on personal growth assume that leaders are deeply in touch with their personal dreams and talents, and that they will act to fulfill them. Therefore , if people

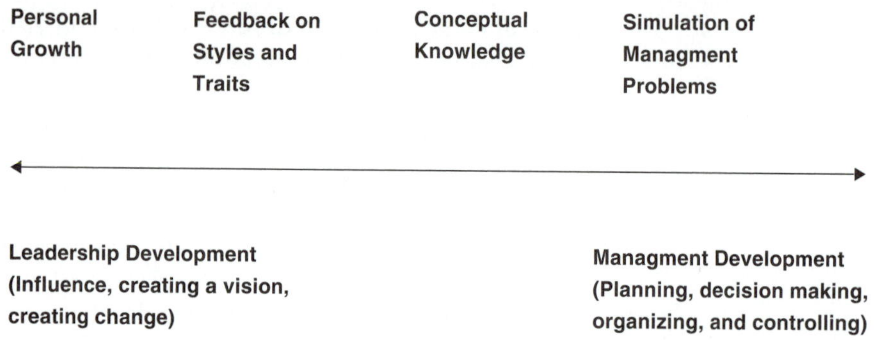

Personal Growth	Feedback on Styles and Traits	Conceptual Knowledge	Simulation of Managment Problems

$$\longleftarrow \hspace{6cm} \longrightarrow$$

FIGURE 15–3

Types of Leadership Development Programs

Leadership Development
(Influence, creating a vision, creating change)

Managment Development
(Planning, decision making, organizing, and controlling)

can get in touch with their inner desires and fulfill them, they will become leaders. A tacit assumption in personal-growth training programs is that leadership is almost a calling. Jay Conger captures the essence of personal-growth programs in these words:

> Using outdoor-adventure activities and psychological exercises, personal growth programs induce participants to reflect on their behaviors (such as their orientation toward risk or personal intimacy) and on their personal values and desires. They also empower participants through experiences that teach them to take responsibility for their situations—rather than blame problems on the job on outside influences or events.[10]

Personal-growth leadership development programs have burgeoned in popularity. (Conger is concerned, however, that they are based on an overly simple conceptualization of leadership.) Most of these programs are established and implemented by business entrepreneurs rather than by professionals in human behavior. The Pecos River Learning Center near Santa Fe, New Mexico, is a well-known leadership program of this type. Two principal aims of the program are developing skills in risk taking and teamwork.

Feedback on Traits and Styles.   A longstanding, yet continually evolving, type of leadership development is to receive systematic feedback on one's personal traits and leadership style. The assertiveness and leadership style tests (Chapters 2 and 5) are representative feedback instruments. As mentioned in relation to diagnostic instruments, self-feedback is supplemented by feedback from workplace associates who complete similar forms. An excerpt follows from a feedback session with a counselor about a discrepancy between self-feedback and feedback from others:

> Your self-feedback suggests that one of your key strengths is sensitivity to people and compassion. I suspect you are quite interested in being sensitive and compassionate. The feedback from others, however, rates you quite low on sensitivity and compassion. Let's see if we can discover the reason for this discrepancy.

The manager in question discovered that part of his problem was that his body language was inconsistent with his thought and actions. For example, he gave encouragement in a manner that was perceived as cold and aloof. By improving his body language—so that he was perceived as sensitive and compassionate—the manager improved his relationships with people.

Conceptual Knowledge. A standard university approach to leadership development is to equip people with a conceptual understanding of leadership. The concepts are typically supplemented by experiential activities such as role playing and cases. Nonuniversity learning firms such as the American Management Association and TPG/Learning Systems also offer conceptually based leadership development programs. Conceptual knowledge is very important because it alerts the leader to information that will make a difference in leadership. For example, if a person studies how a leader brings about transformations, he or she can put these ideas into practice.

The Leadership Challenge program developed by James M. Kouzes and Barry Z. Posner (and stemming from the book of the same name) presents a useful set of concepts for stimulating leadership thinking. The five core practices common to successful leaders are as follows:

1. Challenge the process (don't accept the status quo).
2. Inspire a shared vision.
3. Enable others to act (much like empowerment).
4. Model the way (serve as a positive model).
5. Encourage the heart (leadership involves passion and commitment).[11]

The accompanying Leaders in Action box presents a glimpse of life at the world's most prestigious leadership development program. It combines conceptual knowledge about management with some opportunities for personal growth.

LEADERS IN ACTION

Life at the Advanced Management Program of Harvard University

The Harvard University Advanced Management program is geared to future chief executives and chief financial officers of the world. During the three-month program, class members live in dormitories, away from spouses, significant others, and children. They are given firm instructions not to call the office. Program participants must work exceedingly hard, reveal their weaknesses, and showcase their strengths.

The program, which runs twice a year, requires courage and self-confidence. George Harvin, vice president of Roses Stores Inc., says, "You get put into an environment where you are totally intimidated by everything—by the Harvard name; by being with the top-level folks from very large, successful companies, from all industries, cultures and from many different countries. And you find out how you measure up."

Participants are required to have fifteen to twenty-five years of business experience. Firms carefully choose who will attend and leave little choice to the designate. Being among the 150 participants indicates that a person is on the fast track to the top. The company must invest over $30,000 in tuition per person for the program. In addition, the company must do without the manager's contribution for a quarter of a year.

Jeannette Wagner, one of the two women in her class in 1983, says, "Your boss has to decide to do without your brains for three months and decide not to bug you while you are there." When Wagner attended, she was senior vice president of Estee Lauder International Inc. She is now president.

The key subject areas are finance, marketing, operations and negotiating. Placing the managers under fierce competition in these courses helps them develop leadership skills.

Almost half the class members are from countries outside North America. Consequently, a network is developed among people who may be politically important to each other in the future. Many of the friendships develop as a result of forced, close living composed of eight single rooms grouped around a common living room. Business deals are often made during the course because the participants occupy such high-level positions.

Despite the seriousness of the program, many of the participants get together during late evenings to hold spontaneous parties. Claude Zinngrabe, chairman of Prudential Home Building Investors Inc., recalls fondly a midnight session of singing "Hey Jude" next to a Scotsman playing the piano.

Source: Based on facts reported in Barbara Lyne, "Harvard University's Fast-Track Boot Camp for Rising Executives," *The New York Times* syndicated story, May 31, 1992.

Simulations of Leadership and Management Problems.   Another standard approach to leadership development is to give participants an opportunity to work on a problem that simulates a real organization. Many simulations are computerized, and others reflect the typical scenario of managers making decisions without much assistance from a computer. The Looking Glass, developed by the Center for Creative Leadership, is a carefully constructed simulation of problems facing a real glass manufacturer. (The term *Looking Glass* indicates that participants reflect on their behavior and action, and receive feedback.) The simulation strives to bring the office into the classroom by simulating real job challenge followed by debriefing.

A dominant feature of the Looking Glass is the unrelenting pressure inherent in the simulation. By compressing various organizational roles and demands into six hours, the Looking Glass creates the sense of urgency many leaders and managers face on the job. Other features of executive life incorporated into the simulation are

coming to grips with a new, unfamiliar position

exercising leadership in the face of organizational constraints

being persuasive and influential in the absence of formal authority[12]

The debriefing that follows the simulation is supportive rather than negative and critical. Feedback is based on the observations of peers and trained observers. Many participants in the Looking Glass report that they achieved insight into the human side of management, including the importance of giving effective feedback and resolving conflict.

EVALUATION OF LEADERSHIP DEVELOPMENT EFFORTS

A comprehensive approach to leadership development would include a rigorous evaluation of the consequences of having participated in a developmental experience. Executives and human resource professionals would ask such tough questions as the following:

Do people who receive mentoring actually become more effective leaders?

Do leaders who attend outdoor training become better team leaders than (1) those who do not attend the training, or (2) those whose "team development" consists of playing softball with the office gang?

Does the Advanced Management Program at Harvard improve the decision-making skills of participants?

The evaluation of training and development programs is a comprehensive topic that includes such considerations as the design of experiments, and the development of accurate outcome measures.[13] Here we examine the traditional approach to evaluating training and development outcomes and an approach better adapted to leadership development.

The Traditional Approach to Evaluation

The traditional approach to the evaluation of leadership training and development programs would first specify the program objectives. After training was completed, measurements would be made of the extent to which those objectives were met.[14] Two sets of outcomes are especially relevant. First, an assessment is made of the extent to which the participants acquired new skills during the program. For example, did the seminar participants acquire new skills in giving supportive feedback? Second, an assessment is made of whether the organization has become more effective as a result of this new skill acquisition. Did the bottom line improve because of the new skills? For example, has supportive feedback by leaders resulted in higher quality and profits?

A more rigorous approach to the evaluation of leadership training and development would include an experiment, as shown in Table 15–3. The experimental group would consist of the participants in the development program. Before-and-after measures of skills would be taken to determine if improvements took place. Outcome measures from the experimental group would then be compared to two control or contrast groups. All three groups would be composed of people similar in education, intelligence, job level, job experience, and so forth. People in one control group would receive no special development. Members of the second control group would receive a different kind of development. Instead of training in giving supportive feedback, they might be trained in memo writing. The purpose of the second control (or contrast) group is to determine if training in supportive feedback has an edge over simply sending people to any sensible training program.

The traditional method of evaluation is best suited to evaluating structured, definable skills such as running software or performing a breakeven analysis. Leadership training and development, however, involves much broader, less structured behaviors such as inspiring others and identifying problems. Another problem is that few organizations would be willing to randomly assign managers to expensive and time-consuming leadership development programs.

Domains of Impact of a Leadership Development Program

Researchers at the Center for Creative Leadership decided that the traditional approach to the evaluation of training and development was inadequate for their purposes. Development programs aim to discover and advance the individual potential, especially in interpersonal relationships. These programs are highly personal in nature and will benefit different people in different ways. After participating in the same development program, one leader might become more visionary, whereas another might become more attuned to empowerment.

Members of the Center for Creative Leadership decided to evaluate their Looking Glass program (LGI) by asking, "How did it leave its mark?" rather than "Did it leave this particular mark?" Specifically, the researchers

TABLE 15–3 Evaluating Leadership Development Through the Experimental Method

	Pretraining measures	Training	Post-training measures
Experimental group	Yes	Supportive feedback	Yes
Control group I	Yes	None	Yes
Control group II	Yes	Memo writing	Yes

asked four questions that covered important **domains of impact** (ranges of possible effects) that a program might have:[15]

1. *What did participants learn from LGI?* Open-ended questions were asked about learning outcomes for the development program. The responses related to the domains of *knowledge* (concepts and content) and *self-objectivity* (learning about individual limitations and strengths.)

2. *What impact did the program have on participants' self-objectivity?* Asking about self-objectivity is meaningful because most leadership development programs purport to help participants achieve sharpened self-insights. The participants in the programs themselves, along with peers and superiors, can be asked to contribute input about the participant's self-objectivity after having attended the program.

3. *How was behavior back on the job affected?* Both interviews and questionnaires are used to assess behavioral changes stemming from participation in the Looking Glass program. For example, group members might be asked if the leader had become more adept at helping the group resolve a high-pressure problem such as meeting a challenging deadline.

4. *Was there a relationship between enhanced self-objectivity and behavior change back on the job?* Rather than evaluating the results of the program, this question is aimed at understanding the relationship between two domains (self-objectivity and behavior). The relationship between the two domains might work in this way: A leader develops enhanced insight into her sarcastic behavior when a group member makes a mistake. Back on the job she softens her sarcasm. Constructive change has therefore taken place whether or not this change can be translated into bottom-line results.

Answering these four questions evaluates the essence of the Looking Glass Program. Nevertheless, many top executives will still want to know how improvement in the domains of impact leads to improved productivity and quality.

LEADERSHIP SUCCESSION

In a well-managed organization, replacements for retiring and dismissed executives are chosen through **leadership succession**, an orderly process of identifying and grooming people to replace executives. Succession planning is linked to leadership development in two important ways. First, being groomed as a successor is part of a leadership development through enriched experience. Second, the process of choosing and fostering a successor's development is part of a manager's own development. In a book written for CEOs, Thomas Horton urges them to identify one or more successors before retiring or leaving for other reasons.[16] Identifying a replacement can be regarded as a professional commitment.

The replacement of senior executives and managers with outsiders can reflect either successful or failed succession planning. Bringing in outsiders to replace retiring or dismissed executives reflects successful planning when the board intentionally seeks a fresh perspective. Failed succession planning is indicated when the company has to go outside because no suitable talent is available within the firm.

Replacing top executives with outsiders is typically thought to occur most often when an organization is performing poorly. The reasoning might be that insiders are too closely identified with the CEO's failed strategies and policies. An analysis of 472 succession events at large companies provides a new perspective. The study indicates that poor performance leads to outsider selection only when sociopolitical forces are weak. One factor (or force) prompting the selection of an outsider is the lack of an heir apparent. Another factor is that when the executive holds only the CEO title (and not also chairperson), a replacement might be brought in from the outside.[17]

A firm's succession strategy often mirrors its business strategy. Lynda Gratton and Michel Syrett observe that in a fast-growing and rapidly changing corporate structure, succession methods are temporary and subject to revision. Amstrad, a consumer electronics company, has approximately 1,000 employees. The chief executive takes personal responsibility for the development of high-potential people. He also ensures that they receive the right experience so they are ready on short notice to fill an executive vacancy. A more mature and stable organization, such as Shell Oil Company, has a much more complicated and refined system of succession planning.[18] The system involves human resource specialists, including the use of a computerized human resource information system (HRIS).

The leader who succeeds another, as well as all other existing leaders, must stay alert to new developments that could potentially influence how he or she functions as a leader.

LEADING-EDGE AND FUTURE CHALLENGES

An essential part of developing as a leader is to become sensitive to and prepare for leading-edge and future challenges. Many of these leading-edge trends, such as multiculturalism and empowerment, have been discussed in previous chapters. Here we highlight ten leading-edge and future themes that represent substantial challenges for leaders.

1. *Leaders will serve as role models.* Expectations will rise for leaders to be effective role models in business, not-for-profit firms, and the political arena. Conger believes that for leaders to serve as effective role models, they may need to work with mental health professionals to learn why they are having difficulty with certain interpersonal tasks.[19] For example, some leaders are poor listeners and thus they are poor role models for people dealing with internal and external customers. A counselor might help a leader get to the root cause of the poor-listening habit.

2. *Leaders will liberate and enable people.* A consistent theme of the 1990s has been that managers should deemphasize the control of people and emphasize giving them responsibility. A primary issue for leaders is that their job is to liberate and enable them rather than to supervise. Edward E. Lawler III believes that effective leaders are allowing work team members to make white-knuckle decisions about hiring, firing, and pay. For example, at the Volvo manufacturing plant in Uddevalla, Sweden, work team members receive customer orders and communicate with dealers. They stay in touch with their work output because they are now receiving quality and maintenance data on the cars they build.[20]

3. *Business leaders will be multicultural and diversity experts.* The increasing globalization of business will require mid-level and upper-level managers to relate comfortably to people from other cultures. Managing operations in other countries and negotiating international deals will require cross-cultural insights and wisdom. It will also become more important to work easily with a diverse group of team members, superiors, and colleagues. To gain stature as a leader and influence others (both now and in the future), one must be tolerant of diverse viewpoints.[21]

4. *Effective business leaders will be strategic opportunists.* As worldwide competition continues to increase and profit margins shrink, tomorrow's business leaders will face heavy pressure to locate the strategic opportunities not yet found by competitors. To accomplish this feat, leaders will need penetrating insights into domestic and international markets. They will also need to stay alert to possibilities for improving quality and service and for reducing costs. Peter Drucker recommends that managers walk outside the organization to obtain good insights into the competition. At the same time they will better understand how customers perceive the company's products and services.[22]

5. *Leaders will be adept at building strategic interdependencies and partnerships.* Reuben Mark, the CEO of Colgate-Palmolive, believes that partnerships of all kinds will be the thrust of the future. Strategic interdependencies among companies, governments, and people will become increasingly necessary. Colgate-Palmolive set up such a partnership with two worldwide advertising agencies, who were told: "You set up wherever we do business. You don't have to worry short term about losing our business." Colgate-Palmolive gives agency employees stock in the company. One or two mistakes are forgiven because the emphasis is on a long-term partnership.[23] The Leader in Action box on page 350 describes a leader who thinks in terms of partnerships and is also a diversity expert.

6. *Leaders will encourage others to think of the systems implications of their actions.* According to Peter M. Senge, many organizations can be said to have learning disabilities because their people do not think systemically (in terms of systems). **Systemic thinking** means seeing patterns and the invisible fabrics of interrelated actions that may take years to surface. A systemic thinker will recognize how events throughout the organization are related. For example, a

LEADER IN ACTION

Ernie Lofton of the UAW

Back in 1950, when Ernie Lofton appeared at the Ford Motor Co.'s Dearborn Iron Foundry looking for work, the lines were so long that he was told to return the next day. He did return and was hired. Forty-three years later nobody tells him to come back later. Lofton is the vice president of the United Auto Workers, a union that represents 97,000 workers. Lofton has plenty of power, and the respect of top management at Ford.

Lofton's primary allegiance is to the UAW. He is aware, however, that getting a better contract for union members is linked to company performance. Lofton says that at times Ford and the UAW have disagreements, "but not to the point where it has diminished our ability to look at what's in the best interest of Ford and the UAW."

Lofton's low-key style and communication skills are credited for sustaining a labor-management relationship that began in the 1980s during the wave of plant closings and layoffs at Ford. Membership in the UAW's Ford Department is less than half of what it was in 1979. Yet the crisis years brought the company and union closer rather than creating a wedge between them.

Lofton said that Ford talked with the leadership and membership and explained why they had to downsize the plants. They had too much capacity for their reduced market share. "I think," Lofton continued, "that when you explain your facts to people, they might not relish hearing about them. But at least they can appreciate them and understand them."

Lofton has also exercised leadership in the civil rights movement. "I got involved back in the '50s," he reflected. "You were talking about people who were evicted from homes . . . people who had no jobs . . . racism, bigotry, those kinds of things." Lofton is first vice president of the Detroit chapter of the NAACP. He is also a national board member of the civil rights organization. In 1993, Lofton led a thirtieth anniversary march commemorating the "I Have a Dream" speech of Martin Luther King, Jr.

Lofton believes strongly in encouraging diversity in UAW leadership. He is concerned that very few African American and women leaders have risen through the UAW local ranks. Partly because of his influence, the UAW is committed to having at least one black person and one woman among its international vice presidents.

Source: Adapted from Alan L. Alder, "UAW Leader Is Low-Key, Tenacious," the Associated Press, June 17, 1993.

sales manager who offers generous discounts to customers is placing considerable pressure on manufacturing to lower costs. A leader who helps its organization learn might point out that teaching employees to be better parents might also help them become better managers, and vice versa.[24]

7. *Leaders will direct others in the virtual corporation.* Organizations are becoming more fluid and flexible to adapt to rapidly changing environments and opportunities. The ultimate in such an organization is the **virtual corporation,** a temporary network of independent firms linked by information technology to share skills, costs, and access to each other's markets. After the opportunity has been exploited, the virtual corporation vanishes.[25] The temporary network of companies is typically a strategic alliance. For example, a manufacturer might manufacture and rely on a product-design firm to decide what to make. A marketing firm would then distribute the product.

A leader in a virtual corporation will have to help coach and persuade others because hierarchy and formal authority are minimized. Another challenge facing the leader is a wide span of control, perhaps 70 people. Not being able to supervise people closely, the leader will have to rely on an array of influence tactics. To be credible, the leader will also need to be steeped in information technology.

8. *Leaders will operate comfortably within a flattened pyramid.* Futurists predict consistently that organizational pyramids will become much flatter (as in the virtual corporation). The persistent downsizing of firms has already created a much flatter structure. More leadership and less management are required in these flat structures. The president of Europe's largest container company explains: "You don't order people from the top, you lead them. You give them vision and help. In the past, if a business unit were in trouble, the people at the top dictated the action to be taken. Today, we first help the business unit manager to try to overcome the difficulties. There's only one key decision: whether to replace the manager."[26]

9. *Leaders will be facilitators in the reengineered corporation.* One of the most popular new business concepts of the 1990s deals with organization by process rather than by task. Called **reengineering**, it is the radical redesign of business processes to achieve substantial improvements in performance. Reengineering requires considerable innovation by leaders. They must shake obsolete business processes and the design principles behind them to create new ones. Ford Motor Co. found, for example, that most accounts payable activity could be eliminated by simply paying for goods when they arrived rather than waiting for invoices from suppliers.

Leaders in a reengineered corporation support, coach, and facilitate rather than supervise and control. They help create a permissive atmosphere in which staff members feel free to break loose from outdated rules and assumptions that underlie activities.[27] Leaders at all levels in the organization may have to help team members envision what a radically streamlined process (such as processing a house mortgage application) might look like.

10. *Leaders will become community builders.* The most important skill for leaders of the future is community building, especially when it is combined with

strategic opportunism. According to Conger, community building requires both empowerment and vision. A vision should not only achieve a meaningful goal but also build a community of dedicated people.[28]

Will you be ready to be one of tomorrow's leaders? Use Leadership Self-Assessment Exercise 15–1 to help you answer.

LEADERSHIP SELF-ASSESSMENT EXERCISE 15–1 Checklist for the Future

Directions: To reflect on your readiness to carry out leading-edge and future leadership roles, review the checklist below. Indicate if you believe you are ready, or not yet ready, to occupy each role. Sketch an action plan for developing your leadership skills for roles you are not yet ready to carry out. For example, if you are not ready to be a multicultural and diversity expert, you might participate in diversity training and develop skills in another language. Place your action plans in a safe place, and review them in the year 2000!

Leading-Edge and Future Challenge	Ready	*Not Yet Ready*
1. Serve as a role model	____	____
2. Liberate and enable people	____	____
3. Be a multicultural and diversity expert	____	____
4. Be a strategic opportunist	____	____
5. Build strategic interdependencies and partnerships	____	____
6. Encourage others to think systemically	____	____
7. Lead others in the virtual corporation	____	____
8. Operate comfortably within a flattened pyramid	____	____
9. Be a facilitator in a reengineered corporation	____	____
10. Be a community builder	____	____

Your action plans to achieve competencies in several of these leadership roles may be tentative. Nevertheless, developing these action plans may sensitize you to the requirements for effective leadership in the future.

SUMMARY

Leadership and management development are widely practiced in a variety of organizations and take many forms, including self-development. Self-awareness involves the insightful processing of feedback about oneself to improve personal effectiveness. Single-loop learning occurs when learners seek minimum feedback that may substantially confront their basic ideas or actions. Double-loop learning occurs when people use feedback to confront the validity of the goal or values implicit in the situation; it enables the leader to learn and profit from failure.

Leadership development requires considerable self-discipline. For example, self-discipline is needed to monitor one's behavior to ensure that needed self-development takes place.

Education, leadership experience, and mentoring are all major contributors to leadership development. Most high-level leaders are intelligent, well-informed people who gather knowledge throughout their career. Two important aspects of leadership experience are work associates and the task itself (such as a complex and ambiguous assignment). Broad experience is important for leadership development, as suggested by multifunctional managerial development. A mentor is a more experienced person who develops a protégé's ability through tutoring, coaching, guidance, and emotional support. Mentors can serve as a model of effective (or ineffective) leadership and can coach protégés in leadership skills.

A comprehensive leadership development program includes certain key features: executive involvement; targeting career transitions; addressing current and future organization needs; an appropriate model; diagnostic tools; practical and relevant content; emphasis on interpersonal relations and teamwork; and individual action plans.

Personal-growth experiences for leadership development assume that leaders are deeply in touch with their personal dreams and talents and will act to fulfill them. Outdoor training exemplifies a personal-growth experience. A standard university approach to leadership development is to equip people with a conceptual understanding of leadership. The concepts, such as those included in the Leadership Challenge, can then be applied to leadership situations. Simulations are another standard approach to leadership development, as exemplified by the Looking Glass. The simulation includes practice in exercising leadership in the face of organizational constraints, and supportive feedback on performance.

The traditional approach to the evaluation of leadership development programs includes specifying objectives and then measuring whether they were met. Measures of organizational outcomes, such as increased profits, might also be made. A more rigorous approach to evaluation would be based on an experimental design. An alternative approach to evaluation is to examine the domains of impact (ranges of possible effects) a program might have. Among these domains are concepts and content, self-objectivity, and behavior.

Succession planning (or leadership succession) is linked to leadership development because being groomed as a successor contributes to development. Also, selecting and grooming a successor is part of a leader's development. A firm's succession strategy often mirrors its business strategy.

Many leaders will have to develop to meet leading-edge and future challenges. Among them are serving as a role model, liberating and enabling people, being multicultural and diversity experts, being strategic opportunists, and building strategic partnerships. In addition, leaders must encourage systemic thinking, direct others in the virtual corporation, operate in a flattened structure, be a facilitator in the reengineered firm, and engage in community building.

KEY TERMS

Self-awareness	Domains of impact
Single-loop learning	Leadership succession
Double-loop learning	Systemic thinking
Multifunctional managerial	Virtual corporation
development	Reengineering
Mentor	

GUIDELINES FOR ACTION AND SKILL DEVELOPMENT

An important method for enhancing both the acceptance and effectiveness of leadership development is *needs analysis*, the diagnosis of needs for development. Conducting a needs analysis is based on the idea that individual differences exist among leaders and future leaders. For example, Jennifer might have excellent conceptual knowledge about leadership, but limited team experience. She might be a good candidate for outdoor training. Jack might be an excellent team leader with limited conceptual knowledge. He might be a good candidate for a leadership development program concentrating on formal knowledge about leadership. Sources of data for assessing leadership developmental needs include the following:

1. Self-perceptions of developmental needs, including taking many of the diagnostic instruments presented in this text

2. Perceptions by superiors, subordinates, and peers of the person's developmental needs

3. Psychological evaluation of developmental needs

4. A statement of organizational needs for development, such as the importance of leaders who can deal effectively with diversity (within company, with customers, and globally)

Multiple sources of data are useful because of possible errors in perception, biases, and favoritism.

DISCUSSION QUESTIONS AND ACTIVITIES

1. Many executives believe that playing team sports helps a person develop as a leader. Based on your knowledge of leadership development, where do you stand on this issue?

2. Which aspects of your formal education do you think are making the biggest contribution to your leadership development?

3. How can a person increase self-awareness?

4. Provide a real or hypothetical example of how a leader might engage in double-loop learning.

5. How can a person begin capitalizing on the advantages of multifunctional managerial development early in his or her career?

6. Should the managers who perform the best in a simulation be considered the most eligible for promotion? Why or why not?

7. Is it fair to say a CEO is an ineffective leader when his or her company loses money several years in a row?

8. Assume you were responsible for selecting a leadership development program for your organization. What questions would you ask the potential provider of those services?

9. How do the concepts of "crown prince," "crown princess," and "fast tracker" relate to leadership succession?

10. Speak to a leader who occupies an important position in any organization. Get the person's opinion on the validity of the ten leading-edge and future trends. As an alternative, find an article published in 1994 or later that supports or contradicts the observations about the future. Bring your findings back to class.

LEADERSHIP CASE PROBLEM

"My Leadership Isn't Working"

Sherry Gabrielli had worked as the security supervisor at the regional office of Affiliated Department Stores for six months. She was appointed supervisor after four years of good performance as a security officer. She looked forward with some apprehension to her performance review with her boss, Al Anderson. She felt she was not accomplishing anywhere what was needed.

Anderson greeted Gabrielli with a smile and said, "May I get you coffee, tea, or a soft drink? I want you to relax."

"I will take you up on a decaffeinated, diet cola drink," replied Sherry. "Despite this job, I haven't slipped back to trying to cure my tension with coffee."

"Your health kick must be working, Sherry. You appear quite relaxed on the job to me. One of your strong points as a security supervisor is that you are cool and calm under pressure. In fact, my overall performance rating of you is well above average. Both my boss, the operations chief, and I think you're doing a bang-up job. You can expect an above-average salary increase this next paycheck.

"How do you think you are doing, Sherry? Any problems we may have missed? Anything we can help you with?"

"I'm glad you asked," replied Gabrielli. "I am experiencing one difficulty as a supervisor that may not be showing up in my job performance. My leadership isn't working as well as I would like. The way I see it, our department still isn't acting professionally enough. The men and women are doing a good job, but they are lacking that professional image."

"Sounds like a real concern," said Anderson pensively. "Could you be more specific, though?"

"I can give you a couple of instances," replied Gabrielli. "Mona, one of the security officers, sits in the office with her feet on the desk. And she's forever munching apples. Gordie, our newest security officer, tells about one gross joke each workday. Eduardo, the senior officer who should know better, whistles whenever he's trying to relax."

"What have you done so far about the problems?" Anderson asked.

"I talk about the need for professionalism in security work, but nothing happens. I once even told Eduardo to stop whistling because it gave me a headache. He just gave me a funny look."

"Maybe you and I can talk about this again at a later date. I'll have to give this problem some more thought. In the meantime, we still think you're doing a great job."

1. Is this case simply about supervision, or does it also relate to leadership?

2. What can Sherry Gabrielli do to exert more influence among the security officers?

3. How can her supervisor help her in her leadership development?

4. Which type of leadership development experiences would you recommend for Gabrielli?

LEADERSHIP EXERCISE

The Feedback Circle

Ten members of the class arrange their chairs in a circle. One person is selected as the feedback "target," and the other nine people take turns giving him or her supportive feedback. Assume it is "Ralph's" turn. Each person in the circle gives Ralph two pieces of feedback: (a) his best leadership attribute, and (b) how he needs to develop for the future. The feedback should take about thirty seconds per feedback giver. After receiving input from all the circle members, Ralph is free to comment. It is then the next person's turn to be the feedback target.

Class members not in the circle observe the dynamics of what is happening, and report their observations after the circle finishes. With diligence, the whole process will take about ninety minutes. If time permits, a new feedback circle can form. Alternatively, the class can break into several circles that operate simultaneously, or run just one circle with ten volunteers.

Endnotes

Chapter 1

1. "The Best Managers," *Business Week,* January 11, 1993, p. 114; G. Pascal Zachry, "'Theocracy of Hackers' Rules Autodesk Inc., a Strangely Run Firm," *The Wall Street Journal,* May 28, 1992, pp. A1, A14.
2. W. Chan Kim and Renee A. Mauborgne, "Parables of Leadership," *Harvard Business Review,* July–August 1992, p. 123.
3. Derived from a literature review in Bernard M. Bass, *Bass & Stogdill's Handbook of Leadership: Theory, Research, & Managerial Applications* (New York: The Free Press, 1990), pp. 11–18.
4. Peter Block, *Stewardship: Choosing Service over Self-Interest* (San Francisco: Berrett-Koehler Publishers, 1993), pp. 27–32.
5. Ibid., pp. 29–31.
6. John P. Kotter, *A Force for Change: How Leadership Differs from Management* (New York: The Free Press, 1990); Warren Bennis, *An Invented Life: Reflections on Leadership and Change* (Reading, Mass.: Addison-Wesley, 1993)..
7. Edwin A. Locke and Associates, *The Essence of Leadership: The Four Keys to Leading Successfully* (New York: Lexington/Macmillan, 1991), p. 4.
8. The information about the positive impact of leadership on organizational performance is based on Bass, *Bass & Stogdill's Handbook,* pp. 6–10.
9. Gary A. Yukl, *Leadership in Organizations,* 3rd ed. (Englewood Cliffs, N.J.: Prentice Hall, 1994), pp. 384–387.
10. Jon P. Howell, David E. Bowen, Peter W. Dorfman, Steven Kerr, and Philip M. Podsakoff, "Substitutes for Leadership: Effective Alternatives to Ineffective Leadership," *Organizational Dynamics,* Summer 1990, p. 23.
11. Ibid., pp. 26–27.
12. Bass, *Bass & Stogdill's Handbook,* p. 686.
13. Jeffrey Pfeffer, "The Ambiguity of Leadership," *Academy of Management Review,* April 1977, pp. 104–112.
14. Henry Mintzberg, *The Nature of Managerial Work* (New York: Harper & Row, 1973); J. Kenneth Graham, Jr., and William L. Mihal, *The CMD Managerial Job Analysis Inventory* (Rochester, N.Y.: Rochester Institute of Technology, Center for Management Development, 1987), pp. 2–6.
15. Edwin A. Locke and Associates, *The Essence of Leadership,* pp. 6–11; James G. Hunt, *Leadership: A New Synthesis* (Newbury Park, Calif.: Sage Publications, 1991); John A. Wagner III and John R. Hollenbeck, *Management of Organizational Behavior* (Englewood Cliffs, N.J.: Prentice Hall, 1992), pp. 441–442.
16. Howell et al., "Substitutes for Leadership," p. 21.
17. "Communicate Effectively . . . Manage Successfully" (brochure) (New York: American Management Association, February–May 1993), p. 11.

18. David Greising, "The Toughest #&?!%* in Sports," *Business Week,* June 15, 1992, p. 101.

19. Bass, *Bass & Stogdill's Handbook.*

Chapter 2

1. Edwin A. Locke and Associates, *The Essence of Leadership: The Four Keys to Leading Successfully* (New York: Lexington/Macmillan, 1991), pp. 13–34; Shelley A. Kirkpatrick and Edwin A. Locke, "Leadership: Do Traits Matter?" *The Executive,* May 1991, pp. 48–60.

2. Locke and Associates, *The Essence of Leadership,* pp. 26–27.

3. John Carey, "Is the NIH Doctor In? You'd Better Believe It," *Business Week,* May 18, 1992, pp. 109–110.

4. Julie Cohen Mason, "Leading the Way Into the 21st Century," *Management Review,* October 1992, p. 19.

5. James M. Kouzes and Barry Z. Posner, "The Credibility Factor: What Followers Expect from Their Leaders," *Management Review,* January 1990, p. 30.

6. Morgan W. McCall, Jr., and Michael M. Lombardo, *Off the Track: Why and How Successful Leaders Get Derailed,* Technical Report No. 21 (Greensboro, N.C.: Center for Creative Leadership, 1983), p. 11.

7. Bernard M. Bass, *Bass & Stogdill's Handbook of Leadership: Theory, Research, & Managerial Applications,* 3rd ed. (New York: The Free Press, 1990), p. 90.

8. Locke and Associates, *The Essence of Leadership,* p. 55.

9. "The Hot Seat: Leadership in the '90s Is a Different Ball Game," *Executive Strategies,* September 1992, p. 1.

10. Cited in Glen Collins, "Humor Is the Newest Tool to Lessen Stress, Motivate Workers," *The New York Times,* May 2, 1988.

11. Shari Caudron, "Humor Is Healthy in the Workplace," *Personnel Journal,* June 1992, p. 63.

12. Quoted in "Leadership Concepts," *Executive Strategies,* July 9, 1991, p. 1.

13. Chris Piotrowski and Terry R. Armstrong, "The CEO: An Analysis of the CNN Telecast 'Pinnacle'," *Psychological Reports 65,* 1989, pp. 435–438.

14. Kirkpatrick and Locke, "Leadership: Do Traits Matter?" pp. 51–52

15. Jeffrey Pfeffer, *Managing with Power: Politics and Influence in Organizations* (Boston: Harvard Business School Press, 1992), p. 172.

16. Morgan W. McCall, Jr., and Michael M. Lombardo, "What Makes a Top Executive?" *Psychology Today,* February 1983, p. 28.

17. Locke and Associates, *The Essence of Leadership,* pp. 30–31.

18. Avis L. Johnson, Fred Luthans, and Harry W. Hennessey, "The Role of Locus of Control in Leader Influence Behavior," *Personnel Psychology,* Spring 1984, p. 70.

19. Peter Koestenbaum, *Leadership: The Inner Side of Greatness* (San Francisco: Jossey-Bass, 1991).

20. Warren Bennis and Burt Nanus, "The Leadership Tightrope," *Success,* March 1985, p. 28.

21. David C. McClelland and Richard Boyatzis, "Leadership Motive Pattern and Long-Term Success in Management," *Journal of Applied Psychology,* December 1982, p. 737.

22. Locke and Associates, *The Essence of Leadership,* p. 22.

23. *Ibid,* p. 22.

24. John B. Miner, Norman R. Smith, and Jeffrey S. Bracker, "Role of Entrepreneurial Task Motivation in the Growth of Technologically Innovative Firms," *Journal of Applied Psychology,* August 1989, p. 554.
25. Piotrowski and Armstrong, "The CEO," pp. 436–437.
26. Cited in Cohen Mason, "Leading the Way into the 21st Century," p. 18.
27. Fred E. Fiedler and Joseph E. Garcia, *New Approaches to Effective Leadership: Cognitive Resources and Organizational Performance* (New York: John Wiley, 1987); Robert P. Vecchio, "Theoretical and Empirical Examination of Cognitive Resource Theory," *Journal of Applied Psychology,* April 1990, p. 141.
28. Vecchio, "Theoretical and Empirical Examination of Cognitive Resource Theory," pp. 141–147; Vecchio, "Cognitive Resource Theory: Issues for Specifying a Test of the Theory," *Journal of Applied Psychology,* June 1992, pp. 375–376.
29. "A Tall Order for the Prince of Beers," *Business Week,* March 23, 1992, p. 66.
30. Ray J. Friant, Jr. "Leadership Training for Long-Term Results," *Management Review,* July 1991, p. 50.
31. Pfeffer, *Managing with Power,* p. 168.
32. Sunita Wadekar, "Portrait of a CEO," *Business Week,* October 11, 1993, p. 64; Robert Mims and Ephraim Lewis, "Portrait of the Boss," *Business Week,* October 19, 1990, pp. 10–11.
33. Kirkpatrick and Locke, "Leadership: Do Traits Matter?" p. 59.
34. Gary A. Yukl, *Leadership in Organizations,* 2nd ed. (Englewood Cliffs, N.J.: Prentice Hall, 1989), p. 176; Bass, *Bass & Stogdill's Handbook,* p. 87.
35. Abridged from Robert E. Alberti and Michael L. Emmons, *Your Perfect Right: A Guide to Assertive Behavior* (San Luis Obispo, Calif.: Impact Publishers, 1970), Chapter 2.

Chapter 3

1. Nancy Gibbs, "Truth, Justice, and the Reno Way," *Time,* July 12, 1993, pp. 21–22.
2. Jay A. Conger, Rabindra N. Kanungo, and Associates, *Charismatic Leadership* (San Francisco: Jossey-Bass, 1988).
3. Jay A. Conger, *The Charismatic Leader: Behind the Mystique of Exceptional Leadership* (San Francisco: Jossey-Bass, 1989).
4. Eugene Schmuckler, book review in *Personnel Psychology,* Winter 1989, p. 881.
5. Robert J. House, "A 1976 Theory of Charismatic Leadership," in J. G. Hunt and L.L. Larson (eds.), *Leadership: The Cutting Edge* (Carbondale: Southern Illinois University Press, 1977), pp. 189–207.
6. Jane A. Halpert, "The Dimensionality of Charisma," *Journal of Business and Psychology,* Summer 1990, p. 401.
7. Conger, Kanungo, and Associates, *Charismatic Leadership*; Bernard M. Bass, *Bass & Stogdill's Handbook of Leadership: Theory, Research, & Managerial Applications,* 3rd ed. (New York: The Free Press, 1990), pp. 185–186.
8. Conger, *The Charismatic Leader*; Jane M. Howell and Bruce Avolio, "The Ethics of Charismatic Leadership: Submission or Liberation?" *The Executive* (May 1992), pp. 43–52.
9. Howell and Avolio, "The Ethics of Charismatic Leadership," p. 46.
10. Jay A. Conger, "Inspiring Others: The Language of Leadership," *The Executive,* February 1991, p. 39.
11. Ibid., p. 39.

12. "Management by Anecdote," *Success,* December 1992, p. 35.
13. John J. Hater and Bernard M. Bass, "Superiors' Evaluations and Subordinates' Perceptions of Transformational and Transactional Leadership," *Journal of Applied Psychology,* November 1988, p. 695; Noel M. Tichy and Mary Anne Devanna, *The Transformational Leader* (New York: John Wiley & Sons, 1990).
14. Peter Koestenbaum, *Leadership: The Inner Side of Greatness* (San Francisco: Jossey-Bass, 1991).
15. Hater and Bass, "Superiors' Evaluations and Subordinates' Perceptions," p. 701.
16. Ibid.
17. J. W. McLean and William Wetzel, *Leadership: Magic, Myth, or Method* (New York: AMACOM).
18. Warren G. Bennis and Burt Nanus, *Leaders: Strategies for Taking Charge* (New York: Harper & Row, 1985), p. 223.
19. Robert C. Tucker, "The Theory of Charismatic Leadership," *Daedalus,* Summer 1968, pp. 731–756.
20. Howell and Avolio, "The Ethics of Charismatic Leadership," pp. 52–53.
21. Roger Dawson, *Secrets of Power Persuasion* (Englewood Cliffs, N.J.: Prentice-Hall, 1992).

Chapter 4

1. Ralph M. Stogdill and Alvin E. Coons (eds.), *Leader Behavior: Its Description and Measurement* (Columbus, Ohio: The Ohio State University Bureau of Business Research, 1957); Carroll L. Shartle, *Executive Performance and Leadership* (Englewood Cliffs, N.J.: Prentice Hall, 1956).
2. Andrew W. Halpin, "The Observed Leader Behavior and Ideal Leader Behavior of Aircraft Commanders and School Superintendents," in Stogdill and Coons, *Leader Behavior,* p. 64.
3. Rensis Likert, *New Patterns of Management* (New York: McGraw Hill, 1961); Arnold S. Tannenbaum, *Social Psychology of the Work Organization* (Monterey, Calif.: Wadsworth, 1966).
4. John P. Kotter, "What Leaders Really Do," *Harvard Business Review,* May–June 1990, pp. 104–105.
5. Tim Smart, "GE's Money Machine: How Its Emphasis on Performance Built a Colossus of Finance," *Business Week,* March 8, 1993, p. 64.
6. Thomas J. Peters and Robert H. Waterman, Jr., *In Search of Excellence: Lessons from America's Best-Run Companies* (New York: Harper & Row, 1982).
7. Cited in Jay A. Conger, *Learning to Lead: The Art of Transforming Managers into Leaders* (San Francisco: Jossey-Bass, 1992), pp. 130, 131.
8. "General Magic Invente le Téléphone de l'an 2000," *Enterprises (Le Figaro),* February 22, 1993, p. 7.
9. "Masters of the Game: CEOs Who Succeed in Business When Times Are Really Trying," *Business Week,* October 12, 1992, pp. 113–114.
10. Kotter, "What Leaders Really Do," pp. 105–106.
11. Conger, *Learning to Lead,* p. 131.
12. David S. Brown, "Manager's New Job Is Concert Building," *HRMagazine,* September 1990, p. 42.
13. Conger, *Learning to Lead,* p. 149.
14. Kotter, "What Leaders Really Do," p. 107.
15. Conger, *Learning to Lead,* p. 137.

16. Charles C. Manz and Henry P. Sims, Jr., "SuperLeadership: Beyond the Myth of Heroic Leadership," *Organizational Dynamics,* Spring 1991, p. 18.
17. Ibid.
18. Charles C. Manz, "Helping Yourself and Others to Master Self-Leadership," *Supervisory Management* (November 1991), p. 9.
19. Donald M. Moretti, Carol L. Morken, and Jeanne M. Borkowski, "Profile of the American CEO: Comparing *Inc.* and *Fortune* Executives," *Journal of Business and Psychology,* Winter 1991, pp. 193–205.

Chapter 5

1. Kurt Lewin and Ronald Lippitt, "An Experimental Approach to the Study of Autocracy and Democracy: A Preliminary Note," *Sociometry,* No. 1, 1938, pp. 292–300.
2. Robert Tannenbaum and Warren H. Schmidt, "How to Choose a Leadership Pattern," *Harvard Business Review,* May–June 1973, pp. 162–164, 166–168.
3. "The Airline Mess," *Business Week,* July 6, 1992, p. 52.
4. Donna Brown, "Why Participative Management Won't Work Here," *Management Review,* June 1992, p. 42.
5. Ibid., p. 43.
6. Ibid., p. 44.
7. Robert R. Blake and Anne Adams McCarse, *Leadership Dilemmas and Solutions* (Houston: Gulf Publishing, 1991).
8. Robert R. Blake and Jane S. Mouton, *The New Managerial Grid* (Houston: Gulf Publishing, 1978).
9. Bruce M. Fisher and Jack E. Edwards, "Consideration and Initiating Structure and Their Relationships with Leader Effectiveness: A Meta-Analysis," *Academy of Management Best Papers Proceedings 1988,* p. 204.
10. Meredith Belbin, "Solo Leader/Team Leader: Antithesis in Style and Structure," in Michel Syrett and Clare Hogg (eds.), *Frontiers of Leadership* (Oxford, England: Blackwell Publishers, 1992), p. 271.
11. Based in part on Michael Warshaw, "The Mind of the Entrepreneur," *Success,* April 1993, pp. 28–33; Franck A. deChambeau and Fredericka Mackenzie, "Intrapreneurship," *Personnel Journal,* July 1986, p. 40.
12. Cited in Warshaw, "The Mind of the Entrepreneur," p. 30.
13. Gary N. Powell, "The Effects of Sex and Gender on Recruitment," *Academy of Management Review,* October 1987, pp. 731–743.
14. Judy Rosener, "Ways Women Lead," *Harvard Business Review,* November–December 1990, pp. 119–125.
15. Quoted in Roz Morris, "Management: Why Women Are Leading the Way," in Syrett & Hogg, *Frontiers of Leadership,* p. 309.
16. Cited in "Debate: Ways Men and Women Lead," *Harvard Business Review,* January–February 1991, p. 151.
17. Jan Grant, "Women as Managers: What They Can Offer Organizations," *Organizational Dynamics,* Winter 1988.
18. Bernard M. Bass, *Bass & Stogdill's Handbook of Leadership,* 3rd ed. (New York: The Free Press, 1990), p. 725.
19. Paul Hersey and Kenneth H. Blanchard, *Management of Organizational Behavior: Utilizing Human Resources,* 5th ed. (Englewood Cliffs, NJ: Prentice Hall, 1988), p. 102.

20. Ralph M. Stogdill, "Historical Trends in Leadership Theory and Research," *Journal of Contemporary Business,* Autumn 1974, p. 7. Quoted in Hersey and Blanchard, *Management of Organizational Behavior,* p. 102.
21. Thomas R. Horton, *The CEO Paradox: The Privilege and Accountability of Leadership* (New York: AMACOM, 1992), p. 115.
22. "Directive Management or Not," *Working Smart,* December 1992, p. 3.
23. "Debate: Ways Men and Women Lead," p. 150.

Chapter 6

1. Robert C. Anderson, "Man in Charge," *Success,* December 1982, p. 16.
2. Fred E. Fielder, Martin H. Chemers, and Linda Mahar, *Improving Leadership Effectiveness: The Leader Match Concept,* 2nd ed. (New York: Wiley, 1984); E. Leroy Plumlee, "A Visit with Fred Fiedler," *Management Newsletter* (published by Houghton Mifflin), December 1989, pp. 2–7.
3. Plumlee, "A Visit with Fred Fiedler," p. 4.
4. Robert T. Keller, "A Test of the Path-Goal Theory of Leadership with Need for Clarity as a Moderator in Research and Development Organizations," *Journal of Applied Psychology,* April 1989, pp. 208–212; Robert J. House and Terence R. Mitchell, "Path-Goal Theory of Leadership," *Journal of Contemporary Business,* Autumn 1974, pp. 81–97.
5. House and Mitchell, "Path-Goal Theory," p. 84; Bernard M. Bass, *Bass & Stogdill's Handbook of Leadership,* 3rd ed. (New York: The Free Press, 1990), p. 633.
6. Robert Kreitner, *Management,* 5th ed. (Boston: Houghton Mifflin, 1992), p. 466.
7. Paul Hersey and Kenneth H. Blanchard, *Management of Organizational Behavior: Utilizing Human Resources,* 5th ed. (Englewood Cliffs, N.J.: Prentice-Hall, 1988), pp. 170–177; Oliver Niehouse, "The Strategic Nature of Leadership," *Management Solutions,* July 1987, pp. 27–34.
8. Bass, *Bass & Stogdill's Handbook,* p. 493.
9. Robert P. Vecchio, "Situational Leadership Theory: An Examination of a Prescriptive Theory," *Journal of Applied Psychology,* August 1987, pp. 444–451.
10. Victor H. Vroom, "A New Look at Managerial Decision Making," *Organizational Dynamics,* Spring 1973, pp. 66–80; Victor H. Vroom and Arthur G. Jago, *The New Leadership: Managing Participation in Organizations* (Englewood Cliffs, N.J.: Prentice Hall, 1988).
11. Madeline E. Heilman, Harvey A. Hornstein, Jack H. Cage, and Judith K. Herschlag, "Reactions to Prescribed Leader Behavior as a Function of Role Perspective: The Case of the Vroom–Yetton Model," *Journal of Applied Psychology,* February 1984, pp. 50–60; George Field, "A Test of the Vroom–Yetton Normative Model of Leadership," *Journal of Applied Psychology,* February 1982, pp. 523–532; Richard H. G. Field and Robert J. House, "A Test of the Vroom–Yetton Model Using Manager and Subordinate Reports," *Journal of Applied Psychology,* June 1990, pp. 362–366.
12. George R. H. Field, "A Critique of the Vroom–Yetton Contingency Model of Leadership Behavior," *The Academy of Management Review,* October 1979, pp. 249–257.

Chapter 7

1. Kathleen M. Eisenhardt and L. J. Bourgeois III, "Politics of Strategic Decision Making in High-Velocity Environments: Toward a Midrange Theory," *Academy of Management Journal,* December 1988, p. 737.
2. John R. P. French and Bertram Raven, "The Basis of Social Power," in Darwin Cartwright (ed.), *Studies in Social Power* (Ann Arbor, Mich: Institute for Social Research, 1959); Timothy R. Hinkin and Chester A. Schriescheim, "Power and Influence: The View from Below," *Personnel,* May 1988, pp. 47–50.
3. Gary Yukl and Cecilia M. Falbe, "Importance of Different Power Sources in Downward and Lateral Relations," *Journal of Applied Psychology,* June 1991, p. 416.
4. Sydney Finkelstein, "Power in Top Management Teams: Dimensions, Measurement, and Validation," *Academy of Management Journal,* August 1992, p. 510.
5. Abraham L. Gitlow, *Being the Boss: The Importance of Leadership and Power* (Homewood, Ill: Business One–Irwin, 1991).
6. Finkelstein, "Power in Top Management Teams," p. 508.
7. Jeffrey Pfeffer, *Managing with Power* (Boston: Harvard Business School Press, 1990), pp. 100–101.
8. "Welcome to the Nineties, Donald," *Business Week,* May 14, 1990, p. 119.
9. Morgan McCall, Jr., *Power, Influence, and Authority: The Hazards of Carrying a Sword* (Greensboro, N.C.: Center for Creative Leadership, 1978), p. 5.
10. William Rothschild, *Risktaker, Caretaker, Surgeon, Undertaker: The Four Faces of Strategic Leadership* (New York: John Wiley, 1993).
11. C. R. Hinings, D. J. Hickson, C. A. Lee, R. E. Schneck, and J. M. Pennings, "Strategic Contingencies Theory of Intraorganizational Power," *Administrative Science Quarterly,* 1971, 16, pp. 216–229.
12. The discussion in this section is based on David A. Whetton and Kim S. Cameron, *Developing Management Skills,* 2nd ed. (New York: HarperCollins, 1991), pp. 307–308.
13. Jay A. Conger, "Leadership: The Art of Empowering Others," *The Academy of Management Executive,* February 1989, pp. 17–25; Frank Shipper and Charles C. Manz, "Employee Self-Management Without Formally Designated Teams: An Alternative Road to Empowerment," *Organizational Dynamics,* Winter 1992, p. 59; "Empowered Employees: Rhetoric or Reality?" *Personnel,* September 1991, p. 19.
14. Abraham Zaleznik, "Power and Politics in Organizational Life," *Harvard Business Review,* May–June 1970, p. 47.
15. Eisenhardt and Bourgeois, "Politics of Strategic Decision Making," pp. 737–770.
16. Gregory Moorhead and Ricky W. Griffin, *Organizational Behavior: Managing People and Organizations,* 3rd ed. (Boston: Houghton Mifflin, 1992), p. 302.
17. Gerald Biberman, "Personality Characteristics and Work Attitudes of Persons with High, Moderate, and Low Political Tendencies," *Psychological Reports,* Vol. 57, 1985, p. 1309.
18. Marshall Schminke, "A Dispositional Approach to Understanding Individual Power in Organizations," *Journal of Business and Psychology,* Fall 1992, pp. 63–79.
19. Jeffrey Pfeffer, "Power and Resource Allocation in Organizations," in Barry M. Staw and Gerald R. Salancik (eds.), *New Dimensions in Organizational Behavior,* (Chicago: St. Clair Press, 1977), p. 239.
20. Gerald R. Ferris and Thomas R. King, "Politics in Human Resources Decisions: A Walk on the Dark Side," *Organizational Dynamics,* Autumn 1991, p. 60.

21. Eugene Schmuckler, book review in *Personnel Psychology,* Summer 1982, p. 497.

22. William H. Newman, *Administrative Action: The Techniques of Organization and Management* (Englewood Cliffs, N.J.: Prentice-Hall, 1963), p. 90.

23. Andrew J. DuBrin, *Stand Out! 330 Ways to Gain the Edge with Bosses, Subordinates, Co-Workers, and Customers* (Englewood Cliffs, N.J.: Prentice-Hall, 1993).

24. "The Corporate Elite: Chief Executives of the Business Week 1000," *Business Week,* October 19, 1990, p. 11.

25. "Career 'Insurance' Protects DP Professionals from Setbacks, Encourages Growth," *Data Management,* June 1986, p. 33.

26. "How to Win at Organizational Politics—Without Being Unethical or Sacrificing Your Self-Respect," report published by *Research Institute Personal Report,* 1985, p. 4.

27. Moorhead and Griffin, *Management,* p. 306.

28. Robert P. Vecchio, *Organizational Behavior,* 2nd ed. (Hinsdale, Ill.: Dryden, 1991), p. 282.

29. Gary A. Yukl, *Leadership in Organizations,* 2nd ed. (Englewood Cliffs, N.J.: Prentice-Hall, 1989), p. 44.

Chapter 8

1. Allan R. Cohen, Stephen L. Fink, Hermon Gadon, and Robin D. Willits, *Effective Behavior in Organizations: Cases, Concepts, and Student Experiences,* 5th ed. (Homewood, Ill: Irwin, 1992), p. 139.

2. Gary Yukl, *Skills for Managers and Leaders: Text, Cases, and Exercises* (Englewood Cliffs, N.J.: Prentice-Hall, 1990), pp. 58–62.

3. James L. Bowditch and Anthony F. Buono, *A Primer on Organizational Behavior,* 2nd ed. (New York: Wiley, 1990), p. 4.

4. R. Bruce McAfee and Betty J. Ricks, "Leadership by Example: 'Do as I Do!'" *Management Solutions,* August 1986, p. 10.

5. Gary Yukl and J. Bruce Tracey, "Consequences of Influence Tactics Used with Subordinates, Peers, and the Boss," *Journal of Applied Psychology,* August 1992, p. 526.

6. Bernard Keys and Thomas Case, "How to Become an Influential Manager," *Academy of Management Executive,* November 1990, p. 44.

7. "Build Power and Influence," *Executive Strategies,* June 19, 1990, p. 6.

8. Adapted from ibid., pp. 45–46.

9. Yukl, *Skills for Managers and Leaders,* pp. 62–63.

10. Jeffery Pfeffer, *Managing With Power: Power and Influence in Organizations* (Boston: Harvard Business School Press, 1992), p. 224.

11. Yukl, *Skills for Managers and Leaders,* p. 65.

12. Andrew J. DuBrin, "Sex Differences in Endorsement of Influence Tactics and Political Behavior Tendencies," *Journal of Business and Psychology,* Fall 1989, p. 10.

13. Bernard M. Bass, *Bass & Stogdill's Handbook of Leadership: Theory, Research, & Managerial Applications,* 3rd ed. (New York: The Free Press, 1990), p. 134.

14. David M. Buss, Mary Gomes, Dolly S. Higgins, and Karen Lauterbach, "Tactics of Manipulation," *Journal of Personality and Social Psychology,* December 1987, p. 1222.

15. Chad T. Lewis, Joseph E. Garcia, and Sarah M. Jobs, *Managerial Skills in Organizations* (Boston: Allyn & Bacon, 1990), p. 234.

16. Buss et al., "Tactics of Manipulation," p. 1222.
17. Gary Yukl and Cecilia M. Falbe, "Influence Tactics and Objectives in Upward, Downward, and Lateral Influence Attempts," *Journal of Applied Psychology,* April 1990, p. 133.
18. Buss et al., "Tactics of Manipulation," p. 1222.
19. David Kipnis and Stuart M. Schmidt, "Intraorganizatonal Influence Tactics: Explorations in Getting One's Way," *Journal of Applied Psychology,* August 1980, p. 445.
20. Yukl and Tracey, "Consequences of Influence Tactics," pp. 525–535.
21. Keys and Case, "How to Become an Influential Manager," p. 46.
22. David Kipnis and Stuart M. Schmidt, "Upward Influence Styles: Relationships with Performance Evaluations, Salary, and Stress," *Administrative Science Quarterly,* 1988, pp. 528–542.
23. Keys and Case, "How to Become an Influential Manager," p. 48.

Chapter 9

1. Edwin A. Locke and Associates, *The Essence of Leadership: Four Keys to Leading Successfully* (New York: Lexington Books/Macmillan, 1991), p. 94.
2. Jon R. Katzenbach and Douglas K. Smith, "The Discipline of Teams," *Harvard Business Review,* March–April 1993, p. 112; Chad T. Lewis, Joseph E. Garcia, and Sarah M. Jobs, *Managerial Skills in Organizations* (Boston: Allyn & Bacon, 1990), p. 301.
3. Robert J. Waterman, Jr., "The Power of Teamwork," in Michel Syrett and Clare Hogg (eds.), *Frontiers of Leadership,* (Oxford, England: Blackwell, 1992), p. 489.
4. Peter F. Drucker, "The Coming of the New Organization," *Harvard Business Review,* January–February 1988, pp. 45-53; Deborah Gladstein Ancona, "Outward Bound: Strategies for Team Survival in an Organization," *Academy of Management Journal,* June 1990, pp. 334–335.
5. Irving L. Janus, *Victims of Groupthink: A Psychological Study of Foreign Policy Decisions and Fiascos* (Boston: Houghton Mifflin, 1972); Glen Whyte, "Groupthink Reconsidered," *Academy of Management Review* (January 1989), pp. 40–56.
6. William A. Cohen, *The Art of the Leader* (Englewood Cliffs, N.J.: Prentice-Hall, 1990).
7. Paul S. George, "Teamwork Without Tears," *Personnel Journal,* November 1987, p. 129.
8. Clive Goodworth, "Some Thoughts on Creating a Team," p. 472.
9. Waterman, "The Power of Teamwork," pp. 478–498.
10. Katzenbach and Smith, "The Discipline of Teams," p. 118.
11. Jack D. Osburn, Linda Moran, Ed Musselwhite, and John H. Zenger, *Work Teams* (Homewood, Ill: Business One–Irwin, 1991).
12. "Building Teamwork Takes Some Effort," Rochester *Democrat and Chronicle,* September 23, 1993, p. 8B.
13. Katzenbach and Smith, "The Discipline of Teams," p. 119.
14. Lee G. Bolman and Terrence E. Deal, "What Makes a Team Work?" *Organizational Dynamics,* Autumn 1992, pp. 40–41.
15. Ibid., pp. 41–42.
16. Edward Glassman, "Self-Directed Team Building Without a Consultant," *Supervisory Management,* March 1992, p. 6.

17. Ibid.

18. Frank Shipper and Charles C. Manz, "Employee Self-Management Without Formally Designated Teams," *Organizational Dynamics,* Winter 1992, p. 59.

19. Charles C. Manz and Henry P. Sims, Jr., "Leading Workers to Lead Themselves: The External Leadership of Self-Managing Work Teams," *Administrative Science Quarterly,* March 1987, p. 118.

20. Jennifer J. Laabs, "Team Training Goes Outdoors," *Personnel Journal,* June 1991, p. 59.

21. Jay A. Conger, *Learning to Lead: The Art of Transforming Managers into Leaders* (San Francisco: Jossey-Bass, 1992), p. 159.

22. George Graen and J. F. Cashman, "A Role Making Model of Leadership in Formal Organizations: A Developmental Approach," in J. G. Hunt and L. L. Larson (eds.), *Leadership Frontiers* (Kent, Ohio: Kent State University Press, 1975), pp. 143–165

23. Robert P. Vecchio, "Are You IN or OUT with Your Boss?" *Business Horizons,* 1987, pp. 76–78.

24. Robert C. Liden, Sandy J. Wayne, and Dean Stilwell, "A Longitudinal Study on the Early Development of Leader-Member Exchanges," *Journal of Applied Psychology,* August 1993, pp. 662–674.

25. Waterman, "The Power of Teamwork," pp. 487–488.

26. Conger, *Learning to Lead,* p. 114.

Solution to the Chapter 9 Leadership Exercise

The way to reduce the time to a few seconds per person is for one person simply to run down the group, touching each person's hand. The purpose of this exercise is to demonstrate group brainstorming, a willingness to challenge assumptions, and shared leadership. Above all, observe the amount of teamwork and camaraderie that took place.

Chapter 10

1. Roger D. Evered and James C. Selman, "Coaching and the Art of Management," *Organizational Dynamics*, Autumn 1989, p. 16.

2. A representative example is presented by Fred Luthans, Robert Paul, and Lew Taylor in "The Impact of Contingent Reinforcement on Retail Salespersons' Performance Behaviors: A Replicated Field Experiment," *Journal of Organizational Behavior Management,* Spring/Summer 1985, pp. 25–35.

3. An authoritative source on the use of behavior modification in organizations is Fred Luthans and Robert Kreitner, *Organizational Behavior Modification and Beyond: An Operant and Social Learning Approach* (Glenview, Ill.: Scott, Foresman, 1984).

4. An original version of expectancy theory applied to work motivation is Victor H. Vroom, *Work and Motivation* (New York: Wiley, 1964). Also see Anthony J. Mento, Edwin A. Locke, and Howard J. Klein, "Relationship of Goal Level to Valence and Instrumentality," *Journal of Applied Psychology*, August 1992, pp. 395–405.

5. David A. Nadler and Edward E. Lawler III, "Motivation: A Diagnostic Approach," in J. Richard Hackman, Edward E. Lawler III, and Lyman W. Porter

(eds.), *Perspectives on Behavior in Organizations*, 2nd ed. (New York: McGraw-Hill, 1983), pp. 67–78; Robert E. Quinn, Sue R. Faerman, Michael P. Thompson, and Michael R. McGrath, *Becoming a Master Manager: A Competency Framework* (New York: Wiley, 1990), pp. 65–66.

6. Evered and Selman, "Coaching and the Art of Management," p. 15.

7. Ibid. , pp. 27–28.

8. Sharon Aurelio and John K. Kennedy, Jr., "Performance Coaching: A Key to Effectiveness," *Supervisory Management*, August 1991, pp. 1–2.

9. Richard J. Walsh, "Ten Basic Counseling Skills," *Supervisory Management*, July 1977, p. 9.

10. Gerald M. Sturman, "The Supervisor as Career 'Coach,'" *Supervisory Management*, November 1990, p. 6.

Chapter 11

1. Christopher Knowlton, "Imagineer Eisner on Leadership," *Fortune*, December 4, 1989.

2. Bernard M. Bass, *Bass & Stogdill's Handbook of Leadership: Theory, Research, & Managerial Applications*, 3rd ed. (New York: The Free Press, 1990), p. 216.

3. Richard W. Woodman, John E. Sawyer, and Ricky W. Griffin, "Toward a Theory of Organizational Creativity," *Academy of Management Review*, April 1993, p. 293.

4. G. Wallas, *The Art of Thought* (New York: Harcourt Brace, 1926).

5. Anna Esaki-Smith and Michael Warshaw, "Renegades 1993: Creating the Future," *Success*, January/February 1993, p. 36.

6. Teresa M. Amabile, "The Social Psychology of Creativity: A Componential Conceptualization," *Journal of Personality and Social Psychology*, August 1983, pp. 357–376.

7. Robert Kreitner and Angelo Kinicki, *Organizational Behavior*, 2nd ed. (Homewood, Ill: Irwin, 1992), p. 579.

8. Robert T. Godfrey, "Tapping Employees' Creativity," *Supervisory Management*, February 1986, pp. 17–18; John A. Gover, Royce R. Ronning, and Cecil R. Reynolds (eds.), *Handbook of Creativity* (New York: Plenum Press, 1989), p. 10; Pamela Smith, "Mix Skepticism, Humor, a Rocky Childhood—and Presto! Creativity," *Business Week*, September 30, 1985, p. 81.

9. Teresa M. Amabile, "A Model of Creativity and Innovation in Organizations." In Barry M. Staw and Lawrence L. Cummings (eds.), *Research in Organizational Behavior*, Vol. 10 (Greenwich, Conn.: JAI Press, 1988), pp. 123–167.

10. Woodman, Sawyer, and Griffin, "Toward a Theory of Organizational Creativity," p. 298.

11. Alan J. Rowe and James D. Boulgarides, *Managerial Decision Making: A Guide to Successful Business Decisions* (New York: Macmillan, 1992), p. 172.

12. Edward De Bono, *Lateral Thinking: Creativity Step-by-Step* (New York: Harper & Row, 1970).

13. Anne Skagen, "Creativity Tools: Versatile Problem Solvers That Can Double as Fun and Games," *Supervisory Management*, October 1991, pp. 1–2.

14. Edward Glassman, "Creative Problem Solving: New Techniques," *Supervisory Management*, March 1989, p. 16.

15. Woodman, Sawyer, and Griffin, "Toward a Theory of Organizational Creativity," p. 305.

16. M. Basadur, George B. Graen, and S. G. Green, "Training in Creative Problem-Solving: Effects on Ideation and Problem Finding and Solving in an Industrial Research Organization," *Organizational Behavior and Human Performance,* Vol. 30, 1988, pp. 41–70.

17. Quoted in "Breakthrough Ideas," *Success,* October 1987, p. 50.

18. "Breakthrough Ideas," *Success,* October 1990, p. 38.

19. "Be a Creative Problem Solver," *Executive Strategies,* June 6, 1989, pp. 1–2.

20. Teresa M. Amabile and S. S. Gryskiewicz, *Creativity in the R & D Laboratory* (Greensboro, N.C.: Center for Creative Leadership, 1987).

21. Donald W. Blohwiak, *Mavericks! How to Lead Your Staff to Think Like Einstein, Create Like da Vinci and Invent Like Edison* (Homewood, Ill: Business One–Irwin, 1992).

22. Robert E. Quinn, Sue R. Faerman, Michael P. Thompson, and Michael R. McGrath, *Becoming a Master Manager: A Competency Framework* (New York: Wiley, 1990), p. 255.

23. Amabile, "The Social Psychology of Creativity."

24. Gareth Morgan, *Creative Organization Theory: A Resourcebook* (Newbury Park, Calif.: Sage, 1990).

Solution to Leadership Skill-Building Exercise 11–1, Thinking Outside the Box

Affix the small box to the wall with the thumbtacks. Then place the candle on top of the box. Strengthen the attachment by dripping some wax from the candle, lighting it with the matches. You can strengthen the bond by inserting a thumbtack from underneath, going through the underside of the top of the box.

Solutions to Leadership Skill-Building Exercise 11–3, Word Hints to Creativity

1. party	5. club	9. high	13. make
2. ball	6. dog	10. sugar	14. bean
3. cheese	7. paper	11. floor	15. light
4. cat	8. finger	12. green	

Chapter 12

1. Frank Sonnenberg, "Internal Communication: Turning Talk into Action," *Supervisory Management,* September 1992, p. 9.

2. Bernard M. Bass, *Bass & Stogdill's Handbook of Leadership: Theory, Research, & Managerial Applications,* 3rd ed. (New York: The Free Press, 1990), p. 111; Rosabeth Moss Kanter, *The Change Masters* (New York: Simon & Schuster, 1983).

3. Richard J. Klimoski and Noreen J. Hayes, "Leader Behavior and Subordinate Motivation," *Personnel Psychology,* Autumn 1980, pp. 543–555.

4. M. Remland, "Leadership Impressions and Nonverbal Communication in a Superior-Subordinate Interaction," *Journal of Business Communication,* Vol. 18, No. 3, pp. 17–29.

5. Fred Luthans, Richard M. Hodgetts, and Stuart A. Rosenkrantz, *Real Managers* (Cambridge, Mass.: Ballinger, 1988), p. 68.

6. James M. Kouzes and Barry Z. Posner, *The Leadership Challenge: How to Get Extraordinary Things Done in Organizations* (San Francisco: Jossey-Bass, 1987), p. 118.

7. Jimmy Calano and Jeff Salzman, "Persuasiveness: Make it Your 'Power Booster,'" *Working Woman*, October 1988, p. 124.

8. Personal communication from anonymous reviewer, September 1993.

9. Several of these examples are from "Avoid These Top Ten Language Errors," *Working Smart*, October 1991, p. 8.

10. William Strunk Jr., and E. B. White, *The Elements of Style*, 3rd ed. (New York: Macmillan, 1979).

11. Stephen P. Robbins, *Training in Interpersonal Skills: TIPS for Managing People at Work* (Englewood Cliffs, N.J.: Prentice-Hall, 1989), p. 155.

12. Sherry Sweetham, "How to Organize Your Thoughts for Better Communication," *Personnel*, March 1986, p. 39.

13. Michael W. Mercer, "How to Make a Fantastic Impression," *HRMagazine*, March 1993, p. 49

14. Albert Mehrabian and M. Wiener, "Decoding of Inconsistent Communications," *Journal of Personality and Social Psychology*, 6, 1947, pp. 109–114.

15. Several of the ideas here are from "Body Language," *Executive Strategies*, April 17, 1990, p. 4; *Body Language for Business Success* (New York: National Institute for Business Management, 1989), pp. 28–29.

16. The literature is reviewed in David A. Whetton and Kim S. Cameron, *Developing Management Skills*, 2nd ed. (New York: HarperCollins, 1991), p. 234; and Chad T. Lewis, Joseph E. Garcia, and Sarah M. Jones, *Managerial Skills in Organizations* (Boston: Allyn & Bacon, 1990), p. 24

17. Whetton and Cameron, *Developing Management Skills*, p. 248.

18. "Good Night: Managing a Multicultural Work Force Is Tricky," *Executive Strategies*, August 1992, p. 10.

19. Sandra Thierderman, "Overcoming Cultural and Language Barriers, *Personnel Journal*, December 1988, p. 38–40; Rose Knotts and Sandra J. Hartman, "Communication Skills in Cross-Cultural Situations," *Supervisory Management*, March 1991, p. 12; Sylvie Overnoy, "Cet Été, Je Pars Toute Seule," *Cosmopolitan* (International edition), July 1992, pp. 91–92.

20. "Letitia Baldridge: Arbiter of Business Manners and Mores," *Management Review*, April 1992, p. 50.

21. David P. Tulin, "Enhance Your Multi-cultural Communication Skills," *Managing Diversity*, Volume 1, 1992, p. 5.

22. Roger E. Axtell, *Gestures: The Do's and Taboos of Body Language Around the World* (New York: Wiley, 1991).

23. Jim Kennedy and Anna Everest, "Put Diversity in Context," *Personnel Journal*, September 1991, pp. 50–52.

24. Kenneth Thomas, "Conflict and Conflict Management," in Marvin D. Dunnette (ed.), *Handbook of Industrial and Organizational Psychology* (Chicago: Rand McNally, 1976), pp. 900–902.

25. "Negotiating without Giving In," *Executive Strategies*, September 19, 1989, p. 6.

26. Frank L. Acuff, *The World Class Negotiator: An Indispensable Guide for Anyone Doing Business with Those from a Foreign Culture* (New York: AMACOM, 1992).

27. Adapted from Gay Lumsden and Donald Lumsden, *Communicating in Groups and Teams: Sharing Leadership* (Belmont, Calif.: Wadsworth, 1993), p. 233.

Solution to Leadership Skill-Building Exercise 12–1

quality-driven
customer-driven
viewpoint simply doesn't fly anymore
empowering hourly workers
best steel products possible
take a back seat to
we're becoming a purpose- and vision-driven company.

Chapter 13

1. Cresencio Torres and Mary Bruxelles, "Capitalizing on Global Diversity," *HRMagazine*, December 1992, p. 32.
2. Taylor H. Cox and Stacy Blake, "Managing Cultural Diversity: Implications for Organizational Competitiveness," *Academy of Management Executive*, August 1991, pp. 45–56.
3. Juliane Bailey, "How to Be Different but Equal," *Savvy Woman*, November 1989, p. 47 (cited in Cox and Blake, "Managing Cultural Diversity," p. 48.)
4. Rosabeth Moss Kanter, *The Change Masters* (New York: Simon and Schuster, 1983).
5. Geert Hofstede, *Culture's Consequences: International Differences in Work Related Values* (Beverly Hills, Calif.: Sage, 1980); updated and expanded in "A Conversation with Geert Hofstede" (interview by Richard Hodgetts), *Organizational Dynamics*, Spring 1993, pp. 53–61.
6. Arvind V. Phatak, *International Dimensions of Management* (Boston: Kent, 1983), pp. 22–26.
7. Our analysis of expectancy theory across cultures is based on Nancy J. Adler, *International Dimensions of Organizational Behavior*, 2nd ed. (Boston: PWS–Kent, 1991), pp. 157–160.
8. David Sirota and M. J. Greenwood, "Understanding Your Overseas Workforce," *Harvard Business Review*, January–February 1971, pp. 53–60.
9. Adler, *International Dimensions of Organizational Behavior*, p. 159.
10. Robert Kreitner, *Management*, 5th ed. (Boston: Houghton Mifflin, 1992), pp. 647–648.
11. Phatak, *International Dimensions of Management*, p. 167.
12. Cited in Heidi J. LaFleche, "When in Rome," *TWA Ambassador*, October 1990, p. 69.
13. Benson Rosen and Kay Lovelace, "Piecing Together the Diversity Puzzle," *HRMagazine*, June 1991, pp. 78–84.
14. Taylor Cox, Jr., "The Multicultural Organization," *Academy of Management Executive*, May 1991, p. 34.
15. Joann S. Lublin, "Foreign Accents Proliferate in Top Ranks as U.S. Companies Find Talent Abroad," *The Wall Street Journal*, May 21, 1993, p. B1.
16. Ann M. Morrison, *The New Leaders: Guidelines on Leadership Diversity in America* (San Francisco: Jossey-Bass, 1992).
17. Ibid.; John W. Hodges, "Practical Strategies for Leading Diversity," *HRMagazine*, May 1993, pp. 17–19.

18. Shari Caudron, "Training Can Damage Diversity Efforts," *Personnel Journal*, April 1993, p. 51.
19. Wilcox and Thomas are cited in Caudron, ibid.

Chapter 14

1. Kathleen Driscoll, "Local Firm in Venture in Russia," *Rochester (New York) Democrat and Chronicle*, August 24, 1993, p. 8B.
2. "What Exactly Is Total Quality Management?" *Personnel Journal*, February 1993, p. 30.
3. Thomas H. Berry, *Managing the Total Quality Transformation* (New York: McGraw-Hill, 1991).
4. David L. Calfee, "Get Your Mission Statement Working!" *Management Review*, January 1993, p. 55. The mission statements in the following paragraphs are also from the same source.
5. Cited in David E. Bowen and Edward E. Lawler III, "Total Quality-Oriented Human Resources Management," *Organizational Dynamics*, Spring 1992, p. 34.
6. Del Jones, "1992 Quality Cup Finalists," *USA Today*, April 10, 1992, p. 2B.
7. Patricia Zingheim and Jay R. Schuster, "Linking Quality and Pay," *HRMagazine*, December 1992, pp. 55–59.
8. Timothy L. Ross and Larry Hatcher, "Gainsharing Drives Quality Improvement," *Personnel Journal*, November 1992, pp. 81–89.
9. Oren Harari, "Three Very Difficult Steps to Total Quality," *Management Review*, April 1993, pp. 39–40.
10. Oren Harari, "The Lab Test: A Tale of Quality," *Management Review*, February 1993, p. 55.
11. Oren Harari, "Three Very Difficult Steps to Total Quality," pp. 42–43.
12. Caudron, "Keys to Starting a TQM Program," p. 29.
13. Richard J. Schonberger, "Is Strategy Strategic? Impact of Total Quality Management on Strategy," *Academy of Management Executive*, August 1992, pp. 85–86.
14. David W. Cross, "Building Quality Awareness in Staffers," *Supervisory Management*, June 1991, p. 2.
15. Leonard L. Berry and A. Parasuraman, "Prescription for a Service Quality Revolution in America," *Organizational Dynamics*, Spring 1992, p. 9.
16. David A. Garvin, "How the Baldrige Really Works," *Harvard Business Review* (November–December 1991), pp. 80–84.
17. Robert Kreitner, *Management*, 5th ed. (Boston: Houghton Mifflin, 1992), p. G9.
18. Pier A. Abetti, "Technology: A Key Strategic Resource," *Management Review*, February 1989, pp. 38–39.
19. Cited in "Tom Peters on Managing Technology," *Management Review*, February 1989, p. 39.
20. Gregory B. Northcraft and Margaret A. Neale, *Organizational Behavior: A Management Challenge* (Chicago: Dryden, 1990), p. 644.
21. Ricky W. Griffin, *Management*, 4th ed. (Boston: Houghton Mifflin, 1993), p. 539.
22. Jack Szwergold, "Why Most Quality Efforts Fail," *Management Review*, August 1992, p. 5; Ken Meyers and Ron Askenas, "Results-Driven Quality . . . Now!" *Management Review*, March 1993, p. 40; Oren Harari, "Ten Reasons Why TQM Doesn't Work," *Management Review*, January 1993, pp. 33–38, Harari, "The Eleventh Reason Why TQM Doesn't Work," *Management Review*, May 1993, pp. 31, 34–36.

Chapter 15

1. Based on information presented by Thomas Amirault in *Occupational Outlook Quarterly* (Washington, D.C.: U.S. Bureau of Labor Statistics, 1993.)
2. Chris Argyris, "Teaching Smart People How to Learn," *Harvard Business Review*, May–June 1991, pp. 99–109.
3. Steve Lohr, "IBM Racks Up $8-Billion Loss," *New York Times Service* (*Toronto Globe and Mail*), July 28, 1993, p. B7.
4. Comprehensive self-development books related to leadership skills include Andrew J. DuBrin, *Stand Out! 330 Ways for Gaining the Edge with Bosses, Co-Workers, Subordinates and Customers* (Englewood Cliffs, N.J.: Prentice-Hall, 1993), and Robert L. Genua, *Managing Your Mouth: An Owner's Manual for Your Most Important Business Asset* (New York: AMACOM, 1993).
5. Bernard M. Bass, *Bass & Stogdill's Handbook of Leadership: Theory, Reseach, and Managerial Applications*, 3rd ed. (New York: The Free Press, 1990), p. 173.
6. Richard L. Hughes, Robert C. Ginnett, and Gordon J. Curphy, *Leadership: Enhancing the Lessons of Experience* (Homewood, Ill.: Irwin, 1993), pp. 33–36.
7. Daphna F. Raskas and Donald C. Hambrick, "Multifunctional Managerial Development: A Framework for Evaluating the Options," *Organizational Dynamics*, Autumn 1992, p. 5.
8. Margo Murray with Marna A. Owen, *Beyond the Myths and Magic of Mentoring* (San Francisco: Jossey-Bass, 1991).
9. Marshall Whitmire and Philip R. Nienstedt, "Lead Leaders into the '90s," *Personnel Journal*, May 1991, pp. 80–85.
10. Jay A. Conger, *Learning to Lead: The Art of Transforming Managers into Leaders* (San Francisco: Jossey-Bass, 1992), pp. 46–48. See also Conger, "Personal Growth Training: Snake Oil or Pathway to Leadership?" *Organizational Dynamics*, Summer 1993, pp. 19–30.
11. James M. Kouzes and Barry Z. Posner, *The Leadership Challenge: How to Get Extraordinary Things Done in Organizations* (San Francisco: Jossey Bass, 1987).
12. Ellen Van Velsol, Marian Ruderman, and Dianne Phillips, "The Lessons That Matter," *Issues & Observations*, Spring 1989, pp. 6–7.
13. William R. Tracey, *Designing Training and Development Systems* (New York: AMACOM, 1992); Bass, *Bass & Stogdill's Handbook of Leadership*, pp. 807–856.
14. A. Dianne Phillips, "Taking A Good Look at Development," *Issues & Observations*, Summer 1990, pp. 1–2.
15. Phillips, "Taking a Good Look at Development," pp. 3–4.
16. Thomas R. Horton, *The CEO Paradox: The Privilege and Accountability of Leadership* (New York: AMACOM, 1992).
17. Albert A. Cannella, Jr., and Michael Lubatkin, "Succession as a Sociopolitical Process: Internal Impediments to Outsider Selection," *Academy of Management Journal*, August 1993, pp. 763–793.
18. Lynda Gratton and Michel Syrett, "Heirs Apparent: Succession Strategies for the Future," in Michel Syrett & Clare Hogg (eds.) *Frontiers of Leadership* (Oxford, England: Blackwell Publishers, 1992), pp. 399–407; Jim Spoor, "Succession Planning: Once a Luxury, Now an Emerging Issue," *HR Focus*, December 1993, pp. 1, 4.
19. Jay A. Conger, "The Brave New World of Leadership Training," *Organizational Dynamics*, Winter 1993, pp. 54–55.
20. Quoted in "Today's Leaders Look to Tomorrow," *Fortune*, March 26, 1990.

21. Conger, "The Brave New World," p. 53; the following point about strategic opportunists is also from Conger.

22. Peter F. Drucker, *Managing for the Future: The 1990s and Beyond* (New York: Truman Talley Books/Dutton, 1992).

23. "Today's Leaders Look to Tomorrow."

24. Peter M. Senge, *The Fifth Discipline: The Art and Practice of the Learning Organization* (New York: Doubleday/Currency, 1990).

25. "The Virtual Corporation," *Business Week*, February 8, 1993, pp. 98–102; William H. Davidlow and Michael Malone, *The Virtual Corporation* (New York: Harper-Collins, 1993).

26. "Today's Leaders Look to Tomorrow."

27. Michael Hammer, "Reengineering Work: Don't Automate, Obliterate," *Harvard Business Review*, July–August 1990, pp. 104–112; Hammer and James Champey, *Reengineering the Corporation* (New York: Harper Business, 1993).

28. Conger, "The Brave New World of Leadership Training," p. 56.

Glossary

Achievement motivation Finding joy in accomplishment for its own sake.

Assertiveness Forthrightness in expressing demands, opinions, feelings, and attitudes.

Attribution theory Theory of causality of events.

Autocratic leader The person in charge who retains most of the authority himself or herself.

Bandwagon technique A manipulative approach emphasizing that "everybody else is doing it."

Behavior modification An attempt to change behavior by manipulating rewards and punishment.

Blemish A simple game in which the manager always finds a flaw in a group member's work.

Casual time orientation The view that time is an unlimited and unending resource, leading toward extreme patience.

Centrality The extent to which a unit's activities are linked into the system of organized activities.

Charisma A special quality of leaders whose purposes, powers, and extraordinary determination differentiate them from others.

Coalition A specific arrangement for parties working together to combine their power.

Coercive power Power based on fear.

Cognitive factors Problem solving and intellectual skills.

Cognitive resource theory A theory of leadership emphasizing that intelligent and competent leaders make more effective plans, decisions, and strategies than do leaders with less intelligence or competence.

Collectivism A belief that the group and society should receive top priority.

Commitment The highest degree of success when a leader exerts influence.

Compliance Partial success of an influence attempt by a leader.

Concert building A conception of the leader's role that involves aligning and mobilizing.

Congruence The matching of verbal and nonverbal communication.

Conjunctive communication Communication that is linked logically to previous messages, thus enhancing communication.

Consideration The degree to which the leader creates an environment of emotional support, warmth, friendliness, and trust.

Consensus leader The person in charge who encourages group discussion about an issue and then makes a decision that reflects general agreement and will be supported by group members.

Consultative leader The person in charge who confers with group members before making a decision.

Contingency and situational leadership An approach to leading whereby the leader chooses the right style to match the situation.

Contingency theory of leadership An explanation of leadership specifying the conditions under which a particular style of leadership will be effective.

Creativity The production of novel and useful ideas.

Cultural sensitivity An awareness of and a willingness to investigate the reasons why people of another culture act as they do.

Debasement The act of demeaning or insulting oneself to control the behavior of another person.

Democratic leader The person in charge who confers final authority on the group.

Disjunctive communication Communication that is not linked to the preceding messages, resulting in impaired communication.

Domains of impact In management development, the ranges of possible effects that a program might have.

Double-loop learning An in-depth style of learning that occurs when people use feedback to confront the validity of the goal or values implicit in the situation.

Drive A propensity to put forth high energy into achieving goals, and persistence in applying that energy.

Effective leader One whose actions facilitate group members' attainment of productivity, quality, and satisfaction.

Effort-to-performance expectancy The probability assigned by the individual that effort will lead to performing the task correctly.

Emotional stability The ability to control situations to the point that one's emotional responses are appropriate to the occasion.

Empathy The ability to place oneself in another's frame of reference.

Employee-centered leader One who encourages subordinate participation in goal setting and other work decisions.

Empowerment The process of sharing power with team members, thereby enhancing their feelings of personal effectiveness.

Excursion method A creative problem-solving technique in which the problem solver makes word associations that relate to the problem.

Expectancy theory A theory of motivation based on the premise that how much effort people extend depends upon how much reward they expect to get in return.

Expert power The ability to influence others because of one's specialized knowledge, skills, or abilities.

Farsightedness The ability to understand the long-range implications of actions and policies.

Femininity In Hofstede's research, an emphasis on personal relationships, concern for others, and a high quality of life.

Flexibility The ability to adjust to situations.

Forced-association technique A method of releasing creativity in whch individuals or groups solve a problem by making associations between the properties of two objects.

Formality The attachment of importance to tradition, ceremony, social rules, and rank.

Free-rein leader The person in charge who turns over virtually all authority and control to the group.

Functional fixedness The belief that there is only one way to do something.

Game A repeated series of exchanges between people that appears different on the surface than its true motive.

Gold-collar workers A breed of professionals who combine business knowledge with technical expertise.

Great person theory *See* **Trait approach.**

Groupthink A deterioration of mental efficiency, reality testing, and moral judgment in the interest of group solidarity.

High tolerance for frustration The ability to cope with the blocking of goal attainment.

Individualism A mental set in which people see themselves first as individuals and believe their own interests and values take priority.

Influence The ability to affect the behavior of others in a particular direction.

Informality   A casual attitude toward tradition, ceremony, social rules, and rank.

Information power   Power characterized by formal control over the information people need to do their work.

Initiating structure   The degree to which the leader organizes and defines relationships in the group by activities such as assigning specific tasks, specifying procedures to be followed, scheduling work, and clarifying expectations for team members.

Initiative   The quality of being a self-starter; ability to take action without support and stimulation from others.

Insight   A depth of understanding that requires considerable intuition and common sense.

Instrumentality   *See* **Performance-to-outcome expectancy**.

Internal locus of control   The belief that one is the primary cause of events happening to oneself.

Kaizen   A philosophy of gradual improvement in personal and work life that has become part of the philosophy of total quality management.

Lateral thinking   A thinking process that spreads out to find many different alternative solutions to a problem.

Leader   A person who inspires confidence and support among the people who are needed to achieve organizational goals.

Leader-match concept   The proposition that leadership effectiveness depends on matching leaders to situations where they can exercise more control.

Leader-member exchange model (or vertical dyad linkage model)   A model positing that leaders develop unique working relationships with subordinates, thereby creating in-groups and out-groups.

Leader irrelevance   The position that leaders' actions have almost no impact on most organizational outcomes.

Leadership   The ability to inspire confidence and support among the people who are needed to achieve organizational goals.

Leadership Grid®   (formerly the **Managerial Grid**) A framework for specifying the concern for production and people dimensions of leadership simultaneously.

Leadership diversity   The presence of a culturally heterogeneous cadre of leaders.

Leadership polarity   The disparity in views of leaders: revered or vastly unpopular, but not neutral.

Leadership power   The exercise of position power.

Leadership style   The relatively consistent pattern of behavior that characterizes a leader.

Leadership succession   An orderly process of identifying and grooming people to replace executives.

Leading by example   Influencing others by acting as a positive role model.

Legitimate power   Power granted by the organization.

Long-term orientation   A long-range perspective by workers, thus being thrifty and not demanding quick returns on investments.

Machiavellianism   A tendency to ruthlessly manipulate others in the workplace.

Management by anecdote   The technique of inspiring and instructing group members by telling fascinating stories.

Masculinity   In Hofstede's research, an emphasis on assertiveness, the acquisition of money, and material objects, and a deemphasis on caring for others.

Mentor   A more experienced person who develops a protégé's abilities through tutoring, coaching, guidance, and emotional support.

Micromanagement   The close monitoring of most aspects of group member activities by the manager or leader.

Mission statement   A firm's formal statement of its general field, purposes, values, and direction.

Multicultural organization   A firm that values cultural diversity and is willing to utilize and encourage such diversity.

Multifunctional managerial development   An organization's intentional efforts to enhance the effectiveness of managers by giving them experience in multiple functions within the organization.

Organizational creativity   The creation of novel and useful ideas and products that pertain to the workplace.

Organizational politics   Informal approaches to gaining power through means other than merit or luck.

Outcome   Anything that might stem from performance, such as a reward.

Participative leader   One who shares decision making with group members.

Partnership   A relationship between leaders and group members in which power is approximately balanced.

Path-goal theory   An explanation of leadership effectiveness that specifies what the leader must do to achieve high productivity and morale in a given situation.

Performance-to-outcome expectancy (or **Instrumentality**)   The probability assigned by the individual that performance will lead to certain outcomes.

Personalized charismatic   One who exercises few restraints on the use of power, best serving one's own interests.

Personal power   Power derived from the person rather than the organization.

Pet-peeve technique   A group method of identifying all the possible complaints others might have about one's organizational unit.

Politics   The various methods people use to attain or maintain power and gain other advantages.

Power   The ability (or potential) to influence decisions and control resources.

Power distance   The extent to which employees accept the idea that the members of an organization have different levels of power.

Prestige power   The power stemming from one's status and reputation.

Production-centered leader   One who sets tight work standards, organizes work carefully, prescribes the work methods to be followed, and supervises closely.

Readiness   In situational leadership, the extent to which a group member has the ability and willingness to accomplish a specific task.

Reengineering   The radical redesign of business processes to achieve substantial improvements in performance.

Referent power   The ability to influence others that stems from the leader's desirable traits and characteristics.

Relationship behavior   The extent to which the leader engages in two-way or multiway communication.

Resistance   The state that occurs when an influence attempt by a leader is unsuccessful.

Resource-dependence perspective   The view that an organization requires a continuing flow of human resources, money, customers and clients, technological inputs, and materials to continue to function.

Reward power   The authority to give rewards for compliance.

Self-awareness   Insight into one's own character and talents.

Self-discipline   The ability to mobilize one's efforts and energy to stay focused on an important goal.

Sensitivity to others   Empathy with group members; an understanding of their positions on issues, and how to best communicate with and influence them.

Short-term orientation   A focus on immediate results, and propensity not to save.

Silent treatment A means of influence characterized by saying nothing, sulking, or other forms of passivity.

Single-loop learning A situation in which learners seek minimum feedback that may substantially confront their basic ideas or actions.

Situational leadership model A model that explains how to match leadership style to the readiness of the group members.

Socialized charismatic A leader who restrains the use of power in order to benefit others.

Social loafing Shirking individual responsibility in a group setting.

Social responsibility The idea that organizations have an obligation to groups in society other than owners or stockholders and beyond that prescribed by law or union contract.

Strategic contingency theory An explanation of sources of power suggesting that units best able to cope with the firm's critical problems and uncertainties acquire relatively large amounts of power.

Substitutes for leadership Factors in the work environment that provide guidance and incentives to perform, making the leader's role almost superfluous.

SuperLeader One who leads others to lead themselves.

Supportive communication A communication style that delivers the message accurately.

Systemic thinking Seeing patterns and the invisible fabrics of interrelated actions that may take years to surface.

Task behavior Activity in which the leader spells out the duties and responsibilities of an individual or group.

Teamwork An understanding and commitment to group goals on the part of all team members.

Teamwork pattern A situation in which constructive candor is valued, and collaboration is not an end but a means to goal attainment.

Technology All the tools and ideas available for extending the physical and mental reach of people.

Total quality management (TQM) A management system for improving performance throughout the firm by maximizing customer satisfaction and by making continuous improvements based on extensive employee involvement.

Traditional mental set A conventional way of looking at things and placing them in familiar categories.

Trait approach (or great person theory) The observation that leadership effectiveness depends on certain personal attributes such as self-confidence.

Transactional leader A manager who mostly carries on transactions with people, such as taking care of administrative work and offering rewards for good performance.

Transformational leader A leader who helps organizations and people make positive changes in the way they do things.

Uncertainty avoidance A dislike of—and evasion of—the unknown.

Universal theory of leadership The belief that certain personal characteristics and skills contribute to leadership effectiveness in many situations.

Upward appeal A means of influence in which the leader enlists a person with more formal authority to do the influencing.

Urgent time organization A view of time as a scarce resource, leading to impatience.

Valence The worth or attractiveness of an outcome.

Vertical dyad linkage model. *See* **Leader-member exchange model.**

Vertical thinking An analytical, logical process that results in few answers.

Virtual corporation A temporary network of independent firms linked by information technology to share skills, costs, and access to each other's markets.

Vroom–Yetton–Jago model A leadership theory that identifies five decision-making styles, each reflecting a different degree of participation by group members.

Win-win approach to conflict resolution The belief that after conflict has been resolved both sides should gain something of value.

Work ethic A firm belief in the dignity of work.

Name Index

Acuff, Frank L., 276
Adler, Alan L., 350
Adler, Nancy J., 288
Akers, John, 163
Allen, Bob, 26–27
Amabile, Teresa M., 238, 252
Ammann, Fritz, 300
Argyris, Chris, 332
Armstrong, David, 67, 68
Armstrong, Larry, 177
Armstrong, Terry, 37, 45
Ash, Mary Kay, 67

Baldrige, Letitia, 272
Baldrige, Malcolm, 318
Ballmer, Steven A., 91
Barr, Craig B., 129
Barrett, Craig R., 145
Bartz, Carol, 1, 2, 5, 145
Bass, Bernard M., 59, 70, 72, 113, 258, 335
Belbin, Meredith, 109
Bennis, Warren, 31, 32, 45, 73
Berman, Lyle, 241
Berry, Leonard, 315
Biberman, Gerald, 155
Billard, Mary, 128
Blake, Robert R., 108
Blake, Stacy, 283, 284
Blanchard, Kenneth H., 114, 130, 138
Block, Peter, 2, 3
Blohwiak, Donald W., 252
Bolman, Lee G., 197, 198
Bond, Michael Harris, 291
Brandt, Richard, 328
Branson, Richard, 63, 64, 65, 75, 318
Breen, John G., 47, 48
Brown, David S., 90
Bryant, John, 250
Bryson, Vaughn D., 133, 134
Busch, August A., IV, 49

Calfee, David L., 309
Cameron, Kim S., 269
Canion, Rod, 97, 195
Carlzon, Jan, 85
Case, Thomas, 173, 185
Castellani, Diane, 242
Caudron, Shari, 310

Chemers, Martin M., 123
Clark, Kenneth E., 59
Clark, Miriam B., 59
Clinton, Bill, 161
Cohen, William A., 193
Conger, Jay A., 59, 65, 67, 150, 151, 203, 342, 348, 352
Cowan, Robert, 233, 234, 240
Cox, Taylor H., 283, 284, 297, 298
Crandall, Robert, 102
Crawford, Frederick C., 269
Curtis, Kent, 107

Daly, Chuck, 86
Dawson, Robert, 75
Deal, Terence E., 197, 198
Decker, Sharon Allred, 285
Dell, Michael, 324
Didato, Salvatore, 44
Dilenschneider, Robert, 174
Driscoll, Kathleen, 242
Drucker, Peter F., 189, 349
DuBrin, Andrew J., 157, 171, 227
Dyer, Davis, 269

Eaton, Bob, 13, 14, 20
Eisner, Michael, 48, 232
Elton, Elizabeth, 275
Emshiller, John R., 250
Enright, Paul, 99
Epstein, Cynthia Fuchs, 119
Esaki-Smith, Anna, 241
Evered, Roger D., 211, 219, 220
Exley, Charles E., Jr., 26, 27

Faerman, Sue R., 243
Ferris, Gerald R., 158
Fiedler, Fred E., 122, 123, 125, 130, 138
Field, George R. H., 139
Fonnvielle, William H., 166
Friant, Ray J. Jr., 49, 50

Gardner, John, 60
Gates, Bill, 91, 97, 116, 148, 199
Gerstner, Louis, 333
Gillespie, Marcia Ann, 37
Glasgall, William, 187
Glassman, Edward, 198
Graen, George, 203

Graham, Gerald, 196
Grant, Jan, 113
Gratton, Lynda, 348
Greenberg, Maurice Raymond, 186, 187
Greenwood, M. J., 290
Griffin, Ricky W., 154, 233
Grove, Andrew S., 328
Gryskiewicz, S. S., 252
Guy, Pat, 37

Hallman, Cinda A., 145
Halpert, Jane A., 60, 61
Halpin, Andrew W., 80
Hambrick, Donald C., 336
Hamlin, Richard, 153
Harari, Oren, 84, 314, 316
Harrison, Bennett, 104
Hater, John J., 72
Hawkins, Chuck, 285
Healy, Bernadine, 31
Heller, Andrew R., 255
Hersey, Paul, 114, 130, 131, 138
Hinkin, Timothy R., 183
Hodgetts, Richard M., 258
Hof, Robert D., 328
Hoffa, James R., 65
Hofsess, Diane, 267
Hofstede, Geert, 286, 287, 291
Hollister, Jack, 22
Horton, Thomas R., 114, 347
House, Robert J., 60, 61, 126
Howe, Sally, 202

Iacocca, Lee, 13, 14, 67
Israel-Rosen, David, 250
Iverson, Kenneth F., 140, 141

Jacinto, Bob, 296
Jago, Arthur G., 134, 136
Jobs, Steven, 48
Johnston, Robert W., 115
Jordan, Michael, 86

Karan, Donna, 114
Katzenbach, Jon R., 196, 197
Kazarian, Paul, 179
Kelly, Mark, 200
Kelly, Maryellen, 104

Kerr, Steven, 273
Keys, Bernard, 173, 185
Kidder, Tracy, 197
King, Martin Luther, Jr., 19, 76, 77, 260
King, Thomas R., 158
Kinicki, Angelo, 234
Kipnis, David, 185
Kirchner, Wayne K., 4
Kirkpatrick, Shelley A., 38, 53
Koestenbaum, Peter, 41, 70
Kotter, John P., 3, 4, 85, 89, 91
Kouzes, James E., 32, 59, 343, 372
Kreitner, Robert, 234, 291, 292
Krivnos, Paul D., 260

LaFleche, Heidi J., 293
Lawler, Edward E., III, 349
Lewent, Judy, C., 145
Lewin, Kurt, 100
Lippitt, Ronald, 100
Livingston, Camille, 267
Locke, Edwin A., 4, 38, 53
Lofton, Ernie, 350
Lombardo, Michael M., 39
Lovelace, Kay, 295
Lumsden, Donald, 277
Lumsden, Gay, 277
Lunner, Chet, 241
Luthans, Fred, 258
Lutz, Robert A., 151
Lyne, Barbara, 344

Maccoby, Michael, 5
Machiavelli, Nicolo, 155, 176
Mackoff, Barbara, 36
Madonna, Jon, 119
Mahar, Linda, 123
Manning, Dorothy, 293
Manning, George, 107
Manz, Charles C., 92
Maremont, Mark, 325
Maren, Michael, 71, 111, 223
Mark, Reuben, 349
McCall, Morgan W., Jr., 39
McCanse, Anne Adams, 108
McGrath, Michael R., 243
Mercer, Michael, 265
Milken, Michael, 73
Miller, Naomi, 107
Miner, John B., 102
Mintzberg, Henry, 9
Molloy, John T., 267
Moorhead, Gregory, 154
Morrison, Ann, M., 300
Mukai, Linda, 84

Nanus, Burt, 73
Neuharth, Al, 51
Nienstedt, Philip R., 339, 340

Orr, Robin, 128
Osburn, Alex F., 248

Page, Kagan, 36
Palmer, Ann Therese, 225
Parasuraman, A., 315
Patalon, William III, 294
Pawley, Dennis K., 151
Pennar, Karen, 311
Perdue, Frank, 45
Perot, H. Ross, 42, 43, 51, 62
Petersen, Donald E., 103
Pfeffer, Jeffrey, 9, 39, 51, 175
Pfeiffer, Eckhard, 97, 300
Phatak, Arvind V., 286
Piotrowski, Chris, 37, 45
Pitino, Rick, 222, 223, 229
Poling, Harold A., 7
Posner, Barry Z., 32, 59, 260, 343
Prasad, S. Benjamin, 291
Purcell, Philip, Jr., 6, 26, 145

Quinn, Robert E., 243

Raskas, Daphna F., 336
Raudsepp, Eugene, 249
Reich, Robert, 51
Reinsdorf, Jerry M., 21
Reno, Janet, 58
Riley, Walter, 111
Rivera, Chet, 279
Rivera, Sam, 225
Robbins, Stephen P., 264
Roddick, Anita, 65
Rodgers, T. J., 22, 51
Rodrigues, Carl A., 291
Romerill, Barry, 294
Rosen, Benson, 295
Rosener, Judy, 112
Rosenkrantz, Stuart A., 258
Ross, Steven J., 56, 57
Rothschild, William, 147
Rowe, Alan J., 406
Ruding, H. Onno, 300
Rumsfeld, Donald R., 121

Santora, Joyce E., 296
Sawyer, John, 233
Schipke, Roger, 194, 196
Schminke, Marshall, 155
Schmitt, Warren H., 100, 101, 102, 113
Schonberger, Richard J., 308, 317
Schriesheim, Chester A., 183
Schulze, Horst, 310
Schuster, Jay R., 311, 313
Scruggs-Leftwich, Yvonne, 71
Sculley, John, 23, 38, 87, 176
Selman, James C., 211, 219, 220
Senge, Peter M., 349
Servison, Roger T., 145

Shelby, Richard, 161
Shurtleff, Jill, 325
Sims, Arden C., 321
Sims, Henry P., Jr., 92
Sirota, David, 290
Smith, Douglas K., 196, 197
Smith, Fred, 324
Snow, John W., 89
Stern, Paul G., 29, 30, 40, 70, 145
Stevenson, Howard H., 110
Stodghill, Ron II, 119
Sturman, Gerald M., 228, 229
Sussman, Lyle, 260
Syrett, Michel, 348

Tannenbaum, Robert, 100, 101, 102, 113
Telling, Ed, 6
Teerlink, Richard, 315
Templeman, John, 14
Thomas, Kenneth W., 273
Thomas, Perry, 303
Thompson, Dennis, 198
Thompson, Jan, 177, 186
Thompson, Michael P., 243
Thurow, Lester, 292, 293
Tizzio, Thomas R., 187
Tracey, J. Bruce, 182
Trece, James B., 129
Trump, Donald, 42, 109, 145, 147
Tucker, Robert C., 73
Turner, Danny, 195

Uris, Auren, 107
Usher, Thomas J., 175, 262, 264

Valles, Jean-Paul, 300
van Cuylenburg, Peter, 300
Vecchio, Robert P., 47, 133, 204
Velasquez, Alvero, 208
Vroom, Victor H., 134, 136

Wallace, Don, 71, 111
Walton, Sam, 60
Warshaw, Michael, 241
Waterman, Robert H., Jr., 189, 206
Weber, Max, 59, 62
Weiss, Cyndi, 242
Welch, Jack, 148, 257
Wendt, Gary C., 86
Whetton, David A., 269
Whitemire, Marshall, 339, 340
Wilbon, Michael, 86
Wilcox, Kirby, 303
Woerner, Louise, 306
Woodman, Richard, 233

Yetton, Philip W., 134
Yukl, Gary A., 7, 59, 165, 168, 169, 174

Zingheim, Patricia K., 311, 313

Organization Index

American International Group Inc., 186–187
Anheuser-Busch Companies Inc., 49
Apple Computer Inc., 46, 70, 152
Armstrong International, 67
AT&T, 26–27
Autodesk, 1, 5, 145

Ben & Jerry's, 310
Boeing, 310

Center for Creative Leadership, 32
Chrysler Corporation, 13–14, 20, 151
Compaq Computer, 97, 195

Dean Witter Reynolds, 6, 26, 145
Donna Inc., 114
Duke Power, 285

Eli Lilly, 133
EMI, 63

Fel-Pro Inc., 225
Fit Company, 242
Ford Motor Company, 7, 103, 351

GE Appliance Division, 194
GE Capital Services Inc., 86

General Motors Pontiac, 129
Gillette Co., 325
Glove Metallurgical Inc., 321
Grand Casinos Inc., 241
Guaranteed Overnight Delivery (G.O.D.), 111

Harley Davidson, 315

IBM, 163, 255
Intel Corp., 328

Kentucky Wildcats, 222–223
Kinney Shoe, 296

Lockheed, 310
Lucky Stores, 302–303

Mazda Motor of America Inc., 177
McDonald's Corp., 310
Microsoft Corp., 91, 199
Ms. Magazine, 37

Northern Telcom, 30
Nucor Steel, 140–141

Outward Bound, 201, 202

Peat Marwick, 119
Plantree, 128

Ritz-Carlton Hotel Co., 310

Scandinavian Airline Systems (SAS), 85
G. D. Searle & Company, 121
Sherwin Williams Corp., 48
Sunbeam, 179

TCI West Inc., 202
Time Warner Inc., 56–57
TRW, 269

United Auto Workers (UAW), 350
U.S. Steel Gary Works, 175

Virgin Group, 63–64
Volvo, 349

Walt Disney Corporation, 232

Xerox Corporation, 47, 87, 294

Subject Index

Achievement motive and motivation, 43–44, 110
Achievement-oriented leadership style, 128
Adaptability to situation, 85
Aligning people, 89–90
Assertiveness, 32–35
Authority versus responsibility, 16–17
Autocratic leadership, 102
Autocratic to free-rein continuum, 102–107
Automation and technology, 321–326

Baldrige National Quality Award, 318–321
Bandwagon technique, 178
Behavior modification, 211–213
  rules for use, 212–213
  strategies for, 211–212
Bias-free organization, 298
Brainstorming, 243–244
Bridge burning, 162

Career coaching, 228–229
Cases
  charismatic speech analysis, 76–77
  coaching style, 230
  creative personality, 255
  cross-cultural differences, 304
  decision-making style, 140–141
  devious influence tactics, 186–187
  inspirational language, 279
  leadership change, 97–98
  leadership development, 355–356
  political behavior, 166
  right-stuff analysis, 26–27
  style appropriateness, 119
  teamwork, 208
  technology leadership, 328
  trait analysis of leader, 56–57
Change commitment, 226
Charisma, 59–61
Charismatic and transformational leadership, 58–77
  characteristics of leaders, 62–65
  charisma meanings, 59–61
  communication style, 65–68

concerns about, 72–73
dimensions and content of charisma, 60–61
divine charismatic, 62
empirical studies on, 70–72
evil use of, 73
expert power, 61
gearing language to audience, 67
leadership polarity, 72
management by anecdote, 67–68
managing by inspiration, 65–67
metaphor and analogy use, 67
office-holder charismatic, 62
personal charismatic, 62
personalized charismatic, 62
referent power, 60–61
relationship with group members, 60
socialized charismatic, 62
social responsibility, 73
transformation process, 68–70
type of charismatic, 61–62
Coaching and leadership, 219–226
  advice giving, 226
  career coaching, 228–229
  commitment to change, 226
  emotional support and, 224
  and leadership philosophy, 219–223
  reflection of feelings and content, 224–226
  skills and techniques, 223–226
Cognitive factors, 45–46
Cognitive resource theory, 46–47
Collaborative conflict management, 274
Commitment-compliance-resistance, 168–169, 194
Communication, 258–273
  benefit selling, 264
  congruent vs. incongruent type, 268
  conjunctive vs. disjunctive type, 269
  contextual differences, 272–273
  cross-cultural barriers, 270–273
  evidence about importance, 258
  frontloading of messages, 265
  gearing message to listener, 264
  inspirational and emotion-provoking, 261–262

junk words and vocalized pauses, 263
language errors, 263–264
nonverbal communication, 265–266
objection handling, 264–265
supportive type, 266–270
writing skills, 265
Communication skills, 185, 257–273
Communication style of charismatics, 65–68
Community builder, 351–352
Computer technology, 8
Concert building, 90
Condition interpreting, 87
Conflict and negotiation, 273–276
  styles of conflict management, 273–274
  win-win approach, 274
Conflict resolution skills, 23
Congruent and incongruent communication, 268
Conjunctive vs. disjunctive communication, 269
Consensus leader, 103, 194
Consideration dimension, 80
Consultation as influence tactic, 175
Contextual differences in culture, 272–273
Contingency and situational leadership, 121–141
  decision-making styles, 134–138
  decision style choice, 135–137
  Fiedler's theory, 122–126
  Hersey-Blanchard situational model, 130–133
  leader-match concept, 124–125
  least-preferred co-worker scale, 122–123
  path-goal theory, 126–130
  performance consequences, 129–130
  relationship behaviors, 131–132
  situational analysis, 124
  task behavior, 131–132
  Vroom–Yetton–Jago model, 134–138
Corporate culture, 310–311, 312
Courage, 40–41

Creative problem solving, 22–23
Creativity dampeners, 254
Creativity-enhancing exercise, 247–248
Creativity and leadership, 48–49, 232–256
  characteristics of creative leaders, 234–239
  climate for, 252–253
  cultural diversity and, 284
  dampeners, 254
  enhancing exercises, 247–248
  excursion methods, 246
  explorer-artist-lawyer-judge, 251–252
  forced-association method, 245–246
  functional fixedness, 240
  idea notebook, 251
  knowledge factors, 235
  lateral vs. vertical thinking, 241
  lead users, 250–251
  organizational methods for, 242–247
  personality and, 238
  pet-peeve technique, 245
  self-help techniques for, 247–252
  social habits and upbringing, 239
  steps in process, 233–234
  traditional thinking and, 239–241
Cross-cultural communication barriers, 270–273
Cross-cultural etiquette, 272
Cross-functional teams, 189
Cultural diversity and leadership (see International and culturally diverse leadership)
Cultural sensitivity, 292–293
Customer orientation, 89, 112

Debasement as influence, 180
Decision style choice, 135–138
Democratic leader, 103
Destructive beliefs, 93
Direction setting, 85
Directive leadership style, 127
Diversity policies, 295
Diversity training, 293
Divine charismatics, 62
Domains of impact, 346–347
Dominance and leadership, 32
Door-in-the-face technique, 180
Drive of leaders, 43

Educational background of leaders, 51–52
Effective leader meaning, 79
Embrace or demolish, 162
Emotional stability, 35–36
Emotional support by leader, 92, 224
Emoting-provoking words, 261–262
Empathy, 39

Empowerment, 20, 21–22, 149–153, 311
  SuperLeadership and technique for encouraging, 149–152, 153
  TQM and, 311
Enabling function of leader, 349
Energy and physical stamina, 51
Enthusiasm, 36, 248
Entrepreneurial leader, 110–112
Environmental uncertainty, 154
Ethics test, 170–171
Exchange of favors and bargaining, 173–174
Excursion method in creativity, 246
Exercises and self-assessments
  achievement motive quiz, 43–44
  assertiveness scale, 33–35
  ball handling for teamwork, 209
  brainstorming, 244
  classroom politics, 166
  coach characteristics, 227
  coaching role play, 230–231
  communication effectiveness test, 259–260
  cultural value profile, 289
  decision tree for leadership style, 137, 141
  developmental needs, 356
  diversity circle, 304–305
  effective and ineffective leaders, 98
  emotion-provoking word identification, 262
  empowering manager skills, 153
  feedback circle, 356
  feedback skills, 152
  feedback on traits, 50
  feedback on verbal and nonverbal behavior, 279–280
  functional fixedness overcoming, 240
  future checklist, 352
  humor role play, 57
  influence tactic identification, 183
  influence tactic practice, 187
  influence tactics survey, 170–171
  inspirational leadership role play, 27, 77
  interpersonal skills checklist, 334–335
  leadership criterion of Baldrige, 319–320
  leadership effectiveness, 83–84
  leadership styles role play, 120
  leadership styles test, 105–107
  least-preferred co-worker scale, 122–123
  management by anecdote, 68
  mission statement, 329
  organizational politics questionnaire, 155–157
  personal flexibility, 116
  pet peeve technique, 255–256

power rating of manager, 146–147
readiness for leadership role, 10–11
teamwork checklist, 200
teamwork development, 193
technology attitudes, 322
TQM corporate culture, 312
TQM principles, 307–308
transformational leadership, 66
valences for expectancy theory, 218–219
valuing diversity, 298–299
Vroom-Yetton-Jago model, 135–137
word hints to creativity, 249
Expectancy theory, 214–217, 288–291
  cross-cultural application, 288–291
  effort-to-performance expectancy, 214–215
  leadership skills and, 216–217
  performance-to-outcome expectancy, 215–216
  valence, 216
Experimental method, 346
Expert power, 61

Far sightedness, 49–50
Feedback
  in behavior modification, 212–213
  coaching and, 224
  giving of, 87
  team effectiveness and, 198–199
  on traits and styles, 342–343
Fiedler's contingency theory, 122–126
Financial rewards, 311–313
Flexibility and adaptability, 39–40
Forced-association method, 245–246
Formal leadership, 7
Formality vs. informality, 287
Framework for understanding leadership, 17–23
Free-rein leader, 104
Frustration tolerance, 37
Functional fixedness, 240
Future challenges, 348–352

Game playing, 179–180
Gender differences in style, 112–113
Goal setting and TQM, 316–317
Gold-collar workers, 324
Great person theory, 18–19
Group norms, 192–193
Group recognition, 196
Groupthink, 191, 197

Heredity vs. environment, 52
Hierarchy attitude, 111–112
Hofstede's cultural value dimensions, 286–288
Honesty, integrity, and credibility, 31–32

Idea notebook, 251
Impression management, 160
Individualism vs. collectivism,
    286–287
Influence tactics, 21, 167–187
    bandwagon technique, 178
    coalition formation, 176
    commitment-compliance-resistance,
        168
    consultation, 175
    debasement technique, 180
    devious approaches, 176–182
    door-in-the-face technique, 180
    effectiveness research, 182–184
    ethical test for, 170–171, 183
    exchange of favors and bargaining,
        173–174
    game playing, 179–180
    influence vs. power, 168
    ingratiating behaviors, 181
    inspirational appeal and emotional
        display, 175
    joking and kidding, 181–182
    leading by example, 172
    legitimating a request, 174–175
    Machiavellianism, 176–178
    manipulation of others, 178
    model of power and influence,
        168–169
    network of resource persons, 174
    pressure technique, 178–179
    rational persuasion, 172–173
    silent treatment, 181
    subject matter expert (SME), 173
    team play, 176
    upward appeal, 180–181
Ingratiating behaviors, 181
Initiative by leaders, 38–39
Insight, 49
Inspirational appeal, 175
Inspiring others, 90
Intergroup competition, 197
Internal locus of control, 40
International and culturally diverse
        leadership, 281–305
    bias-free organization, 298
    competitive advantage of diversity
        management, 283–284
    cultural factor influences, 285–292
    cultural sensitivity, 292–293
    dimensions of value differences,
        286–288
    diversity policies, 295
    diversity training pitfalls, 302–303
    expectancy theory application,
        288–291
    formality vs. informality, 287
    individualism vs. collectivism,
        286–287
    leadership diversity, 300–301

leadership style and national group,
        291–292
    masculinity vs. femininity, 287
    multicultural organization, 297–298
    pluralism, 297
    power distance, 287
    time orientation, 287–288
    uncertainty avoidance, 287
    work force diversity, 282–283
Intrinsic satisfaction, 8

Jargon and teamwork, 197–198
Joking and kidding to influence,
    181–182
Junk words and vocalized pauses, 263

Kaizen, 311
Knowledge of the business, 47

Lateral vs. vertical thinking, 241
Leader-member exchange model,
    203–205
Leaders in Action
    Craig Barr of GM, 129
    Lyle Berman of Grand Casino, 241
    Richard Branson of Virgin Group,
        63–64
    John Breen of Sherwin Williams, 48
    John Bryant, self-employed, 250
    Vaughn Bryson of Ely Lilly, 133–134
    Rod Canion of Compaq, 195
    Frederick Crawford of TRW, 269
    Chuck Daly of New Jersey Nets, 86
    Sharon Allred Decker of Duke
        Power, 285
    Bob Eaton of Chrysler, 13–14
    Bill Gates of Microsoft, 91, 199
    Marcia Ann Gillespie of *Ms.*, 37
    Harvard Advanced Management
        program participants, 343–344
    Lee Iacocca of Chrysler, 13–14
    Bob Jacinto of Kinney Shoes, 296
    Donna Karen of Donna Inc., 114
    Paul Kazarian of Sunbeam, 179
    Ernie Lofton of UAW, 350
    Management team at TCI West, 202
    Robin Orr of Plantree, 128
    Dennis K. Pawley of Chrysler, 151
    Donald Peterson of Ford, 103
    Rick Pitino of the Kentucky Wild-
        cats, 222–223
    Philip J. Purcell of Dean Witter, 6
    Walter Riley of Guaranteed
        Overnight Delivery, 111
    Sam Rivera of Fel-Pro, 225
    Barry Romeril of Xerox, 294
    Horst Schulze of Ritz Carlton, 310
    Yvonne Scruggs-Leftwich of a
        Buffalo bank, 71
    Jill Shurtleff of Gillette, 325

Arden Sims of Globe Metallurgical,
        321
    Paul G. Stern of Northern Telcom,
        30
    Richard Teerlink of Harley-David-
        son, 315
    Jan Thompson of Mazda, 177
    Cyndi Weill and Diane Castellani of
        the Fit Company, 242
Leadership behaviors and practices,
    78–98
    adaptability to situation, 85
    aligning people, 89–90
    concert building, 90
    consideration dimension, 80
    customer orientation, 89
    destructive belief problem, 93
    direction setting, 85
    effective leader definition, 79
    emotional support, 92
    feedback giving, 87
    initiating structure, 79–81
    inspiring people, 90
    interpreting conditions, 87
    mobilizing people, 90
    need satisfaction, 91
    Ohio State studies, 79–81
    performance standards and, 85
    pioneering research, 79–83
    positive self-talk, 93
    production-centered leaders, 82
    relationship-oriented behaviors,
        89–92
    risk taking and bias for action, 87
    situational influences, 93–94
    stability of performance, 88
    SuperLeadership, 92–93
    task-related attitudes and behaviors,
        83–89
    University of Michigan studies,
        81–82
    vision and strategy shaping, 91–92
    visualization technique, 93
Leadership development, 330–356
    conceptual knowledge, 343
    domain of impact, 346–347
    education role, 335–336
    experience and, 336–338
    feedback approaches, 342–343
    mentoring, 336–337
    multifunctional managerial de-
        velopment, 336–338
    needs analysis for, 354–355
    personal growth experiences,
        341–342
    program characteristics, 339–341
    program evaluations, 345–347
    program types, 341–345
    self-awareness, 331–333
    self-discipline and, 333

simulations, 344–345
single-loop vs. double-loop learning, 332–333
Leadership experience, 336–338
Leadership Grid (or Managerial Grid), 107–109
Leadership irrelevance, 9
Leadership and leaders
  behaviors and attitudes, 78–92
  behaviors and practices, 19–20
  charismatic and transformational leadership, 58–77
  communication skills, 23, 258–266
  computer technology and, 8
  conflict resolution skills, 23, 273–276
  contingency and situational leadership, 20, 121–141
  contingency theories, 122–126
  creative problem solving, 22–23, 232–256
  definitions of, 2
  development of leaders, 331–347
  diversity enhancement, 300–301
  empowerment and, 20–22, 149–152
  entrepreneurial style, 110–112
  framework for understanding, 17–23
  future and, 348–352
  importance of, 3–7,
  influence tactics for, 21, 167–187
  international and culturally diverse aspects, 281–305
  irrelevance of, 9
  leader-member exchange model, 203–205
  learning and development orientation, 23
  loneliness of leaders, 17
  vs. management, 3–5
  meaning of, 2–5
  motivation and coaching, 22, 210–231
  multicultural skills, 23
  organizational performance and, 5–9
  as partnership, 2–3
  politics involved, 17
  power and politics and, 20–21, 142–166
  right stuff for, 29
  roles, 9–13
  satisfactions and frustrations, 14–17
  situational influences, 93–94
  situational leadership model, 130–133
  styles, 20, 99–120
  substitutes for, 7–9
  succession, 347–348
  SuperLeadership, 92–93

teamwork development, 188–209
teamwork and empowerment, 21–22
technology fostering, 321–326
total quality management and, 307–318
trait approach, 18–19
traits, motives, and characteristics, 28–57
Leadership polarity, 72
Leadership power, 145
Leadership roles, 11–13
  coach, 12
  entrepreneur, 12–13
  figurehead, 11
  negotiator, 12
  spokesperson, 11
  team builder, 12
  team player, 12
  technical problem solver, 12
Leadership styles, 20, 99–120, 291–292
  autocratic-participative-free rein continuum, 102–104
  best style selection, 109, 113–115
  boss-centered vs. employee-centered, 100–102
  consensus leader, 103
  customer orientation, 112
  democratic leader, 103
  entrepreneurial style, 110–112
  free-rein leader, 104
  gender differences, 112–113
  Leadership Grid, 107–109
  national group adaptation, 291–292
  participative leader, 102–104
  situational factors, 101
  stress relationship, 113
  team leader, 109
  team vs. solo leadership, 109
Leadership succession, 347–348
Leading by example, 172, 193
Leading edge and future challenges, 348–352
  community building, 351–352
  enabling people, 349
  multicultural and diversity experts, 349
  reengineered corporation, 351
  role model, 348
  strategic interdependence, 349
  strategic opportunists, 349
  systemic thinking, 349–351
  virtual corporation, 351
Lead users, 250
Learning and development orientation, 23
Least-preferred co-worker scale, 122–123
Legitimating technique, 174–175

Loneliness of leaders, 17

Machiavellianism, 155, 176–178
Management by anecdote, 67–68
Managing by inspiration, 65–67
Manipulation of others, 178
Masculinity vs. femininity, and culture, 287
Mentoring, 338–339
Metaphors and analogies, 67
Micromanagement, 199–200
Mission statement, 191, 309–310
Mobilizing people, 90
Motivation and coaching skills, 22, 210–231
  behavior modification, 211–213
  cross-cultural factors, 288–291
  expectancy theory, 214–217, 288–291
  extinction, 212
  negative reinforcement, 211–212
  positive reinforcement, 211
  punishment, 212
  Pygmalion effect, 217
Management vs. leadership, 3–5
Modeling of performance and behavior, 226
Motives of leaders, 41–45
Multicultural skills, 23
Multicultural organization, 297–298
Multifunctional managerial development, 336–338

Needs analysis, 354–355
Need satisfaction, 91
Negotiating and bargaining, 274–276
  interests vs. positions, 276
  international differences, 276
  plausible demand or offer, 275
Networking method, 174
Nonverbal communication, 265–266, 272–273

Ohio State studies, 79–81
Openness to experience, 50
Opportunity recognition, 233
Organizational climate and creativity, 252–253
Organizational creativity, 233–234
Organizational politics, 17 (see also Politics)
Outdoor and wilderness training, 201–203

Participative leadership style, 102–104
Partnerships of leaders, 2–3
Path-goal theory, 126–130
Performance consequences of leadership, 5–9, 129–130
Performance (organizational), 309–313
Performance stability, 88

Personal growth programs, 341–342
Personalized vs. socialized power motive, 42–43
Personal power, 144–145
Pet peeve technique, 245
Physical factors of leaders, 51–52
Pluralism, 297
Political blunders, 161–162
Politics (organizational), 152–164
  back stabbing, 162
  blunders and, 161–162
  bridge burning, 162
  communication lines and, 159
  contracts and, 159
  control over, 163–164
  contributing factors, 152–158
  embrace or demolish, 162
  ethical issue, 158–162
  impression management and, 160
  information control and, 159
  Machiavellian tendencies and, 155
  quick-showing technique, 160
  top management tactics, 149–152
Position power, 144
Positive reinforcement, 211
Positive self-talk, 93
Power, 143–152, 168
  and closeness to power, 148
  coercive type, 144
  empowerment and, 149–152
  information and, 144
  leadership type, 149–152
  legitimate, 144
  model of, 168–169
  opportunity capitalizing, 147–148
  ownership type, 145
  personal type, 144–145
  plan for increasing, 149
  prestige type, 145
  from providing resources, 145–147
  sources and type, 143–148
  strategic contingency theory and, 148
  suggestions for using, 165
  reward type, 144
Power distance, 287
Power and influence model, 168–169
Power motive, 42–43
Power and politics, 20–21
Pride within teams, 193
Production-centered leaders, 82
Professional norms, 8
Punishment, 212
Pygmalion effect, 85, 217

Rational persuasion, 172–173
Readiness and leadership, 132
Reengineered corporation, 351
Referent power, 60–61
Relationship-oriented attitudes and behaviors, 89–92, 131–133

Resiliency, 41
Resource dependency perspective, 145
Rewards
  cross-cultural application, 290–291
  innovation and, 325–326
  "Right stuff," 29
Risk taking and bias for action, 87
Risk-taking mistakes, 317–318

Satisfactions and frustrations of leaders, 14–17
Self-awareness, 37–38
Self-confidence, 31
Self-discipline and development, 333
Self-objectivity, 37–38
Sense of humor, 36
Sensitivity to others, 39
Simulation and development, 344–345
Single-loop vs. double-loop learning, 332–333
Situational influences, 93–94
Situational leadership model, 130–133
Six-Sigma quality standard, 316
Socialized vs. personalized charismatic, 62
Social loafing, 190
Social responsibility, 73
Strategic contingency theory, 148
Strategic interdependencies, 349
Strategic opportunism, 349
Stress and leadership, 113
Subject matter expert (SME), 173
Substitutes for leadership, 7–9
SuperLeadership, 92–93, 152
Supportive communication, 266–270
Supportive leadership style, 127–128
Systemic thinking, 349

Task behavior, 131–133
Team play and influence, 176
Teamwork patterns, 189
Team vs. solo leadership, 109
Teamwork and teamwork development, 188–209
  behavior and attitudes for, 191–200
  consensus leadership for, 194
  feedback for, 198–199
  group recognition, 196
  groupthink and, 191, 197
  intellectual challenge in, 197
  intergroup competition for, 197
  jargon for, 197–198
  leader-member exchange model, 203–205
  micromanagement and, 199–200
  mission statement, 191
  model for, 193–194
  norm for, 192–193
  outdoor training for, 201–203

pride in accomplishment, 193
ritual and ceremony for, 198
teamwork advantages and disadvantages, 189–191
teamwork pattern, 189
we-they attitude, 194–196
work standards for, 196
Technology leadership, 321–326
  automation role, 324
  gold-collar workers, 324
  potential pitfalls, 326–327
  rewards for innovation, 325–326
  strategy for, 323–324
  training and, 324
Tenacity and leadership, 45
Time orientation and culture, 287–288
Total quality management (TQM), 306–320
  advocate, facilitator, and cheerleader roles, 317
  Baldrige award, 318–320
  culture of quality, 310–311
  empowerment, 311
  extraordinary goals and, 316–317
  financial rewards and, 311–313
  immersion in quality, 314
  kaizen, 311
  leadership practices for, 307–318
  measurement of quality, 317
  mission statement, 309–310
  organization-wide principles and practices, 309–313
  review of principles, 307–308
  risk-taking mistakes, 317–318
  service-operation contacts, 318
  6-sigma standard, 316
  at team and individual level, 313–318
  top-level commitment to, 309
Traditional mental set, 240
Trait approach, 18–19, 28–57
Traits, motives, and characteristics of leaders, 28–57
  achievement motivation, 43
  assertiveness, 32–33
  cognitive factors, 45–50
  cognitive resource theory, 46–47
  courage, 40–41
  creativity, 48–49
  dominance, 32
  drive and achievement motivation, 43
  education, 51
  emotional stability, 35–36
  energy and physical stamina, 51
  enthusiasm, 36
  extroversion, 32
  far sightedness, 49–50
  flexibility and adaptability, 39–40
  frustration tolerance, 37

general personality traits, 30–38
height of leaders, 51
heredity vs. environment, 52
honesty, integrity, and credibility, 31–32
initiative, 38–39
insight into people and situations, 49
internal locus of control, 40
knowledge of the business, 47
motives, 41–45
openness to experience, 50
personalized vs. socialized power motive, 42–43
physical and background factors, 51–52
power motive, 42–43
resiliency, 41
school attended, 52

self-awareness and self-objectivity, 37–38
self-confidence, 31
seniority factors, 52
sense of humor, 36
sensitivity to others and empathy, 39
strengths and limitations of trait approach, 53
task-related traits, 38–41
tenacity, 45
universal theory of leadership, 29
warmth, 36
work ethic, 44–45
Transactional leader, 62–64
Transformational leader, 62

Uncertainty avoidance, 287
Universal theory of leadership, 29

University of Michigan studies, 81–82
Upward appeal, 180–181

Vertical dyad linkage model, 203–205
Virtual corporation, 351
Vision and strategy shaping, 91–92
Visionary perspective, 111
Visualization technique, 93
Vroom–Yetton–Jago decision-making model, 134–138

Warmth, 36
"We-they" attitude, 194–196
Win-win conflict style, 274
Work ethic, 44–45
Work standards, 196